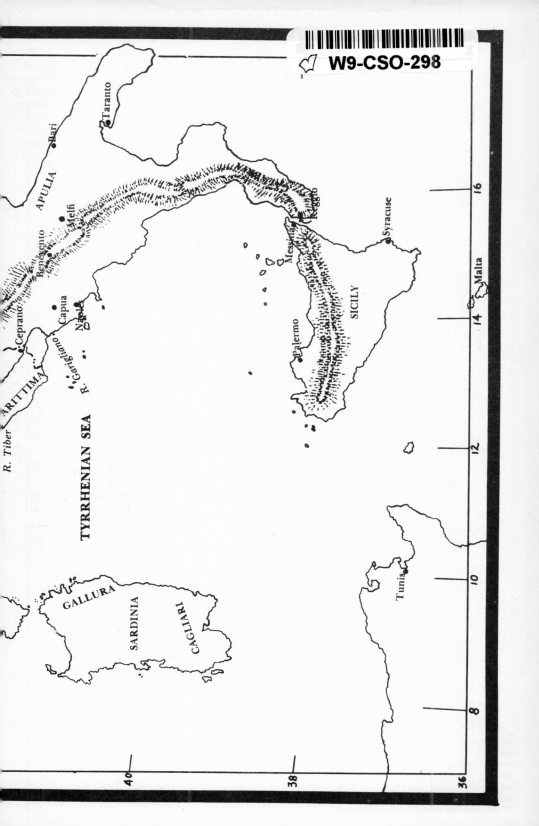

TYRRHENIAN SEA

R. Tiber

MARITTIMA

Ceprano

R. Garigliano

Capua

Napoli

Benevento

Melfi

APULIA

Bari

Taranto

Reggio

Messina

Palermo

SICILY

Syracuse

Malta

GALLURA

SARDINIA

CAGLIARI

Tunis

16

14

12

10

8

40

38

36

Henry VII in Italy

WILLIAM M. BOWSKY

Henry VII in Italy

The Conflict of Empire and City-State,
1310-1313

UNIVERSITY OF NEBRASKA PRESS
LINCOLN   1960

Publishers on the Plains

UNP

The publication of this book was made possible by a Ford Foundation grant.

To the memory of
THEODOR E. MOMMSEN

Preface

"Rejoice, O Italy! Though now to be pitied even by the Saracens, soon you will be envied throughout the world! For your bridegroom, the solace of the world and the glory of your people, the most clement Henry, Divine and Augustus and Caesar hastens to the nuptials!" Joyously Dante Alighieri acclaimed the arrival in Italy in 1310 of the Emperor-elect, Henry of Luxemburg. The poet anticipated that his eagerly awaited *alto Arrigo* would succeed in pacifying the turbulent Italian peninsula and inaugurate an era of universal peace and justice. This dream was not fulfilled: Henry VII died less than three years later—the last emperor to undertake seriously the pacification of strife-torn Italy and its inclusion as an integral part of the Holy Roman Empire.

The fact that the Emperor Henry VII occupied a prominent place in the life and writings of Italy's greatest literary figure would in itself be sufficient grounds for supposing that there exist detailed modern historical studies illuminating every facet of the monarch's career. The truth is that in the past hundred years only one major study of his life has been published, while not a single monograph deals with his relations with Italy in their entirety.

This neglect is the more surprising if we consider something of the nature of Henry's Italian expedition. After the collapse of Hohenstaufen power in the middle decades of the thirteenth century, the disappearance in practice of legitimate imperial authority in Italy left men and cities free to act as if they were the lawful masters of their own destinies without a denial of the concept of the Empire. When Henry of Luxemburg appeared in Italy this convenient fiction had to end: men were forced to choose between the concept and exercising their local independence. The expedition of Dante's Emperor brought temporary order out of political confusion, and crystallized and intensified the issues dividing political loyalties and plaguing consciences on the eve of the Renaissance.

This book is a study of Henry VII's attempt to revive the medieval Empire in an Italy dominated by secular city-states and beset by the demands of nascent lay kingdoms and dynasties and a new-born Avignon Papacy. It is dedicated to the memory of Professor Theodor E. Mommsen, who first suggested to the author the need for such a study and offered the continuous encouragement of his scholarly counsel and criticism and his warm friendship. Professor Joseph R. Strayer merits special thanks for his advice and assistance while the author was a candidate for a doctoral degree at Princeton University and during the more advanced stages of research and manuscript preparation. The author is grateful to Professor Ernst H. Kantorowicz for suggestive ideas based upon his wide and penetrating knowledge of the period. Professor Glenn W. Gray has the author's particular thanks for reading the entire manuscript and offering many excellent suggestions. The author gladly acknowledges his debt to these and other friends, recognizing that all errors or shortcomings in this book are wholly his own.

The staffs of the Princeton University Library and the University of Nebraska Library provided generous aid in obtaining published materials, while those of the Archivi di Stato of Florence and Reggio Emilia extended the author every courtesy in allowing him to use and obtain photographic reproductions of manuscripts.

The author has been kindly granted permission to use copyrighted material from E. H. Kantorowicz, *The King's Two Bodies* (Princeton: Princeton University Press, 1957); W.

Bowsky, "Clement V and the Emperor-Elect," *Medievalia et Humanistica*, XII (1958), 52-69; *id.*, "Florence and Henry of Luxemburg, King of the Romans: The Rebirth of Guelfism," *Speculum*, XXXIII (1958), 177-203; *id.*, "Dante's Italy: A Political Dissection," *The Historian*, XXI (1958), 82-100, which forms the basis for much of the Prologue.

A fellowship from the Princeton Graduate School, a Fulbright Grant for study in Italy, 1954-1956, and a grant from the University of Nebraska Research Council have all facilitated this project and are greatly appreciated.

Finally the author wishes to thank his wife and his mother, both of whom have provided inspiration and assistance essential to the writing of this book.

WILLIAM M. BOWSKY

Contents

Henry VII in Italy

Prologue: Italy

All Italy anxiously awaited a great new event throughout the spring and summer of 1310: for the first time in nearly a century a King of the Romans, Henry of Luxemburg, was about to make the traditional journey to Rome to receive the crown of the Holy Roman Empire at the hands of the Supreme Pontiff.

The last crowned emperor, Frederick II, had died sixty years earlier, and few living men could claim to have witnessed the devastating wars that he had waged against the Holy See and the communes of the Lombard League. During the two decades following Frederick's death in 1250, an implacable Papacy and its knightly champion, Charles I of Anjou, had hunted down and crushed the Hohenstaufen "brood of vipers." When the ensuing imperial interregnum ended in 1273 with the election of Count Rudolf of Habsburg, the Empire had already suffered severe damage that could not easily be repaired. The very nomination of the Habsburg demonstrated the new-found power of the German electoral princes to control the selection of an emperor, and to make certain that no candidate would be chosen whose independent strength was great enough to endanger their special privileges. The post-interregnum Empire, moreover, was still the object of many misgivings at the papal curia, and the apparent pontifical policy of looking more and more to the kingdom of France for support weakened the Empire's remaining

diplomatic power. Pope Boniface VIII had openly sided with the
Empire against the individual kingdoms of Europe in his efforts
to win increased freedom of action and independence for the
Papacy, but such policies seemed doomed after the crushing
French victory over the Pope at Anagni in 1303.

The Empire faced more than political and constitutional difficulties in the early fourteenth century: it was buffeted by ideological attacks that threatened to undermine its prestige and
authority. Since Pope Innocent III issued the famous decretal
Per Venerabilem in 1202, the Papacy and many of its canonists
had frequently led the attack. It was another pope, Innocent IV,
who openly challenged the imperial claim to universal jurisdiction on the grounds of right as well as of actual practice. By the
latter part of the thirteenth century the increasingly powerful
and self-assertive nascent nation-state of France was the scene of
a mighty political and juristic assault upon the integrity of the
Holy Roman Empire. As early as 1254, St. Louis had indicated
that he did not believe himself subject to the Emperor. The
struggle between Philip IV and Boniface VIII gave rise to a
number of outspoken tractates asserting the rights of the French
king against the Emperor on historical, legalistic, and sociologi-
cal grounds.[1] But it was still to be seen how much harm these
attacks had done the Empire, and in 1310 all Italy was astir
with the news of the imminent arrival of an emperor-elect.

Even the southernmost lands responded to the general excite-
ment. Sicily, long contested between Empire and Papacy, had at
last been ceded to the Holy See in 1275. In August 1309 Robert
of Anjou, the leading member of a cadet branch of the French
royal house, followed in the footsteps of his father and grandfather and did liege homage to Pope Clement V for the Kingdom of Sicily. Bitter papal experience with the successors of
Frederick Barbarossa caused the Pope to include in the oath of
homage solemn promises that the Kingdom of Sicily would never
be united with the Empire, and that Robert and his heirs would
never become emperors, Kings of the Romans, rulers of Tuscany
or Lombardy, or even accept office in any other papal lands.[2]

Robert, the new Angevin king of Sicily, possessed only half
his kingdom. The island itself and much of the province of
Calabria was ruled by Frederick of Trinacria, younger brother

of James II of Aragon. After a series of futile Angevin attempts to oust the usurper, Frederick's *de facto* possession of the island had been sanctioned by the Treaty of Caltabellotta (1302), with the stipulation that on his death it would revert to Robert or his heirs. This arrangement left the Angevin unsatisfied, but he lacked the means necessary to overthrow it.

The area remaining to Robert included part of Calabria and most of present-day Apulia, Campania, and Abruzzi, and was called the Kingdom of Naples or simply the *Regno*. That kingdom was socially, politically, and economically unsettled, and by itself could not provide Robert with the strength necessary to maintain great military ventures. Social strife prevailed and the non-noble classes were at times oppressed by the royal officials sent to bring them relief. Private warfare, frequent rebellions, and a nobility that had not submitted to effective Angevin rule added to the kingdom's troubles. The King, moreover, was almost continually in debt, and could not easily ignore the desires of his Florentine creditors. The fact that Robert was also Count of Provence, Forcalquier, and Piedmont distracted rather than helped him in administering the Regno. He could impose his will upon a large portion of the Italian peninsula only if he exercised great astuteness and force of character, or if the course of external events came to his aid.[3]

The Angevin king and his rival Frederick both attempted to win military predominance in large part by launching and supporting powerful fleets. Their naval ventures, however, seem puny when compared with those of Venice, the undisputed mistress of the Adriatic and the mightiest sea power in the Mediterranean. A contemporary of Dante, the Bishop Nicolas of Butrinto, could only describe the Venetians as "a fifth essence, that wished to recognize neither God, nor Church, nor Emperor, nor sea, nor land, unless insofar as pleased them."[4] Venice had amassed a considerable collection of privileges from popes and western emperors and yet never recognized their sovereign temporal jurisdictions. Its citizens devoted their energies to maintaining and increasing the city's commercial and maritime supremacy—a goal that involved Venice in numerous wars with rivals that ranged from the commune of Genoa to the Papacy itself.

Political power in Venice rested with a merchant oligarchy which had established such rigid constitutional barriers in the last years of the thirteenth century that it was almost impossible for new families to enter the charmed circle. During the summer of 1310 Venice crushed the most serious rebellion yet to occur in its history. The aftermath was the creation of a commission possessing extraordinary powers for the protection of the public safety. This new Council of Ten soon received permanent status and became the government's most effective instrument for discovering and suppressing conspiracies. Venice was a great independent naval power whose assistance could be courted or purchased by all, but commanded by none.

The remainder of Italy comprised two political regions: the northernmost, subject in theory to the direct jurisdiction of the Holy Roman Emperor, and the southern section, dependent upon the Pope.[5] The very nature of those two sovereigns had an important effect upon their Italian lands. The Papacy and the Empire were more than local or regional institutions for exercising political control. Each purported to be a special entity, created by God and charged with the good of Christendom. Popes and emperors claimed a right of allegiance and an authority over their Italian subjects both as immediate overlords and as the supreme spiritual or temporal rulers of Christendom. These rulers, moreover, could not deal with their Italian holdings on the basis of local, regional, or dynastic needs alone: they had to consider the requirements of all the Christians whom God had placed in their care, and at times this worked to the disadvantage of their immediate Italian possessions.

The lands subject to direct papal jurisdiction included much of present-day Lazio, Umbria, the Marches, and the Romagna with the valuable city of Bologna. The heart of the papal possessions was Rome, from which popes ruled their temporal domains and gave universal spiritual guidance.

Since the death of Pope Boniface VIII this situation had changed. Clement V, crowned in Lyon in 1305, had not left the Rhone Valley, and for five years there had been no pope in Italy. The Gascon pontiff found it difficult to manage the varied and turbulent elements in papal Italy by means of couriers and directives sent across the Alps. The political vacuum left by the

absence of direct pontifical control was filled by the most law-
less groups. Rome itself was racked by continual feuding among
noble families and by fighting between these and the more well-
to-do merchant groups. Clement was also unable to maintain
order in the Romagna, and his appointees to the Rectorship
had accomplished little.[6] Included in the papal lands were self-
governing communes, treated at times as though they were independent states, and feudal nobles independent of the Papacy.

The Italian lands subject to papal jurisdiction, though extensive and important, did not include the present-day provinces
of Piedmont, Lombardy, Veneto, Emilia, Liguria, and Tuscany.
These territories were theoretically subject to the Holy Roman
Empire, and at times were included in a general appellation,
"The Kingdom of Italy." [7] Whether regarded from an economic,
political, or literary viewpoint, in many respects they were the
most flourishing part of the Italian peninsula during the first
decade of the fourteenth century. In art and literature seeds
were sown that would soon bear fruit in the Italian Renaissance. Cities in imperial Italy ranked among the world's greatest
commercial, industrial, maritime, and banking centers. Men
strove towards new goals, driven on by new aspirations that
could not easily be recognized and often masqueraded under old
names. Families, cities, and provinces seethed with factionalism
and internecine conflict.

At the heart of all this vitality and energy were the Italian
city-states. Imperial Italy contrasted with much of northern
Europe, where urban political development was often impeded
by a powerful feudal nobility or growing national monarchies.
For more than two centuries the cities of imperial Italy had been
assuming an increasingly prominent role in every aspect of life.
In 1310 Genoa was a naval power second in importance only to
Venice. The metropolis of Milan in central Lombardy, one of
the great industrial centers of western Europe, produced textiles
and armor for an international market. The commune of Florence, straddling the Arno River in Tuscany, was far more than
the birthplace of Dante Alighieri and the cradle of an incipient
renaissance in arts and letters. Florence was a mighty industrial,
mercantile, and banking center, whose gold coin, the florin, was
winning universal recognition as the best currency in Europe.

Florentine banking firms like those of the Bardi and the Peruzzi counted the kings of England and Naples among their debtors, while other Florentines were private bankers of the King of France.

These Italian cities, however, were not free to develop and expand, or to deal with their own problems in the manner of independent kingdoms or states, since theoretically they were subject to immediate imperial control and jurisdiction. Even communes that dated their legitimate existence as semiautonomous political entities to the Peace of Constance (1183) were still legally subject to the emperor's supervisory powers. The Italian imperial cities confronted a problem similar to that of their counterparts in the Papal States: they could be used as the tools of a supranational institution whose goals did not necessarily coincide with their best interests. But while the Pope ordinarily dwelt in Rome and was Italian, the Holy Roman Emperor often was a German who resided north of the Alps and was less inclined than the Pope to give primary consideration to Italian problems and needs.

Since the death of Frederick II in 1250 Italy had experienced more than half a century of relatively great freedom from imperial control. The expected advent of the Emperor-elect Henry of Luxemburg in 1310 seemed about to put an end to this *de facto* independence; and it was not inconceivable that once again, as in Hohenstaufen times, the question of the validity and enforcement of imperial rights and jurisdictions was to complicate the intricate and difficult problems confronting the inhabitants of imperial Italy.

Imperial connections with Italy had already contributed greatly to the discord that plagued the land. By the mid-thirteenth century in many cities Guelfs and Ghibellines (Italian supporters of the Papacy and of the Empire respectively) had formed two distinct political organisms, each with its own institutions, party chiefs, and nominal leader—pope or emperor. When a party lost control of a city and its members were forced to leave as exiles, they often remained together, frequently uniting with exile groups from other communities and attempting to re-enter their native city by force of arms.

Within city walls factionalism manifested itself frequently in

warfare and street fighting, while murders and blood feuds per-
petuated dissension. With strife so intense it is difficult to con-
ceive how any ruler, even an emperor, could long remain above
parties unless he commanded a large military force and considerable economic resources.

By 1310, the various factions distinguished as Guelf or Ghibelline were seldom primarily interested in asserting papal or
imperial predominance in Italy.[8] The ancient meanings of those
party labels served at times only to intensify and continue discord, for they obscured the fact that most so-called Guelfs and
Ghibellines now quarrelled over strictly local questions whose
resolution did not turn upon the position of either the Papacy or
the Empire. So little did the pristine significance of the term
"Guelf" indicate the real issues dividing men that even where a
Guelf party emerged victorious it often disintegrated into opposing factions. The best-known example of this is the appearance of the White Guelfs and Black Guelfs in Florence in the
first years of the fourteenth century. Even during the opening
decade of that century the term "Guelf" was not customarily
applied to the Della Torre, ruling family in Milan. Only during
the summer of 1310 were the Torriani again called Guelfs as
they had been in the thirteenth century—and this because their
leader Guido set himself against the coming of the Emperor-
elect.[9]

Not all internal problems facing the Italian city-states could
be ascribed to imperial pretensions. Quite as serious were difficulties that arose from the clashing ambitions of rival families,
social groups, and economic interests. Too many historical accounts treat these dissensions as a single phenomenon: the opposition of old feudal nobility to a new rising order of wealthy
bourgeoisie called *popolo* or *popolo grasso*.[10] To single out a
struggle between magnates and *popolo grasso* as the chief cause
of communal strife may be to oversimplify dangerously a complex social, economic, and political structure. An examination
of the origins of families classified as noble by the ruling Florentine bourgeoisie in the last decade of the thirteenth century,
and thus disqualified from public office, reveals that the back-
grounds of many so-called nobles, the Bardi, Frescobaldi, and
Cerchi, for example, differed in no way from other houses that

were to remain *"buoni popolani."* Nobles had many close connections with the wealthy elements who directed the gilds or
arti, and many of the *popolo grasso* were related to magnates by
marriage. Magnates also participated in communal financial and
commercial ventures. Nor did the magnates present a serious
threat to Florence's control over its *contado,* or surrounding
district, and only a few parts of the *contado* remained in the
hands of nobles hostile to the commune.[11] Late nineteenth-
century accounts of other Italian cities, with their heavy emphasis upon the theme of noble-*popolo* antagonism, should perhaps
be read with some reserve until the approach used so fruitfully
in the case of Florence is applied elsewhere.

The briefest survey of communal governmental organization
should make one leary of superficial generalizations about complex social, economic, and political relationships. For while
communal governments shared many basic similarities, most
cities differed noticeably from their neighbors in their political
constitutions and practices. Thus in Florence, as elsewhere, the
podesta and the captain of the people were the chief communal
magistrates. They held office for six months and could not be
Florentines. They were assisted by staffs of judges who, together
with a few servants and police officials, comprised their official
"families." The podesta possessed more extensive powers than
the captain of the people, although both magistrates had certain jurisdiction in civil and criminal cases, led their own councils, and could command Florentine citizenry in time of war.

Far more important than both of these officials was the Florentine Signory, the commune's chief executive body. The Signory enjoyed a two-month term of office and was composed of
the Priors (chosen by leaders of the greater gilds and by certain
men selected by the outgoing Priors) and the Standard-Bearer
of Justice. Without the Signory's consent no legislative or delib-
erative assembly could be summoned, be it that of the podesta,
the captain, or the General Council of Florence attended by all
citizens. And depending upon their character and importance,
legislative measures had to be approved by one or more of some
half-dozen councils before becoming law.

The nature of a city's ties with the Empire also were to prove
to be directly related to the resolution of one basic issue: the

form of government that was to predominate throughout imperial Italy: republican commune or despotic signory.[12]

Most important Italian cities were in practice self-governing communes by the early thirteenth century. Citizens elected their own magistrates and had a voice in the councils where all important policy decisions affecting the entire commune were made. During the second half of the century, however, another form of government, the signory, appeared with increasing frequency. It was particularly evident in Lombardy, where the communes of Verona, Treviso, and Mantua were all replaced by signories.

When the people of a commune wearied of continual factional and family strife and of battles with neighboring feudal lords and cities, they often desired above all else tranquility and an opportunity to develop their economic energies. They then lost interest in civic life and resigned their commune's hard-won autonomy and liberties to the care of a single ruler or *signore*. Such a change of government could come about in many ways. In some places it occurred slowly, through a gradual transferring of powers from the commune to a *signore*. In others military conquest cancelled communal autonomy at a single stroke, substituting for it the dictatorship of a man, a party, a group of citizens, or a society of magnates. A podesta, a captain of the people, a *contado* noble, a wealthy merchant who had become the leader of the city's gilds, or an imperial vicar or governor might succeed in establishing a signory.

The new ruler was often acclaimed in a tumultuous public assembly that was not really a normal session of the commune's General Council. For the exercise of his absolute powers the *signore* usually adopted a title such as "Captain General" or "Perpetual Lord," although it was possible to wield the same authority without the benefit of any special appellation. Most *signori,* in fact, preferred to leave virtually intact the institutional forms of government by which the commune had ruled itself, perhaps so that the citizens would not be forcefully reminded that their liberties were now lost.[13]

The *signori* were basically insecure, however, as they lacked certain attributes conducive, if not essential, to permanent rule. The signory was not supported by tradition or by the divine

sanction that strengthened the Empire and Christian monarchies. A *signore* could not claim to rule *"Dei gratia,"* nor could
he trace his authority back to Charlemagne, Constantine, and
Augustus.

Despite the grants of power given to *signori* by communal
assemblies, the juridic authority of the *signore* remained uncertain. The plebiscites that so vigorously acclaimed the new rulers
could only sanction, not change, an already existing condition. A
signore could justify his position only by receiving a grant of
authority from the power to which the commune was ultimately
subject. He needed a specific concession from the city's lay or
ecclesiastical lord, which, in the case of most independent communes, meant a grant from the Pope or the Emperor. The reception of an imperial vicarship could appear to justify a *signore*'s
rule over a commune, and freed him from the restriction of
having to base his absolute dominion upon a donation of authority from his subjects—a donation that they might at any
time pretend to retract. If a *signore* succeeded in gaining control
over several cities and towns, an imperial vicarship might allow
him to unite them all in some measure into a single lordship.
Imperial policies could even assist in the creation of new signories, as the man commanding a city as its imperial vicar or governor might be in an excellent position to maintain and fortify
that rule for his own personal advantage.[14]

The connection that existed between the Holy Roman Emperor and imperial Italy seriously affected all attempts to solve
still another major problem confronting Italian city-states in the
early fourteenth century: defining the relationship between an
individual city and its surrounding *contado*.[15]

Throughout the thirteenth century Italian cities had engaged
in a bitter struggle for existence. More fortunate communes succeeded in establishing their domination over large areas of the
countryside surrounding them, their *contadi,* forcing nobles,
villages, and small cities in those districts to recognize their
authority. Control over its *contado* meant life and expansion to
a city, for it guaranteed a supply of food and of military man-
power, while denying rebels a place of refuge. It meant that
roads were free from attacks. It meant the elimination of count-

less tolls on travellers and merchandise, and provided new sources of taxable revenue.

Often, as in the cases of Milan, Florence, and Genoa, the recognition of a city's authority over the towns and nobles of its *contado* represented more than a century of effort and warfare. Yet the ultimate validity of these acquisitions did not lie in concessions forced from *contado* inhabitants but could be obtained only through an imperial grant. For in the final analysis a *contado* did not belong to the city that it surrounded, but, like the rest of imperial Italy, it was dependent directly upon the Emperor or his representatives. Thus the arrival of each imperial candidate upon Italian soil threatened to reopen the delicate issue of the legitimacy of communal control over *contado* lands, lands that in fact had been usurped from the Empire. The appearance of a new representative of imperial power raised the question of his policy with regard to those usurped imperial rights and jurisdictions. Would Henry of Luxemburg sanction the existing situation and allow communities to purchase the legitimization of their hard-won acquisitions, and at what price? Or would he try to regain those usurpations even at the cost of precipitating another bloody upheaval in Italy?

Italian cities cannot be conceived of as individual points on a map, each the center of a large circle that delineated its *contado*. A city ordinarily exercised the greatest command in the lands immediately adjacent to its walls, and the farther one went out from the walls the more a city's influence diminished, until an area was reached where that influence was contested by another city. As many cities lay close together, they were often engaged in a series of wars with their neighbors, caused in part by a struggle for the lands lying between them. The city winning those territories gained a vital source of strength, while the loser was left at a severe disadvantage. Thus did Florence cripple and then dominate neighboring Pistoia during the first decade of the fourteenth century.

Each of the stronger cities of imperial Italy was engaged in a battle for regional hegemony, and the outcome of that contest meant life or death to a great commune. In Tuscany the thirteenth-century rivalries of Florence with Siena and Pisa with

Lucca resulted in the victories of Florence and Pisa. The four-teenth century was to witness a war between the victors for the domination of Tuscany, a struggle for independent existence in which the vanquished would be drawn into the economic, military, and political orbit of the victor.

This process was being repeated throughout Italy as different communities clashed on the battlefield and in the market. Gradually certain cities, favored by location, natural resources, political astuteness, or good fortune, gained the upper hand over a large number of their neighbors. Such growing loci of power were Florence in Tuscany, Milan in central Lombardy, Genoa in Liguria, and Padua in the Trevisan March.

The emergence of these powerful cities helps to explain the fact that many neighboring cities changed their political allegiances at almost the same time. Small communes located in the sphere of influence of one of the great urban centers could not easily risk opposing the masters of those powerful cities on many important issues. When one local faction gained power in Milan, for example (as did the Della Torre in 1302), its allies and supporters soon came to the fore in the governments of such satellite cities as Lodi, Novara, and Vercelli.

This struggle for regional hegemony was directly affected by the relation of Italy to the Holy Roman Empire. Concessions extorted from a defeated rival might be challenged on the grounds of imperial privileges and diplomas held by the vanquished. If an emperor took a serious interest in Italian affairs, each contestant in the battles for local domination was forced to take a stand towards the Empire. One city might court imperial support in the form of military aid and diplomas legitimizing its past and future acquisitions; another might even oppose an emperor—despite the risk that it might appear to be a rebel against legitimate, God-given authority. With the advent of Henry of Luxemburg, all of these problems, and possibilities, would have to be faced and solved.

Italian cities and the Emperor were far from free to settle the many existing problems by themselves. In addition to the Empire, the Papacy, Venice, Robert of Anjou, and Frederick of Trinacria possessed lands and jurisdictions that entitled them to intervene in Italian affairs. This did not prevent several non-peninsular powers from interfering in the game of Italian politics when they considered it expedient.

Such an interested power was the Kingdom of Aragon. King James II relinquished his claims to Sicily only in return for the investiture of Corsica and Sardinia by Pope Boniface VIII. But investiture was not equivalent to effective occupation, and ever since 1295 the Aragonese monarch had been plotting the seizure of Sardinia from the maritime commune of Pisa, and the resulting Aragonese machinations, intrigues, and alliances further complicated peninsular politics.[16]

The French court too could display a great interest in Italian affairs. The mere fact that the Angevins of Naples were cousins of the Capetian kings would have sufficed to provoke French interest in Italy. Perhaps equally decisive were French relations with Germany and the Holy Roman Empire. Recent French rulers had made serious efforts to limit and contain the strength of their eastern neighbors, and to whittle away at imperial borderlands and incorporate them into their own realm.[17] The Capetian monarch could ill afford to ignore imperial Italy, as it might provide his rival with a source of great military and economic strength. Paris might be counted upon to keep a close watch upon the activities of Henry of Luxemburg in Italy.

The Italian peninsula presented a maze of problems and complexities to a visiting northerner. Regardless of success or failure, the future of Italy would be shaped by Henry's personal abilities, the knowledge he could gain of a complex and unfamiliar region, his conception of the rights and duties of an emperor, and by the program which, as a result of all these factors, he adopted for imperial Italy.

I

Planning an Expedition

HENRY OF LUXEMBURG: THE NEW EMPEROR-ELECT

Henry Count of Luxemburg and La Roche and Marquis of Arlon stemmed from an ancient and noble lineage, but until his election as King of the Romans and Emperor-elect in the fall of 1308 he had never been a major figure in European politics.[1] His holdings, smaller than those of his Habsburg predecessors or Adolf of Nassau, lay between the Mosel and the Meuse. While Henry held the County of Luxemburg as a direct fief of the Empire, he was also a vassal of the King of France and of his own cousin, John of Flanders, Count of Namur. Henry had the reputation of being a brave and honest ruler, with lands unusually free of brigandage and crime. As his territory contained no great natural or geographical resources while his expenses were considerable, he had difficulty making ends meet. Yet economical management had enabled him to collect money to purchase the feudal allegiance of persons living beyond the borders of his lands, especially in the nearby cities of Trier and Metz. Henry attempted to avoid the many wars that raged around his small territories. Through a cautious policy based upon negotiation and alliances, he escaped serious involvement in the fierce disputes of France and Hainault with the Counts of Flanders and Namur. Henry even made peace with his father's victorious opponent, the Duke of Brabant, whose daughter Margaret he wed in 1292.[2]

Luxemburg was indeed an imperial fief, but Henry's court language was French, and he may even have been knighted by Philip the Fair, to whom he was bound by treaties and vassalage. He had appeared frequently at Paris and signed the protest of French nobles against Boniface VIII in 1302. Four years later he and his youngest brother, Baldwin, pledged their loyalty to Philip IV. The only flaw in Henry's attachment to France was that he did not take great risks on its behalf, and ordinarily worded his treaties so as not to force himself to fight against such powers as Flanders, England, or the King of the Romans.[3] Henry's real exertions had been for the advancement of his own house and lands. Yet even benevolent neutrality had aided Philip, and early in 1308 the French monarch procured Baldwin's appointment to the Archbishopric of Trier, thus making him one of the three ecclesiastical electors of the Holy Roman Empire. Philip doubtless considered that he had placed another supporter in a high ecclesiastical post.

The new archbishop soon received a chance to demonstrate his worth. On 1 May 1308 a group of discontented Swabian-Swiss nobles assassinated Albert, King of the Romans. Philip the Fair saw an opportunity to secure the election of one of his followers to the German throne. He could then annex imperial territories on the French borders without encountering serious opposition, while Flemings, English, and others who might oppose him would be deprived of a powerful ally. Philip's candidate for emperor was his brother Charles of Valois.

Philip immediately claimed papal support for the Valois candidacy. Clement V, former Archbishop of Bordeaux, had been counted as one of Philip's supporters since his election. The Pope had not left the Venaissin since his coronation, and ignored Italian pleas to return the Papacy to its traditional home. Physically ill, Clement did not desire to expose himself either to the notoriously unhealthy Roman climate or to the Italian political turmoil and wars. Yet Philip's constant and urgent demands oppressed even the Gascon pontiff, and Clement favored the election of an emperor who might at times help him resist French influence. The Pope gave Charles of Valois only token support so that he could not be accused of openly opposing Philip's interests.[4]

The electoral princes too did not desire a Capetian emperor, and only the Archbishop of Cologne strongly favored Charles of Valois. This repugnance on the part of the electors came from the fear that a very strong king might severely limit their powers in Germany, and not from a resurgence of German nationalism. The same attitude resulted in the unfavorable hearings given to various Habsburg candidacies. During the summer of 1308 the situation remained confused, as a host of aspirants sought the electors' votes with bargains and promises.

The man who did the most to defeat the French aspirations was none other than the newly appointed Archbishop of Trier. Baldwin focused attention upon a new candidate, his older brother Count Henry IV of Luxemburg. Henry gained greatly from the support of the Archbishop of Mainz, the widely travelled and experienced statesman Peter of Aspelt, whose family came from a small Luxemburg town.[5]

There is no evidence that Henry himself had nourished aspirations to the throne before the unexpected demise of the late incumbent. Shortly after the assassination he participated in a meeting of six leading nobles of the Lower Rhine at Nivelles in Brabant.[6] These men concluded a pact for mutual military aid, agreeing that if one of them became King of the Romans he would confirm the feudal possessions of the others.

By the fall Henry's electoral campaign was in full swing. A series of astute negotiations and many lavish promises won the needed votes. On 27 November 1308 the electors unanimously chose him "to be elected King of the Romans, in the future to be promoted to Emperor, advocate of the sacrosanct Roman and universal Church, and defender of widows and orphans." [7] Henry was crowned King of the Romans and anointed by the Archbishop of Cologne in Aachen on Epiphany, 6 January 1309.[8]

The new Emperor-elect was in his middle thirties, well proportioned, of medium height, and slightly short-sighted in one eye. He was clean shaven and wore his reddish-blond hair cropped short in the contemporary French manner.[9] Modern historians variously describe this French-speaking King of the Romans as a Lowlander and a half-Frenchman.[10]

Even Henry's enemies acknowledged his noble virtues, his valiance, courage, magnanimity, and generous pacific intentions, although at times they mentioned his ingenuousness.[11] Clerical chroniclers praised his piety and Catholicity, and joyously noted his regular attendance at divine offices.[12] But since our sources do not indicate how the new ruler conceived of his position and of the role of the Empire at the time of his accession, we can only safely examine his *subsequent* actions and writings as King of the Romans and later as emperor.

Henry's chief concern during the first year of his reign was to establish his relations with the major European princes and with the more important imperial feudatories and cities and to fulfill the promises that had gained him the election.[13] He tried to set Germany in order and began to seek ways to increase the possessions and prestige of his house.

Although the failure to procure his brother's election disappointed Philip IV, he did not look with disfavor upon the new King. Considering their previous relations, Philip need not have been disturbed by visions of aggressive anti-French alliances or wars. When Henry sent an embassy to Paris, Philip responded with a cordial message of congratulations and expressed the hope that France and the Empire would prosper and remain at peace.[14] It remained to be seen whether the French monarch would actually change his policy toward the Empire in any way.

Henry soon achieved a great diplomatic success at the imperial Diet of Spires (late August—mid-September 1309), where he effected a reconciliation with the house of Habsburg.[15] He acceded to requests that the late King of the Romans be solemnly interred in the ancient Cathedral of Spires. Henry then confirmed Albert's oldest son Frederick and his brothers in the possession of their imperial fiefs and indemnified them 50,000 silver marks for the renunciation of their claims to Moravia. The Emperor-elect also conceded the Habsburgs the territories of their father's assassins, whom he duly proscribed and condemned to death. The Luxemburger, moreover, arranged to receive substantial military service from the Habsburgs. He must have been well satisfied with the outcome of these delicate negotiations.

As soon as he could free himself from these affairs, Henry of

Luxemburg set about planning a project that he held close at heart: his triumphal voyage to Italy to receive the crown of Empire. He had many reasons for desiring that the coronation take place at the earliest possible moment.[16] Once crowned emperor, he would obtain greater respect and obedience, particularly from the ignorant masses who might look with less deference upon a King of the Romans, and create disturbances or even rebellions, he said at one point. "Since many barons, because of the modes, forms, and conditions of their fiefs, and others by strength of privileges and from custom, are bound to perform many services and to make financial grants to the Emperor after his coronation and not before," Henry added, "it would redound greatly to his disadvantage should the coronation be delayed." [17] The monarch realized also that his stay in Italy must be brief, as it would be unwise to leave the northern nobles to their own devices too long.

The weakness of his dynastic and military position and the many concessions with which he had purchased electoral support in the Rhineland may have led Henry to believe that he needed some new source of strength and prestige if he were to be king in more than name alone, or if he wished to check French attrition of imperial lands. A *Romzug* might bring him both increased prestige from the imperial coronation and financial strength if he could revive imperial rights and administration in Italy. Perhaps, as some scholars maintain, Henry even now hoped to play the righteous sovereign and judge who remained above parties and brought peace to a warring Italy.[18] But while this analysis may provide clues for understanding Henry's future behavior, let us recall that, in the absence of documentation for this early period, our hypotheses concerning the monarch's earliest motivations and plans are based upon a study of later writings and deeds which occurred in new and changed situations.

Italy first received official word of the great advent in early July 1309 when messengers arrived with copies of a royal encyclical announcing that Henry, "divinely elected King of the Romans," had "placed upon his shoulders the burden of so great a rule and taken up the yoke of regal dignity." Even now he was "preparing the benefit of desired quiet for the cities and happy peoples of the Empire in the parts of Italy," and soon "the horrors of rivalries and tribulations" would be things of the past.[19]

This fine-sounding proclamation could not itself cause the wicked to tremble or the righteous to rejoice. Italy had seen similar encyclicals, proclamations, and couriers, vicars had been appointed and proctors had received homage for Kings of the Romans who had never set foot south of the Alps. Much like Henry in 1309, Adolf of Nassau had dispatched messengers to Italy in 1294, and he too spoke of bringing peace to Italy and putting an end to rivalries.[20]

More significant than his encyclical was the delegation Henry dispatched to Avignon early in June 1309.[21] Composed of men neither strongly French nor German in origin or outlook, and well known to the Luxemburger, the embassy was charged with securing papal approval and recognition of his election and coronation as King of the Romans, and with settling upon a date for the imperial coronation in Rome.[22]

The embassy offered Clement V the inducement that, once crowned, Henry VII would immediately lead a crusade to liberate the Holy Land.[23] On 26 July the ambassadors swore in the King's name that he would not usurp papal jurisdiction in Rome or in the States of the Church, that he would defend these and the Church itself, and that he would personally renew this oath after his imperial coronation. Clement thereupon officially recognized Henry. Yet despite the embassy's entreaties, the date conceded for the coronation was over two and a half years away, with the Pope retaining the right to change it if he saw fit. Clement explained that he would be occupied until then with important business, especially the coming Council of Vienne. Later in the same day Clement published an encyclical "to all persons, ecclesiastic and secular, subjects of our dearest son in Christ, Henry, illustrious King of the Romans," and announced the Holy See's acceptance of the royal election, and the decision that the imperial coronation was to take place in Rome on 2 February 1312.

The Pope demonstrated benevolence towards the new monarch in the very wording of the 26 July encyclical, which carefully avoided any expression that might indicate the subordination of the Empire to the Papacy. The encyclical clearly emphasized the divine origin, separateness, and collaboration of the *imperium* and *sacerdotium* as elaborated in the Gelasian theory.[24]

Clement recognized Henry's new status within a relatively short time,[25] but even if it was his sincere desire, he could not easily have set an earlier date for the coronation. He was busy trying to satisfy in part Philip the Fair's insistent demands that he proceed more vigorously against the order of the Knights of the Temple, and that he openly condemn his predecessor, Boniface VIII, as an heretic. Although Henry offered the Papacy a possible point of support in its dealings with the French court, the Pope proceeded cautiously, both from a realization of the power of the Capetian monarch, and from a desire not to lose the fruits of his patronage. Much could happen between the summer of 1309 and the day of the coronation, and time would be gained to observe how well Henry established himself in the sphere of European politics and what sort of ambitions he was nourishing. For the present it sufficed to pronounce him worthy of the imperial diadem and to grant him a coronation date, a date which could be advanced or retarded as conditions required. Control over the imperial coronation date was a weapon that Clement had over Henry, and he was not yet ready to give it up.

And in no way could a project that Clement presented to the royal embassy be construed as hostile to the Luxemburger. The Pope revived an old plan that Pope Nicolas III had advanced in 1277: an alliance between the imperial ruling house, the Habsburgs, and the Angevins, to be cemented by granting the Kingdom of Arles as a dowry to the heir to the Anjou fortunes.[26] Clement adapted the details of this scheme to fit present needs, and proposed an alliance based upon the marriage of Beatrice, a daughter of Henry of Luxemburg, to Charles of Calabria, a son of Robert of Anjou, with the Arelat as the dowry.[27]

According to a statement made by Pope Clement himself on 8 November 1310, the principal object of the proposed union was the healing of the breach between the Guelfs and Ghibellines in Italy through a reconciliation of their respective natural leaders in the peninsula: the House of Anjou and the King of the Romans–Emperor-elect.[28] Nor could it have escaped Clement that the marriage of a daughter of the Emperor-elect with a great-grandson of Charles I of Anjou might end the split between the Angevins and the Empire which had existed since that very Charles had executed the Hohenstaufen Conradin in 1268.

The plan had much to recommend it to Henry of Luxemburg. He would profit in Italy, as the Guelfs would see their leader removed from them and hear him openly requesting that they obey the Emperor-elect. For prior to his accession to the Sicilian throne Robert of Anjou had appeared several times in the role of nominal chieftain of the Italian Guelfs. The sight of the imperial candidate travelling to Rome in the company of his Angevin kinsman might seriously dampen enthusiasm for rebellion among recalcitrant Guelfs. Dynastically also these propositions contained advantages for Henry, as they offered the possibility of allying his noble but little-known house with one of the most important families in western Europe. Nor would the loss of the Arelat actually entail a great sacrifice, since in fact imperial power was almost nonexistent there, while Robert of Anjou already controlled a portion of it in his role of Count of Provence and Forcalquier. An independent kingdom of Arles might form a buffer between France and the Empire, providing an impediment to Philip's policy of encroachment.[29]

The Pope favored an increase in Angevin power. Since the days when Charles I had defeated the last Hohenstaufen in Italy, the Angevins had been the most faithful and effective papal vassals. The proposed alliance would place the Emperor-elect in a position of partial dependence upon Robert with regard to his activities in Italy, creating a safeguard for the Papal States as well as for the Regno. The alliance would also help the Papacy in that it tended to isolate Frederick of Trinacria, the Aragonese who was holding half the Kingdom of Sicily against papal wishes. Henry's pact with Robert would deny Frederick the possibility of imperial support.

For Clement V the creation of a kingdom of Arles had the added attraction of diminishing the relative power of Philip the Fair, who at times could press even the Pope too hard. Perhaps Clement felt that the French monarch would be pleased to see a branch of his own family strengthened at the expense of the Empire; but could the Pope have closed his eyes to Philip's intention to absorb the Arelat into his own territories? Or did Clement further the Luxemburg-Anjou marriage alliance in part to force concessions from Philip? On this we can only conjecture. But even if Clement advanced this project with the principal aim of relieving French pressure upon the Papacy, it could not be construed as an attempt to obstruct or harm the Emperor-elect.

Shortly after he received the news of Clement's proposals and actions at Avignon, Henry officially notified the princes of the Empire assembled at Spires of his intention to undertake the traditional *Romzug* to Italy in the fall of the following year. There is a lack of adequate documentation on the initial reactions of the northern nobles to the news that a King of the Romans planned to lead imperial troops over the Alpine passes for the first time in over half a century.[30] It may well be true, as told in the report of Dino Compagni, Florentine White Guelf merchant and retired statesman, that the Archbishop of Mainz urged the Luxemburger not to attempt the perilous journey south, but to content himself with being King of Germany. Peter of Aspelt had lived in Italy and probably realized that even an astute and well-prepared northern monarch might easily become mortally enmeshed in its violent and seemingly endless wars.[31] But Henry was not to be dissuaded.

After the meeting at Spires, non-Italian business kept Henry occupied. An attempt to establish his dynasty as one of the most important in western Europe involved him in a complicated contest for the crown of Bohemia. By careful planning, patience, and practical bargaining Henry concluded the project with the success that marked most of his efforts north of the Alps.[32] There he was familiar with the lands, problems, and ways of thinking. He knew how to wait and compromise, and understood the necessary techniques of diplomacy. In the north Henry appears as an intelligent politician, balancing opposed interests, buying friends, and seeking steadily to strengthen the position of his own house.

LEGATIONS TO ITALY

During these busy months Henry devoted little time to the Italian expedition one year away. Yet he did receive a promise at Spires on 17 September 1309 that one hundred heavily armed cavalry and one hundred knights equipped with bows and led by Duke Leopold of Austria would serve him for six months in

Italy at Habsburg expense.[33] There is evidence too that the King ordered the entire "Lombard" population of many Lowland cities and towns, as well as many individual Italians, to appear before him in Cologne on 23 December 1309.[34] Even persons summoned were not clearly informed as to the purpose of the meeting. Among those called were many representatives of banking houses and individual merchants, while of the twenty-eight single individuals cited by name, twenty-five came from the city of Asti. No other Italian city was named, while not a single person listed is called a Florentine. If Henry's purpose was to gather information on the state of Italy, he should have desired to hear from Tuscans as well as Lombards; but this would not necessarily have been the case if he was seeking to arrange for loans, as he could expect little assistance from Guelf banking houses that lent their gold to the Angevins and Capetians. While the assembly of Lombards at Cologne may have been designed to further a large loan for the Italian expedition rather than to investigate political conditions in the peninsula, we cannot be certain of this until more evidence is available.

Even at this early stage in his career, however, Henry knew personally several Italians who for reasons of business or politics were north of the Alps and placed themselves at his disposition. Henry heard their political interpretations, their hopes and aspirations, and their conceptions of the task to be accomplished in Italy. Perhaps his own views became slightly colored and biased in their favor. The Luxemburger, moreover, would be judged in part by those men, especially Italians, who accompanied him into the peninsula and seemed to enjoy a close relationship with the Emperor-elect at the outset of the expedition.

We know little with certainty about two Italians who served Henry in the summer and fall of 1309, Henry of Ralvengo of Asti, and Bassiano de' Guaschi, Doctor of Law, perhaps from Alessandria or Savoy.[35] We are more fortunate concerning one Italian legate whom Henry dispatched from Spires to procure Mantuan aid for the Pope's battle for Ferrara. Ugolino da Vico, papal knight, was a Ghibelline exile from Florence. Condemned to banishment, he saw in Henry's expedition a means for re-entering his native city. Such a man would be sure to urge the

King to readmit exiles to their native cities, and if the Priory ignored such a royal command, Ugolino might hope to return home in the wake of a victorious imperial army and even secure a position in a Ghibelline regime that would surely follow. Ugolino served his new master well in September 1309, and received an even more important commission before he accompanied the imperial expedition across the Alps.[36] Another Florentine exile, Vermiglio degli Alfani, also offered Henry his services early. This former banker for Albert of Habsburg quite naturally sought to establish similar relations with the new King of the Romans.[37] Yet the open use and favoring of such men, despite their experience and competence, might give the Italian expedition an aggressive and anti-Guelf appearance and expose the Emperor-elect to dangerous hostility.

In the spring of 1310 Henry began to make serious preparations for the great *Romzug*. Two imperial legations left Germany to visit the lords and cities of Tuscany and Lombardy. Each legation was composed of two Swiss or German bishops and two laymen. Gerard, Bishop of Constance, led the embassy to Lombardy, and was accompanied by Siegfried of Gelnhausen, Bishop of Chur, and two Italians, Ugolino da Vico and Henry of Ralvengo. To Tuscany went Gerard of Wippingen, Bishop of Basel, Philip of Ratsamhausen, Bishop of Eichstädt, and the layman Bassiano de' Guaschi. The other lay legate was the far more important Louis of Savoy, Lord of Vaud and nephew of Count Amadeus V. He had recently been elected Senator of Rome, and received papal approval to assume office on 1 August during the course of his mission to Tuscany.[38]

Both embassies had the same charge: to announce and prepare the way for the forthcoming expedition. They proclaimed that the Emperor-elect would arrive in Italy no later than 29 September 1310, and declared that all men must receive him as they were bound to do. Every city was to send him armed escorts and proctors empowered to hear and promise to fulfill his commands. All roads and bridges must be put in good repair and victuals set aside for the imperial expedition. Moreover, all warfare must cease and a truce be maintained until 1 November, by which time Henry would be on the scene and could resolve all existing difficulties. Any violation of this truce would be punished by banishment or other such penalty as pleased the Emperor-elect.[39]

There is no indication that the embassies strayed from the missions assigned them. They did not delve into the political and military conditions of the land, nor attempt to study its economic or social structure. They were to prepare for the coming expedition and collect promises of obedience to the Emperor-elect, and not to investigate and analyze the many complex problems that awaited him.

Fortunately we are well informed as to the progress of the embassy to Lombardy and its reception in more than twenty-five cities and towns as it travelled eastwards across the Po valley, arriving at Venice and the extreme limits of the Trevisan March and circling back through Modena, Reggio, and Parma on the Via Emilia.[40]

The great masses of people almost universally greeted the embassy with enthusiasm. But it is difficult to say whether this was done more from a fickle readiness to see a change of rulers, as claimed by the Guelf chronicler Ferreto de' Ferreti of Vicenza, or from a desire to see justice done to tyrants, or from a general hope that the advent of an emperor would inaugurate a new era of peace and prosperity.[41] For while ruling factions and *signori* might be greatly interested in the maintenance of city "liberty" and independence (and their own positions), many ordinary citizens fervently hoped that the arrival of that mysterious figure, the Emperor, might augur a return of peace.[42]

Throughout its travels the embassy received promises of obedience from numerous counts, barons, and castellans in every part of Lombardy. Political exiles showed particular zeal in searching out the legates and loading them with the strongest oaths and vows. Members of defeated political factions "of Bologna and of all the other cities of Lombardy" rushed to offer their services to the Emperor-elect.[43] Some perhaps desired the beginning of a reign of peace, tranquility, and justice, while others sought only to re-enter their native cities, regain their property, offices, and positions and avenge themselves upon their enemies.

Normally when the legates arrived in a city they addressed the assembled populace and clergy in a large palace, church, or central square. Later the podesta, captain of the people, or vicar of the place, together with its wise men or ancients, delivered a prepared answer in the name of the city at a private meeting with the legates.

Many cities paid the legates' expenses during their stay and several added handsome personal presents in order to make a favorable impression. Even a brief examination of the legates' reception in various cities makes it clear that blandishments were not offered, or withheld, in accordance with the supposed Ghibelline or Guelf political allegiance of ruling communal factions. And of course a city like Venice had long ago learned the advantages to be gained from favorable popes and emperors, and made certain to entertain the embassy in the best fashion.[44]

Nor is it strange to find that the Ghibelline *signori* ruling Modena, Mantua, and Verona paid the legates' expenses and feted them royally, the Scaligers of Verona adding personal gifts. The lords of these cities might win legal or military support from the presence in Lombardy of an Emperor-elect, even if he came under papal auspices and bearing standards of peace. Such possible advantages were well worth the game.

Some so-called Guelf *signori* did not lag behind their Ghibelline counterparts, and Pavia and Piacenza in central Lombardy created excellent impressions upon the embassy. The legates reported that at Pavia they were received

> honorably above all other places. . . . the bishop and Count Philippone [Langusco] and the major part of the people of the city, on horse and on foot, came before us, and there we solemnly proposed our chapters. They responded that they wished to serve our lord as their natural lord and to carry out and obey all his commands, and to do even more if they were able. And they paid our expenses. The bishop and all of his people responded similarly.[45]

This reception by the nominally Guelf lords of Pavia may appear particularly strange when we recall that Philippone Langusco was father-in-law of the great Guelf captain Guido della Torre of Milan. But the Langusco Guelfism was scarcely three decades old, and for centuries the Langusco Counts Palatine of the Lomello had proudly maintained their imperial allegiance. Ideals of feudal chivalry in part moved the count, and he did not wish to contemplate disobedience to his liege lord. Moreover, Philip could gain much from loyalty, including the sought-after confirmation of many imperial grants.[46] And anything less than a zealous reception of his sovereign would play into the hands of Langusco's exiled Ghibelline rival for rule of Pavia. Thus the Langusco decided immediately among themselves to give the embassy excellent treatment, without waiting to hear the opinions of neighboring Guelf chieftains as did so many other Lombard *signori*.

The embassy received an equally enthusiastic reception from Alberto Scotto, "magnificent and honorable citizen . . . [and] governor of the city" of Piacenza.[47] This so-called Guelf lord had reversed political alliances more than once, and his only constant policy was a determined zeal to establish his rule in Piacenza. Since the Emperor-elect might further Scotto's life-long ambition, appearance at the royal court, or even playing the Ghibelline, was a small enough price to pay.

In like fashion Ghiberto da Correggio, nominal Guelf ruler of Parma, received the embassy in royal fashion, paid its expenses, and promised to obey all of its commands.[48] This political opportunist was severely menaced by his Ghibelline sons-in-law, the *signori* of Mantua and Verona, and by his exiled Parmesan Guelf rivals. Ghiberto did not want to incur the royal wrath, or to overlook the possibility of enlisting powerful support.

The course pursued by Richard da Camino of Treviso, greatest Guelf *signore* of the March, is particularly interesting. His position was extremely difficult, as he had risen to power with the support of the Trevisan Guelf nobles, and he could not afford to offend nearby Padua, the stronghold of Guelfism in eastern Lombardy. Nevertheless, when the *signore* of Treviso realized that the imperial visit to Italy would actually materialize, he rapidly attempted to gain favor with the King of the Romans. Less than a week before the embassy's arrival he installed as podesta of Treviso Galeazzo Visconti of Milan, eldest son of Lombardy's leading Ghibelline chieftain. The legates' report of Da Camino's response, made after a requested delay of several days, showed the still-unresolved ambiguity of his position:

> [Treviso and Richard da Camino] are very happy at the coming of the lord [Emperor], and greatly hoped that it would be to the honor and reverence and peace of the Holy Church and of the Empire. They responded to our other chapters that they intend to honor and serve our lord the Emperor in all things that they could and should. And they paid the expenses of our going and coming for five days, and gave us each a silver cup.[49]

Whatever misgivings and preoccupations existed in Guelf Padua, that city too received the embassy honorably, congratulated Henry upon his good fortune, welcomed him to Italy, and augured him a long life. The Paduans expressed their pleasure at Henry's good relations with the Church, and carefully pointed out their own long and faithful allegiance to it. But then the Paduan response proceeded to much more dangerous ground, and recalled that the Church had been Padua's great defense against the "evil tyrant" Ezzelino da Romano—the imperial vicar of Frederick II.[50] Nevertheless a Cremonese chronicler probably recalls a state of mind prevalent among Padua's ruling classes, rather than the actual negotiations with the embassy, when he relates that the Paduans openly declared that, as they were already in a state of peace and tranquility, there was no need for the Emperor to come and pacify them, and concluded bluntly, "Therefore we do not want him to come."[51]

Padua might well fear the advent of an Emperor-elect, especially one who was concerned with maintaining and restoring imperial rights, since Padua had been holding the imperial city of Vicenza in protective custody for almost half a century. Vicenza greeted the news of Henry's coming with tremendous joy, as many citizens hoped that it would mark the end of Paduan domination. But for the present, Vicenza could only place its official response in the hands of its custodian.[52]

Two other localities dominated by an overpowering neighbor greeted the embassy enthusiastically, and expressed veiled hopes that the arrival of their titular sovereign would mean renewed independence. A vicar of Guido della Torre openly ruled the castle of Vigevano southwest of Milan, despite the fact that

Vigevano possessed imperial diplomas stating that it pertained
directly to the Empire as part of the *camera regis*. Although
Vigevano could not respond officially to the embassy until it
received word from Milan, its statement added that if it could
say what was in its heart it would at once declare a readiness to
do everything asked of it, and even more, "for the said Lord
Emperor is its lord in all and for all." [53] Monza, which not only
pertained to the *camera regis* but claimed to be the "seat of the
Kingdom of Italy" and the rightful coronation place of kings,
was ruled by a Torriani podesta. The embassy reported that the
men of Monza were highly pleased at the announcement of "the
Emperor's approaching arrival, but at present they could neither
give nor make a response unless they first spoke with Lord Guido
della Torre of Milan, who is at present lord of the said place." [54]
But if forts and towns dominated by great cities or *signori* welcomed Henry's arrival in hopes of being liberated, what fears
and distrust arose in Padua or Torriani-ruled Milan? [55]

On Monday 8 June 1310 the embassy entered Milan, a pivotal
city upon whose reaction much of Henry's success or failure
would depend. The Bishop of Constance delivered the royal
requests before a huge throng of citizens, and tried to recall
Milan's imperial allegiance by evoking memories of its past
glories and promising that the King of the Romans would be
crowned in Milanese territory and by the Milanese archbishop.
A speaker for Guido della Torre then replied that as such
weighty matters had to be considered in council, an official
response would be communicated in a fortnight.[56]

The legates visited other cities while they awaited the Milanese
answer, but in fact they could accomplish little. Neighboring
towns, whether nominally Guelf or Ghibelline, depended upon
Milan and were more or less tightly subjected to its hegemony.
Novara could only tell the legates that it could not answer clearly
because of its obligations "to many other cities of Lombardy." [57]
Lodi begged to be excused from answering because it was

> a modest city and a modest commune and can and could do
> little, and the communes of Milan, Cremona, Piacenza, Pavia,
> and Bergamo surrounding the city of Lodi are great and most
> powerful communes, and the commune of Lodi could not resist

them. And because the ambassadors of the commune of Lodi
and other ambassadors of the communes of the Lombard
League are in the city of Milan for the purpose of considering
the answer to be made to the said lord ambassadors of the Lord
Emperor.[58]

We may wonder whether the embassy recognized the implications
of the use of the designation "Lombard League," an ominous
reminder of struggles of the twelfth and thirteenth centuries.

Ambassadors of the interested cities duly assembled, indeed,
but the conferences that were to have decisive effect were those
in Guido's private hall attended by the most powerful Guelf
lords in central Lombardy.[59] Present were Count Philippone
Langusco of Pavia, William Cavalcabò of Cremona, Antonio
Fissiraga of Lodi, Simone degli Avvocati di Colobiano of Vercelli, Alberto Scotto of Piacenza, and Guido himself. Count
Philippone seems to have thrown the meeting into partial confusion when he refused to hear of opposition or rebellion against
his feudal lord, the Emperor. Cavalcabò and Della Torre tried to
dissuade him, perhaps aided in their efforts by Fissiraga. They
saw in Henry's advent a serious menace to their positions, but
felt that with resolute military action they could prevent his
entry into Lombardy. Scotto argued that craft was the only means
for successful resistance. There was even a risk, he said, that any
who tried to oppose the Emperor's coming with armed resistance
might be overthrown by the very people of the communes who
seemed to be eagerly awaiting the new ruler. The best course,
counselled Scotto, was to accept Henry with the most benign
appearance possible. Guido was infuriated and would have none
of this. "Tell me," he cried, "are we bound to Henry of Luxemburg, to an unknown German or Allobroge!"

But Guido did not prevail. The meeting could not decide
upon a common program satisfactory to all, since it was in actuality a temporary, uneasy union of several lords, each looking
out for his own selfish interests and willing to sacrifice his associates in an effort to make the best possible bargain with the
coming Emperor-elect.[60] The one important action taken at
Milan was the decision to send messengers to the Pope from
Guido, Milan, Pavia, Novara, Como, and Crema (representing

also Vercelli, Lodi, Tortona, Piacenza, and Cremona), requesting
assurances that they would not be harmed by Henry, and asking
Clement's advice as to how they should receive the coming
monarch.[61]

Guido was compelled to follow Scotto's tactics, and thus it was
that on 22 June 1310 the imperial messengers were told that the
Milanese were prepared

> to come to the lord king honorably and decently, and to re·
> ceive the same lord king magnificently, and to honor him with
> all their forces, and to do all things to which they are held,
> and to conserve his honors and rights according to their ability.
> They hold firm confidence that the said lord king will con-
> serve and maintain the said lord captain [Guido della Torre]
> and the Milanese commune and its friends in its every honor
> and in the condition in which they are and [in] all of their
> rights and privileges, the immunities, honors, and conventions
> that . . . the Milanese commune has and was accustomed to
> having from the Empire.[62]

Guido della Torre had decided that it would be most prudent
to welcome this foreign ruler whose coming he could not prevent.
This he did in flowery and rhetorical terms, linked with the
veiled threat that any effort to remove him or his followers from
power, to weaken seriously his position, or to upset the hard-won
Milanese hegemony in central Lombardy and rule in its own
contado would be met with resistance. Already two other Lombard cities had requested similar respect for their privileges.[63]

The imperial legates could not have been fully informed as to
the proceedings in Milan. They might, however, have noted the
interesting fact that almost half a dozen Lombard cities responded in the same form: they welcomed the Emperor's advent
inasmuch as he was coming with the full approval and blessing
of the Holy Church, to which they were especially devoted.[64]
While the legates need not have taken umbrage since Henry did
have papal sanction, this type of answer might well mask a strong
antipathy at the prospect of the arrival of another emperor in
Lombardy. The qualified welcome given the embassy by the
"modest city" of Lodi may have been more a sign of deference
to the Della Torre than a defiant expression of opposition to the

King of the Romans. The same did not hold, however, for Cremona, ruled by the fierce Guelf *signore* William Cavalcabò. Immediately upon hearing the embassy's propositions the Cremonese officials dryly responded that

> they wish to notify the Lord Pope of the aforesaid things, and to have the counsel of the said Lord Pope concerning the said embassy, and if it be the decision and wish of the Lord Pope that they obey the said Lord Emperor, they will be prepared to do the bidding and the mandates of the same Lord Emperor and the said Lord Pope.[65]

Yet Cremona remained one of the only places with whose answers the legates do not appear to have been fully satisfied.[66]

Many questions concerning the embassy to Lombardy cannot be answered from the extant evidence, but we are still less equipped to study the activities and fortunes of the legates sent to Tuscany. On 28 May 1310 the exiled Ghibelline chief of Vercelli, Richard Tizzone, wrote the Emperor-elect from the region of Feltre in the Trevisan March that he had recently met the royal embassy and pledged the monarch a military escort and firm support and obedience.[67]

Our next evidence of the embassy places it in the Piedmontese commune of Asti in mid-June.[68] It arrived at a crucial moment. The air buzzed with rumors that the city, long pressed by Savoyards and Angevins, was about to give up its liberty and become a vassal of Robert of Anjou. Philip of Savoy himself had come to Asti, threatening and cajoling the magistrates to swear never to elect Robert as their king, "for he was Philip's enemy." According to the contemporary anti-Savoyard chronicler Guillelmus Ventura, the imperial legates proposed that Asti "not be subjected to anyone, and especially not to the yoke of the King of Sicily." Asti then answered the embassy and the Savoyard, "We are servants of the Lord Emperor, and we do not have, nor will we have, any other lord before him all the days of our lives." Considering the bias of our source (and its tendency to sacrifice some accuracy for the sake of drama and synchronism), we can safely conclude only that in Asti the embassy enjoyed the aid of Philip of Savoy, who in turn used its presence to further his own purposes. The city's past maneuverings and policies indicate the sincerity of the promise to take no other lord.[69] Asti desired to maintain its actual independence and its communal institutions, and its leaders saw in the Angevin only a military ally against the city's exiles.

When the embassy left Asti it travelled to Cuneo, a small commune belonging to Robert as Count of Piedmont. But unfortunately we do not know what took place there, or in Savona and Genoa, which it visited later.

On 20 June the embassy received a royal welcome as it entered Pisa, close to the mouth of the Arno River in Tuscany.[70] The announcement of the coming expedition reawakened old enthusiasms for Ghibellinism and Empire, both intimately associated with the age of Pisa's greatest glories. The city took new hope in its fight for survival against Florence, with its Tuscan Guelfs and Catalan mercenaries, and against the persistent designs of James II of Aragon upon Sardinia, a major source of Pisan revenue. Pisa offered Henry of Luxemburg the handsome gift of tents for himself and ten thousand of his followers, at a cost of four thousand gold florins. The King's tent became a masterpiece of craftsmanship, decorated with golden silk, adorned with precious stones, and surmounted by a golden imperial eagle.

The preparation of the gifts was to be supervised by Giovanni de' Cerchi, a prominent Florentine White Guelf exile.[71] He was only one of many enemies of Florence who had taken refuge in Pisa and there plotted revenge. On 30 June, a hundred Luccan White Guelf exiles in Pisa appointed proctors to appear before the embassy, do allegiance to Henry, and promise to obey his every command upon the pledge of all their property.[72]

Large portions of Tuscany, however, did not receive the legates in the same spirit as Pisa. Even before the embassies set forth, important groups within Italy prepared for the arrival of the Emperor-elect and tried to foresee what difficulties might arise from his presence in the strife-torn peninsula. Behind much of this activity lay the commune of Florence, whose Black Guelf rulers quickly realized what dangers the imperial expedition could entail. They had no desire to see their monopoly on the city's government broken, or to share rule with the men whom it had exiled and deprived of their property—and such a peril existed if the Emperor-elect intended to implement his announced program of pacification. Any effective imperial intervention in Italian affairs might destroy the great gains that the commune had made in its century-old struggle for the hegemony of Tuscany. Large portions of the Florentine *contado* by right were directly dependent upon the Empire and had been subjected to Florence by force. An emperor might well attempt to regain them.

The unconfirmed report of the Florentine Dino Compagni indicates that as early as the summer of 1309 Florence had made diplomatic efforts to stave off the coming expedition, counselling the Luxemburger not to undertake the perilous journey to Italy and baldly stating that it sufficed for him to be King of Germany. This Florentine tactic, if such it actually was, failed completely.[73]

More successful were attempts to protect Florence by military alliances with friendly Italian cities. Florentine control had already been established over small nearby communes such as Prato and San Gimignano, while Lucca and Siena followed the Florentine lead almost invariably in foreign affairs. During the late winter and early spring of 1310 Florence, together with its satellites and followers, sought to join in a military league with the powerful Guelf city of Bologna, a strategic link along the Emilian Way. By mid-March 1310 these Florentine efforts resulted in the creation of a military league by means of a pact binding upon its members for five years.[74]

When Florence built military leagues for the suppression of Pistoia or Arezzo, it used the nominal Guelfism of its allies as the common element binding them together, and claimed to be acting as the leader of a Guelf league or party, and not merely in its own interest. Similarly, this league of March 1310 joining Bologna to Florence and its followers was made firm by conjuring up the common element of Guelfism. The documents creating the alliance were written to protect the interests of the Guelf Party as well as those of the individual league members. All differences between the member communes or their citizens, if these were Guelfs, were to be laid aside.

The newly formed association was in essence a defensive military alliance, whose members were bound to consult with each other on problems touching their common welfare. A league army of four thousand cavalry was to be created by 1 May 1310, and its disposition lay with the more important participants— Bologna, Florence, Lucca, and Siena. The way was left open for the expansion of this league, since Bologna reserved the right to invite representatives from Lombardy and the Romagna to future meetings.

The emphasis upon a common Guelf name was not the only hint of the league's orientation. A still surer indication was contained in the *arenga* of the pact, stating that it was written in honor of Christ and the Church, the Pope and the cardinals, and King Robert of Sicily. An article of the convention provided that the allies were to send common representatives bearing the same instructions to the Pope, the cardinals, and King Robert. It would appear that the allied cities naming themselves Guelfs were calling upon the very forces that had traditionally succored the Guelf Party in the thirteenth century—the Papacy and the Angevins of Naples.

But what was the league's attitude towards the Empire and the Emperor-elect? These are not mentioned in the extant documents; yet there is no doubt that it was the forthcoming imperial expedition of Henry of Luxemburg that had called forth this alliance. There was no other new or serious menace to the security of Florence and Bologna. Parties friendly to them controlled most of the leading cities in Tuscany, the Romagna, and Lombardy. Their reluctance to declare openly against the Emperor-elect is understandable when we recall that he had received the blessings of the Pope, and was negotiating with Robert of Anjou for a marriage alliance which the Angevin seemed eager to conclude.[75] Neither of the principal powers upon which the league had called as its protectors was ready to listen to threats against the Emperor-elect.

The following months saw a spate of meetings of the Bolognese–Tuscan Guelf League, and events demonstrated that the omission of a statement against the Emperor-elect in the pact of mid-March 1310 was caused by more than the realization that it would have been imprudent in view of papal and Angevin attitudes. The Guelfs of Tuscany, led by Florence, did not seek war with their temporal sovereign. They were willing to obey the

King of the Romans, provided that he grant their fundamental political desires.

In order to achieve this, Florence was perfectly satisfied to show Henry the greatest respect and to shower him with promises. This becomes clear when we examine the Tuscan Guelf treatment of the imperial embassy during the summer of 1310. Florence wrote to Lucca that

> the ambassadors of the said king should be honored, and that they should be answered with elegant and general words, especially showing sufficient devotion, [and they should be told] that your commune is joined to many other communes by the insoluble bond of a society, league, and fraternity, as ancient as it is new, without whose assent and unanimous and common deliberation you cannot give a response to the . . . aforesaid ambassadors; and that also above all, together with the other aforementioned partners or communes, you intend to send solemn ambassadors to the Lord Pope, with special regard to the aforesaid cause. And you should also use other finer words concerning these things, such as seem most suitable according to your wisdom, provided that you do not obligate yourselves in anything.[76]

It comes as no surprise then that the imperial embassy was received magnificently by the Tuscan Guelf cities, and was showered with fine words and gifts.[77] Only at Florence itself, where the embassy arrived on 3 July, was there any slip in the prearranged plans for the legates' festive and honorable reception. The legates delivered their message at a meeting of the Great Council, but with the additional request that Florence abandon a siege it was conducting against its enemy, Ghibelline Arezzo. This was a natural corollary to Henry's order that a general truce be instituted at once and remain effective until 1 November. But the distinguished chieftain Betto Brunelleschi had heard as much as he could stomach. He had seen an imperial embassy enter the city, accompanied by Ghibelline and White Guelf exile enemies of every true Florentine. So far he had maintained silence, and, following the policy laid down by the Priory, had even feigned pleasure at all this. When called upon to respond

for the commonwealth, Brunelleschi answered the embassy in
words *"superbe e disoneste,"* [78] crying out that "the Florentines
have never lowered their horns to any lord." [79] The Priory's
efforts to repair this tactical error were not very successful.

What was the purpose of the vague promises, the false show
of respect and love, and the embassies to Avignon and Naples?
What did Florence and its allies hope to win from the Emperor-
elect? Dino Compagni provides us with an answer in a brief
passage discussing the attitude of Lucca towards the Luxemburger: "Several times they [the Luccans] said that they would
obey him, if he conceded them letters [stating] that they could
keep the lands they held of the Empire and that he would not
restore the exiles [to Lucca]." [80] The terms of Florence itself are
neatly outlined in a letter written to several of its agents little
more than two weeks after Henry's arrival in Italy.[81] The commune desired

> that the Emperor himself . . . leave [*dimittat*] those cities and
> communes [of Florence, Lucca, and Siena], with the districts,
> *contadi,* and lands which they hold, in free jurisdiction and in
> their present state, and that he concede to those communes . . .
> the *contadi,* districts, and lands which they hold, as they now
> hold them.

If he were willing to grant these terms, and only in that case,
the Tuscan Guelf communes would give "the Emperor" cash
payments and troop service, the letter continued.

The letters written in connection with the imperial embassy
of the summer of 1310 and the Florentine correspondence of the
following fall reveal another important side of the Tuscan Guelf
position: it did not rest in any sense either upon a denial of the
rights of the Emperor-elect in Tuscany or upon a refusal to
recognize Henry of Luxemburg as the rightful head of the Empire. He was continually referred to as either "King of the
Romans" or "the Emperor," and his rights were not denied. No
distinction was made between the rights of the King of the
Romans–Emperor-elect and those of the crowned Emperor.[82]
The Florentine Priors were no revolutionaries. Here was no open
ideological clash between the rights of free communes and those
of the Empire. Men in power were trying to conclude a practical

LIBRIUM®

A valuable adjunct in the treatment of alcoholism

bargain that would legitimize their continued rule and assure the well-being of their communes. While these men sought the necessities of life and expansion for their secularized city-states, they still appeared willing to attain their goals within the framework of the medieval Christian Empire. But if the acknowledged representative of imperial authority denied their claims, they would be forced to choose between the independence of their city-states and continued allegiance to the concept of Empire.

The aims and stratagems of the Tuscan Guelf cities captained by Florence must not, moreover, be confused and equated with "Italian Guelfism." Despite the provision made in March 1310 that representatives from other regions might attend meetings of the Bolognese–Florentine league, Tuscan and Lombard Guelfism did not present a united front with regard to the Emperor-elect. And while in Tuscany parties had a reasonably broad base of support within their cities and could therefore unite behind Florence, in Lombardy Guelf control rested upon a very personal basis, and policy was based largely upon the desires of a few individual *signori* and would-be *signori,* who at times could not even count upon the majority of their own families for support.[83] These differences in the composition of political parties and governments in the major regions of imperial Italy may help to explain why an anti-imperial league could materialize in Tuscany, but not in Lombardy.

Henry of Luxemburg, however, did not have the benefit of either our investigatory techniques or our hindsight. Few signs of possible difficulty filtered back to the royal court with the returning embassies in late August 1310. In the north several cities leagued with Milan had desired to consult together before answering the legates. Similarly in Tuscany many cities leagued with Florence had delayed in answering, while in both regions men had sought reassurances from the Supreme Pontiff. There had been definite evidences of hostility manifested in Florence, the government of Cremona (though not the populace) had been decidedly cold, and that of Padua less pleased than was desirable. Exiles had given dire warnings, along with profuse offers of aid, but much of this might be discounted as biased and partisan attacks by bitter and disillusioned men. On the other hand, the announcement of Henry's coming had been almost univer-

sally received with overt signs of joy and welcome, and his embassies had been showered with gifts and promises of allegiance
and obedience.[84] We have no indication that Henry did not
think that all was well, or that he took any special precautions
as a result of his embassies' reports.

The embassies sent to Italy in the spring of 1310 perhaps serve
the modern historian more than they did their originator. Henry
had little time to study the many documents that his legates
brought back and to analyze the nuances of meaning in carefully
and subtly worded responses. His future actions indicate that he
passed over many fine points which might have given him a better understanding of the complex situations into which he was
about to enter. But the Emperor-elect had other pressing business to conclude before starting south, and he devoted much
time to such affairs as negotiating a peace pact with Philip the
Fair, coming to an agreement with the Pope, dealing with the
Bohemians for their crown, with the German nobles and cities,
and finally making the necessary arrangements for the Italian
expedition.

FINAL PREPARATIONS

Henry expedited much varied business at two great imperial
diets held during the summer of 1310.[85] At Frankfort, during
the second half of July, provisions were made for maintaining
peace and order in Germany during the King's absence. Henry's
son John, elevated to the rank of Count of Luxemburg and La
Roche and Marquis of Arlon, was to administer the lands north
of the Alps with the aid of Peter of Aspelt, Archbishop of Mainz.
The oath rendered by the Bohemians to Henry, Duke of Carinthia and Count of Tyrol, was declared invalid, and the wedding
of John of Luxemburg with Elizabeth, heiress to Bohemia, was
set for 30 August at Spires. The wedding took place as planned,
and the young King was duly enfeoffed with Bohemia and
Moravia. At Spires too Henry undertook to assure peace in Germany and made more grants to leading nobles and prelates, the
Archbishops of Mainz and Cologne receiving the lion's share.
The Archbishop of Cologne, who had by previous agreement
been named Archchancellor of the Empire for Italy, announced

that he would be unable to go south and appointed as his vicar Henry, Abbot of the Cistercian monastery of Villers.

Henry of Luxemburg made a critical error in judgment in his haste to become emperor. A large number of German nobles suggested that he delay the Italian expedition and receive the crown on 2 February 1312, as fixed by Clement V; [86] but Henry desired to advance the coronation date as much as possible. Thus he spent the remaining days at Spires preparing for not one but three military expeditions. First, King John had to occupy Bohemia in the face of resolute opposition from Henry of Carinthia and his supporters. This action deprived the Italian expedition of many valuable soldiers and counsellors, among them Peter of Mainz, Duke Rudolf of Bavaria, and Philip of Eichstädt, recently returned from Tuscany. A second army, composed largely of Swiss and Swabian contingents, was organized to combat that perennial enemy of the Kings of the Romans, Count Eberhard of Württemburg, who was now declared to be in contumacy and ban of the Empire.[87] Henry had recruited a few participants for the third military expedition, that to Italy, as early as the summer of 1309, but he only began to pursue the matter in earnest a year later at the second Diet of Spires. And far from being the entire imperial army, or *Reichsheerbann,* it was only a contingent of about five thousand troops that prepared to accompany Henry of Luxemburg across the Alps. His soldiers were mostly Luxemburgers, Lowlanders, Lorrainers, Alsatians, Swiss, Savoyards, Burgundians, and men from the Dauphinate. Moreover, while younger sons and brothers of great nobles frequently volunteered for this Italian campaign, Henry ordinarily did not obtain the services of even the greatest lords in those lands most heavily represented in his army.[88]

Examination of the promises of military service makes one fact clear: Henry lacked funds even before he started to cross the Alps. His own possessions were hardly rich, and the electoral campaign had been costly. The Emperor-elect was obliged to reimburse most of the nobles who accompanied him for at least the maintenance of their following of cavalry or foot soldiers. He sought to do this by granting the right to collect tolls rather than by making money payments—and in at least one case he said that this was because of a shortage of cash. This lack of

money could prove a serious disability in Italy. Should he en-
counter strong resistance or actual rebellion that necessitated
mercenary soldiers or extra service from his feudal levies, the
Emperor-elect might be compelled to accept the aid of any who
came to him, in return for almost any favors that they might ask.
But records do not indicate that Henry anticipated such difficulties, and he probably assumed that the expedition would pay for
itself from Italian taxes and requisitions.

Since the Brenner Pass in the east was vulnerable to attack by
Duke Henry of Carinthia, the Luxemburger chose another route
into Italy. He decided upon the pass of Mount Cenis in Savoy
because his brother-in-law Count Amadeus and his nephews held
all its approaches. Nor did Henry omit to ingratiate himself with
the Savoyards on the eve of the expedition. On 2 July 1310 he
told Philip of Savoy that he would assist his efforts to secure the
cash payments due him from Robert of Anjou for his renunciation of the title "Prince of Achaia." If the Angevin did not pay,
Henry would personally make good the sum.[89]

The Emperor-elect wished to take all reasonable precautions
for safeguarding the lands north of the Alps before leaving for
Italy. In the spring of 1310 he sent a second embassy to Paris,
charged with concluding treaties of peace and alliance with
Philip IV. On 27 June proctors signed pacts which provided for
a commission to arbitrate any border disputes.[90] But such promises should not have deceived Henry for long. A meeting scheduled for 22 August never took place, and Philip revealed his true
intentions by capturing the city of Lyon after a brief campaign
in the summer of 1310—a campaign in which, we may note, Amadeus of Savoy assisted the French king against his own nephew
the Archbishop of Lyon.[91] Here the Count placed his own interests before kinship—and it is not unreasonable to assume that he
assisted Henry of Luxemburg in the Italian expedition more
because he hoped to gain more influence and holdings in the
peninsula than because of ties of kinship or friendship.

During the late spring and summer of 1310, however, Henry
entrusted Count Amadeus V with a crucial mission. The King of
the Romans was preparing to depart for Italy and the Roman
coronation. It was essential that his arrival be preceded by a clear
pronouncement of papal approval, coupled with unequivocal

pontifical commands that all obey the coming monarch. Only thus could Henry insure the good will, or at least the neutrality, of papal supporters and deprive any who might wish to oppose the presence of an emperor in Italy of an excellent rallying cry and the claim to be the defenders of the Holy Roman Church. Count Amadeus headed the embassy that arrived in Avignon in June 1310, commissioned to hear the Pope's desires and obtain the needed papal blessings for the coming expedition.[92]

The envoys brought with them a series of royal requests, to many of which Clement V acceded.[93] The Pontiff further demonstrated his good will towards Henry by approving the election as Senator of Rome of Louis of Savoy, a man sure to favor the Luxemburger's interests, and by granting Henry the right to fill fifteen ecclesiastic positions in "the Kingdom of Germany." [94]

Clement refused, however, to grant the one request that called upon the Papacy to make a financial sacrifice. More than half of the document containing the papal responses to Henry's petition is filled with an involved argument in which Clement explained that, much as he desired to do so, he was unable to comply with secret petitions that the Emperor-elect be given the tithes and annates for one year, as that would greatly jeopardize the crusade that the Pope planned to organize at the Council of Vienne.

The Pontiff added that the King would hear in person certain other things which it would be indiscreet to commit to writing. One of these became public indirectly in another papal writing of 1 September.[95] Royal envoys had requested that the coronation date be advanced. This was not done. Clement knew that Philip IV had no desire to see the King made emperor, and the Pope had no reason for opposing the French king at this point.

The Pope's letter of 27 June, containing his responses to the royal requests, closed with the exhortation that Henry be an imitator of the King of Peace (*ut sis Regis pacifici imitator*), an indication of the role that Clement expected Henry to play in Italy.

The King of the Romans need not have been dissatisfied with the papal reception of his requests, for there had been little chance that he would receive the tithes and annates, and the coronation date might still be advanced once he crossed the Alps —the Pope might decide to expedite Henry's leaving Italy as soon as possible in order to avoid any misunderstandings or disturbances.

The returning embassy brought with it a document containing Clement's demands upon Henry. These had to be complied with before the Italian expedition could be further considered at Avignon—and therefore before the precious papal approval would be forthcoming.

The Pope drove a hard bargain. His first request was that Henry take an oath to aid the Church at all times, not to harm it in any way, and to confirm all privileges granted it by previous Kings of the Romans and emperors—particularly those conceding jurisdiction over lands in Italy.[96] But the list of lands claimed for the Church was more detailed and farther reaching than even the most extensive of the concessions made by that most generous of Roman kings, Rudolf of Habsburg.[97] Henry was asked to concede the cities of Perugia and Città di Castello and the entire Romagna, to acknowledge papal rule over each of the key communes and areas of the Patrimony of St. Peter in Tuscany, and to grant specifically all the rights and jurisdictions pertaining to all the territories listed.

In a copy of the promises that he signed at Hagenau on 17 August 1310, Henry did not include the city of Bologna, Orvieto in the Patrimony, the County of Bertinoro, and Arce Cesarum —a fortress near Terni. Nor did he retain the clause "integrally with all the cities, lands, limits, boundaries, and confines, and with all the rights and jurisdictions of the same" which Clement had so carefully inserted after each of the major cities and regions.

The Pope was not to be thwarted. A month later he wrote Henry recognizing the receipt of the promises, which, he reminded the King, would be filed in the papal archives. However, he regretted to state that the document contained a few very minor omissions, doubtless due to the carelessness of a scribe. He would appreciate it if Henry would send other, complete copies.[98] Despite any personal misgivings and the objections that he probably heard from various princes of the Empire, Henry gave in completely and sent a satisfactory form from Lausanne on 11 October, complying in every particular with the curial desires.

The papal form contained yet another clause that is to be found in no previous imperial concession. This was a promise that "the devoted and faithful of the Church," that is, the Italian Guelfs, "even those constituted within the Empire," would be treated benignly and not oppressed by Henry, nor would he permit their oppression, but he would conserve them in their rights and jurisdictions.[99] Never before had an emperor bound himself in this way. Henry agreed to this on 17 August, as he had absolute need of the Pope's support.

Clement realized the novelty of his demands. Following the receipt of the promise of Lausanne, the Pope sent Henry a letter that was intended to make him feel that he had made no new or major concessions. The Pope began by citing many imperial grants on file in the papal archives. Clement pointed out that his special love and esteem for Henry was to be seen in that he tolerated with equanimity the royal advance into Italy although the coronation date was yet far off. He ignored the fact that Henry was to traverse mostly imperial and not papal territory. The King was further assured that by his promises he had removed the possibility of discord between Pope and Emperor in Italy, a spectre that haunted the steps of every *Romfahrt*.

A separate paragraph was devoted to the promise to maintain the Guelf partisans of the Church within the Empire. This, said Clement, was included "both because of his solicitude for the Emperor-elect and for giving security to the devoted of the Church in Lombardy and Tuscany, who [in the past], terrified at the advent of the King of the Romans, have broken relations with him, and from such breaking have prepared themselves for rebellions and disobedience against him." [100] In other words, Henry was being told that any attempt to interfere with the status quo would probably be met by rebellion. The papal explanation avoided pointing out the theoretical implications of the term "even within the Empire."

The Pope was absolutely sure of his position and certain that Henry must agree to all his demands, for in late June 1310 Clement had already bound Henry to more specific promises in favor of the Guelfs in imperial Italy. In an open session of the papal court, in the presence of the royal embassy, the Pope responded to the envoys sent him by Guido della Torre, Milan,

Pavia, Novara, and other Lombard cities. Clement assured these Italians of his support of and affection for Henry, and testified to the King's good character. Then the Pope promised categorically that Henry would take to his breast Guido della Torre and all of the aforesaid cities and their friends, both within their walls and throughout all Lombardy and Tuscany. He would cherish and love them (*fovere* and *diligere*), preserving them in their present condition and rights as a just king and a pacific lord.[101] Only three and a half months later, on 8 October 1310, did Clement think it necessary to communicate to the King of the Romans the full details of these specific promises made at Avignon in that monarch's name.

Clement could have done no more for the Italian Guelfs than to guarantee them that their temporal lord would leave them absolutely untouched. Yet even this action need not be interpreted as done in hostility to Henry of Luxemburg, but may be seen as an attempt by Clement to help secure peace in Italy, in his view the principal function of the forthcoming imperial expedition.

Indeed, once he acceded to Clement's demands, Henry received his reward. Already the Pope had approved of a Senator of Rome friendly to the imperial cause and had appointed a legate to assist the expedition in Italy. On 1 September 1310 a lengthy papal encyclical was sent to all cities and prelates subject to the King of the Romans and Emperor-elect in Italy, ordering them to receive Henry peacefully and obediently as their temporal lord.[102] Clement again expressed the Gelasian ideals concerning the separateness and collaboration of *sacerdotium* and *imperium* which he had included in the encyclical (26 July 1309) announcing papal acceptance of Henry's election. The Luxemburger was said to have full papal approval. The just and pacific ends of his expedition were outlined, and special assurances were given to the Italian Guelfs that they would be cherished and not unjustly offended. As he had many times assured the Pope, the King would show positively no partiality in his affections. This encyclical was what Henry had been waiting for. It paved the way for his peaceful reception in Italy, and seriously hampered any who planned to oppose him in the name of the Holy Church and the Guelf Party.

The promises made to the Italian Guelfs by the Pope showed that Clement was not interested in any plans that Henry might have had for reorganizing imperial administration or restoring usurped imperial rights in Italy. He saw in the Luxemburger a means for pacifying the unruly peninsula, and for crushing rebels of the Church and restoring usurped lands to the Papacy in Italy. He emphasized these aims both in public manifestoes and in orders to the papal legates who were to meet and accompany the imperial expedition.[103]

The Pontiff did not place all of his eggs in one basket. On 19 August 1310 he named Robert of Anjou Rector of the entire province of the Romagna and the County of Bertinoro, with the exception of Bologna, Ferrara, and their surrounding districts, for an indefinite length of time.[104] Both Clement and Robert chose to ignore the fact that less than a year earlier the latter, as King of Sicily, had sworn in his oath of liege homage that he would never accept any other papal office or dignity. In the light of Clement's other actions, and particularly in view of his desire for an Anjou-Luxemburg marriage alliance, this appointment may not have been intended as a threat to the Emperor-elect. The Pope was perhaps attempting to secure a firmer hold over the unruly cities of the Romagna in order to discourage misguided Ghibellines from rebelling against the Church while imperial forces were present in Italy.[105]

With the publication of the papal encyclical of 1 September, Henry appears to have been satisfied that all was in order, and by the thirteenth he sent another encyclical to Italy.[106] The Emperor-elect announced the appointment of John of Bohemia as vicar in Germany and Arles, and apologized for delaying his own arrival in the peninsula. Now he was on his way to Lausanne, and from there he would cross the mountains at once. He again reminded his Italian subjects to prepare to meet him upon his arrival in Italy and to embrace his happy advent.

Many, in fact, prepared to meet Henry of Luxemburg in the spirit of "the humble Italian, Dante Alighieri, Florentine and guiltless exile," who wrote to all Italy:

> Behold, now is the acceptable time, wherein arise the signs of consolation and peace. . . . Rejoice, O Italy, though now to

be pitied even by the Saracens, for soon you will be envied throughout the world, because your bridegroom, the solace of the world and the glory of your people, the most clement Henry, Divine and Augustus and Caesar, hastens to the nuptials. Dry your tears and remove the marks of grief, O fairest one, for he is near who will liberate you from the prison of the impious, who striking the malignant with his sword's edge shall destroy them, and shall give out his vineyard to other farmers such as who render the fruit of justice at harvest time.

But will he then be merciful to none? On the contrary, he will forgive all who implore mercy, for he is Caesar and his majesty flows from the fount of compassion. His judgment abhors severity; always punishing short of the median, it places itself beyond the median to reward. . . . You, too, who mourn oppressed, raise up your spirits, for your salvation is near at hand . . . awaken, all you dwellers in Italy, and rise up before your King. You are reserved not only for his commands, but, as free men, for his guidance.[107]

Dante closed his letter with a joyous allusion to the pontifical acceptance of Henry of Luxemburg in the encyclical of 1 September 1310.

When Dante briefly treated the nature and scope of imperial authority (c. 1307) in the *Convivio,* he described the Roman Empire as founded by God for the perfection of human life and possessed of universal legal jurisdiction:

Imperial majesty and authority is shown to be the highest in human company. . . . one can almost say of the Emperor . . . that he is the rider of the human will. How that steed goes across the field without its rider is manifest, especially in wretched Italy [*misera Italia*], which is left without any means to its own governance.[108]

Dante eagerly seized upon the appearance of Henry of Luxemburg in 1310 as the possible actualization of the divinely ordained universal ruler who could bring peace and justice to Italy and restore a guiltless exile to his native Florence. For three years the poet was to praise and exhort his *alto Arrigo* and write passionately in defense of Roman Emperor and Empire.

Henry VII in Italy

A Fourteenth-Century Pictorial Account

The following photographs are taken from the manuscript illustrations of the *Codex Balduini Trevirensis* (Staatsarchiv Koblenz 1 C No. 1). The drawings on parchment form a pictorial account of Henry's Italian expedition and may well have been executed by an eyewitness to many of the scenes portrayed. The anonymous artist probably participated in the expedition and drew the illustrations in Germany under the personal supervision of Archbishop Baldwin of Trier (d. 1354).

The following twenty-nine scenes are selected from the seventy-three portrayed on thirty-seven pages of the *Codex*. The number accompanying each figure indicates its place in the entire series. For a detailed discussion of all the illustrations see G. Irmer, *Die Romfahrt Kaiser Heinrich's VII. im Bildercyclus des Codex Balduini Trevirensis* (Berlin, 1881).

FIG. 1 [3B] The election of Henry of Luxemburg as King of the Romans, 27 November 1308.

FIG. 2 [4B] Henry crowned King of the Romans at Aachen by the Archbishop of Cologne, 6 January 1309. The Queen is kneeling beside him.

FIG. 3 [6B] The treasure wagon that accompanied the imperial expedition into Italy.

FIG. 4 [7A] The King ascends Mt. Cenis. Pictured behind Henry are his brother, Baldwin, Archbishop of Trier, and his Queen, Margaret of Brabant.

Fig. 5 [8A] Henry receives the keys to Asti.

Fig. 6 [9B] The Coronation in Milan, 6 January 1311.

FIG. 7 [10A] The Milanese uprising of February 1311.

FIG. 8 [10B] Henry holding court in Milan.

FIG. 9 [11 B] The royal judgment of Cremona.

FIG. 10 [12 B] The siege of Brescia.

FIG. 11 [13A] The capture of the Brescian captain, Theobald Brusati (third from right).

FIG. 12 [13B] "Justice Done": the execution of Theobald Brusati.

FIG. 13 [14A] The death of Henry's brother, Walram of Luxemburg, at the siege of Brescia.

FIG. 14 [17A] The expedition in Genoa: the death of Queen Margaret, December 1311.

Fig. 15 [17B] Henry sails to Pisa.

Fig. 16 [19B] The entry into Rome: fighting at the Milvian Bridge.

FIG. 17 [22B] The Battle for Rome, 26 May 1312. Archbishop Baldwin of Trier, mounted in the center, splits an Orsini helmet with his sword.

FIG. 18 [23B] Henry crowned Emperor by three cardinals, Rome, 29 June 1312.

FIG. 19 [24B] The coronation banquet.

FIG. 20 [24A] Henry VII and the Jews of Rome.

FIGS. 21, 22 [27A, 27B] Imperial victories in the Florentine *contado* (September 1312).

FIG. 23 [29A]   The Siege of Florence.

FIG. 24 [30A]   A clash between imperial and Florentine knights.

FIG. 25 [34A] Entertainment for the royal court at Pisa: a joust between Baldwin of Montcornet and Count Henry of Flanders, Marshal of the imperial army.

FIG. 26 [35A] The imperial army marches against the Regno, August 1313

FIG. 27 [36A] The body of Henry VII is returned to Pisa.

FIG. 28 [36B] Funeral services for Henry VII in Pisa.

FIG. 29 [37] An idealized representation of Henry VII in his sarcophagus. Above the canopy the black imperial eagle is flanked by the lions of Bohemia (l.) and Luxemburg (r.).

Some of Dante's ideas and hopes were shared in various forms and attenuations by certain men of letters, scholars, jurists, and notaries. More numerous were those men who approached the coming ruler with a decidedly partisan spirit, seeking to win favors or avoid harm. Thus even before the dispatch of the imperial embassies to Italy, Modena named a proctor on 4 May 1310, to appear before Henry, hear and obey his orders, and secure his favor for Modena, and of course for its Ghibelline captain Francesco della Mirandola.[109] The young Ghibelline *signore* of Verona decided to reach the royal ear as soon as possible, to win favor and precede his enemies, the exiled Counts of Sambonifacio, who would surely try to win Henry's sympathy. Can Grande (Francesco) della Scala therefore sent an embassy to Spires during the imperial diet of August-September 1310, with the message that the Scaligers had been supporting the imperial cause in the March almost single-handed since the downfall of the Hohenstaufen. Now, said the Veronese legates, Alboin and Can Grande eagerly awaited the arrival of their new sovereign.[110]

To Spires came the colorful Ghibelline, Francesco da Garbagnate, a close friend of the exiled Milanese chieftain Matteo Visconti. Lecturer at the University of Padua, Garbagnate sold his books and purchased arms and horses with the money when he heard of the coming expedition. With these and a single mount given him by Galeazzo Visconti, he hastened north to plead the cause of the Lombard Ghibellines and in particular of Matteo Visconti—or at least so some chronicles would have it.[111]

As for Guelf exiles who presented their cases at Spires, we have only rather weak evidence that perhaps one, Theobald Brusati of Brescia, sent couriers to offer Henry his services and request that he and his followers be reinstated in their native city.[112] Perhaps many so-called Guelfs feared that their very party designation, reminiscent of opposition to the Empire, would deny them a fair hearing before the Emperor-elect. But let us recall too that the great majority of Italian cities were controlled by Guelf factions, so that there were far fewer Guelf than Ghibelline exiles, and those few could find refuge in a host of powerful and thriving cities, often quite close to their old homes. Of those Guelfs in power, some, such as the governments of Bologna and

San Gimignano, sent couriers to Germany during the spring and summer of 1310 in order to learn more accurately Henry's disposition towards them.[113]

The Milanese *signore* Guido della Torre also sent scouts to Germany—but for a different purpose. Since he viewed the coming expedition as a serious threat to his own position, Guido not only tried to counter the stories that his enemies would surely bring to the Luxemburger but also attempted to lull Henry into a false sense of security and make him appear in Lombardy with as small an army as possible. He sent the Prior and Sub-prior of the Milanese Dominicans to Spires with the message that no one had so great love for the King as Guido, and that Guido would meet Henry at Lausanne with his sons and a thousand armed men, and conduct him through Lombardy unarmed with a single hunting falcon on his arm. An eyewitness to the interview at Spires, Nicolas of Butrinto, adds that when the messengers told Henry that Guido intended to keep his word, the monarch believed them the more readily as one claimed to be Guido's private confessor.[114]

At home, however, Guido and several neighboring *signori* labored to secure their rule and prevent the news of the King's advent from having any insurrectionary repercussions. They attempted to stifle public discussion of the coming expedition, and issued strict orders that no one leave his own bishopric in order to meet the Emperor-elect upon his arrival in Lombardy. Even Count Philippone Langusco of Pavia considered this a necessary precaution; and he later backed his word by ruining a Pavian who disobeyed the order.[115]

From May to November 1310 Robert of Anjou, King of Sicily, Count of Provence and Forcalquier, took the precaution of making a grand tour from Provence through Piedmont and parts of Tuscany to the Regno, in order perhaps to consolidate his prestige and holdings against any disturbances that might arise from the imperial expedition. Robert received almost universal acclaim, concluded an advantageous treaty with Asti, accepted the homage of Alessandria, and was showered with substantial cash presents by the Guelf cities through which he passed.[116] Yet the new Rector of Romagna had excellent reasons for keeping on the best of terms with Henry of Luxemburg during the papal-sponsored *Romzug,* particularly since he was actively negotiating for a marriage alliance that could bring him the Kingdom of Arles. Why should Robert play the rebel chief in Italy? The outcome was unsure, the risk great, and the advantages questionable. Moreover, the Angevin was quite occupied with administering his far-flung possessions and watchfully eyeing Frederick of Trinacria. For the present he waited to see what the future would bring. And Robert did not have long to wait: the Italian stage was set for the entry of Henry of Luxemburg, King of the Romans and Emperor-elect.

II

"The Emperor Henry's Most Auspicious Entry into Italy"

THE ARRIVAL IN ITALY

Dante exultantly hailed "the Emperor Henry's most auspicious entry into Italy," and the monarch's appearance indeed seemed to mark the beginning of an imperial restoration in the peninsula.[1] Unfortunately our knowledge of Henry's first encounters with his Italian subjects is very meagre, and for the reconstruction of important episodes we must utilize inaccurate and contradictory sources.[2] The generally accepted account is based (with slight modifications) upon the Florentine chronicler, Giovanni Villani (IX, 7), who reports that while Henry assembled his forces at Lausanne he received embassies from many Italian cities, including Rome and Pisa. The latter sent him sixty thousand florins in order that he might cross the mountains, and promised another sixty thousand upon his arrival in Pisa. Florence, Lucca, Siena, and other Tuscan Guelf communes prepared to send embassies too, but at the last moment abandoned the plan since it might lead to the restoration of political exiles and the destruction of partisan rule. Henry heard of this change and was deeply disappointed, declaring that he had planned to honor Florence above all other cities of the Empire.

Only in the case of Pisa, however, where the coming imperial expedition reawakened old Ghibelline fervor, can we speak with some certainty of an embassy being sent to Henry while he was still in the vicinity of Lake Geneva.[3] Documentary evidence rules out the sending of a Roman embassy,[4] while certain later events cast doubt upon Villani's solitary testimony regarding Florence and its allies.[5] The great majority of Italian cities simply carried out the instructions they had received during the summer of 1310, and dispatched proctors and escorts to the Emperor-elect once he arrived in Italy.

On 23 October 1310 the imperial army completed the long Alpine crossing and arrived at the small commune of Susa in the foothills.[6] There Henry spent the next six days resting, reorganizing, and planning for the future. In Susa he probably received the ringing greeting from the proctor of the town of Casale in Monferrat, "To the most excellent prince, his singular lord, lord Henry, by the grace of God invincible King of the Romans always Augustus," telling how his letters had brought "vehement joy" to the souls of Casale's inhabitants. Henry's descent into Italy was likened to Christ's descent into the underworld "for the well-being of the human race, that he might snatch it forth from the snare of diabolical servitude." [7] Such a reception might well please the Emperor-elect; it was to remain the most lofty, imaginative, and laudatory accolade that he received while in Italy.

Henry could use good auguries. His force of about five thousand men, with less than five hundred cavalry, was not imposing. With the King and Queen were Henry's brothers, Baldwin of Trier and Walram of Luxemburg. Close to Henry were his brother-in-law, Amadeus V of Savoy, and his cousins, Theobald of Bar, Bishop of Liège, and Counts Henry and Guy of Flanders. Other leading royal counsellors were the Bishops of Geneva, Constance, and Basel, Duke Leopold Habsburg of Austria, and Counts Hugh and Guy of Vienne. The expedition also included foot soldiers, squires, the Queen's personal cortege, and court and chancellery personnel such as the jurisprudent Henry of Geldern, twice imperial legate to Italy. The Emperor-elect does not appear to have counted upon having to spend much money in Italy, for the greater part of his liquid assets was carried across the Alps in one lovely treasure wagon. The monarch probably assumed that he would receive an adequate income from obedient and well-administered Italian cities once he had swiftly set things in order.

To comprehend the relative strength and potentiality of the imperial force, we might recall that Guido della Torre, *signore* of Milan, alone disposed of a personal following of a thousand mercenaries, while the Guelf cities of Pavia, Vercelli, and Lodi could muster more than seven hundred cavalry for escort duty. Henry could ill afford to rely primarily upon force to obtain his objectives.[8]

Of great importance was the week spent in Henry's next place of call: Turin in Savoy. There he received oaths of fealty from a Roman delegation and the proctors of Chieri, but only the oath rendered by the small commune of Valenza north of Alessandria is extant.[9] Its proctor, appointed only four days earlier, recognized Henry as the city's immediate lord, having rights of high and low justice (*merum et mixtum imperium*) and every jurisdiction (*omnimodam jurisdictionem*). Valenza swore loyalty to Henry against all men, and promised to give him aid and counsel and never to harm him or the Empire, but rather to reveal any knowledge of planned conspiracy at once and render him all possible assistance. Valenza pledged to assist Henry to recover and retain everything (thus comprehending the *regalia* as well as territories) that he had at present, or might acquire in the future, and lost in any way whatsoever. The commune further bound itself to abide by all things contained in the old and new forms of homage.

Most vassals who swore fealty in Italy, both nominal Guelfs and Ghibellines, promised to aid the King or Emperor in recovering even those things acquired in the future and then lost.[10] Some persons and communities, such as Count Amadeus of Savoy, Marquis Theodore of Monferrat, Padua, and Milan at one time, swore an oath worded slightly differently, which bound them to aid in recovering and maintaining the rights and *regalia* of the Empire.[11]

Yet contemporaries could not base their ideas of the new ruler's actual intentions upon the wording of these oaths, which did not vary significantly from traditional forms. The clause referring to the recovery of things that the King of the Romans acquired in the future and then lost was taken from the New Form of the Vulgate of Lombard Feudal Law; while even Rudolf of Habsburg, who had alienated large portions of imperial Italy, had exacted oaths to maintain "the Roman Empire and its *regalia* especially in Italy." [12] Only his future actions would reveal Henry's plans, if indeed they were yet clearly formulated.

While few communal proctors appeared in Turin (since most cities only appointed them after the King arrived in Italy), Henry spent much time meeting those Italians who first presented themselves to their French-speaking sovereign.[13] And here some of his greatest difficulties began. Their nature becomes clear when we read the name of the single Italian witness to an instrument drawn up at the conclusion of Valenza's act of fealty: Palmieri degli Altoviti, jurisprudent, White Guelf exile condemned to death by his native Florence in 1302.[14] The presence of such a man in the inner circle of the royal court might easily create suspicion in the minds of those who as yet had no fixed opinions about the new ruler, and confirm the worst fears of those who already believed that he would automatically favor Ghibellines and destroy Guelfs simply because of the labels they bore.

Since the majority of Italian cities were at least nominally Guelf, flourishing economically, and were not subject to continual pressure as were the Ghibelline strongholds of Pisa, Arezzo, Verona, Mantua, and Brescia, inevitably there were far more Ghibelline than Guelf exiles. In fact, the only important exile to present himself in Turin was Richard Tizzone, Ghibelline of Vercelli, who appeared with the promised escort of one hundred knights. He declared publicly that he had been ruined because of his adherence to "the Party of the Empire," and affirmed that he was prepared to serve his lord, Henry, to the death.[15] Tizzone represented his misfortunes not as failure in a struggle of local families or factions for political, military, social, or economic power, but as the consequence of his adherence to the Ghibelline, or imperial, cause in Italy. The Vercelli chieftain was only one of many exiled Italian politicians who tried to make the Emperor-elect feel that, as a matter of personal honor and for the good of the Empire, he had no choice but to support them and reinstate

them in their native cities for the simple reason that they be-
longed to a group of loosely allied factions and individuals
traditionally designated as Ghibelline.[16]

On the other hand, the so-called Guelfs who came to Turin
were not exiles, but leading *signori* of central Lombardy.[17] Count
Philippone Langusco saluted his feudal lord with the entire
Pavian militia, over four hundred strong. With him came Simone
degli Avvocati di Colobiano of Vercelli with two hundred
knights, and Antonio Fissiraga of Lodi with more than one
hundred. These men had consulted with Guido della Torre in
Milan, sent embassies to Avignon for advice, and taken measures
at home to secure their rule against possible rebellion. But they
had acted primarily to protect themselves. They hoped that the
Emperor-elect might aid them, and even legally sanction their
signories, despite their bearing the Guelf label. If he received
them well, they were prepared to serve him, and meanwhile they
could observe his behavior and decide upon a course of action.

All Italy watched Turin, eager to see what the new monarch
would do, whom he would favor and heed, and what his plans
were. Henry recognized the importance of these first weeks in
Italy and demonstrated his desire to maintain an honest impartiality in the factional disputes that racked the country. He
scrupulously avoided giving biased or unconsidered judgments
in favor of either Guelfs or Ghibellines. He raised the hopes of
those who wanted peace by replying to Richard Tizzone of Vercelli that although he sympathized with his misfortunes, he did
not feel culpable for the exile's predicament. He had come to
Lombardy for no one party, but for all.[18] Similarly, when the
Ghibelline Marquis Manfred of Saluzzo appeared in Turin and
requested permission to do fealty for his holdings, Henry refused
because the marquis had already done homage to Robert of
Anjou. On the same grounds the Emperor-elect would not accept
the fealty of Alba. Henry carefully respected Robert's rights, and
publicly declared his intention to conclude a marriage alliance
with the Angevin. He particularly pleased the Guelfs by using as
one of his chief advisers his brother-in-law, Count Amadeus of
Savoy, a prince who, although sympathetic to the Guelfs, had
never antagonized their opponents. The three Lombard Guelf

signori, Langusco, Avvocati, and Fissiraga, were so pleased that they wrote directly to Guido della Torre in Milan praising Henry's conduct.

Before he arrived at Chieri, only eight miles from Turin, he again displayed his impartiality. Both the Cathedral of Turin and the Count of Savoy claimed Chieri; but despite his affinity to the Count, Henry decided that neither party should possess the small commune since the privileges offered in proof had been issued by Frederick II after his papal excommunication. Henry sustained Chieri's claim to be a direct appurtenance of the Empire, thus giving further proof of his impartiality, and making a good start in the "recovery of the rights of the Empire." [19]

When he entered Chieri on 6 November Henry took a critical step: he restored the long-exiled Ghibellines to the city. Italian exiles had eagerly awaited such a move—it was a sign of their salvation. What years of suffering, battles, and bloodshed had not achieved was at last to be accomplished by this ruler from the north, who had come from Mt. Cenis with his colorful court, its gaily caparisoned knights and finely dressed ladies.

But the restoration of the Chieri exiles was a great shock and disappointment to the onlooking Guelf chieftains. They had pleaded with Henry that he restore no exiles until after his Roman coronation. Since such restoration could threaten their tenuous and hard-won supremacy, it might turn many Lombard *signori* against the Emperor-elect. Henry, however, chose to heed the majority of his non-Italian counsellors, who urged that he assert his rule swiftly and unequivocally, as hesitation would be interpreted as weakness and inspire disobedience. The northerners' experiences and ways of thinking were his own and their advice convinced the Luxemburger.[20]

Henry still further disturbed his Guelf followers before he left Chieri by placing the city and its *contado* in the care of an imperial vicar. This official, directly dependent upon the Emperor-elect, replaced the communal podesta, and was indiscriminately entitled "vicar," "podesta," or "rector" of the commune.[21] Chieri was to provide the vicar's stipend, fixed at five hundred florins a year—the same sum the city had paid its podesta.[22]

Henry decided against the appointment of a foreign vicar, and selected an Italian, as he could understand the language, quickly grasp local problems, and probably would arouse less distrust or animosity. Henry also wanted the vicar to be a man whom he knew and could trust to be efficient. As he was closely acquainted with few Italians, he quite naturally turned to one who had twice served as imperial legate to Italy: Ugolino da Vico, Ghibelline exile from Florence.

This solution of its problems satisfied the small Piedmontese commune; for although it lost many customary attributes of self-government, Chieri was placed under the immediate protection of the Emperor. It might at last be safe against the intrusions of powerful Savoyard and Turinese neighbors who had already destroyed much of its internal autonomy. Chieri soon legislated the severest penalties against those who attempted to undermine its new-found "liberty . . . a most precious treasure." [23]

All Italians did not share Chieri's enthusiasm. We can imagine the disappointment of the Lombard Guelf chiefs as they saw the King first reject their advice that he not disturb the status quo until after the Roman coronation, and then name as his first vicar a professed Florentine Ghibelline exile. Was this not exactly what Guido della Torre had warned of in June? But the Guelf lords did not lose hope; they remained with Henry and tried to convert him to their point of view. Moreover, they could better quash their enemies' accusations if they remained close to the King. They might still gain much from a friendly monarch, and it was no time for rash or unplanned opposition.

Henry had no desire to anger his Italian subjects, or to create a new and effective anti-imperial Guelfism. Yet at his coronation in Aachen he had been told that he was a God-appointed monarch, and now he acted as though he believed it his task to rule as well as reign. Through his positive acts of restoring exiles and installing an imperial rector in Chieri, Henry indicated that he preferred to fit an Italian city-state into a larger imperial regime rather than adjust the imperial system so as to accommodate a large measure of local autonomy and practical independence. His solution suited the needs of the small, hard-pressed Piedmontese commune to which it was first applied. But would Henry try to repeat it without exception throughout imperial Italy? and would it suit a Florence or Milan?

HENRY IN ASTI

The Emperor-elect left Chieri on 11 November and journeyed twenty miles southeast to Asti, where representatives of the commune came forth and offered him the keys to the city.[24] Henry now showed that his actions in Chieri had been only a preview of his general intentions for other Italian cities, for he brought with him into Asti its long-banished Ghibelline exiles. Those exiles themselves had contributed to this event: two weeks earlier they had appointed proctors to appear before Henry, recognizing him as immediate lord of Asti and its district, with rights of high and low justice and every jurisdiction, and naming him arbiter of all quarrels with their enemies within the city.[25] They swore to obey the admonitions and mandates of the King and his vicars so long as he should live, to preserve his state and honor and that of the Empire, and to observe the dispositions that he made for Asti, its castles and *contado*, pledging all their possessions that these promises would be maintained. The exiles would promise to do anything so long as they could return home.

The factions in power saw things differently. Only after Henry was in Asti four days did they name proctors, and they assigned them a different task.[26] The party in power desired primarily to reaffirm and strengthen the commune's independence and control of its *contado,* and to secure its own position. Already Asti had entered into a military pact with Robert of Anjou with these ends in view. Thus in addition to taking an oath of fealty, its proctors requested the confirmation of Asti's imperial grants and privileges, together with official ratification of the communal customs and usages. This last would include, of course, recognition of Asti's statutes and ordinances—even of those fines and sentences directed against the returning political exiles. In addition, Asti's proctors were to accept any new privileges that Henry might grant. This divergence in the orders given the two sets of proctors reflects the difference in immediate aims between a group of outcasts and persons established in power in a flourishing commune, much more than it marks any discrepancy between nominal Ghibellines and Guelfs.

On Sunday 15 November the entire populace of Asti assembled in the central square in front of the cathedral. Henry of Luxemburg, King of the Romans, sat on a raised platform flanked by members of his entourage, among them the same Philip of Savoy who had recently aided the imperial legates within the city and had tried to prevent the conclusion of its alliance with Robert of Anjou. The newly appointed communal proctors swore fealty for Asti and its district, and promised to aid Henry in reacquiring and reoccupying the rights and honors of the Empire.[27] They did not, however, specifically declare that Henry was the commune's immediate lord, with complete jurisdiction, but adhered to their less comprehensive instructions. The proctors then knelt and kissed the monarch's feet in sign of obedience, and the assembled crowd cheered loudly in approval.

Asti had made a good start in establishing friendly relations with its ruler, for he immediately approved and confirmed all its imperial privileges.[28] Yet on the next day he was forced to repeat officially a request that his council be given those privileges for examination, as the communal podesta had ignored an earlier request.[29]

The magistrates of Asti had several reasons for their reluctance to display the city's privileges. Those documents might be amended, or even confiscated and annulled, if they seemed too extensive for the royal taste, or if they conflicted with valid grants held by other cities or persons. The city's leaders also wished to conceal how many of the commune's *contado* possessions were not legally justifiable but represented promises of obedience forcibly extracted from direct vassals of the Empire.

Still, all proceeded well. On 18 November Henry requested the citizenry of Asti to assemble in a great market place.[30] Once again the monarch displayed his peculiar talent for placing in the public eye just the sort of men who would displease most of the populace and watching Guelf chieftains like Count Philippone Langusco of Pavia, Simone degli Avvocati of Vercelli, and Antonio Fissiraga of Lodi. As in Turin, the condemned Florentine exile Palmieri degli Altoviti sat with Henry and his court. The King's official spokesman was Niccolo di Bonifazio de' Buonsignori, an exiled Sienese Ghibelline banker condemned to death as a tyrant and traitor by his native city.[31] He explained that

Henry wished to restore peace and order to Asti and its district and to settle the quarrels that had for so long created factional dissension. The King, he continued, already possessed the right to provide the necessary remedy "from the plenitude of his power" (*ex plenitudine sue potestatis*), but wanted the faithful to concur in this action. Buonsignori then asked the citizenry to concede to Henry, in the name of the commune, the fullest and most general authority and power for pacifying, reforming, and ordering Asti and its district, and this despite any statutes that might exist forbidding such a delegation of authority. When Buonsignori stopped speaking, a cheese dealer, William de Vayo, mounted a table and proposed that the King be given such authority. Buonsignori put the question to the assembly, which cried out in the affirmative—and the deed was done.[32]

Less than five days later events took an unexpected turn for the worse. This change had little to do with the fact that the incumbent leaders of the city were nominally Guelfs, for that was equally true of Chieri, just left, and of Vercelli and Novara, soon to be visited. It seems rather connected with the treaties recently concluded between Asti and Robert of Anjou. The general rumor circulating in Asti, that the angry Philip of Savoy informed Henry of the existence of those pacts, may be true.[33] It is certain that Henry did read those documents in the presence of the Queen, his two brothers, the Bishop of Geneva, and his Dominican counsellor, Nicolas of Ligny, later Bishop of Butrinto. Henry immediately ordered Nicolas to burn the documents. Butrinto explains that Henry did not want the treaties to come to light because of his plans for a marriage alliance with the Angevin, and excused Robert before his own counsellors, saying that a man with such illustrious parentage, bearing "the blood of St. Louis," could not have performed such acts, and no doubt his council was to blame.[34]

Another factor must be considered in any analysis of Henry's hardening attitude towards Asti, even if the demonstration of its existence rests largely upon logical inferences. The Emperor-elect may not have known that a Florentine spy had been placed in Asti before his arrival in order to watch and report upon his plans and actions. Yet it is possible that he heard indirectly of the very severe terms (announced to certain Florentine agents

10 November) upon which Florence and its allies were prepared to serve him. An awareness of Tuscan Guelf hostility may
have helped Henry to decide to secure Asti as firmly as possible,
in order to forestall similar recalcitrance and obstruction in
northern Italy.[35]

On 23 November the citizens of Asti were again ordered to
assemble in the market place.[36] A royal spokesman requested
that they renew the earlier grant of authority to Henry for pacifying and reforming the city. This time, however, the grant was
spelled out and extended to permit the King to do whatever he
saw fit in the commune and its *contado* without any contradic-
tion—even to the point of removing Asti's officials and changing
its statutes. Immediately upon receiving the crowd's assent, the
spokesman read and promulgated a previously prepared list of
orders and dispositions. The assembly found itself in the same
position as those assemblies that had appointed and designated
numerous *signori* in other Lombard cities: it could only assent
to an existing state of affairs and could not make a free decision.
In this case the presence of five thousand imperial troops and
numerous returned exiles within the city walls reinforced the
arguments presented in favor of the Emperor-elect.

Far-sweeping and extensive changes were made in Asti's constitution that afternoon. Men who thought that the commune
was a faithful vassal of the Empire which still possessed a large
measure of autonomy quickly apprehended their error. Henry
nullified not only the recent treaties concluded with Robert of
Anjou but all pacts, conventions, laws, and statutes made in
Asti during the preceding eight years. He ordered the seques-
tration of Asti's official records and documents, and the removal
of all communal officials, including the podesta and the captain
of the people. The King took personal charge of appointment
to and direction of the city's executive council. He opened
prisons and subjected the inmates to royal justice. Men banished
for political reasons had their sentences cancelled, and all persons forced to leave the city or its surrounding villages and forts
since the preceding Christmas received permission to return with
their families and possessions. Henry announced that Niccolo
de' Buonsignori of Siena, royal spokesman on 18 November, was
constituted vicar of Asti from that day (23 November) until

1 January 1312, or more or less at the King's pleasure. Henceforth no one was to belong to any party or show any partiality, but all should strive to maintain and defend the honor, utility, pacific state, and good condition of the King, the commune of Asti, its people and *contado*. The syndics of every village belonging to the city had to swear to uphold these new regulations— an indication that Henry did not completely accept Asti's claim to rule and act for its *contado*. Finally, the monarch reserved for himself the right to change or interpret these rulings in any way he saw fit.

Supplementary measures soon followed. Two days later, on 25 November, Henry officially cashiered the podesta and captain of the people, along with the podestas of the *contado* towns. He declared that those *contado* officials would no longer be elected in the council of the city of Asti as had been customary.[37] This decision, a serious blow to the commune's control over its *contado*, was reinforced the following week when the King received various *contado* forts and castles into his own hands.[38] Ventura adds that Henry garrisoned those forts with imperial troops to be maintained at the city's expense, while within the commune he adopted severe police measures and forbade groups of more than three men to gather in the streets.[39] Henry feared possible opposition to his new regime, salutary and necessary though he judged it to be.

Yet the Emperor-elect's displeasure with Asti passed almost as quickly as it had come, and during the last week of his stay his relations with the commune improved notably.

On 5 December he tried to end once and for all the difficulties caused by the perennial struggles between the city's two leading factions, the Solari and the newly returned De Castello.[40] Leaders of the rival groups appeared before Henry and members of his court. It was stated that the King was acting as much on the strength of his royal power as from the authority conceded him by the commune. This first peace arbitration that we possess which was promulgated by the Luxemburger in Italy is disappointing. Vague, verbose, poorly organized, with topics ill defined, it is another evidence of Henry's unpreparedness for the task he had undertaken. Over half the document contains a lengthy confirmation of a pact made between the warring parties the preceding winter by the Savoyards, Amadeus and Philip, who had ever been eager to exploit Asti's troubles to their own advantage. Henry ignored this aspect of the situation and regarded his brother-in-law as merely a wise, experienced counsellor and friend.

The remaining clauses elaborate a complicated and unsatisfactory method for restoring former holdings to the returned exiles. The complainant, though he might be a propertyless exile, was bound to give security to the vicar of Asti in order to regain possession of his property. The arbitration made no provision for dealing with disputes that might arise as to the rightful ownership of property. This could be an extremely complicated matter, since lands had changed hands many times during the preceding decades, as one faction and then another reigned supreme and ousted its rivals, condemned them to heavy fines and confiscated their property. Some lands had been confiscated legally by the commune after its owners had been duly condemned, and then they had been sold to the present owners. Such owners would feel that they had a rightful title. Still other lands were held by second or third purchasers.

These problems did not exist for Henry. He apparently saw legal issues in simple terms of justice and injustice, honesty and dishonesty, black and white with few shadings of gray in between. He desired decisions that were simple and swift. In many later peace arbitrations he ordered that any controversies arising as to goods or rights be judged simply and quickly by the city's imperial vicar alone, without the "clamor and formality" of a normal legal case—a desire for equity perhaps, but in fact an unworkable oversimplification.[41]

Henry soon performed another act that showed his rapidly improved disposition towards Asti. On 8 December he issued a second confirmation of the city's imperial privileges, much more generous than that of 15 November, as it specifically ratified and regranted control and all rights, including the dispensing of high and low justice, that the commune and its citizens exercised in the Asti *contado* over vassals, towns, forts, and castles.[42] This was a great gain for the commune, and if granted earlier would probably have been saluted with demonstrations of joy and affection. But the harsh measures of the past few weeks remained uppermost in men's minds.

Henry had felt constrained to depart from his self-appointed role of the generous, peace-bringing arbitrator in dealing with Asti. He seems to have believed that the city had not dealt fairly with him or with the Empire, and hence it had needed to be taken in hand and set on the right path. This done, Henry bore no animosity towards the commune. He made no effort to punish the perpetrators of the treaties with Robert of Anjou, and even included one of the signers, Bonifazio Solari, on the list of counsellors for the city that he compiled on New Year's Day 1311.[43] Much of Asti, however, still bore a grudge against the Emperor-elect and his new regime. Reduced to the status of private citizens and forced to accept the return of their rivals, the Solari awaited an opportunity to overthrow Henry's forced settlement.

As in Chieri, so in Asti Henry failed to take his subjects' sensibilities into account. When he removed the chief communal magistrate, the podesta, and substituted an imperial vicar, he acted in part from sheer ignorance of the communal forms of government and of their psychological importance. Even shortly before he arrived in Italy the Luxemburger did not know how to address correctly the various officials and councils of the Italian cities.[44] In official documents issued during three weeks while Henry sojourned in Asti we find Niccolo de' Buonsignori designated indiscriminately as "podesta," "rector," and "vicar" of the city and its district,[45] while he appears several times as a witness without any title.[46]

Despite his inadequacies, and the difficulties with Asti, Henry achieved much while in the city. Proctors from four more communities appeared. On 14 November he received the fealty of Casale in Monferrat.[47] Proctors from Ghibelline Modena, Mantua, and Verona did fealty on 2 December. Long before their less fortunate Guelf exile rivals they sought the sympathy of the Emperor-elect and assured him of their support.[48] The Scaliger and Bonacolsi lords wanted to be sure of success. Their agents had harangued the Luxemburger at Spires. Now their embassies brought him a letter from "the captains, communes, and cities

of Verona and Mantua," which captains and their predecessors
had always been "most faithful and devoted followers of the
Sacred Empire, for whose name they had undertaken many long
labors." [49] Like Richard Tizzone of Vercelli at Turin, these
signori attempted to bind the fate of the Empire in Italy to their
own personal and factional fortunes and struggles for power.
They invited the Emperor-elect to visit Verona and Mantua,
where he and his court might expect a splendid reception if one
were to judge by that given the imperial legates a few months
earlier.

More numerous than official delegates of Lombard communes,
however, was the swarm of political exiles who thronged to the
court in Asti. The disappointment and consternation of the
watching Guelf *signori* and their friends must have been great
as Matteo Visconti of Milan arrived in the company of the
Veronese and Mantuan legations.[50] The Emperor-elect's appearance in Italy spurred the former imperial vicar and exiled Ghibelline *signore* to attempt a return to public life and political
power. Matteo hastened to do fealty to his new sovereign, and
he quickly perceived Henry's naïveté in Italian affairs. He decided to convince the monarch of his wholehearted adherence
to the ideal of making peace with his enemies, laying aside hates
and grudges, and henceforth living quietly under the supervision
of the Emperor and his officials. The crude honesty and lack of
wiliness displayed by his opponents aided Matteo's efforts. In
Henry's presence he attempted to embrace two of the Lombard
Guelf *signori,* Count Philippone Langusco and Antonio Fissiraga, and both spurned his overtures. They addressed him
angrily and accused him of having caused all the troubles in
Italy while he was in power, permitting rest to no city. And now
he requested peace and quiet! Matteo only answered humbly,
"Now is the time to put an end to our evils." The Luxemburger
completely missed the significance of this exchange. Contented,
he said with a smile, "Peace between you is already half made." [51]

Other important exiles appeared in Asti. Manfred Beccaria,
Ghibelline rival of Philippone Langusco of Pavia, pleaded a tale
of woe to win the monarch's sympathy. The Genoese exile Opizzino Spinola de Lucolo attached himself to the imperial entourage, where he found great favor and was promised readmission

to his native city. The Emperor-elect was particularly conspicuous in his enthusiastic reception of the one Guelf exile chief who came to Asti, Theobald Brusati of Brescia. Henry was probably eager to demonstrate again his impartiality.

To Asti too came the long-awaited papal legate, Arnald Pellagru, Cardinal Deacon of Santa Maria in Portico, nephew of Pope Clement V. The violent pro-Florentine was not the man to give the Emperor-elect wholehearted aid and counsel.[52] Nevertheless, before he left Asti the Cardinal assisted Henry in the resolution of technical problems concerning the forthcoming coronation in Lombardy, which would precede the imperial coronation in Rome.[53]

The Emperor-elect believed that his work of pacification in Lombardy would be successfully completed within a very short time, and he made plans to depart rapidly for Rome and an early imperial coronation. On the very day that Cardinal Pellagru entered Asti, 19 November, a royal embassy headed by John, Deacon of Trier, and Nicolas of Ligny (later Bishop of Butrinto) left for Avignon to convince the Pope that he should advance the coronation date from 2 February 1312 to 30 May 1311.[54] Since the Pontiff was occupied with the Council of Vienne, Henry wanted cardinals appointed and dispatched to Italy at once, empowered to conduct the ceremony. As one of many inducements, Henry offered to aid the Papacy by subduing rebels in the Papal States after he became Emperor.

Even outside of Lombardy Henry had reasons for satisfaction. His son John's army was progressing well in Bohemia. Negotiations were well under way for a marriage alliance with Robert of Anjou. The most difficult point remained that of a dowry. Robert insisted on receiving the Kingdom of Arles, while Henry was unwilling to alienate permanently this portion of the Empire. But there was no reason for discouragement at this stage of the proceedings.[55]

Meanwhile in Asti the Emperor-elect continued (despite several errors) to renew the hopes of onlooking Guelfs, and to demonstrate his desire to act the impartial arbiter superior to party strife. He justly settled a dispute over the possession of Monferrat in favor of the rightful claimant, the Guelf Marquis Theodore Paleologus. On 25 November Henry accepted the new marquis' fealty, together with his offer of the service of one hundred knights for one year.[56] Paleologus appeared to have decided that his interests in Piedmont and western Lombardy would best be advanced by adherence to the imperial cause.

Four days later Henry took an important step designed to give more formal organization and structure to his court. He swore in twenty-eight men as members of the royal council.[57] Half were Italians or Savoyards, half northerners. Included were the King's two brothers, his brother-in-law Amadeus, his cousin Theobald of Bar, Bishop of Liège, the chancellor Henry of Trent, the jurist Henry of Geldern, Cassone della Torre, Archbishop of Milan, the Bishops of Geneva and Basel, and the Dauphin Counts, Guy and Hugh. Among the Italians were four known Ghibelline ambassadors of Pisa, one Florentine Ghibelline exile, and three Lombard Guelf *signori,* Count Philippone Langusco of Pavia, Antonio Fissiraga of Lodi, and Simone degli Avvocati of Vercelli. The political allegiance of four of the Italian councillors is unknown.

These men swore fealty to Henry, much after the New Form of the Vulgate of Lombard Feudal Law. They pledged their advice and counsel, and promised to help recover and retain for all time anything that the monarch held in the present or the future and should lose. Those nobles who had previously sworn liege homage to another lord made certain reservations.

If the list of royal councillors had fairly represented the men whose advice Henry frequently demanded and heeded, the Lombard Guelf chiefs might have had some cause for satisfaction. But several days later the newly arrived Ghibelline exiles, Matteo Visconti of Milan and Manfred Beccaria of Pavia, received places on this council, and the Guelf captains found themselves seriously outnumbered. The council, moreover, did not include all those who had easy access to the Emperor-elect—men such as the acting treasurer, Simon Philip of Pistoia, and the exiled Florentine judge, Palmieri degli Altoviti. And could the Ghibellines and White Guelfs who had come to Lombardy and Tuscany as imperial legates during the past summer have been forgotten, especially as one of them had been the first vicar appointed by Henry in Italy? Less than a week before the swearing in of the royal councillors, the Ghibelline Sienese exile,

Niccolo de' Buonsignori, had become vicar of Asti. While to Henry of Luxemburg these Ghibelline and White Guelf exiles may have seemed to be merely experienced soldiers, administrators, and politicians whose services could prove useful, the factions ruling the majority of cities in imperial Italy saw in them only hated rivals for political power.

As the expedition prepared to leave Asti, the royal councillors engaged in a trial of strength. The Lombard Guelf *signori* attempted to persuade the King to turn toward Pavia on the Ticino River, stronghold of Count Philippone. Matteo Visconti counselled him to go directly to Milan. Judging from Henry's actions in Chieri and Asti, he would reduce the Torriani to the rank of private citizens, and reintroduce the Ghibelline exiles, Matteo among them, into the city. Visconti held out to the monarch the lure of receiving homage and holding court in the most important city of all Lombardy. We do not know what arguments the Guelf leaders used. It seems that they wished to gain time, to create a favorable impression in Pavia, and to persuade the Emperor-elect to make no further changes in the constitution of Lombardy for the present. The astute Visconti won this contest for influence with Henry of Luxemburg and his northern counsellors. The expedition was going to Milan.[58]

Until the arrival of Matteo Visconti, the Guelf *signori* of Pavia, Lodi and Vercelli had entertained high hopes of guiding or even dominating the policy and tactics of the Emperor-elect in Italy.[59] They wanted to lead him rapidly and safely out of Lombardy, southwards towards Rome and the imperial coronation, leaving behind their own possessions untouched. Henry's displays of impartiality and his cordial reception of their own overtures in Turin had boded well. In Asti he had performed several acts that pleased them and had given them honorable positions in his council. Now the situation had changed. The Guelf chiefs found a worthy rival in Matteo Visconti and they had lost a first, and important, round.

Henry's decision not to bypass Milan cannot, however, be ascribed simply to his desire for a Lombard coronation or to the Visconti's wiles. Until the Pope advanced the coronation date the Emperor-elect had no pressing incentive to hasten to Rome. Milan's military and economic superiority over Pavia

made the Guelf plan appear less advisable than that of the
Visconti. With the allegiance of Count Philippone seemingly
secure, Henry's failure to proceed to Milan might have been
interpreted as yielding to the veiled threat expressed in the
Torriani response to the imperial legates during the preceding
summer. Thus it is possible to argue that Henry merely chose
the sounder of the two alternatives offered him, and in no way
cast aside his Guelf counsellors.

Count Philippone doubtless realized that his son-in-law, Guido
della Torre, Captain of Milan, was in danger. But the Lombard
signori in Asti had much to gain by continuing to remain with
their somewhat ingenuous northern ruler, and to act as faithful
vassals and counsellors. Nor could they have relished the prospect that open rebellion would bring down upon them a horde
of eager Ghibelline rivals who possibly awaited just such a move.

From Asti to Milan

On 11 December 1310 the imperial expedition left Asti for
Casale, some twenty miles to the north.[60] As Henry and the
main body of troops prepared to spend the first of two nights in
that small town, a small contingent left the main force and
occupied the castle of Vigevano, lying between Vercelli and
Milan. Although this castle possessed diplomas designating it as
part of the "chamber of the Empire" and guaranteeing it direct
imperial jurisdiction, it had actually been controlled by Guido
della Torre, Lord of Milan.[61] Occupying Vigevano, Henry
seemed to give notice that he was set upon assuming control
over lands and jurisdictions usurped from the Empire. Furthermore, he was menacing the authority of the mightiest Guelf
signore in Lombardy.

The occupation of Vigevano must have caused some doubts,
too, as to the real efficacy of papal supervision and influence
over this expedition. Clement V had personally guaranteed, in
the name of the Emperor-elect, that rights and jurisdictions of
the Torriani and their friends and allies would be left intact.
It appeared that Henry construed this promise to include only
those rights and jurisdictions whose just possession could be
clearly demonstrated by imperial grants and privileges. It still

was to be seen, however, whether the occupation of Vigevano was an isolated incident, or part of a consistent policy.

At the very time of the Vigevano incident Henry began to demonstrate misgivings as to the loyalty of the Italian Guelf *signori* accompanying him. Perhaps the insinuations and warnings of the Ghibellines and White Guelfs who had flocked to his court began to tell. Henry took no chances, and ordered spies to watch the three Guelf chieftains on the royal council. But even if the spies succeeded in hiding their work, the Guelfs had cause for misgivings when Henry denied their request that Simone degli Avvocati precede the expedition to his native Vercelli to prepare a suitable welcome.[62] These signs of suspicion and distrust might easily serve to push the Guelf captains into the arms of Guido della Torre, the Florentine Priory, and other more determined opponents of the Emperor-elect.

On 13 December the entire expedition entered Vercelli, and with it the city's Ghibelline exiles led by Richard Tizzone. Whereas in Asti the promulgation of a pact reconciling the city's opposing factions had been one of Henry's final acts before leaving, in Vercelli the Emperor-elect confronted this problem at once. On 15 December the podesta of Vercelli, the bishop-elect, members of the communal councils, and leaders of the rival factions appeared before the monarch, whom both parties recognized as arbitrator of their disputes. The peace arbitration promulgated on the following day was a marked improvement over that for Asti—less verbose and more neatly organized.[63]

The document's greater simplicity, however, makes even clearer Henry's continued ignorance of the size and complexity of the problems with which he was dealing. The arbitration was a pious hope that all would now live in peace, that past quarrels would be forgotten, and that exiles would receive their rights and property. Henry perhaps believed that an imperial vicar left behind in Vercelli would have the time needed to eliminate intelligently the causes for discord and to solve the many problems entailed in restoring the exiles to the community.

The arbitration, and all later ones, began "In the name of the King of Peace. Amen." Henry seems to have taken seriously the papal injunction that he be a *Regis pacifici imitator*. The document then explains that the lord King, wishing mercifully to return the long-warring factions to peace, pronounced this sentence as much from his regal authority as from the power granted him by the contending factions. Henry orders that there no longer be two separate parties in Vercelli, but that there be peace. Citizens are to abstain from actions conducive to a violation of the peace, and to forgive each other for damages done to persons or property. The King himself liberally pardons such past acts. Exiles are to receive back unimpaired all their former possessions and rights, with no resistance from anyone. A person breaking this peace pact is subject to a fine of one hundred gold pounds and the royal indignation. The pact did not specify whether any of that fine was to remain in the city treasury. As in Asti, Henry reserved the right to make changes in or interpretations of this pact.[64] When the arbitration had been read, representatives of the rival Tizzoni and Avvocati factions embraced and exchanged the kiss of peace.

Only after he had publicly reconciled the quarrelling parties did Henry accept an oath of fealty from the proctors of Vercelli.[65] On 18 December he appointed a "podesta or vicar" for the city and its district. This man should not have proven personally undesirable to Vercelli's dominant Guelfs, as he was a vassal of Louis of Savoy, nephew of Amadeus and presently Senator of Rome. The appointment also reflected the great influence of Henry's brother-in-law and his Savoyard kinsmen.[66]

The new vicar's background could not change the fact that Vercelli's chief communal magistracy had been eliminated, and that the royal councillor and *signore* of Vercelli was reduced to the status of a private citizen. Yet Simone remained loyal to the Emperor-elect. An unplanned revolt by a single city was doomed to failure. Sulking would only harm his position with the Luxemburger and his northern advisers and appear to confirm his enemies' accusations. The best policy was to act as a faithful vassal and adviser to Henry. Nor did the monarch show himself ill-disposed towards the Avvocati. The King and Queen royally feted the new bishop-elect of Vercelli, an Avvocato, and even promised him a place next to the Archbishop of Milan in the forthcoming Lombard coronation.[67]

On 18 December the imperial expedition journeyed from Vercelli to Novara, less than fourteen miles northeast. It need hardly be added that the Ghibelline Novarese exiles entered the city with the imperial troops. It was Henry's misfortune that the exiled factions of the first four imperial cities that he had visited, as well as that of Milan, were all nominally Ghibellines. This was not the result of any particular scheming or the design of the route of travel. The simple fact was that since Milan, the most powerful city in the region, had been in the hands of the Torriani, almost all of western Lombardy was dominated by their allies or satellites. Henry probably did not take account of this circumstance in selecting his route of entry into Italy and his itinerary, but was guided by the fact that the Mt. Cenis pass lay safely in the hands of his Savoyard relatives. But Henry's ignorance of Italian politics did not detract from the fact that his enemies could capitalize splendidly upon his reintroduction of a series of Ghibelline exile bands into Guelf-dominated cities, as well as upon his open use of the many Ghibelline and White Guelf exiles who offered him their services.[68]

While the expedition was still in Vercelli, the Novarese exiles appointed a proctor to pledge fealty to Henry and appoint him the arbitrator of their disputes. The party in power, however, the Guelf Brusati, only accomplished this formality the day after the Emperor-elect entered their city.[69] As in Vercelli, Henry's first care in Novara was to conclude a peace between the warring factions. The peace pronounced in the cathedral of Novara on Sunday 20 December (in the name of the King of Peace) was almost identical with that promulgated four days earlier in Vercelli, except that now the clause of 18 December cancelling fines and bans against the former exiles was included in the body of the text.[70] Yet although the two instruments were almost identical, this pact had a much better chance of succeeding than its predecessor. The difference was due to the political situation within Novara. The ruling faction was led by an old man, and did not have so strong and forceful a leader as Simone degli Avvocati. Unlike the Avvocati in Vercelli, and the Langusco in Pavia, the leading Novarese Guelf family did not have one of its members as bishop of the city. The maintenance of peace within a city depended at least as much upon the will (and power) of the local factions and citizenry as upon royal fiat or ordinance.

On the same day that the peace pact was concluded, proctors for Novara did fealty to the King.[71] As in Vercelli, Henry removed the podesta from office and placed the city's dominant faction upon a legal par with the other citizens. As vicar of Novara and its *contado,* Henry selected the Genoese Guelf, Albert de Maloselli, relative and probably the choice of Amadeus of Savoy. Henry's treatment of Novara is significant as it indicates that he had established a pattern in Vercelli, and that he would most probably reform the other cities he visited, reintroducing exiles, removing *signori* from power, and replacing communal magistrates with imperial vicars. But would he apply these policies universally, even to cities he did not visit, and would he make any exceptions or special arrangements to fit local conditions—or Ghibelline *signori?*

While in Novara the King of the Romans decided upon the matter of his Lombard coronation. Since an iron crown was not to be found, he commissioned the goldsmith Lando of Siena to fashion a new diadem. Despite the claims and pretensions of Monza, Henry heeded the learned opinions of the men whom he had sent to investigate the matter.[72] On 20 December he issued joyous letters to all important vassals in imperial Italy, inviting them to come to Milan for participation in the coronation ceremonies to take place there on Epiphany, 6 January 1311.[73] We might note that this decision to favor Milan over Monza need not be explained as a pragmatic seeking of political support, since the metropolis in actuality did possess the better historical claims.

Only now that the royal cortege was in Novara, less than thirty miles from Milan, did Henry receive official notice from Guido della Torre, the *signore* who had promised to meet him at Lausanne with a thousand armed men and lead him across Lombardy with a hunting falcon on his fist. Protests and excuses made for the Captain of Milan by the Luxemburger's three Guelf councillors could not have countered completely the bad impression created by Guido's absence, his obvious silence, and the stories told by his enemies—among them his own cousin the Archbishop of Milan. Henry himself publicly defended Guido against all accusations, but whether he did this because he actually believed that the Guelf lord would obey him in good faith or for reasons of tactics and diplomacy we cannot know.[74]

As the Emperor-elect and his officers disposed their troops for the march from Novara towards Milan, on 22 December, Henry concluded an agreement that was to have enormous repercussions. Matteo Visconti promised to pay him sixty thousand florins after he was readmitted to his native city.[75] The Ghibelline exile was well aware, both from Henry's previous actions and from public declarations of policy, that he would be able to re-enter Milan without making any payment. This gesture, made on the eve of an already certain return home, must have created an excellent impression on Henry and his northern relatives and advisers. It had the special advantage of touching one of their weakest points—their purses, ever empty.

The imperial expedition left Novara behind, forded the Ticino River, and marched towards Magenta, more than thirteen miles northeast. As the main body of troops neared that town on the cold and snowy evening, runners came in with letters from the Marshal, Henry of Flanders. He had been sent ahead to provide for food and lodging in Milan and reported dissatisfaction with the state of the city and the attitude of its captain, Guido della Torre. The *signore* had refused to leave his residence at the Old Palace of the Broletto and place it at the King's disposal. Guido also appeared unwilling to dismiss his personal mercenaries, almost a thousand strong. Disconcerting rumors circulated in the imperial camp: in one square alone ten thousand Torriani, foot and horse, had assembled and declared their opposition to a reconciliation with the Archbishop and the Visconti. Henry decided to camp at Magenta for the night. Perhaps more important in his calculation than rumored stories of Torriani opposition was the fact that it was more than fourteen miles from Magenta to Milan. The army had already travelled thirteen miles and was not accustomed to marches of over twenty-seven miles in a single day, and the inclemency of the weather alone might have counselled a stay at Magenta.[76]

As the imperial army marched towards Milan the following morning, the city's nobles and populace lined the road to view the novel sight. At last Guido della Torre appeared before the sovereign whom he had not known how to deter nor how to accept as lord. As he approached the King with his companions, Guido inadvertently forgot to order his standards lowered before the imperial eagles. An enraged German sprang forward, tore the offending banner from its carrier, and thrust it into the mud. Guido himself leaped down from his horse and kissed the feet of the Emperor-elect. According to Cermenate, Henry then smiled and said, "Henceforth, Guido, be pacific and faithful, and recognize as lord him whom it is sinful to deny." [77]

IN MILAN

Before sundown 23 December 1310 the Emperor-elect triumphantly entered Milan.[78] First on the royal agenda was the pacification of the opposing factions. The Guelf Torriani had no choice but to grant Henry power to arbitrate their disputes.[79] The royal court met in a solemn session on Sunday 27 December in the Palace of the Broletto. The imperial chancellor read aloud the peace arbitration for Milan in the presence of Matteo Visconti and two of his sons, Guido della Torre, Cassone della Torre—Archbishop of Milan, and other leading members of both parties.[80] Although worded more tightly, the pact was almost identical in form with that decreed a week earlier at Novara. But the penalty for single breaches of the peace was multiplied tenfold, to one thousand pounds of gold, an indication of the importance of Milan in the monarch's reckoning. Partisans present at the reading of the arbitration pledged all their goods that they would personally observe it.

At the conclusion of the reading the onlookers in the Broletto Palace were treated to the spectacle of Guido della Torre and Matteo Visconti, mortal rivals for the signory of Milan, embracing and exchanging the kiss of peace. The city witnessed another stirring scene on the following day when Henry, King of the Romans, enthroned upon a raised platform and surrounded by leading members of the court, received an oath of fealty from the proctors of the commune.[81] Seated peacefully at his feet were Guido and Matteo.

In view of Henry's actions in the communes already visited,

it was no surprise to see Guido, captain of the people, removed from office along with the podesta. The city was to be ruled by an imperial vicar, this time not an Italian but the Burgundian noble Jean de Chaux. Ill-equipped to handle this huge responsibility, he was replaced a few weeks after his appointment by none other than the exiled Ghibelline Sienese banker, Niccolo de' Buonsignori, vicar of Asti since 23 November.[82] Henry must have been well satisfied with Buonsignori's performance to give him this fine promotion.

Henry soon took other measures to ensure the smooth functioning of the new regime in Milan. As in Asti, he emptied the city jails of political prisoners. He consigned the communal statutes to a commission of jurists who were to purge them of the signs of eight years of Torriani rule. This was the way in which the Emperor-elect saw fit to honor the pointed request made of his legates in June, that he "maintain the said lord captain [Guido della Torre] and the Milanese commune and its friends in its every honor and in the condition in which they are." The assurances made in Henry's name by Pope Clement V to the Guelf lords and communes [83] were to be applied in terms of strict adherence to ample theoretical and legalistic interpretations of the rights of the Holy Roman Empire.

From all Italy bishops, feudal lords, and communal delegates began to appear in Milan for the festive coronation. Venice made certain to be represented by a splendid embassy, although it did not swear fealty to Henry. Lombardy had almost perfect representation, and even the proud republic of Padua sent envoys. Francesco della Mirandola, *de facto* lord of Modena who came to Milan as a communal representative, must surely have encountered the proctors sent by his city's exiles. Similarly, Can Grande and Alboin della Scala, *signori* of Verona, might have seen their noble Guelf exile, Vinciguerra, Count of Sambonifacio. Some exiles, born since their families had suffered expulsion, had never been within the walls of their "native" cities.[84]

Chroniclers noted that Bologna was not represented in Milan, since they thought of it as still being an imperial city. But one absence could not fail to be marked by all: Florence and its

Tuscan Guelf allies. Perhaps the positive measures adopted by Henry in assuming control over and reforming Chieri and Asti had convinced Florence that it was useless to hope that the King of the Romans would accept its terms—terms that amounted in fact to granting the commune autonomy and self-government and abdicating imperial rights in Tuscany. As we have noted, the Florentine conditions were already drawn up by 10 November, and although the advisability of sending an embassy from the Tuscan Guelf League to the Emperor-elect was discussed throughout that month, the project was finally abandoned.[85] By not sending an embassy empowered with doing fealty to the Luxemburger, Florence and its allies patently disobeyed the orders brought to them, and to all the cities and lords of imperial Italy, by Henry's legates during the past summer.

Florence sent spies to watch Henry.[86] The city's dislike for the northern monarch became more apparent when Florence and its allies failed to send representatives to honor his coronation in Milan on 6 January 1311. The Priory adhered to what seemed to be its chosen policy of avoiding all direct contact with the commune's temporal lord.

Rather than entrust its security to the Emperor-elect, Florence preferred to rely upon other methods. It gave large gifts to insure the good will of friendly members of the papal curia and of Robert of Anjou, whom the Guelf republic was determined to have on its side in the case of an eventual conflict.[87] The Angevin was barraged with letters and urged to support Florentine diplomacy.[88] But Robert refused to commit himself against the King of the Romans, and not even the Florentine plea that "our every hope rests in your hands and power" moved the cautious Angevin.[89] Simultaneously with these negotiations, envoys from the Tuscan Guelf cities and Bologna went to the Pope, pleading for his protection and support.[90] Already orators of these allied cities had enlisted the sympathies of Philip the Fair and were working in close liaison with French representatives at the papal curia.[91] In Italy itself the papal city of Perugia in Umbria was gained for the Florentine cause.[92]

Let us consider why Florence and its allies so desperately sought to postpone the arrival of the Emperor-elect in their own

Tuscany and if possible to escape it completely.[93] Their complaints and worries were made quite clear in a letter sent by the Priory to Robert of Anjou. They expressed their anger at

> those things that [the Emperor] did and effected in the other lands that were ruled by Guelfs devoted to you and to the Church, especially in replacing Ghibellines in those [lands], in annulling laws, statutes, and orders, and in [removing] their rectors, podestas, and councillors, and in placing them almost beneath the yoke of servitude, and reorganizing them with Ghibelline rectors and personnel, and that he follows the counsels of these latter for the most part.[94]

The Priory added that Florence would prepare to resist subjugation by "the Emperor" with all the means at its disposal.

The Tuscan Guelf communes feared that Henry would introduce into Tuscany exactly those measures being enforced in Lombardy, that party rule would be ended, exiles restored, and communal autonomy restricted. They were afraid that their feudal lord, whose legitimacy and claim to rule they had not denied, would exercise the rule that was rightfully his according to tradition and imperial law. The fact that they were opposing the legitimate use of authority made it difficult for the Guelf cities to gain aid outside imperial Italy or from any but those who felt their own positions similarly threatened.

In order to win all possible support, Florence based its resistance to the Emperor-elect upon a general principle, such as that of "liberty," that could embrace more than the selfish interest of a single political faction desirous of maintaining power. Florentine ambassadors were urged to protect "our liberty and status and that of the other communes of the Guelf Party of the League of Tuscany and of our other friends." [95] Bologna was begged to act in defense of its "customary liberty." [96] Robert of Anjou was politely requested to aid Florence and its allies so that they "might remain in their accustomed liberty, and in most faithful devotion to your majesty." [97] Siena, Perugia, and Città di Castello were called upon in the name of their own welfare and that "of the Guelf and Church Party." [98] It did not matter that the Emperor-elect had received the support of the Papacy and had entered Italy under papal sponsorship. Reference to the Party of the Church made it seem as if the Tuscan cities in their disobedience were part of a more general movement and could expect powerful assistance from the Church. Similarly, in stressing the welfare of the Guelf Party, Florence could appeal to all factions throughout imperial Italy bearing that name, playing upon fears that they too might be mistreated by a King of the Romans who listened to their enemies and political exiles. The Guelf name gave a note of respectable antiquity to the present conflict and called forth heroic memories of battles waged for liberty against the Hohenstaufen. The cause of practical local independence needed such a cloak of respectability if it was to contest traditional concepts of the medieval Christian Empire and the majesty of the imperial name.

Tuscan Guelf fears and machinations had little effect in Milan, where all efforts were concentrated upon last-minute preparations for the climax of Henry's triumphal march across Lombardy: the coronation on Epiphany 1311. On that day, two years after Henry's elevation to the Kingship of the Romans in Aachen, he and his queen entered the Church of St. Ambrose, accompanied by the entire court and dignitaries from almost all parts of imperial Italy. Behind the high altar stood two newly erected statues of the King and Queen.[99] As Henry knelt, the Archbishop of Milan consecrated him and placed upon his head the new crown glittering with pearls and precious stones. The Queen, Margaret of Brabant, received a golden diadem.[100] For some Lombards this coronation was highly important, perhaps even outranking the ceremonies in Aachen, and the Reggian statutes compiled in 1311 date Henry's reign as beginning only in that year.[101] Despite the vagueness of the Italian coronation tradition, the rites in Milan helped make this French-speaking ruler from north of the Alps more acceptable to certain Italians.

Joyous festivities followed the solemn coronation ceremony. Henry created at least one hundred and fifty new knights and gave to each the regal gift of a palfrey and three complete military outfits. Most of these knights were Italians, and, according to the recollection of Nicolas of Butrinto, the majority were Ghibellines. The Guelfs, he reported, though more numerous, powerful, and rich, did not want to receive their knighthood at the King's hands. Among those knighted in Milan were Matteo Visconti, the nominally Ghibelline chief of Brescia Matteo Maggi, the nominally Guelf lord of Parma Ghiberto da Correggio, and Ponzino Ponzoni, convinced Guelf of Cremona.[102] Henry clearly stated that he did not want to hear the names "Guelf" and "Ghibelline," but we can believe Dino Compagni's statement that the members of each faction loudly accused the King of favoring the adherents of the other.[103]

The Emperor-elect received a pleasant surprise soon after the coronation. The Milanese had decided to give him a gift. The matter was discussed in council and the elderly Guillelmus de Pusterla entrusted with deciding the amount. He proposed fifty thousand florins. Matteo Visconti then rose and declared that the city should not neglect the Queen, and requested that she be given ten thousand florins. Then Guido della Torre sprang up in a rage, asked cynically if so small an amount was a fitting gift for so great a city as Milan to give its ruler, and proposed the round sum of one hundred thousand florins. The council tried to ignore this outburst, but it was too late. Henry's notaries present in the room had heard all, and taken down the last sum. In vain a delegation asked the King to permit a reduction. The coronation had cost a fortune, and Henry needed more money for the court, troops, and the general maintenance of the expedition.[104] The Milanese gift seemed a godsend to the hard-pressed monarch, and he would not let it slip by. The northern counsellors who understood little of the actual play of events or politics of the city now lavished praise upon Guido della Torre. But actually the former Guelf *signore* had only let a few words escape in anger.[105] Matteo Visconti, on the other hand, had played a shrewd game. This was his way of keeping the promise he had made to the Emperor-elect on the eve of his re-entry into Milan that he would pay sixty thousand florins. The Luxemburger might yet pay dearly, however, for this gift which made the Milanese populace grumble under the burden of new taxes.

Henry of Luxemburg, his court, and his chancellery had little time now for such worries. Proctors from the remaining Lombard cities and from numerous groups of exiles came to do fealty. Among the exiles were Alberto Scotto of Piacenza, who had so magnificently received the imperial embassy during the past summer, and the Guelf Theobald Brusati of Brescia, who had made so fine an impression upon the monarch in Asti. Only the cities of Alba and Alessandria were absent, due, it was said, to their having performed homage to Robert of Anjou, and thus no longer being directly dependent upon the Emperor-elect. A splendid embassy arrived to do fealty for Genoa, a city that had resisted the threats and blandishments of Frederick II. Arezzo in Tuscany sent a proctor to Milan, while the Pisan delegation paid that city's debt to the monarch with 29,400 gold florins. Leo Lambertenghi of Como, replaced in his see by the Emperor-elect, was one of several bishops who did homage for their imperial holdings. Nor did Henry neglect to invest Cassone della Torre with a useful fortification.[106]

The monarch threw his energies into settling the disputes of the numerous Lombard cities that were split into factions in power and others without the walls trying to fight their way in. The complex problems raised by the return of political exiles and the rightful restitution of their property and rights still troubled Henry. His chancellery had made several different attempts to solve these difficulties in peace pacts promulgated since the complicated judgment given at Asti on 5 December. On the second and third of January 1311 Henry issued a special declaration concerning the Milanese arbitration and ordered that no one unjustly take possession of the rights or goods of another.[107] Complaints arising in this respect had to be taken to the vicar of Milan, who would judge the cases without recurring to any of the usual legal procedures. The party adjudged guilty had to pay all court expenses and a fine of one hundred imperial pounds for every day that it persisted in resisting the vicar's sentence. In his desire for swift and simple justice, Henry placed tremendous power in the hands of the vicar. A man who was less than honest might profit considerably from this situation, to the misfortune of the city and its district.

The treatment of disputes over properties and rights that would certainly arise between the newly returned exiles and the factions that had remained in power was still the greatest problem facing the notaries and jurists who drew up the peace arbitrations delivered in the name of Henry of Luxemburg. The peace of Milan, with its addition of 2–3 January, was extremely important, and appears to have been adopted in unchanged form as the solution to the problems of at least five other communes.[108]

The first changes made in the peace arbitrations since the pact for Milan appear in the pacts pronounced for Cremona and Reggio on 14 January. Henry had at first thought to give Cremona a pact no different than those issued previously.[109] We do not know why or at whose suggestion this decision was changed. The new document set the fine for each breach of the peace at three hundred pounds gold, rather than the one thousand set for Milan or the one hundred for Vercelli and Novara.[110] Several of the innovations in the Cremonese pact remained unique and were applied to no other cities. Provision was made to assure the readmission to the city of the son of a famous exile. Here at least imperial officials were acquainted with the groups contending for power and had bargained seriously with both sides, for the pact represented a compromise between opposing interests, as a limitation was placed upon the rights of the returned exile. Other clauses dealt with deciding disputes between the returned exiles and the hitherto dominant factions. Arrangements were included to provide reasonable reimbursement to the present holder for improvements he had made upon an exile's lands. One unique provision in this pact left room for great abuse of authority. Instead of fixing the penalty for the loser of a dispute at legal costs plus one hundred imperial pounds for each day of recalcitrance, the vicar of Cremona received the right to set whatever fines he saw fit for the loser of a dispute. Perhaps this was intended to be a deterrent to unnecessary litigation, but it left the door open for financial extortion by the imperial vicar. Fortunately this clause never found its way into later documents.

The arbitration for Reggio, also made on 14 January,[111] was even more important for the development of imperial policy than that for Cremona. The Reggian document was like that for Milan with two exceptions. The fine for a breach of the peace was three hundred pounds of gold, and this remained the standard amount in other peace arbitrations. It was also stated that the Reggian vicar had to settle each dispute brought to him concerning property and rights between former exiles and mem-

bers of the parties in power within one month of receiving the
case. This was an obvious improvement. The penalty for the
loser of litigation remained that established in 2–3 January for
Milan: the cost of legal expenses plus a fine of one hundred
imperial pounds a day for refusal to abide by the vicar's judgment. But still, as in earlier pacts, the vicar alone retained the
power of decision, even though it was easily subject to abuse.
This clause nevertheless remained unchanged in future pacts.[112]

Two other extant peace arbitrations from this period demonstrate that the imperial chancellery did not arrive at a formula
with which it was satisfied, and yet did not return to the attempt
(made in the case of Cremona) to treat each city individually
on the basis of an investigation into its special local problems.
The pact announced for Lodi on 15 January differed somewhat
from those given to Reggio and Modena the day before.[113] Actions taken by the commune prior to Henry's reform were officially recognized to have legal validity, to the extent that the
present possessors of exiles' property were to be repaid the purchase price if they had bought those holdings directly from the
commune. As a safeguard against legal hair-splitting it was explicitly stated that an exile's heirs had legal title to his property
and rights. The pact decreed, moreover, that only half of the
three-hundred-pound fine for each breach of the peace should
go to the imperial fisc. The remaining one hundred and fifty
pounds was to be given to the commune itself. Thus the Lombard city received a solid interest in the maintenance of the
peace, and leaders of the communal council would have a reason to occupy themselves with enforcing the observance of the
imperial arbitration. This clause also appeared in the peace
established for Crema two days later.[114] Perhaps complaints from
communal representatives forced the omission in the Crema
document of the provision for the reimbursement of those who
had purchased exiles' property from the commune.

We do not have peace treaties for all the Lombard cities, yet
those remaining permit some useful generalizations. Henry's
first effort in this field, made in Asti, was actually only the re-
newal of an earlier Savoyard arbitration combined with a complicated and unsure attempt to deal with the return to the city
of the exiled De Castello faction. The pact made at Vercelli

marked the beginning of a line of development that continued for approximately one month. During that time Henry issued peace pacts to almost all the more important Lombard cities. Promulgating these in the name of the "King of Peace," the Emperor-elect appears to have attempted to play the role suggested to him by the Pope. Perhaps Henry made certain to secure the consent of the affected parties to his arbitrations so that there could be no question or cavilling as to the validity of his settlements, but nevertheless, that desire for consent may indicate an element of unsureness or even weakness on the monarch's part. As Henry and his northern advisers gradually became aware of some of the problems confronting the royal program of peace, love, reconciliation, and the return of political exiles, they attempted various solutions.

It may be that no completely satisfactory solution could have been found. Endless confusions were certain to arise in determining the just owner of lands or rights in cities where rival factions had by turns been vanquished and victors for many decades, where goods had been sold, exchanged, resold, at times by the communal government itself. These problems ordinarily were simply lumped together and classified as disputes to be settled by an imperial vicar. In the interest of speed normal legal procedures and officials were sidetracked. Enormous power and discretion were given to the imperial vicars—men often foreign to the local situation and ignorant of the histories of the cases presented them, and thus likely to make judgments on the strength of favors and graft rather than on the merits of the extremely complicated and emotionally charged issues involved. But one of the greatest flaws in the peace arbitrations may be the attempt made to find a single formula, or perfect peace pact, rather than to combine certain general remedies or formulae with particular clauses directed to the special local problems of each particular city.

Even at the conclusion of this cycle of pacts, in essence they remained too much merely pious hopes that all would turn out for the best. The pro-imperial Milanese notary Cermenate wrote of Henry: "His simple soul wholly aspired to give peace to the world." [115] And the monarch seems, indeed, to have expected to establish a new era of peace, tranquility, and imperial order in

Italy largely by imperial fiat. He showed little understanding of
the situations with which he dealt. Opponents of years standing
were told that parties were no longer to exist within commune
or *contado*. Past injuries were ordered forgotten. Proctors present at the reading of peace arbitrations were then ordered to
"kiss and make up," and the matter was considered closed, except for tying up a few loose legal ends and fining some re-
calcitrants.

In considering these arbitrations that were to form the base
for a new age of peace and to be one of the pillars of a new, firm
imperial administration in Lombardy, we must recall that Henry
and many of his northern advisers did not speak the local ver-
nacular and had not resided in Italy. They were accustomed to
dealing with cities of a different character, located in lands
where the most powerful military forces did not lie in the hands
of truly independent communes and signories. Many Italians in
the court, among them most of the Guelf and Ghibelline counsellors, were *signori* or would-be *signori,* at times too interested
in their own political affairs to give unbiased, honest advice.
Those bulwarks of Henry's counsel, the Counts of Savoy, did not
have all the answers, even had they been able to make their
voices continually prevail. Their intimate knowledge was confined to Piedmont and western Lombardy, and there they had
their own interests to further.

What alternative remained to Henry? He did not have time
to visit every city in northern Italy and remain long enough to
acquaint himself with its peculiar problems. He had to hope
that the imperial vicar assigned to each city would be able to
deal intelligently, justly, and firmly with the many difficulties
that hampered the re-establishment of peace, justice, and an
imperial administration. Another approach, that of fitting his
imperial designs into the present situation, sanctioning the status
quo, and permitting the Italian cities local autonomy and practical independence, might have simplified Henry's administrative
task and even guaranteed him a measure of certain military and
financial support. Such an approach would have been consonant
with the Florentine policy statement of 10 November 1310. But
Henry of Luxemburg could not accept this alternative—or perhaps could not even recognize it. For it would have denied him

the role of a supreme ruler, *Dei gratia,* an arbiter who stood above parties and commanded imperial lands as a Holy Roman Emperor.

In justice we must add that Henry and his court could not devote sufficient time to this problem of peace arbitrations. Other matters called for attention.

The peace pacts themselves had to be implemented. Much to the amazement of contemporary chroniclers, exiles returned to almost every Lombard city swiftly and without bloodshed.[116] Only two major cities kept their gates barred against the exiles during Henry's stay in Milan. One of these was Padua, which the Emperor-elect treated as a semiautonomous power. He engaged in delicate negotiations with its representatives in order to effect the installation of an imperial vicar on terms acceptable to the proud Guelf republic.[117] The case of Ghibelline Verona was more serious. There the Scaliger lords actually disobeyed imperial orders and refused to permit the return of their enemies, offering as an excuse their condemnation as rebels by Frederick II. Here too Henry did not press the issue, as he was carrying on dealings with the Veronese that would soon bear fruit in an advantageous financial arrangement.[118] Again, as with the Milanese gift, Henry overlooked the possible implications and consequences of his action and concentrated upon immediate gain. By allowing Verona, the most important Ghibelline city in northern Italy, to ignore the order to accept the return of its exiles, the Emperor-elect severely marred his record for impartiality.

A royal decree issued 23 January 1311 admitted the monarch's failure to solve the complex problem of reconciling the warring factions.[119] When he had come to Italy, said Henry, he had found it violently agitated by party strife. Moved by partiality, the rulers of cities passed harsh and unjust sentences against exiles who could not defend themselves, and had even burdened persons within the cities with unreasonable taxes and fines. The King, deeply moved by this state of affairs, had sought to separate the just from the unjust sentences. But there had been too much confusion for this method to succeed. Thus it was ordered that all criminal sentences be cancelled in all the Lombard cities where Henry had made or would make peace. Ex-prisoners and

their families were to be undisturbed and could never be condemned again for the same crimes. Books listing the sentences
were to be destroyed. This ruling was to prevail over all local
laws, ordinances, or customs, and communal statutes existing to
the contrary were automatically cancelled. On the same day, 23
January, Henry cancelled all reprisals granted in Lombardy.[120]
In his zeal for reform Henry had originally intended that these
measures be applied to Tuscany as well, but he decided to deal
with all the affairs of that province at one time in the future.

The drastic remedies of 23 January probably had several important effects. A wholesale opening of the jails would not only
liberate unjustly condemned political prisoners, but would turn
loose upon the population a considerable number of thieves,
highwaymen, and murderers. In abolishing the rubrics of communal statutes so openly Henry risked offending popular sentiment, sentiment that cherished traditional communal organization and methods—defective though they might seem to a
noble count and marquis from Luxemburg. Even when native
signori made changes in communal usages they often did so over
a period of many years, making use of the customary councils
and magistrates so as to give their actions the appearance of
legal, traditional normality. Henry, on the other hand, seems to
have assumed that as King of the Romans and Emperor-elect his
actions automatically became acceptable. He forgot, perhaps,
that Italians were not accustomed to seeing or thinking of an
emperor as a functioning, integral part of their lives. It was still
an open question how well an active monarch would mesh into
the normal routine and ways of thinking of Italian political life.

The decrees of 23 January did not, however, remain mere
commands on paper. In Parma the *signore,* Ghiberto da Correggio, who was extremely anxious to make a perfect impression
on Henry, executed the orders before the arrival of the first imperial vicar. In Modena a newly appointed vicar executed the
decrees almost immediately upon his arrival.[121]

Henry had decided even before the Milanese coronation to remove the podestas, captains, and any other rulers in the Lombard
cities, and assign them instead "competent podestas, rectors,
vicars, and prefects at the royal pleasure." [122] In a general coun-

cil held only four days after that coronation Henry announced
that a vicar would be appointed to preside in each of the Lombard cities.[123] By mid-February he had given vicars to almost
every major city in the province.[124] The King of the Romans also
removed any thoughts that the seizure of Vigevano on 11 December had been an isolated phenomenon. He showed that he
intended to assert strictly the rights of the Empire, assigning
individual vicars to at least three more places that had previously
been controlled by larger neighboring communes.[125] And even
so-called Ghibelline cities and lords might react strongly against
the reassertion of imperial rights in their *contadi*.

Half the vicars named on an official list of mid-February 1311
cannot be identified. Five of the remaining twelve were well-
known Tuscan Ghibelline or White Guelf exiles, and one was a
leading Pisan Ghibelline.[126] Henry of Luxemburg was still using
those men to whom he was attracted, regardless of their partisan
affiliations or of the possible effect upon pronounced Guelfs or
men undecided in their allegiance. Three other vicars had probably been chosen at the suggestion of the Savoyards and the
Marquis of Monferrat, while the brother of the Bishop of Parma
was sent to nearby Borgo San Donnino.[127]

One fact is striking: not one of the great tyrants in power or
aspiring *signori* of Lombardy had received an imperial vicarship. One looks in vain for the names of the Scaligers, the Bonacolsi, Matteo Visconti, Richard da Camino, Francesco della
Mirandola, or Alberto Scotto. The vicars were imperial functionaries, and no more. Appointed for terms of one year or six
months, as had been the communal podestas and captains, they
could be removed or kept longer in office at the royal pleasure.
They derived their powers from their imperial mandate and not
from local holdings or from a large personal following in the
commune they ruled. Nor were they very powerful lords in their
own right. Although some communes and *signori* had certainly
discussed the selection of vicars with Henry and his council, the choice rested entirely in imperial and not local hands.
Yet ordinarily the communes paid the vicars, whose salaries
might be determined by the Emperor-elect beforehand (as perhaps was the case in Chieri) or be left to bargaining between
the vicar and the commune. Possibly some of the money col-

lected in imperial fines or from the rights and *regalia* of the Empire in a city and its district could be used towards the vicar's salary, but we find no specific mention of the practice for this early in the expedition.[128]

The vicar's powers were far from all-inclusive, and roughly comprehended those of the podesta and captain whose place he took. Vicars could execute orders sent them by the Emperor-elect, his council, or a high official delegated by one of these. Ordinarily vicars did not possess the rights of dispensing high and low justice, or the more important *regalia,* such as the right of coinage. One could appeal from a vicar's sentence to the Emperor-elect or his council. This entire system, however, was very vague, general, and flexible, or perhaps better, was not completely determined.[129]

Some cities, such as Cremona in early 1311, received a "vicar-general," an official whose competence extended to a larger area than that of a city and its *contado* or whose city was of particular importance. If we may judge by later conditions, vicars-general had only supervisory and inspectorial functions and not compulsory authority over other vicars in their area. Only to a very limited extent did some of the vicars-general enjoy the right to appoint sub-vicars. But this office was ill-defined and the official himself was ordinarily addressed merely as "vicar." [130]

Frederick II had first attempted to assign to each province a captain general or vicar, who had all military and civil authority and was aided by minor imperial officials and communal podestas. When this system proved unsatisfactory, he reverted to that used by his grandfather after the Peace of Constance (1183) and invested authority in city chieftains chosen by the people.[131] Henry of Luxemburg did not continue the Hohenstaufen tradition—rather he made general for the first time vicarships over individual cities instead of over provinces. But would this arrangement succeed any better than its predecessors—and with what ramifications for Italian political development?

The newly installed vicars quickly complied with their initial orders. They saw to the resignation of communal podestas and captains, opened the city prisons, and effected the return of exile factions. Some vicars went much further and altered and reorganized the entire constitutional and political functioning of their cities. Although we have no direct evidence, it may not be amiss to conjecture that such action depended more upon the strength and purpose of individual vicars and upon local conditions than upon special mandates. As the Milanese statutes were taken in hand and purged of traces of Torriani rule, so in Reggio and Chieri (and later in Vicenza) communal statutes were studied, revised, and amended under the vicars' supervision.[132]

We are provided with an interesting account of the inception of the new imperial regime in Parma.[133] The peace pact concluded for the city in Milan on 10 January was read and promulgated in a public council in Parma three days later and the populace acclaimed it joyously. The following week end Parma's jails were opened, and at the same time political exiles began returning home. On 27 January 1311, two weeks after the reception of the peace arbitration, the new imperial vicar, Guido Cocconato Count of Radicate, arrived in the city and mounted the steps of the Palace of the Podesta. The podesta and captain of the people then turned the rule of the city over to the vicar, were paid, and departed. Four days later the populace saw the most important of the exiles, the Guelf Rossi, return to Parma from their stronghold in Borgo San Donnino, unarmed and festooned in garlands. During February the vicar reformed the city's most important council, that of the ancients, and replaced it with a group of *popolani,* four from each of the "gates" or quarters of the city. The larger Council of the Four Hundred remained the same size it had been since 1308, but now was presided over by the vicar. At the same time men were appointed to review and draw up new copies of the Parmesan statutes, eliminating objectionable rubrics, that is, those impinging upon the rights of the Empire in Parma and its district.

Naturally the process was not the same for all cities, and in some, statutes remained as they were and councils were not altered. And although the examples we have considered provide a general idea of the vicars' tasks and the means they adopted to accomplish them, it is essential to remember that great variety existed. The vicar of the small Piedmontese commune of Chieri, desperately eager for imperial protection, could act with much greater ease and freedom than Vanni Zeno of Pisa, sent to the Scaliger stronghold of Verona, and he would meet with far less resistance than would the vicar in Cremona, city of the fierce Guelf Cavalcabò.

On 10 January 1311 Henry of Luxemburg put the crowning touch on the new edifice of imperial administration in Lombardy. At the same general council during which he announced the policy of assigning separate vicars to each city, the Emperor-elect declared that he would appoint a Vicar-General to administer Lombardy in his absence.[134]

Within four days Henry appointed his brother-in-law, Count Amadeus V of Savoy, to the post.[135] At a later date the monarch wrote the Pope that he had made the appointment in order to please the Guelfs.[136] But in reality Henry had little choice. For besides his acceptable political "complexion," Amadeus combined the advantages of being the monarch's kinsman, an experienced diplomat and conciliator, speaking the language of the country, and having a fair knowledge of the Italian political situation, and yet being disinterested enough in many Lombard affairs to command general respect. True, he always had an eye open to possibilities for expanding Savoy and furthering the interests of his dynasty, but in the light of his qualifications—and in the absence of any other likely candidate—this was a relatively minor defect.

The Vicar-General was to administer the entire northern portion of imperial Italy during the monarch's absence, from Piedmont to the Veneto. He would hear and settle any disputes that arose, supervise the conduct of the local vicars, see to the collection of imperial revenues, and generally insure the continuance of peace and the enforcement of the rights and *regalia* of the Empire.

The Emperor-elect had already revived the payment of many dues and taxes legally owed the Empire. Now the staggering sum of close to 300,000 florins a year required to support the Vicar-General and his 1,500 cavalry was added to the tax burden. This amount Henry apportioned among approximately fifty Lombard cities and lords, assigning each a quota roughly proportionate to its relative power and importance.[137] Even Venice was hopefully included. Highest taxed was Genoa with its Riviera, at 40,000 florins. Milan, second at 29,760 florins annually, had to contribute its regular one-quarter or 7,440 florins within three months. Such was the price of the newly established era of peace and brotherly love in northern Italy.

Henry of Luxemburg, at any rate, had little doubt that his new regime would function smoothly. During the first half of February 1311 he made the final preparations for the journey south to Rome and the imperial coronation. Although he had not yet received pontifical approval for an advancement of the coronation date, Henry expected that it would soon be forthcoming. Since the *Regis pacifici imitator* had completed his task in northern Italy, why should Clement V object if he proceeded directly to Rome? Henry decided to take with him the party leaders of the major Lombard cities, both in order to honor his coronation and to leave Lombardy in as secure a condition as possible. All would leave Milan on 14 February, and any who failed to appear were subject to severe penalties.[138]

In the fall of 1310 an ill-informed French-speaking King of the Romans had entered Italy, armed with few soldiers and with a simple, legalistic, and somewhat vague program of peace, justice, and imperial restoration. Yet his solutions had often been met with great general enthusiasm. But would they function well in their day-to-day application? And would the men of the Italian city-states be willing to pay the price in money and in lost freedom of political action needed to maintain the new imperial structure? If Henry of Luxemburg had done his work well, then all the machinations of his enemies would avail little.

III

The First Troubles: From Milan to Genoa (February-October 1311)

February Rebellions

One month after the magnificent coronation in St. Ambrose, the joyous spirit that had welcomed Henry's arrival in Milan had all but disappeared. Resentment steadily increased against the heavy financial burdens imposed by the city's gift to the Emperor-elect, the stipend of the Vicar-General, and the daily maintenance of the imperial forces. Nicolas of Butrinto relates that he lacked the courage to make the trip from his lodgings to Henry in the Broletto Palace because of curses and vituperation in the streets against the King and his foreigners who were forcing the Milanese to make exorbitant payments.[1] And great though Henry's expenses were, they would increase within a few months, when in order to retain their services he would be constrained to pay those vassals who had fulfilled their feudal duty. On 30 January alone the monarch requested funds from half a dozen Lombard cities.[2] The Milanese notary Cermenate nicely observed that the King, "truly magnanimous and rich in all virtues, was very poor in money and gold." [3]

The Emperor-elect ignored the accumulating anger. When the Milanese selected to accompany the expedition to Rome requested that the commune reimburse their expenses, Henry heeded only the limited legal question involved and recognized the correctness of the petition, thereby still further burdening the irritated citizens of Milan.

A new and serious source of complaint appeared in the comportment of the vicar of Milan. Niccolo de' Buonsignori intended to exercise his powers fully. He severely threatened the commission of jurists charged with revising the Milanese statutes when they balked at granting him absolute power over the commune. Buonsignori rightly argued that he sought no more than the Torriani had possessed for eight years. But the city had not suffered the overthrow of a native tyranny simply to see itself subjected to a possibly worse one over which it would have no control. The vicar's methods, as much as any changes he made, turned nearly all Milan against him.[4] Henry, however, retained him in office since he appeared to be an efficient administrator.

One of the Emperor-elect's chosen policies threatened to undermine and perhaps destroy completely a condition essential to Milan's safety and prosperity—the city's control over its *contado*. The favor shown Asti had not marked the beginning of a general policy; rather, Henry had demonstrated his intention to restore to the Empire rights and places usurped by local cities and lords. Witness his judgment of Chieri, the seizure of Vigevano, and the removal of certain *contado* towns and forts from the jurisdiction of Brescia and Reggio.

Despite Milan's generosity the monarch made no real exception for the Lombard metropolis, although on 24 January, as a mark of special favor, he did grant the city the right to appoint captains and officials in *contado* towns and castles "for this time only." [5] He had indicated his general attitude two weeks earlier when he accepted homage from one of the Milanese *contado* towns. Other communities took courage from this example and appointed proctors to appear before the vicar of Milan and its district to swear fealty and promise all that might be required of them.[6]

Henry's position was decisive regarding the two most important cities in the Milanese *contado*, Monza and Treviglio. In Monza he installed an imperial vicar. Less than a week after conceding Milan special authority over its *contado*, the King confirmed all of Treviglio's imperial privileges.[7] Continued Milanese efforts to maintain control over that town provoked him to pro-

vide Treviglio with a letter addressed to Milan, stating clearly
that Treviglio's privileges had been confirmed and that it was
to be in no way molested.[8]

While almost all Milanese agreed that the city's well-being
necessitated its continued control of the *contado,* the Torriani
had a private grudge against the new imperial regime. At a touch
of the royal sceptre those lords of Milan had become private citizens and been forced to accept with a smile the return of their
hated rivals, the Visconti. Now a Ghibelline Tuscan exile commanded the city. Might even the wily Matteo Visconti succeed in
regaining his former position? The ex-*signore* of Milan, Guido
della Torre, might have reflected bitterly upon his own words of
the previous June: "I see that we are procuring our own death
with great zeal." [9]

The order that all party chiefs accompany the imperial expedition to Rome was the final action needed to throw the Torriani
headlong into plans for revolt. They would rise in arms and,
gathering almost universal Milanese support, drive the northern
monarch and his followers out of the city. It is possible that
Florence greatly encouraged and urged this rebellion in an effort
to work the destruction of the Emperor-elect or at least to delay
his entry into Tuscany. But there is no evidence for this, and the
uprising is explicable as a purely local phenomenon.

Matteo Visconti knew of the Torriani plans and found himself
in a difficult predicament. He and his eldest son, Galeazzo, were
to accompany the expedition to Rome, leaving in Milan a pre-
ponderance of Torriani supporters and men tired of the new
regime. Yet the outcome of the revolt was too uncertain for
Matteo to commit himself by revealing the plot to the Emperor-
elect. Visconti shrewdly succeeded in convincing the Torriani
that he would join them in ousting the Germans from Milan,
while he secretly resolved to await the outcome of events before
declaring himself. He ordered his partisans to go about their
normal routine and not to arm publicly.

The great rebellion was scheduled for 13 February, the day
before the imperial expedition accompanied by the Lombard
party chieftains was to leave for Rome. But on the morning of
12 February someone warned the Luxemburger of trouble, and
imperial patrols set out to inspect the quarters of the Torriani

and the Visconti.[10] The Ghibelline Visconti passed muster, and Matteo himself was seen seated unarmed on his own porch. The Torriani, taken by surprise and disorganized, resisted the imperial troops. The situation was confused, and the rebels were heard to shout, "Death to all the Germans! There is peace between lord Guido and lord Matteo!" [11] This battle cry was soon belied: despite Matteo's orders, groups of Visconti fought side by side with the imperial troops. Nevertheless it is worth noting the Torriani war cry and the absence of that ominous phrase "Death to the Ghibellines!," for it underlines that this first uprising against the King of the Romans was not a Guelf rebellion. A Milanese noble faction, tricked into believing that it had the support of its rivals, had attempted to gain control of the city.

The bitter combat continued for several hours before the Torriani fled discomfited, and the northerners and their Italian allies gave themselves over to several days of pillage. The Torriani were hunted down in city and *contado,* and even innocent members of the family and their friends and neighbors suffered. Men took advantage of the chaos to satisfy personal vendettas and sent imperial soldiers to sack the homes of enemies not even remotely connected with the ill-fated uprising.

Henry of Luxemburg acted with fairness and calm. He temporarily banned the absent Torriani until the origins of the rebellion could be better determined. Since it appeared that they might have been implicated, he also banished Matteo and his son Galeazzo. He did not terribly inconvenience the Visconti, however, as he sent Matteo to Asti and ordered Galeazzo to Treviso where he still held the office of podesta.

Inside Milan itself Henry created a special league of citizens dedicated to assuring the maintenance of peace and order.[12] Led by more than fifty nobles, judges, merchants, and doctors, it was bound to obey and uphold the Emperor-elect in Milan, to the exclusion of all other allegiances, blood relationships, partisan oaths, personal loves and hatreds, and the possibility of financial gain. Contrary to what might have been expected, Henry exercised moderation and forbearance and soon reaccepted Milan into his good graces. Only a month after the uprising he ratified all of the commune's earlier imperial privileges.[13]

Henry's moderation could not prevent the Milanese tumults

from having dire repercussions. The Torriani insurrections gave
the spark of life to opposition to the Emperor-elect in northern
Italy. Many parties that had been in sole power before the
Luxemburger's arrival ousted their newly returned political
rivals and cast off imperial rule. Factions bearing the Guelf name
had controlled almost all Lombardy before the advent of the
Emperor-elect, and since it was these factions that rebelled during
the second half of February 1311, the entire movement took on
the appearance of a Guelf rebellion against the Empire. In
Crema, Brescia, Cremona, and Reggio the Ghibellines were violently expelled along with the imperial vicars. Parma and Lodi
ejected only the Ghibellines, allowing the vicars, representatives
of imperial authority, to remain. In Asti the nominally Guelf
faction was exiled after an abortive uprising, while in Mantua
the Ghibelline Bonacolsi shrewdly maneuvered their enemies into
a compromising situation and then expelled them as troublemakers.[14]

An incident connected with the rebellion of Lodi may have
warned the King of possible future developments.[15] The royal
councillor Antonio Fissiraga requested Henry's permission to go
to his native Lodi and attempt to persuade his kinsmen and
friends to desist from their folly and recommend themselves to
the royal mercy. Once inside the city, however, his fellow citizens
persuaded Fissiraga to take over the leadership of the revolt.
Attachments to city, family, and friends outbalanced the new-
found allegiance to Henry of Luxemburg and the Empire.

The Lombard uprisings had a profound importance. The
northern Guelfs' dissatisfaction with the imperial regime and
their consequent rebellion seemed to bear out Florentine charges
that the Emperor-elect was set upon ruining the Italian Guelfs
simply because they bore a party name reminiscent of defiance of
the Empire.

What was to be the official reaction to this series of rebellions?
Italian advisers favored a policy of severe repression, arguing that
mildness would only be interpreted as a sign of weakness. Most
of the northern counsellors disagreed. Now Henry could prove
that the appellation *Regis pacifici imitator* and his encyclicals,
proclamations, and speeches were more than empty rhetoric. The
Guelfs had bolted from the new imperial regime because of fear

and misunderstanding. They should be gathered back to the fold as stray lambs, not hunted down and destroyed as rabid beasts. Impartiality and justice tempered with mercy might prevent later acts of folly. To imprison or hang all traitors as they so richly deserved would only incite other cities to rebellion, destroy whatever hopes remained of peacefully reorganizing Tuscany, and perhaps incur the hostility of Robert of Anjou or alienate Pope Clement V.

Henry of Luxemburg acceded to the counsels of temperance, and to demonstrate his good faith and impartiality he leaned over backward to favor the Guelfs in his entourage. He made generous grants to Count Philippone Langusco of Pavia and Simone degli Avvocati of Vercelli, and even forgave Antonio Fissiraga his treason.

The King's first major task, however, was to persuade the Torriani to return to Milan and trust themselves to royal clemency. Henry entrusted the delicate negotiations to his cousin the Bishop of Liège and his brother-in-law Amadeus of Savoy, the Vicar-General of Lombardy and a known friend of the Guelfs.[16] They were assisted by five Lombard Guelf chiefs—the three royal councillors and two Novarese. Henry offered the Torriani and the rebel cities generous terms. If Guido and his sons came to Milan they were guaranteed security of their persons and property. Later they would have to remain in certain other cities for a stipulated time, as had Matteo and Galeazzo Visconti. The monarch promised to restore the goods seized from the Torriani and their friends in Milan, except for those taken by the imperial forces. The five Guelf chiefs would try to persuade the Torriani and the rebel cities to return to their imperial allegiance. Should these efforts fail, the Guelf chiefs would sever their friendship with the rebels and pursue them as commanded by the Emperor-elect and his vicars. If the five Guelf leaders did not comply with these promises they would immediately be treated as rebels of the Empire. To support their oaths these chieftains had to provide oath guarantors (*fideiussores*) from their own cities.

Although it seemed sensible that Henry deal with the rebels through his Guelf counsellors, their own townsmen entertained serious doubts as to the strength of the counsellors' attachment to the imperial cause, since one month later only Antonio Fissiraga had found men willing to risk their lives and property as security for his word.[17]

To the monarch's surprise the Torriani refused to accept his terms. Henry had played a good hand and lost. The Milanese rebels took refuge in Cremona, and from this new center of Guelf rebellion they scornfully rejected Henry's promises and offers, accusing him of desiring to destroy Italian Guelfism and exalt the Ghibellines as had his Hohenstaufen predecessors.

The Emperor-elect now adopted a severer tone in Milan. As a precautionary measure he sent Torriani who still remained in the city and its *contado* to Ghibelline Pisa or to the lands of his Savoyard relations.[18] Henry appointed a Pistoian judge to study the condition of the rebel goods in Milan and its district, and to make confiscations for the royal fisc in those cases where they were legally justified.[19] As Henry soon restored order in Milan he saw no reason for removing its vicar, Niccolo de' Buonsignori, despite his general unpopularity.

Elsewhere in Lombardy the royal policy of clemency and impartiality met with greater success than among the Torriani. Reggio and Parma soon returned to the fold, and the Emperor-elect allowed their disobedience to go unpunished. They received new vicars who the monarch hoped would be more effective than their predecessors. Exiles once more entered these cities, while many rebels submitted and some fled. Lodi and Crema sought reconciliation with the King of the Romans, and by mid-April they too were obedient. And once again Henry was clement and punished no one.[20]

The Emperor-elect planned to move at once to the only remaining centers of opposition, Cremona and Brescia, where he expected the same contrite recognition that had come from Reggio, Parma, Crema, and Lodi. Then he would march towards Rome and the coronation in the Basilica of St. Peter.

The reconciliation of almost all the rebel communes was not Henry's only significant achievement in these months. As early as 4 February the Ghibelline Scaligers of Verona had promised Henry the city's imperial income and renounced the right to levy new taxes there. They accepted an imperial vicar and secretly resigned their captainships. But the Scaligers still hoped to acquire the imperial vicarship of Verona and its *contado* for themselves. This could place them once more at the head of the commune, and with official sanction. Their power might seem legally restricted and diminished because the authority of a vicar was far less comprehensive than that of those full-fledged *signori*. But the vicarship would provide a legal basis for their rule, a basis all the more valuable as it did not depend upon the will of their subjects. And who would have the opportunity to scrutinize carefully the documents or instructions in which their vicarial authority was specified?

Henry had hitherto refused to grant any vicarships to powerful native *signori*, choosing rather minor nobles whose strength was derived from their imperial appointments. To have done otherwise would have exposed the monarch to the charge of bringing to Italy tyranny and not peace, justice, and imperial liberty.

After the mid-February rebellions the Scaliger persuasions took on new appeal. The existing vicars had been unable to prevent the outbreaks and at times had comported themselves dishonorably in the face of difficulties.[21] Might an exception be made in the case of the Scaligers? These vassals, acting in the name of the Empire, could provide a bulwark of strength in the March. Was there not an advantage in making an already established power responsible for the maintenance of the peace in that region? Certainly such an appointment brought with it the risk that neighboring Guelfs might begin to fear for their own safety and to doubt the King's honorable intentions. Such a move would not reassure the republic of Padua. But the Scaligers once more struck upon an argument that had hitherto found great success with Henry: a financial compensation for his kindness and understanding. The Ghibelline lords promised the imperial treasury a large sum of money in return for the vicarship. On 17 March 1311 amidst great festivities it was announced in Verona that Alboin and Can Grande della Scala had been named vicars-general of that city.[22]

The Ghibelline Scaligers did not long remain the only *signori* to become imperial vicars. Throughout the early months of 1311 representatives of Richard da Camino worked assiduously to procure him the vicarship of Treviso. The Lombard insurrections probably influenced Henry of Luxemburg here as they had earlier in the case of the Scaligers. Signs of Paduan hostility to the new

imperial regime in north Italy also made the monarch seek
every possible point of support. And Da Camino had the special
advantage of being called a Guelf, established and maintained in
power by the leading Guelf nobles of his city. If these men could
be held for the Empire by Da Camino, a pro-imperial Treviso
might balance Padua's attraction for Guelfs in the March.

The Da Camino promise, moreover, to pay sixteen thousand
florins for the vicarship probably influenced the Luxemburger's
calculations. In a letter of 10 May 1311 Henry promised that
Richard would remain in office for life.[23] Should he be removed,
sixteen thousand florins would be returned to him. This type of
vicarship was new. Richard was no longer a mere imperial official
appointed by the Emperor-elect and removable at will. He had
purchased his position and it was his for life, as possibly was
that of the Scaligers in Verona (where our investigation is hampered by insufficient documentation). Henry of Luxemburg con-
ferred this new type of vicarship upon few men. But all were the
same type of persons, whether called Guelf or Ghibelline: powerful *signori* in their own right, who disposed of large military
forces and practically ruled their own cities. Numerically these
new vicars were insignificant, and the great majority of vicarships
remained what they had been when first introduced by the King
of the Romans in the winter of 1310–1311. The importance of
these few special vicarships, however, is incalculable.

The appointment of such vicars made it appear that after
much fanfare and the arousal of false hopes the loudly heralded
monarch had done nothing more than give supreme sanction and
approval to Italian tyrants. These actions doubtless caused other
signori and would-be *signori* to hope that faithful service to
Henry, large cash payments, and a bit of fortune could secure
them too the blessings of an imperial vicarship. Perhaps Count
Philippone Langusco of Pavia and Simone degli Avvocati di
Colobiano of Vercelli, recently rewarded with money and fiefs,
would now hope for even better things and remain loyal to the
Emperor-elect. For the present situation it was rather unimportant that Henry himself may have believed that these new arrangements were only temporary, and that after the imperial
coronation and the complete pacification of Italy (with the consequent flow of imperial income) he would be able to reassert his

authority and reduce all vicars to obedience and dependence.[24]

The northern monarch probably did not appreciate all the implications of his actions. The financial payments made by the newly appointed vicars might be conceived of as manifestations of gratitude, such as a prelate might make to the man who had secured his elevation to a high ecclesiastical post. And why should these vicars exercise their office in any way other than that expected of all vicars? The security against removal or loss of the payment made to the treasury should have proven sufficient to satisfy these men.

But vicars were not bishops. For the men of early fourteenth-century Italy this was a new experience. Most had never seen an emperor. The vicarships themselves, as conceived and used by Henry, were a novelty. The Hohenstaufen had never adopted the general system of appointing imperial rectors for each of the Italian communes. The vicars or captains general of Frederick II had been the chief military and civil authorities of entire provinces, and not the supplanters of podestas and captains of the people. Henry's policies did not even coincide with the tradition of the vicarships and rectorates that existed in the Papal States or the Regno.

The Italian *signori* named as vicars by Henry of Luxemburg had made a large investment, and it was not unnatural that they should want to realize a profit upon it. The vicarships might be regarded by the Scaligers or Da Camino as costly acquisitions of increased legal validity for their signories. Certainly heriditary investiture as a marquis, duke, or prince would be better, but an imperial vicarship was a temporary workable substitute. As long as the interests of the Empire coincided with the dynastic interests of the new vicars all would go smoothly, but should the two come into conflict, which would prevail?[25]

Such possible conflicts of interest were problems for the future. At present, despite his strange methods and lack of knowledge of Italian politics or psychology, Henry of Luxemburg seemed on the verge of succeeding where the greatest German emperors before him had failed in pacifying northern Italy and re-establishing imperial administration. By mid-April only two important communes had not submitted peacefully to the Emperor-elect. Thus far his policy of mildness toward the rebels of February had achieved excellent results. The dire predictions of his Italian counsellors, the fulminations of the exiled Torriani, and the machinations and embassies of the troubled Florentines all appeared to have been in vain.

Even the mighty Padua, which had shown reluctance to deal with the King of the Romans, had been brought to terms. The commune had rejected an exceptionally liberal "Privilege of Liberty" in which the monarch substantially granted it continued internal autonomy and legalized its possession of Vicenza in return for an annual cash payment. Then while Padua plotted rebellion, Henry chastened the Guelf republic by liberating Vicenza from its control on 15 April 1311 and placing it under the supervision of the Pisan Ghibelline Vanni Zeno, former vicar of Verona.[26] On 9 June 1311 a much sobered Padua received a far more limited "Privilege of Liberty," and Henry of Luxemburg had stifled a dangerous insurrection at its birth, liberated an imperial commune, and gained a large sum of money.[27]

Outside Italy too in early April 1311 the Emperor-elect had little cause for dissatisfaction on the basis of that information available to him. Since mid-January at the latest, admittedly he had been aware of the papal decision to refuse the imperial expedition permission to pass through Bolognese territory on the southward journey from Lombardy to Rome.[28] This greatly inconvenienced the King of the Romans, making impossible the use of the traditional and best route of travel. But it would be unwarranted to assume that Clement was acting from a motive of hostility towards Henry. Rather he may have taken a sensible precaution for securing the safety and calming the fears of Bologna. That city was surrounded by Ghibellines who might have exploited the presence of imperial forces in the vicinity to renew their attacks upon the commune. Bologna had done yeoman service in the war against Venice for Ferrara, and Clement probably wished to assure the Bolognese that they had not been forgotten.

The only overt action taken by Clement during this period that might be construed as unfriendly to Henry is the papal denial of requests made in November 1310 that the coronation date be advanced to 30 May 1311. In a very polite letter of 28 February 1311 Clement rejected that date as being too early, and not allowing sufficient time for all the necessary preparations.[29] This explanation taken by itself must have seemed quite plausible to Henry of Luxemburg; the Emperor-elect was probably unaware of a letter written on 19 January 1311 by Pope Clement to Philip the Fair. In answer to a letter from the French monarch, Clement stated that both he, the Pope, and the curia had held many discussions on the subject of Henry's request, and come to the conclusion that it should be granted despite Philip's opposition.[30] Perhaps during the weeks between 19 January and 28 February Philip was able to find arguments more convincing to the papal curia. Yet this is mere conjecture. We do know for a certainty that by 17 April papal proctors had given sanction (subject to Clement's official publication) for the coronation to take place in Rome on 15 August 1311, only two and a half months later than the date requested by the King of the Romans in November 1310.[31]

Papal policy towards Henry's activities in Italy did not remain static. Events occurred during the late winter and spring of 1311 that indicate a change in Clement's attitude, and at the very least a marked decrease in his sympathy for the cause of the Emperor-elect. New circumstances arose which called into play and strengthened certain papal attitudes and interests that hitherto had been for the most part only latent potentials, attitudes, and interests that would work to the disadvantage of the Emperor-elect.

In March and early April 1311 Clement sent the Emperor-elect two important pieces of misinformation. The Pope directed that Henry be informed that there was absolutely no truth in stories then circulating that Philip the Fair or any members of his family or council had listened to anything said contrary to the interests of the Emperor-elect; nor, affirmed Clement, had any of the aforementioned Frenchmen ever spoken against Henry.[32]

We have already seen that Philip did not hide from the Pope his displeasure at Henry's rapid advance in Italy. Clement himself admitted having heard all of the above-mentioned stories, and men such as the Ghibelline Cardinal Nicolas, of Prato, or Cardinal Stefaneschi, originator of the Anjou-Luxemburg alliance plan of 1309, would have been quick to tell him tales of any negotiations that were actually taking place at the French court.[33]

Similarly, the pro-French Cardinal Pierre de la Chapelle,[34] the Pope's own nephew Cardinal Pellagru, only recently returned from Florence,[35] and the French councillor Enguerrand de Marigny [36] were busy furthering the views of the French court as to the dangers involved in continuing to support the enterprise of the Emperor-elect in Italy.

It is difficult to believe, in the light of the contents of a letter sent Henry by Clement on 30 March 1311, that the Pope was ignorant of the conditions which the Tuscan Guelfs demanded of their temporal lord.[37] The Pope related that before Christmas Day 1310 he had received the ambassadors of Florence, Lucca, Siena, and other Tuscan Guelf communes at Avignon. He had heard the favors they sought of Henry, and had offered his pontifical intercession with the Emperor-elect on their behalf, in order that Henry might more freely carry on his affairs. Nothing sought by these communes should prove unsatisfactory to the King of the Romans or should prejudice his position, said Clement. The Pope added that the ambassadors had requested permission to consult their governments for further instructions before continuing the negotiations, and had been told to return to Avignon by 25 January. Although, surprisingly, they had not yet arrived (by 30 March), Clement still strongly advised Henry to grant all their petitions. In the event that the Emperor-elect gave an affirmative reply, noted the Pope, the communal ambassadors had promised to give Henry the obedience that they had rendered his predecessors. This might not have sounded quite so reassuring to any who thought back to the desperate resistance encountered by the Hohenstaufen.

Clement's firm support of the Tuscan Guelf interpretation of the correct relationship between the Emperor and the Italian communes shows the Pontiff's absolute refusal to support Henry's program for imperial restoration in Italy. It can even be argued that Clement was subordinating all interests but papal ones to the goal of peace in Italy. It does not seem unreasonable to connect the papal favoring of the Guelf cause during the winter of 1310–1311 with Clement's unprecedented efforts, in the summer of 1310, to maintain the gains made by Italian Guelfs in the face of the approaching arrival in Italy of their temporal sovereign. The first Avignon pontiff had a special predilection for the Italian Guelfs, and associated their well-being with that of the Papal States—a group of territories in which he was soon to show a renewed interest.[38]

Clement's devious methods in his dealings with Henry can be explained in part by his desire to see the conclusion of binding peace pacts and alliances between France and the Empire. Urgent requests to sign such pacts made up a good part of Clement's messages to Henry in March and early April 1311.[39] Yet the fact remains that the report of political events given by the Pope to the man who was acting in Italy under the aegis of pontifical approval and sponsorship was inaccurate and slanted. Against this fact we should recall the extremely accurate and up-to-date account of the current state of papal negotiations with Henry of Luxemburg that Clement officially provided the French king.[40]

The key to understanding the weaknesses of Henry's position *within* Italy (weaknesses that existed despite his reconcilation of almost all the rebellious Lombard cities) is to be found by examining the activities of Florence. That Tuscan Guelf city and its followers had been subjecting Robert of Anjou to ever-increasing pressure to declare himself publicly as their ally and protector against the Emperor-elect. They wanted him to play the role of the Prince who nominally led and united the forces of Italian Guelfism. As its desperate pleas for increased military aid and armament went unanswered, the Black Guelf Priory tried to force the Angevin's hand by a daring *tour de force*. On 1 April the Priory wrote Robert that his brother, Philip of Taranto, had been chosen to captain the armies of the Tuscan Guelf League, and asked him to persuade Philip to accept the post. Simultaneous letters were sent to the Prince of Taranto himself and to Florentine ambassadors in Naples.[41] Robert's only response was complete silence. This provoked the Florentines to write Robert that harmful rumors were circulating that he had decided to desert his Guelf allies, and request him to gainsay them. The Priory argued that Henry's imperial expedition contained an inherent threat to the stability and peace of the Angevin's own territories. "There is need for deeds and not for words," it reprimanded.[42]

Robert's position was extremely difficult. Some of his past actions, the geographic location of Guelf Tuscany, and his indebtedness to Florentine bankers all pushed him towards playing the defender of Italian Guelfism. But his liege lord, the Pope, had openly supported the Luxemburger's expedition, and if negotiations for a Luxemburg-Anjou alliance succeeded, Robert would gain an entire new kingdom, the Arelat. Thus the Angevin tried desperately to stall for time and to hide from both Florence and the Emperor-elect the extent of his dealings and commitments with the other. Robert undertook only limited defensive troop movements and attempted to safeguard his holdings in Piedmont, the Romagna and the Regno against possible insurrections or attacks.[43]

Of far greater immediate danger to the Emperor-elect than the clandestine negotiations between Florence and Robert of Anjou was a closely guarded success of Florentine gold and secret diplomacy. By mid-April Florence had contacted Ghiberto da Correggio, the most powerful individual in the Emilia. That nominally Guelf lord was disappointed at the treatment given him by the King of the Romans. His knighting after the Milanese coronation could not compensate for the loss of rule in Parma and the failure to receive an imperial vicarship. And as the opportunist Da Correggio showed increasing interest in Florentine promises and proposals, Henry of Luxemburg remained unaware of these attempts to subvert the allegiance of one of his most important north Italian vassals.[44]

Henry was aware of one important success of Florentine diplomacy. On 1 April 1311 the Priory announced that Bologna had finally been won over to complete alliance with Florence and its anti-imperial followers.[45] The Romagnol city had participated actively in the planning and dicussions of the previous spring and summer, and had itself been the scene of numerous assemblies and conferences. Until now, however, secure in its immunity from imperial jurisdiction, Bologna had not openly and absolutely committed itself to the Florentine cause. The Bolognese had been seriously perturbed by the Lombard rebellions of February 1311, and deemed it prudent to reject a Cremonese request that they provide that rebel city with a podesta.[46] Bologna then tried to gain the protection of Robert of Anjou (papal Rector of the Romagna) and offered him the captainship of the people. It was after the Angevin refused this offer[47] that Bologna strengthened its ties with Florence and its allies by openly joining the Tuscan League. Although Bologna was a papal city and had received assurances that the imperial expedition would not pass through its territory, the commune's Guelf rulers decided that the peril of renewed Ghibelline attacks warranted public Bolognese adherence to the Tuscan League.[48] The open hostility of Bologna, immune from reprisal because of its papal allegiance, was a severe blow to the Emperor-elect.

At this same time the Florentine Priory attacked the monarch along still another front. Until now all had admitted that Henry of Luxemburg, rightful King of the Romans, was the legitimate lord of imperial Italy. This made direct resistance quite difficult. As we have noted, some Lombard rebels in February 1311 even allowed imperial officials to remain in their cities after they had expelled their political enemies. A change in the line of Florentine propaganda seems to have been introduced in order to eliminate this difficulty: Florence no longer conceded that Henry of Luxemburg had a legitimate right to rule imperial Italy. It accomplished this by denying him the titles "King of the Romans" and "Emperor" that it had hitherto accorded him unquestioningly. This new Florentine tactic was indeed revolutionary, particularly in view of the fact that Henry was still publicly accorded papal blessings.

This change in Florentine tactics is first noticeable in the correspondence of 1 April 1311. In a series of letters written to describe the course of events in Lombardy and to solicit aid for Florence we find the Luxemburger almost always called "King of Germany," and in one document he is given the untraditional title of "Emperor of the Germans." [49] This change demonstrated that, at least in Florentine eyes, Henry of Luxemburg was a foreign ruler come to Italy, and not a rightful king of Italy or of Italians. The change also indicates that the Priory believed that the appellation "Emperor" still retained significant traditional and symbolic attraction for many Italians; and Florence wished to deny its enemy this strength. During the month of April the Florentine chancellery switched to the new form of designation, and it was as "King of Germany" that it continued to refer to Henry until his death.[50]

Using this new tactic, Florence tried to escape the stigma of

disobeying its temporal overlord, and to rally support against
the foreign invader who was unlawfully disturbing the cities of
Italy. No longer need possible supporters withhold their aid because of a reluctance to assume the role of rebels against a
legitimate king. They could now pose as loyal sons of the Guelf
Party and of the Church protecting their customary liberty
against a foreign tyrant and helper of Ghibellines [51]—completely
ignoring, of course, the Papacy's apparent continued satisfaction
with Henry's activities in Italy.

Florence immediately complemented its new ideological and
propaganda line with a hardening of its diplomatic position.
On 1 April 1311 the Priory sent new instructions to its embassy
at the papal curia.[52] The terms demanded of Henry were far
more severe than those of November 1310. Florence and its allies
would no longer even consider permitting him to enter their
districts or communes.

There is no evidence that in mid-April 1311 Henry knew of
the many maneuverings at Avignon and Florence, or tried to
counter directly those few Florentine machinations of which he
was cognizant. The Emperor-elect turned rather to the immediate task of ending the two remaining Lombard rebellions.

As he approached Cremona on 26 April 1311, more than two
hundred of the city's leading citizens came forth to meet him
and plead for mercy.[53] Led by the Guelf chieftain Sopramonte
Amati, they were barefoot, dressed only in gowns, with heads
uncovered and halters about their necks. Judging from the monarch's treatment of the other rebel towns that had sued for
mercy, these Cremonese did not expect to be disappointed. To
the great surprise of all, the King of the Romans unsheathed his
sword and made the Cremonese pass under it in sign of absolute
submission. He then ordered the immediate incarceration of the
penitents who had come to meet him. With drawn sword Henry
of Luxemburg entered Cremona.

The Emperor-elect spared the lives of those within Cremona,
but commanded that the city walls and gates be demolished
along with the houses and palaces of the rebel Guelf Cavalcabò
faction which had fled before his entry. Only the Queen's suppli-
cations prevented further destruction and the horrors of pillage.

Henry deprived the commune of its imperial rights and privileges, fined it one hundred thousand florins, and reassumed its *contado* into the imperial fisc.[54]

On 10 May the monarch promulgated a lengthy sentence against seventy-one escaped Cremonese rebel leaders and Guido della Torre and his sons. All were branded rebels of the Empire guilty of lese majesty and might be injured or killed by anyone with impunity. No one was to aid or shelter them, their property was confiscated by the imperial fisc, and their debtors became debtors of the fisc. Imperial grants and privileges they had hitherto enjoyed were cancelled. This sentence included Cremona's most powerful and influential Guelf leaders, William Cavalcabò and his brother Jacob, Pino Vernazzi, podesta of Florence in 1294,[55] and Ponzino Ponzoni, knighted by Henry himself at Milan four months earlier.

Before he left Cremona, Henry installed there as imperial vicar none other than Richard Tizzone, militant Ghibelline leader and former exile of Vercelli. It was too soon for men to have forgotten how Tizzone had swept into Turin with one hundred knights, pledged his life in Henry's service, and publicly proclaimed that all his ills derived from his attachment to the Party of the Empire. With the new vicar the Emperor-elect left the Proctor-General of the Fisc in Lombardy and the March, Giovanni da Castiglione, charged with collecting the fines and taxes laid upon Cremona and with the confiscation of rebel goods and property. Da Castiglione was a Luccan exile who had come to Henry early in the fall of 1310. Now, only six months later, he occupied one of the most important offices in imperial Italy. Da Castiglione was noted for his efficiency, lack of scruples, ferocity, and ruthlessness. The Bishop of Butrinto described him as "the cruelest man I have heard of since Nero." [56] Yet Henry kept this proctor in Cremona even after he replaced the vicar Tizzone late in the summer of 1311.[57] The Emperor-elect demonstrated little solicitude for the sensibilities of his Cremonese subjects, men among whom Guelf sympathies ran high. But how well would the new regime flourish in this unhappy commune on the Po? And how might the rest of Italy react to the appointment of violent Ghibelline partisans as imperial officials in Cremona?

Why did Henry suddenly abandon his policy of clemency and mildness towards repentant rebel cities in the case of Cremona? For one thing, Cremona had given immediate and generous hospitality to the fugitive Guido della Torre and his sons. Fretting under heavy financial burdens placed upon it by the King of the Romans and goaded on by the fiery Marquis William Cavalcabò, Cremona had been the first city to follow the Milanese example and rebel. During the rebellion it had received a Florentine podesta, and accepted an embassy from the Black Guelf enemy of the "King of Germany." Cremona assumed the role of rebel chief in northern Italy and sent its own embassies to encourage neighboring cities in their rebellion.[58] The Emperor-elect had cause for specially hating Cremona.

Henry's severity seems as much the result of considerations of policy as of anger, impatience, and self-righteousness. He only refrained from meting out stronger punishments because of the insistent pleadings of many of his counsellors and of several papal representatives present, and particularly because of the entreaties of his gentle Queen. Perhaps Henry believed that his harsh handling of Cremona would serve others as a warning against disobedience and insurrection. But even writers such as Giovanni da Cermenate of Milan and the Bishop of Butrinto who sympathized with the Emperor-elect reproved his treatment of Cremona. The moderate Guelf Sopramonte Amati and his followers had just persuaded the populace to ignore the warlike Cavalcabò and to trust its fate to the mercy of the King of the Romans. In his ignorance Henry turned against the men who might have helped him retain the obedience and regain the affection of the commune. The real leaders of the Cremonese insurrection remained unpunished, for they had fled to Brescia, the last major city still in rebellion.

By punishing Cremona harshly Henry of Luxemburg risked placing himself in the role of the Teutonic barbarian intent upon destroying Italian Guelfism. He seemed to justify the stream of propaganda which the Florentine chancellery poured forth in increasing volume. Where was the *Regis pacifici imitator* now? Was the Black Guelf republic the bastion of liberty that it claimed to be?

Henry had committed a serious tactical error. Frightened at

the severe punishment meted out to the last city that had returned to obedience, Brescia refused to yield. The Emperor-elect
had accepted Theobald Brusati, the exiled Brescian Guelf captain, with open arms at Asti, and had replaced him with his
followers in their city. Considering Henry's treatment of Sopramonte Amati, a man who owed him little, Brusati well imagined
the terrible punishment that would be reserved for his own
ingratitude. So reasoned even that staunch imperial partisan
Cermenate.[59]

Brescia presented the monarch with serious problems.[60] Since
it had gained sufficient time to put its walls and fortifications in
good repair and to gather in a large store of food and military
supplies, it could withstand a long siege. When the leading Guelf
noble families seized control of the commune, exiled their Ghibelline rivals, and raised the standard of rebellion, Brescia became the fulcrum for all resistance to imperial authority in
northern Italy. Brescia eagerly received a podesta from Florence,
as well as a host of rebel Guelf chiefs who had fled their native
cities at the approach of the Emperor-elect. Almost to a man the
rebels within Brescia were members of the Guelf Party.

Florence had several reasons for offering the Brescian rebels
moral and financial aid. The Priory wanted to create all the
trouble possible for the Emperor-elect, and to delay his march
south to Tuscany in order to win time to repair its own defenses.
Throughout the winter and spring of 1310–1311 workers had
labored feverishly to enclose the westernmost part of Florence
with moats and to raise the height of the walls from Porta San
Gallo to the Porta dal Prato d'Ognissanto along the Arno.[61]

Henry of Luxemburg faced a crucial decision: should he turn
north from Cremona and engage in a decisive action against
Brescia, or march southwards towards Tuscany and Rome?
Many argued that it would be wise to leave Brescia temporarily
to its obstinate disobedience in view of the smallness of Henry's
army. Once he had acquired glory, prestige, and increased power
from his imperial coronation, it would be simpler to bring the
solitary rebel commune to its knees. Indeed, Brescia might then
throw itself upon the Emperor's mercy and eliminate the need
for a major military operation.

The numerous Tuscan exiles in and around Henry's court had

a special reason for pleading this course of action. Tuscan Ghibellines and White Guelfs desired to follow the example of the former Lombard exiles and return to their native cities. Communes that would not accept them at once would be forced to submit to imperial arms.

The Tuscan exiles had a strong argument, and nowhere is it expressed more clearly or forcefully than in an urgent letter that Dante wrote to the King of the Romans on 17 April 1311.[62] He chided the monarch, "so long a victor in the Po valley," for his neglect of Tuscany, and reminded him that the rights of the Empire were to be defended beyond the confines of northern Italy. "Tuscan tyranny," he cried, drew force from "Augustus'" delay and daily grew stronger:

> Do you delay at Milan throughout the winter and spring, and believe that you will destroy the pestiferous hydra by cutting off her heads? What will you proclaim to have accomplished, O sole ruler of the world, when you have twisted the neck of contumacious Cremona? Will not the sudden madness then swell up at Brescia or Pavia? Indeed, even when that will have sunk down beaten, at once another will arise at Vercelli or Bergamo or elsewhere, until the fundamental cause of this suppuration be removed, and the root of so great an error torn forth, the thorny branches withering with the trunk. . . . and perhaps you are unaware?—this pestilence is named Florence. This is the viper turned upon the entrails of its mother. . . . The viper . . . with her false blandishments and fictions gathers her neighbors to her, and gathered bewitches them. . . . Come then, break off delay, O new offspring of Jesse. . . .

Against Dante's impassioned pleading others may have argued that it would be disastrous for Henry to leave an active center of insurrection behind in Lombardy, a gathering place for Torriani and Cavalcabò, and a breeding ground for other rebellion. We should also recall, however, that the metropolis of Milan, now in the hands of its imperial vicar and strengthened by the recently recalled Visconti,[63] was probably capable of holding Brescia in check until the arrival of the crowned Emperor. The Vicar-General of Lombardy alone, Amadeus of Savoy, disposed of fifteen hundred armed men.

When Henry of Luxemburg decided to turn against Brescia, he appears to have acted from other considerations: rebellious subjects had thrown down the gauntlet; could the King of the Romans and Emperor-elect ignore this brazen challenge to his authority? [64]

THE KING OF THE ROMANS BEFORE BRESCIA

By 19 May 1311 the King of the Romans was encamped before Brescia. Men and supplies streamed into the imperial camp. Soon Henry commanded a considerable force, composed mainly of northern troops and Italian Ghibellines, supplemented by a few Guelfs. Four Ghibelline lords commanded the detachments from their native cities: Matteo Visconti led the Milanese, Alboin and Can Grande della Scala captained the Veronese, while Modena's contingent was headed by Francesco della Mirandola. The nominally Guelf Ghiberto da Correggio led the Parmesans. Louis of Savoy, nephew of Count Amadeus and Senator of Rome, appeared together with the Ghibelline Roman noble Stephen Colonna. The commune of Genoa supplied a force of excellent bowmen. Even Padua sent gifts to the royal advisers and gave to the King of the Romans its most precious military trophy: the crown of Frederick II, captured at Victoria in 1248. In addition to a host of Tuscan and Romagnol Ghibellines, contingents from Spires, Strassburg, Cologne, and other Rhenish cities served with the Emperor-elect before Brescia.[65] On the other hand, as we have noted, the Brescian defenders were almost all members of the Guelf Party.

The besieged but well-prepared city fought hard. Henry was bitterly disappointed by his failure to penetrate the Brescian defenses. When the Brescian captain, Theobald Brusati, fell prisoner after an unsuccessful sortie, even the Queen's pleading could not save him from the enraged monarch's vengeance. Henry had received the outcast Guelf exile like a prodigal son in Asti, and had quickly restored him to his native city. And the recompense? Treason.

The royal sentence pronounced against the rebel leader on 20 June 1311 began with a long list of his crimes: ingratitude, a broken oath of fealty, aiding rebels, and rebellion that had caused the deaths of many men during the present siege. Theobald Brusati was declared guilty of lese majesty.[66]

The King of the Romans preceded the rebel's punishment with a declaration that he desired to make an example of Brusati in order to dissuade others from similar conduct. Placed inside an oxskin, the Brescian was dragged about the siege camp by a wild ass, then hung upon a gallows "in order that he may die slowly." Executioners then tied his hands and feet to the necks of four horses and violently quartered his still warm body. Each quarter was placed upon a wheel for display in the camp, while fire consumed Brusati's heart and entrails. His head was impaled upon a lance and paraded before the walls of Brescia to strike terror into the hearts of his beleaguered comrades.

In the absence of documentary evidence, we can only speculate as to Pope Clement's reaction upon hearing of this latest achievement of his *Regis pacifici imitator*. There is a hiatus in the collection of Florentine correspondence for May-August 1311, but it seems reasonable to imagine that the Priory did not overlook this opportunity to commiserate with and strengthen the resolve of its Brescian brothers, and to send numerous letters with detailed accounts of the "King of Germany's" treatment of the Guelf captain to Italian communes and rulers.[67] While some imperial partisans argued that another Judas had received his just deserts,[68] other men became convinced that both they and Italy would be better off if a successful conspiracy or military league were organized against this new tyrant in Lombardy.[69]

We should note, if only in passing, that Brusati's captor did not long remain unscathed. Only a month after the Brescian's execution, the King's own brother, Walram of Luxemburg, was slain by an arrow, and at the request of the Scaliger vicars was buried in Verona.

Brusati's execution did not bring the Emperor-elect his expected victory. After the failure of a major attack in mid-August, Henry decided to leave the Vicar-General of Lombardy in charge of what he hoped would be the final weeks of the siege. The King, Queen, court, and the rest of the army would leave at once for Rome and the imperial coronation.

This was not to be. Before Henry could depart, plague broke out in the besieging camp. Aggravated by unsanitary conditions, it spread like wildfire. Although it struck persons of every rank and quality, the northerners, unaccustomed to the broiling Italian sun, were particularly vulnerable. Shallow trenches that served as graves soon filled to overflowing, and the air was filled with the foulest stenches from the corpses of decaying horses. The Bishop of Geneva and Henry's cousin, Guy of Flanders, both died during the first fortnight of October. The Habsburg, Duke Leopold of Austria, was one of many northern nobles who left the battlefield and sought to return home in order to escape a similar fate.

Even before the outbreak of plague Henry began to fear desertion, or worse, on the part of many Lombard soldiers in his army. On 9 August he made almost fifty leading citizens, Guelf and Ghibelline, from Asti, Pavia, and Vercelli swear that they would not leave camp without his express permission and supply oath guarantors (*fideiussores*) for their word. A four-thousand-florin fine was the penalty for disobedience. So troubled was Henry that he ordered these men to appear in person before his tent at least twice a day! [70] And the King of the Romans had some cause for worry. His camp swarmed with spies and informers sent by Florence and its allies; and only a few of them suffered the fate of the unlucky Bolognese "Jack the Blind" whom the Marshal, Henry of Flanders, caught and hanged during the earliest stage of the campaign.[71]

The line of huts and tents that surrounded Brescia did not circumscribe Henry's difficulties. Guelfs and Ghibellines alike exploited his preoccupation with Brescia to create disturbances in half a dozen Lombard cities. At the very outset of the siege only the resourcefulness of the vicar of Bergamo prevented a serious rebellion.[72] In Como and Novara recently restored Ghibellines expelled their Guelf rivals.[73] Pavian Ghibellines attempted a similar coup; but they failed, and a judgment given by the Archbishop of Thebes in the name of the Emperor-elect severely restricted their freedom of movement.[74] The late summer saw new clashes between rival factions in Vercelli.[75] Trouble even appeared again in Milan, where old political enemies were at loggerheads. The King of the Romans could take no risks with this key city. He temporarily left the siege to promulgate a new pact between the Visconti and the Torriani Arch-

bishop, and threatened the staggering fine of twenty thousand
florins for each breach of the peace.[76] Here a menacingly clear
division between Guelfs and Ghibellines appeared in the lists
of the men acting as security for both sides. The Guelf chieftains
of Pavia, Vercelli, and Novara and several Milanese Torriani
pledged security for the Della Torre Archbishop and his partisans. Among those who pledged for Matteo Visconti were Francesco della Mirandola of Modena, leading Ghibellines of Vercelli
and Asti, and Matteo's own relatives and Milanese followers. As
the Brescian siege dragged on, the terms Guelf and Ghibelline
took on increasingly dangerous significance in Lombardy.

Regardless of its importance, however, no single matter could
receive the monarch's full attention during the summer of 1311.
As Henry desired not only to restore peace and order but to
create an effective imperial regime in Italy, he issued a series of
monetary decrees from August to October.[77] Thenceforth no
gold or silver coins were to be minted in imperial Italy other
than a new imperial coinage issuing only from royal mints. If
this program succeeded, it would be the end of the most desired
and successful money circulating in western Europe, the gold
florin. Henry's new monetary policy was a direct challenge to
Florence, and further evidence that the King of the Romans
intended to rule effectively and reassert imperial rights in Italy.
A northern Emperor-elect who had not yet been able to subdue
the single commune of Brescia ordered monetary measures that
could revolutionize the entire economic life of a peninsula containing many of the world's greatest banking, commercial, and
industrial centers. It is difficult to understand how the Luxemburger could have ignored both Italian financial realities and
necessities and his own weak position.

Outside Italy Henry's situation had become even more
difficult than he could have suspected. During the late winter
and spring of 1311 a definite improvement took place in the
relations between the French and papal courts.[78]

The Pope had manifested his displeasure with Philip the Fair
by the definitely cold reception given the French embassy that
visited Avignon in November 1310,[79] and it was not to Philip's
advantage that strained relations continue. He wished to see
the imperial coronation delayed as long as possible, and to have

the King of the Romans tied down indefinitely by Italian affairs. Moreover, the French monarch was firmly set against the Anjou-Luxemburg alliance, a combination that would certainly put an end to his hopes for absorbing the Arelat, and might even tend to isolate France. In view of such considerations Philip moved towards a reconciliation with the papal curia. By mid-February he had relaxed the pressure on the Papacy for the trial of Boniface VIII for heresy. The result was a rapprochement between King and Pope. On 27 April, Clement V publicly proclaimed in the bull *Rex gloriae* that the French king bore none of the responsibility for the heinous attempt against Boniface at Anagni in 1303, and the Pope ordered the destruction of all acts of Boniface VIII and his short-lived successor, Benedict XI, that were directed against Philip the Fair.

Four days later Philip received another clear sign of returning papal favor. Clement wrote him stating that because of hatreds and quarrels that might otherwise arise, he would not consent to the granting of the Arelat to any person or entity except the Holy Roman Church.[80] This newly adopted papal policy, while pleasing to the French king, seriously damaged Henry's position. It greatly diminished the prospects of successfully concluding the marriage alliance negotiations with Robert of Anjou, since that monarch had been largely attracted by the possibility of gaining the Arelat kingdom. And only a few months earlier, on 8 November 1310, this same Pope had fervently exclaimed "that he believed that he would sin mortally if he should impede that matrimony, from which might come peace between Ghibellines and Guelfs." [81]

The Pontiff's sympathy and enthusiasm for Henry of Luxemburg declined noticeably during the spring of 1311, while his interest in both the King of France and the Italian Guelfs increased. Was this partially due to a papal disillusionment in the King of the Romans as a result of the rebellions that broke out in northern Italy in February 1311? Desirous of peace above all, was the leader of Christendom losing faith in an Emperor-elect who brought only war and trouble to Italy? Such an interpretation places Clement V in a favorable light—but it is not justified by the evidence available, and is contradicted by certain of the Pope's actions during the summer of 1311.

Very revealing for an understanding of Clement's basic ways
of thinking and his fundamental policies are two letters that he
wrote during the summer of 1311. The first letter, dated 4 July
1311, directed to "[our] dearest son in Christ, Henry, illustrious
King of the Romans," concerned the Guelf rebels in Brescia.[82]
It was these Italian Guelfs whom Clement had striven to protect
by binding the Emperor-elect with novel promises during the
summer of 1310, and it was their cause that he had so warmly
espoused with Henry of Luxemburg during the winter and
early spring of 1311. The papal letter of 4 July dealt exclusively
with the Brescian rebels against imperial authority in Italy. "It
is befitting the clemency of royal benignity that you shower an
abundance of mercy upon your subjects, whom the blindness of
error is leading away from royal fealty," the Pope wrote Henry.[83]
Clement requested and commanded "with paternal affection,"
from the depths of his spirit, that the King act with piety and
give praiseworthy evidence of his regal mercy in dealing with
his erring subjects.[84] This letter was a touching plea for Christian forgiveness and moderation.

The hard-pressed Emperor-elect was not alone in facing rebellion in his Italian lands during the summer of 1311. In July
and August the forces of Robert of Anjou, papal Rector of the
Romagna, were attempting to subdue a new outbreak of violence and insurrection among the lords and communes of that
province.[85] The letter which Clement sent to the King of the
Romans on 10 August 1311 concerned the men who had led an
unsuccessful rebellion against the papal authority in the city of
Ferrara, only recently restored to the Holy See after a war that
had lasted more than three years.[86]

This letter of 10 August was far different in tone and spirit
from that of 4 July concerning the Brescian rebels, although
some of the phrases may strike a familiar chord. "Straying into
error through the blindness of a horrible ingratitude," wrote
Clement, those "traitors" (*proditores*) from Ferrara had tried
to destroy the peace and order existing in that commune. Many
of their leaders had been captured, and "by the just judgment
of God, finally handed over for capital punishment because of
their misdeeds."[87] Unfortunately others had escaped, and Clement had been informed, he wrote, that they were taking refuge

in imperial Lombardy, especially in Mantua, Verona, Modena, and Reggio—all but the last, we may note, were strong centers of Ghibellinism—and there, together with their hosts, they were devising new plots, leagues, and conspiracies against Ferrara. Knowing the sincerity of Henry's devotion to himself and to the Apostolic See, wrote the Pope, he found it difficult to give credence to such reports. However, he requested and commanded, "with paternal affection, that you [Henry] cause the aforesaid traitors . . . to be banned, as manifest and public enemies of ourselves and of the aforementioned See." [88] The Emperor-elect, furthermore, was to give specific orders that no one join with the escaped rebels in any conspiracy against Ferrara, or give them any aid or succor whatsoever. This last papal injunction calls to mind the request made of Clement by the King of the Romans less than two months earlier, that the Pope order all vassals of the Church not to favor or aid the rebels and enemies of the Emperor-elect, impede imperial military operations or troop movements, or receive those men banned by the King—a request that had gone unanswered.[89]

For Clement V a rebel was not always a rebel. His virtues and vices were not to be deduced from the act of his rebellion against rightfully constituted authority, but from a consideration of *which* ruler he rebelled against.

This double standard employed by Clement can best be explained in terms of his material interests in the holdings of the Papacy in Italy. Despite the fact that this Gascon pope had never visited Italy since his election, he had not ignored the welfare of the Papal States. His sustained and ultimately successful efforts to regain Ferrara for the Church, involving as they did a full-scale war and the declaration of a crusade against Venice, testified to his seriousness of purpose. We have already seen how Clement did not hesitate to appoint the powerful Angevin, Robert of Sicily, as papal Rector of the Romagna in 1310 in order to assure as great a measure of control and order as possible in that province, in view of the dangerous situations that might arise from the presence of the Emperor-elect and imperial forces in the vicinity. This desire to safeguard the Papal States had even overcome the fears demonstrated by this very Pontiff that the King of Sicily might himself become too strong to be

managed successfully from Avignon.[90] Perhaps Clement realized
that Robert of Anjou could not commit his forces too heavily
outside his own turbulent kingdom because of the constant
threat from his southern neighbor, Frederick of Trinacria, the
actual possessor of half the Kingdom of Sicily.

Just as the existence of an allied and friendly power on their
southern border made the papal lands in Italy more secure, so
it was to Clement's advantage that imperial Tuscany on their
western border remain under the hegemony of Florence and its
allies, all professedly Guelfs and faithful to the Holy Roman
Church. Similarly, the very events referred to in the letter of 10
August seemed to bear out the fact that the papal territories were
better guaranteed when Lombardy, on their northern border,
was in Guelf hands than when it was dominated by Ghibellines.
It is impossible to decide on the basis of the existing evidence
whether Clement would have been satisfied with a Lombardy
and a Tuscany kept peaceful and orderly by the *Regis pacifici
imitator* whose expedition to Italy he had strongly supported in
earlier public statements. But clearly a disorderly and warring
imperial Italy was a threat to the security of the lands of the
Church.

While all of these considerations probably contributed to
bringing about the disparity in Clement's policies towards the
rebellions in the imperial commune of Brescia and in the papal
city of Ferrara, Henry of Luxemburg took less notice of the letters of 4 July and 10 August than he did of another event—the
arrival in the siege camp during the first half of August of the
cardinals who had been sent to carry out his coronation in Rome.
Two of these, Nicolas of Prato, Cardinal Bishop of Ostia and
Velletri, a proven friend of Tuscan White Guelfs and Ghibellines, and Luca Fieschi, Cardinal Deacon of Santa Maria in Via
Lata, a Count of Lavagna (an important family of the eastern
Genoese Riviera), were to assist Henry greatly in Italy.[91]

The Emperor-elect soon derived a direct advantage from the
arrival of these princes of the Church as they tried to persuade
the beleaguered city to yield. Cardinal Luca Fieschi, whose house
was closely bound with the Brusati and other Brescian Guelf
nobles, was particularly effective. It was in part due to the prelates' efforts (as well as to the ravages of plague and exhaustion

within the city) that Brescia agreed to surrender in mid-September 1311.

Henry of Luxemburg entered the conquered city on 19 September, through a breach that he ordered made in the walls that he had been unable to penetrate during the entire summer of hard fighting. Whatever safeguards or reservations the Brescians thought they had obtained from the cardinals in Henry's name did not trouble the Emperor-elect. Henry wrote to his son John, King of Bohemia, that the city, its inhabitants, and their goods had been ceded into his hands "free of any conditions." [92] Yet he actually punished the rebel commune little more severely than he had far less culpable Cremona five months earlier—a most uneven and unpredictable discipline.

The official sentence was pronounced on 1 October.[93] All the Brescian fortifications, walls, and towers were ordered destroyed, and the city gates were to be sent to Rome as trophies. But there were no death sentences; the instigators of the costly rebellion suffered exile and banishment. While the commune lost all its imperial rights and privileges along with its *contado,* the goods and properties of all remained intact, and the city retained the right to contract legal agreements. A fine of seventy thousand florins was levied upon those who had been inside the city at the time of the siege, thus exempting the Brescian Ghibellines. Judges and notaries had their right to practice suspended, and men who had served as officials during the past four months could hold no other office in Brescia.

Before he left Brescia the Emperor-elect gave it a new vicar, Moroello Malaspina, friend of Dante and one of the Ghibelline marquises from the Lunigiana. When he departed on 2 October Henry took with him seventy leading Brescian Guelfs, both to honor the imperial coronation in Rome and to insure Brescia's good conduct. But, left unguarded, the seventy Brescians soon returned home without having received permission—perhaps another sign of Henry's lack of consistency or merely of his inefficiency.[94]

The four-month siege had cost the King of the Romans dearly in time, treasure, and troops. As much as two-thirds of his originally small army perished to make possible the pyrrhic victory over Brescia.[95] As the campaign had drawn on, the Emperor-elect had found it increasingly difficult to remain above party strife and partiality. He was compelled to assume more and more the role in which Florence had cast him—the chief of the Ghibellines and the tyrannical oppressor of communal liberties. Desperate need for an ever-increasing number of soldiers and for larger amounts of money left Henry little choice. He turned to the only persons willing and able to give him such aid, for the most part Italian Ghibelline lords, and these were not so idealistic or chivalrous as to serve their feudal lord gratis and let slip by this marvelous opportunity for increasing their own prestige, importance, and legal authority. Besieged by difficulties that he did not know how to meet in any other way, Henry resorted to granting legal authority and power to those Italians who offered him support. Thus on 1 August 1311 Francesco della Mirandola, Ghibelline lord of Modena, re-entered his native commune bearing the title of imperial vicar.[96] A little earlier Walter de Curte, a Pavian Ghibelline, took command as imperial vicar-general in Como.[97] The Mantuan Ghibelline chief, Passerino Bonacolsi, purchased the vicarship of his native city from the hard-pressed Emperor-elect for twenty thousand florins.[98]

The weightiest of these appointments was made on 13 July 1311 when the great Ghibelline rival of the Torriani, Matteo Visconti, received the vicarship of Milan in return for the promise to pay fifty thousand florins.[99] Thus far had Matteo advanced three months after his banishment for suspected complicity in the Milanese tumults of February. Monza and Treviglio were excluded from his jurisdiction, however, and Henry retained them in the *camera regis*. In exchange for the payment of twenty-five thousand florins a year to the imperial treasury Matteo received permission to keep all of the imperial income from Milan and its *contado*. The monarch probably wished to guarantee the imperial treasury a fixed income from Milan while sparing it the headaches of collection.

Along with these Ghibelline *signori* and would-be *signori* the King of the Romans chose to honor a nominally Guelf lord who participated in the siege of Brescia. Ghiberto da Correggio of Parma was permitted to purchase the vicarship of Reggio and its district.[100] But still he withheld the prize that Ghiberto desired above all others, rule of Parma. Da Correggio, who had labored continuously to fulfill Henry's every command, found the Reggian vicarship a mean compensation for his efforts and continued to treat secretly with the Florentines.

Not to be omitted in the distribution of rewards was Philip of Savoy, a "free-lance" Piedmontese feudal lord whom we could not with any accuracy label as a Guelf. After the conclusion of siege operations, in the second week of October, Philip was appointed vicar-general of Vercelli, Pavia, and Novara, which office, Mussato states, cost twenty-three thousand florins.[101]

Yet although they served alongside the Emperor-elect at the siege of Brescia and comported themselves as faithful vassals, the Guelf lords Count Philippone Langusco of Pavia and Simone degli Avvocati of Vercelli received relatively slight compensations. Like the other Guelf royal councillor, Antonio Fissiraga of Lodi, these men had been deprived of their special ruling status in their native cities, and this Henry had not restored them.[102]

These actions did not mark simply the continuation of the policy of making the mightiest men in the various regions responsible for keeping the peace. The Emperor-elect had passed over too many Guelf lords. Contemporaries saw a deliberate effort to reward and elevate Ghibelline followers and a mere legalization of tyranny, rather than an attempt to harness all existing political leadership and authority in Lombardy regardless of partisan affiliation for the good of the Empire.[103]

Whatever misgivings others might have had, Henry's actions after leaving Brescia on 2 October indicate that he at least was relatively content. During a stop of less than four days at Cremona he considered it safe at last to release the unfortunate Cremonese who had greeted him upon the road in April and implored mercy for their city. Few had survived the hardships and tortures of five months' imprisonment.

The Emperor-elect believed that peace in Lombardy was sufficiently secure for him to leave the province. He planned to proceed to Rome and the imperial coronation, with a brief stop at Genoa. On 5 October Henry commanded that the representatives of each commune who were to attend and honor the festivities in Rome be in Genoa by 21 October.[104]

Henry's itinerary contained one important stop before Genoa:

Pavia, where he would make final dispositions for administering Lombardy and keeping peace during his absence. But several events which occurred in Pavia should have warned the Emperor-elect that all was not in order. First, despite royal commands and pleas, Count Philippone Langusco of Pavia refused for three days to permit the Ghibelline Matteo Visconti, imperial vicar of Milan, to enter Pavia, and then only let him enter alone and unarmed. Within Pavia the presence of numerous Guelf partisans and the lack of imperial troops made Henry's northern followers feel insecure. The Bishop of Butrinto claimed that the court even uncovered a plot to kill the King of the Romans.[105] And according to a Parmesan chronicle, while in Pavia Henry became aware that Ghiberto da Correggio of Parma was dealing with his Tuscan Guelf enemies. Although this notice is not completely certain, the vicar of Reggio himself feared that his treachery had been exposed and abruptly interrupted his journey to Pavia, hastening back to Parma for fear of arrest.[106] Actually the Emperor-elect probably had received only a very vague account of Ghiberto's activities, as he took no action against him and ordered no special measures for safeguarding Parma and Reggio.

In Pavia delegates from nearly every Lombard city assembled to hear that now that Henry had restored peace and order to their province he would hasten to Rome. On the trip north from Rome the crowned Emperor would pause to settle any difficulties that still troubled northern Italy. Particularly disappointed were many Lombard exiles who had followed Henry as far as Pavia. They realized that despite his noble speeches and promises, the monarch was not about to readmit them to their native cities. The multitude of delegates saw their demands for redress of grievances ignored at the assembly, where the Emperor-elect formulated no new plans for improving imperial rule in Lombardy, but simply reinstated the regime of city vicars.[107]

Henry of Luxemburg further demonstrated his belief that Lombardy was at last in order by beginning to act upon Tuscan affairs. He sent a vicar to Ghibelline Arezzo, together with orders that the commune's Guelf exiles be readmitted to the city at once.[108] Thus he would prove to his Tuscan Guelf subjects that their sovereign had not become embittered by his experiences in the north and still intended to remain above party and mete out equal justice to all.

"Unawareness" perhaps best characterizes Henry's understanding of his position as he left Pavia and northern Italy. He did not recognize the important alteration in the Pope's attitude towards him and his expedition. While Henry had heard rumors that Philip the Fair was listening to hostile Tuscan Guelf embassies, he did not comprehend the full extent of the opposition at Paris. As late as May 1312 the Emperor-elect sent Philip IV copies of important and delicate negotiations so that the French king might remain informed of his progress and activities.[109] Unaware was the King of the Romans also of the double game that Robert of Anjou was playing. Henry's information was more complete concerning Tuscan Guelf plans to block his journey south, but he showed no awareness of the desperately serious nature of the Florentine-led conspiracy. He had not acted upon the rumors challenging the fidelity of Ghiberto da Correggio, a ringleader of the anti-imperial plot.

The fall of Vicenza in mid-April, the capitulation of Cremona, and Henry's march upon Brescia had severely frightened Florence and its allies. Their defenses were inadequate and they feared that the Luxemburger might arrive in Tuscany before he could be successfully resisted. Florentine control over the small communes surrounding it was far from complete, and as early as April 1311 the Priory worried that San Gimignano and Colle di Val d'Elsa might defect to the Emperor-elect.[110]

While the Guelf rulers of Siena sent the remaining Ghibellines of that once imperial stronghold to the *contado* as a security measure,[111] Florence reacted differently. The commune needed every fighting man it could obtain and wanted to deny "the King of Germany" the services of a large body of its citizens. During the last week of April the Priory initiated a policy that it pursued ever more zealously throughout the summer and fall. Florence offered a general amnesty to Guelf exiles from both city and *contado*, regardless of their crimes. Sentences were cancelled, and the banished could return home upon payment of a small fine. In September this policy was extended to neighboring towns within the Florentine orbit.[112]

Meetings of the Guelf League were held, and innumerable

messengers went back and forth among Florence, Siena, Lucca, Bologna, Perugia, and their lesser allies. League delegations pleaded at Avignon and Naples and maneuvered to stop Henry's course southwards.[113] The allied cities themselves acted militarily to impede his transit from Lombardy in the early fall. Bolognese troops guarded the northern approaches to the Magra Valley, while Luccans strengthened their fortifications in the treacherous hills of the Lunigiana.[114]

Fortunately for Henry, even now the League was uncertain of its own strength. In mid-October Florence took over the castle of San Miniato al Tedesco, fearing its defection, and wrote menacingly to Volterra not to rebel in favor of the Ghibellines for the imperial candidate.[115] Only a few days later Bologna increased the fines and exactions levied upon those within the city who were believed to be opposed to the present regime.[116]

No such unsureness, however, marked the Priory's propaganda campaign. The scope of Florentine propaganda now widened and encompassed more than pleas to battle for "your and our liberty" or for "the Guelf Party." The rebels were urged to resist "the King of Germany and his people" for "your and our status, liberty, and defense, and [that of] the Guelf Party of all Italy." [117] Yielding could bring "death and peril to you and us and all the [Guelf] Party, of all Italy." [118] At last the Florentine government had formulated a program embracing more than local city or regional interests, one that professed to have at heart the interests of all Italy.

While it remained true that farther north, despite all Florentine efforts, Lombard cities once more obeyed the Emperor-elect and his vicars, even there powerful and influential Guelf factions such as the Torriani and the Cavalcabò still warred against Henry. And in the papal city of Bologna many Lombard Guelfs joined their confreres from other parts of Italy to conspire and plot against the Emperor-elect.

Nor did the re-establishment of relatively settled conditions in the north hide the fact that numerous Italians of varying political complexions had shown clearly that they were not entirely enthusiastic about an Emperor-elect who really intended to rule. A host of peace arbitrations had not ended discord. The installment of city vicars and tampering with communal usages and traditions had not proven a great success, and not a few men considered the granting of vicarships to local *signori* to be simply a sanctioning of tyranny. The loss of some two-thirds of an originally small fighting force before Brescia made Henry's position all the more precarious. A major question remained as the King of the Romans hastened to the imperial coronation in the fall of 1311: Would the re-established peace prevail in Lombardy against the pressures of a newly crystallized Guelf opposition?

IV

Winter Storms: The Emperor-elect in Genoa and Pisa

THE EMPEROR-ELECT, GENOA, AND IMPERIAL POLICY

Representatives of a proud Genoese commune that had steadfastly resisted Emperor Frederick II presented Henry of Luxemburg with the keys to their city on 21 October 1311.[1] The monarch planned to pacify rapidly Genoa's internal strife and then hasten south to Rome;[2] but it was only on 16 February 1312, nearly four months after his arrival, that the Emperor-elect left the Ligurian seaport. Let us attempt to determine the reasons for this radical change in the imperial timetable.

Events since the Milanese coronation had not caused Henry to alter his tactics significantly: Genoa's political exiles accompanied him into their native city. The ambitious exile Opizzino Spinola de Lucolo, nominally Ghibelline ally of Lombard Guelfs and Robert of Anjou, had been close to the Luxemburger's court since November 1310. Henry perceived that if Genoa was to serve his cause he had first to make peace between its leading rival Ghibelline factions, the Spinola de Lucolo and the Doria. The Emperor-elect entrusted his brother-in-law, Amadeus of Savoy, Vicar-General of Lombardy, with the major responsibility for effecting this delicate reconciliation.[3]

The task of bringing order to Genoa was far from simple.

For decades internal divisions had torn the city, and numerous expedients at government had failed. Henry's court undertook elaborate investigations and questioned leading nobles and representatives of the commune's trade gilds as to the best approach to adopt.[4] At the end of a month the Emperor-elect had still not altered Genoa's constitution nor removed its podesta and abbot of the people.[5]

It was 14 November when the King of the Romans publicly brought the Genoese oath of fealty in line with those sworn by most other communes, by including the promise to aid the King in the recovery of even those things that he acquired in the future and then lost.[6] Immediately after this action the Guelf noble William Fieschi rose and requested that Henry be given authority for pacifying the city. Hardly had he finished when Opizzino Spinola strengthened the proposal by advising that the King receive complete power over Genoa and its forts, with the right to dispose of the city and *contado* as might please him. These propositions were at once put to the onlooking multitude, which responded in the affirmative.[7]

This event, apparently so similar to that which had occurred almost exactly a year earlier in Asti,[8] was actually quite different. Like the official pronouncements and the reception of authority that followed a week later, the Genoese act resulted from weeks of discussion and negotiation between the Emperor-elect and his Genoese subjects, and not from a unilateral ukase.[9] Matters were apparently concluded when Nicolas of Prato, Cardinal Bishop of Ostia and Velletri, announced on 21 November that Henry would rule the city, its *contado,* and forts for twenty years, and that this should create no precedent and not prejudice the commune's liberties and privileges. The Cardinal added that the Emperor-elect would install a just vicar in Genoa and place its forts in the custody of wealthy Genoese *popolani.*

This last provision met the swift and determined opposition of the city's leading noble families, eager to increase their strength in the republic and the Riviera. The following day the official reception of authority was repeated, with the significant difference that now the Genoese forts were to be entrusted to wealthy men "who themselves and their fathers were born in Genoa or its district, and who live in the city of Genoa." The word *"popolani"* had disappeared, and the door was opened to the scions of the noble houses that for generations had battled for the domination of the maritime republic. The warring noble chieftains had removed a possible threat to their predominance.[10]

The Emperor-elect then reorganized the constitution and political practices of the commune. To assist the imperial vicar, he created a group of twenty-four councillors or Ancients (twelve nobles and twelve *popolani,* three from each quarter of the city) whose membership would change every three months. The vicar and the outgoing Ancients would choose the new Ancients, and no man could serve more than once a year, nor could he serve if any member of his family had been in the outgoing group of Ancients. Interestingly, Henry hand-picked the first group of Ancients and exempted them from these restrictions. The Genoese councillors, moreover, had very limited powers and could not discuss critical matters such as justice, and the sale or donation of offices, jurisdictions, lands, and castles in the city or Riviera.

Whereas other north Italian cities lost their captains of the people, the Genoese abbot of the people, with his constables, remained in office as a special concession to the Ligurian republic. But even the Genoese magistracy did not go unscathed, and henceforth the manner and form of the abbot's election was left to the vicar's discretion, so that the imperial official could in fact select the candidates he desired.[11] The Genoese podesta did not fare so well as the abbot. The office lapsed when the incumbent completed his term, and an imperial vicar installed shortly before the expedition left the city assumed his duties.[12]

One of Henry's actions is significant both for clarifying his relationship with Genoa and for the light that it sheds upon some of his more general aims. On 22 November the Emperor-elect ordered the destruction of a series of open treaties which Ghibelline Genoa had concluded with Charles II, father of Robert of Anjou.[13] These pacts, said Henry, had been "contracted to the grave prejudice and injury and in diminution of the rights and *regalia* of the Holy Roman Empire." He particularly deplored a promise that Genoa would provide Charles and his heirs with from ten to one hundred galleys against anyone, as this might be taken to include even the pledge of aiding

Robert of Anjou against the Emperor should the two ever come to blows.[14]

In the opening lines of the instrument ending the Genoese-Angevin agreement, Henry of Luxemburg clearly stated one of his principal aims:

> that the rights and *regalia* of the Roman Empire perpetually be preserved uninjured . . . . Therefore among the imperial cares, it should be pre-eminent, to keep unharmed the rights and *regalia* pertaining to the Roman Empire, to recover and increase them when they are occupied, and having been increased, to maintain and defend them with a double protection, namely, of arms and of laws. Indeed we, Henry, by grace of God King of the Romans always Augustus, after we arrived at the height of regal dignity with the favor of divine clemency, thinking about the conservation, recovery, [and] acquisition of those rights and *regalia* of the Roman Empire, and also of the tranquility and peace of our subjects, and their custody, [turned our attention to Genoa].[15]

By the fall of 1311, at least, the Luxemburger had come to believe that his duties as ruler demanded that he conserve the rights of the Empire and the peace of the subjects of the Empire, and take custody and care of those subjects. That the primacy given to the preservation of imperial rights in this statement was not mere oratory or verbal decoration is shown by the fact that even Milan, the greatest power in Lombardy, had received only minor concessions when a matter of usurped or injured imperial rights was involved.

The Emperor-elect demonstrated his continued adherence to these same ideals. He refused to be swerved by possible advantages to be gained from giving special treatment to Genoa, which, together with Venice and Pisa, could give him undisputed mastery at sea. Even the exaction of an annual sixty-thousand-florin tribute from Genoa did not make Henry deviate from this policy,[16] although he deemed it either just or prudent to respect twelfth-century privileges that strictly limited Genoese military obligations to the Empire on land and sea.[17]

The monarch displayed his attachment to the goals indicated in the declaration of 22 November by his treatment of Genoese

petitions submitted shortly before he left the city.[18] Granting
those requests would have greatly curtailed the effectiveness of
his control of Genoa and the surrounding district, and would
have placed the entire Riviera coast in Genoese hands—giving
the commune far greater legal authority than even Frederick
Barbarossa had conceded it. The Genoese boldly petitioned that
Henry confirm even those communal acquisitions that represented feudal holdings and could not legally have been alienated without royal consent. Still more audacious was the request
that he revoke all grants to individuals or cities of all lands and
jurisdictions that Genoa held, or should hold, "or almost" held
at the time of his arrival in Italy, and in all places where Genoa
had the right of *chevauchée*. The Genoese further desired that
their petitions be granted in a privilege that did not mention
Henry's twenty-year rule of Genoa.

The King of the Romans did not believe that he was in such
dire straits as to have to comply with proposals so obviously
detrimental to the rights and *regalia* of the Empire. Although
Genoa was stronger than the towns and persons in the Riviera
who would have been adversely affected, Henry preferred to risk
the displeasure of the maritime republic. His decision on this
question accorded with those he had taken in respect to such
Lombard cities as Chieri, Reggio, Brescia, and Milan.

During his stay in Genoa the Emperor-elect gave still other
signs of his attachment to the same policies. Nobles from the
contado of Ghibelline Arezzo complained that officials in the
city were molesting them in property and person "contrary to
their ancient immunity, observed by right and custom." Henry
responded on 22 January 1312 with the order that "our beloved,
our vicar, the governors, council, people, and commune of the
city of Arezzo" desist from this conduct upon the pain of a
one-hundred-mark fine for each act of disobedience.[19] Less than
a fortnight later the Emperor-elect granted the plea of a knight
in the Vercelli *contado* that he no longer be forced to do military service to that commune, since the obligation had been
imposed by force.[20]

As for Genoa itself, Henry's denial of the commune's many
claims and requests was only one cause of a rapid deterioration
that took place in the republic's relations with its sovereign.
The new imperial regime and the changes made in the com-

munal constitution soon produced loud complaints. Other cries arose against the harm done trade and commerce because of worsened relations between the King of the Romans and the Guelf League.[21]

But the event that caused the greatest anger, and brought the entire population to the verge of despair, was the sudden outbreak of the plague in Genoa, an evil carried to the city by the imperial expedition from Brescia. A great procession led by the Archbishop of Genoa, in which relics of St. John the Baptist and other saints were paraded through the city to gain God's mercy, was to no avail. The disease was at its height in December, and on the thirteenth of the month it took the life of the Queen, Margaret of Brabant.

All, including Guelf chroniclers, praised the merciful and mild Queen.[22] For Henry of Luxemburg, however, her death was more than a personal loss. Margaret had partaken actively in her husband's activities and decisions. She had tried to calm Henry and make him show forgiveness and mercy towards even those who had offended him. With her death a gentle and useful influence disappeared from the inner circle of the monarch's advisers.[23]

The Emperor-elect needed the best counsel he could obtain, for throughout the fall and winter of 1311 complex diplomatic problems demanded his attention.

To the court at Genoa came envoys from Frederick of Trinacria, archenemy of Robert of Anjou, with the proposition that Henry conclude a marriage alliance with the Aragonese. The Luxemburger replied that his daughter Beatrice was in the hands of the Pope, who was negotiating a marriage alliance with Robert, and as the matter appeared to be on the point of a successful conclusion he would not deal with Frederick until it was settled.[24] Other issues also appear to have been discussed, but we are uninformed as to their specific nature.[25]

Robert himself sent two separate missions to Henry in Genoa to further the marriage alliance negotiations.[26] The first, dispatched in November, returned to Naples without achieving any results. Robert then became suspicious of Henry's intentions, and his doubts were not allayed upon learning of the reception of the Aragonese embassy in Genoa.

The Emperor-elect increased the Angevin's suspicions by re-

newing the demand, made several times before, that Robert
appear in person (not represented by a proctor) at the Roman
coronation, and there do homage for his imperial fiefs of Piedmont, Provence, and Forcalquier. As the Milanese notary Cermenate neatly phrased it, Henry "was waking a sleeping dog." [27]
To do homage before anyone other than his liege lord, the Pope,
would injure Robert's position and dignity. And for the Angevin
to appear so closely bound to Henry would severely compromise
him with his Florentine Guelf banking creditors.

At this point Clement V interceded on behalf of his vassal.
In a letter to the King of the Romans (8 January 1312) he reviewed the efforts Robert had made during the past two years
to do homage through duly appointed proctors, and concluded by
urging Henry to desist at once from demanding an act of personal homage.[28] Clement argued that the presence in Rome of the
supporters of both Robert and Henry might too easily lead to
disturbances and fighting because of the diversity of the peoples, "especially of the Guelfs and the Ghibellines." The Pope
seemingly placed the need for peace above the right or wrong
of Henry's case, or his desire to increase the glory and prestige
of his coronation; but it is impossible to say how much Clement's
decision was influenced by the wish to protect his most important Italian vassal, the King of Sicily.

Matters were further complicated by the fact that the negotiations between Henry and Robert gave rise to doubts and suspicions on both sides. The Angevin's balking over homage may
have troubled Henry less than the knowledge that Robert's Marshal, Diego de la Rat, daily increased the size of the Florentine
army while flying the Angevin's banners. When questioned
point-blank about this, the first embassy that Robert sent to
Genoa in November 1311 only replied that its mandate was
insufficient to treat the affair.[29]

News that came to Genoa in December was graver still: Robert's brother, Duke John of Gravina, had arrived in Rome with
a large body of troops. The first story to spread through Genoa
—that those men had come to Rome in order to honor the imperial coronation and give aid against the rebellious Tuscan
Guelfs—was soon belied.[30] Duke John had other plans. He spent
money lavishly buying the services and allegiance of Roman

nobles loyal to Henry of Luxemburg. Even vicars left in Rome by its Senator, Louis of Savoy, seemed to have been corrupted. Aided by the Roman Guelf Orsini, John soon controlled the powerful fortress of Castel Sant' Angelo overlooking the Tiber. His troops seized the famous Milvian Bridge (Ponte Molle) and barred passage. Late one evening as reports of these occurrences streamed into Genoa, Robert's embassy secretly slipped away from the city and Henry's feared wrath. Despite this rude turn of events, the Emperor-elect did not break off negotiations with Robert of Anjou, and continued to broadcast his belief in the sincerity of the explanation that the Angevin troops were in Rome in order to honor his coronation.

In the light of later happenings it is easy to claim that as early as November or December 1311 Henry was no longer deceived by Robert's devices.[31] It can be argued that he continued the negotiations for a marriage alliance and made no hostile moves towards Robert because he did not want an open conflict with a specially favored vassal of the Pope, upon whose good will much of his chance for success depended. Similarly, one might claim that the Emperor-elect did not wish to push Robert completely into the arms of Florence and its allies, and was stalling for time until after the imperial coronation.

The plain fact is that Henry of Luxemburg did not act against the Angevin during his stay in Genoa. Until this time, moreover, Henry had spoken openly against all whom he knew to have opposed or treated him unjustly. He was to continue this policy to the end of his life, regardless of the persons or states he offended. It might be nearer the truth to state that although Henry now doubted Robert's loyalty, he was not certain that the Angevin had determined to oppose him. Caution was called for, but not an open declaration of war.[32]

THE GREAT CONSPIRACY

Genoa and Robert of Anjou presented the Emperor-elect with serious problems, but more immediate and pressing difficulties arose in the winter of 1311–1312, and prevented Henry from concentrating upon and solving one issue at a time.

Throughout the fall and winter Florence and its allies prepared furiously for open resistance to the northern monarch. They blocked passes in the Lunigiana and roads from Genoa to Pisa, Henry's next port of call.[33] In mid-October Florence refused to receive two imperial legates sent to receive homage from the Tuscans and arrange for their appearance at the coronation in Rome.[34] One of these messengers, Nicolas of Butrinto, describes vividly how he was first menaced by the Bolognese and then narrowly escaped death at the hands of the Florentines. From the same report we learn that the rulers of Florence had told the populace that Henry was a tyrant [35] who had destroyed the Guelf Party in Lombardy and was about to descend upon Tuscany in order to do the same there. Florence, it was said, was the special object of his hatred.

The Black Guelf republic went even further in its opposition to the Emperor-elect. All Florentine subjects were given the right to rob or kill messengers of the "King of Germany" or of his allies with complete impunity. As a crowning gesture Florence solemnly banned him.[36] From having been the recognized lord of Florence in 1310, Henry of Luxemburg was now relegated to the status of an outlawed public enemy. Any attempt to gain obedience from Florence would be met by force.

Banishment by the commune of Florence was not the most serious peril facing the Emperor-elect. His victory over Brescia had come too late. The long and cruel campaign had produced the very condition that was bound to prove fatal to plans for the establishment of an impartial, suprafactional imperial regime in Italy. Guelf opinion finally united against Henry of Luxemburg. Worst of all for the Emperor-elect, his opponents were at last working together through a single organization.

The instrument of that organization was the Guelf League, and it was Guelfism, anti-imperial champion of local independence, that formed the bond unifying Henry's enemies. The defensive alliance formed between Florence and Bologna in the spring of 1310 was expanded to include the leading Guelf opponents of the Emperor-elect in Lombardy—exiled Milanese, Cremonese, and Modenese Guelfs, as well as some of the most important citizens of Parma and Reggio. The League enlarged its objectives as well as its size. Its immediate aim was to effect the rebellions of Reggio and Parma and to secure their adhesion to the League. This was conceived of as the opening blow in a campaign that would wrest all Lombardy from imperial control. The actual uprisings were scheduled for early December 1311.

The man designated to trigger the conspiracy was none other than the imperial vicar of Reggio, the nominal Guelf captain Ghiberto da Correggio. This would-be *signore* was dissatisfied with the rewards that he had received for service to the Emperor-elect, and most particularly disappointed at not having been given the rule of his native Parma. After the planned rebellions Ghiberto claimed that he had not rebelled for money or position, but because the King of the Romans had offended him by reintroducing his enemy, the Marquis Pallavicini, into Cremona. But we may note that since the marquis' reintroduction in January 1311 Ghiberto had not sulked in his tent like Achilles, but had served Henry before Brescia and received the fief of Guastalla and the vicarship of Reggio. Perhaps more instrumental in attracting Ghiberto into the conspiracy was the offer of thirty thousand Bolognese pounds, payable in Bologna after he had effected the insurrections of Parma and Reggio. It was also probably understood that Da Correggio would captain the Lombard Guelf forces in the war that would surely follow in northern Italy.[37]

Florence and its allies did well to entrust the actual execution of the coup to Ghiberto da Correggio, for in reality he was still the most important person in Parma, where he held the office of *podestà della mercanza* or leader of the city's gilds.[38] In Reggio, the second target for rebellion, he was imperial vicar, and could count at least one-fifth of the members of the all-important Reggian Council of the Twenty Wise Men among his fellow plotters during the critical month of November 1311.[39]

The conspirators projected the formation of a society or league that was to endure until their goal had been attained. Although we have no direct evidence, it is reasonable to ascribe this project to Florence in view of its past activities—its secret discussions with Da Correggio, its aid to Cremona and Brescia, its attempts to strengthen the Guelf League in Tuscany, and its constant opposition to and propaganda against Henry of Luxemburg and his expedition. The formation of this anti-imperial league can be followed in the negotiations carried on with Ghiberto da

Correggio during the winter of 1311–1312. Plans for such an organization were already outlined in the pact made with the then vicar of Reggio on 1 November.[40] Ghiberto pledged to enter Parma and Reggio into a league with Bologna, Florence, Lucca, Siena, Guido della Torre, the Milanese Guelf exiles, and the Cremonese Guelf exiles. The organization of the league was not yet complete, for provision was made for including the Modenese Guelf exiles.

A week before the first rebellion, proctors of all the interested parties once more assembled at Bologna. Also present were representatives of the Modenese Guelfs and certain men from Parma and Reggio. All of these contracted a "real society, fraternity, union, and league, to endure so much time . . . [as will be arranged] in a congress to be held by the ambassadors [of the members]." [41] The organization's aims were then set forth. The members promised

> legally and in good faith, mutually to aid and maintain each other, [and] to defend their state and that of the Guelf Party of Tuscany and of the Holy Mother Church, and of the Geremei [a leading Bolognese Guelf family], and of the cities of Bologna, Lombardy, and all of Italy, and of their friends, followers, and those adhering to them . . . . And also to treat friends as friends and enemies as enemies, understanding as enemies all followers of the King of the Romans and of his adherents, which enemies, according to their [the League members'] power must be put to flight, pursued, and brought to extermination and death.[42]

The contract became more explicit, eliminating any grounds for equivocation: "That war will be understood to be finished when the King of the Romans is dead, or has receded from the parts of Italy, or even when the province of Lombardy is pacified." Thus in the most formal document of the Guelf alliance, Henry of Luxemburg was accorded his correct title, "King of the Romans." Florence, leader of the campaign against the Luxemburger, was still ahead of its allies in the strength of its anti-imperial and untraditional ideology. Yet by conceding Henry his correct title Florence and its allies clearly highlight for us the direct opposition that had developed between allegiance to medieval concepts of the Empire and to the claims and needs of local political entities, Italian city-states.

The failure of any of the parties contracting to the Guelf alliance to fulfill its obligations was punishable by a fine of twenty thousand florins. To carry on the battle Da Correggio was promised two hundred well-armed mounted knights and three hundred infantry. Further, plans were made to hold future meetings of the League.

After the successful rebellions of Parma and Reggio on 4 and 6 December 1311, those two cities entered the League, whose existence, scope, and organization were confirmed in a pact made in Bologna on 16 December.[43] The society's duration was fixed at ten years, alterable at a congress of its members. Now included on the list of declared enemies were the exiles of all the member cities.

In the pact of 16 December the League members specifically pledged themselves "to return the province of Lombardy entirely to the Party of the Holy Mother Church and of the Guelfs." [44] As in the case of the original Florentine-Bolognese pact of March 1310, this connecting of the Church with the objectives of the League was not simply a vague definition of an ideological attachment. It was a citation of one power from whom this combination of communes and Guelf exiles hoped to receive active support in its fight against the Emperor-elect. The introduction and dedication of the pact by which the League was formed on 27 November 1311 presents a revealing list of the forces, celestial as well as terrestrial, in which the allies placed their hopes.[45] Immediately following Christ, the Virgin Mary, and all of the saints and angels in heaven are ranked the Holy Mother Church, Pope Clement V, the cardinals, Robert of Anjou and his brothers and descendents, and all the royal house of France. This same invocation appears with only slight variations in wording in the pact of 16 December. We know too that these powers were not called upon only through the dedicatory lines of a military convention concluded long after Henry's arrival in Italy. The many Florentine embassies sent to Avignon, Naples, and Paris, the gifts to divers cardinals, and other efforts to lure those mighty powers to the anti-imperial cause have already been noted.

The conspiracy of the Guelf League immediately presented the Emperor-elect with immense practical military difficulties. The spirit of rebellion manifested in Parma and Reggio during the first week of December quickly found sympathetic acceptance in other Lombard communes.

First to react was Brescia.[46] There the recently returned Ghibelline Maggi and their followers, alone exempted from contributing to the crushing seventy-thousand-florin fine levied upon the vanquished commune in October, sustained the imperial cause almost singlehanded. And Brescia had sufficient cause for lament. The onerous terms imposed upon the city made difficult even earning a living. Imperial officials continued to aggravate the situation. They called upon the poverty-stricken, plague-ridden, indebted commune less than two months after its surrender to supply military aid against Guelf exiles ravaging the Cremonese *contado*.[47]

The only recorded response to this request did not come from the commune of Brescia itself, but was a promise of compliance by "Bertolinus Maggi for himself and for, and in the name of, all the faithful friends of the Party of the Roman Empire recently re-formed in the city of Brescia." [48] We may note that this Ghibelline chief considered it wise to observe scrupulously the forms set and followed by the Emperor-elect. He avoided using the term "Ghibelline" as being notedly displeasing to his sovereign. Even during this period of crises and rebellion Henry of Luxemburg still consciously and steadfastly avoided the charged words "Guelf" and "Ghibelline," preferring such phrases as "faithful" and "rebels" of the Empire.[49]

The Brescian Guelf leaders who slipped away from the imperial expedition after being forced to accompany it to Genoa had returned home and, together with Guelf exiles from Milan, Cremona, and Brescia itself, plotted their return to power. The conspirators succeeded—how we do not know—in corrupting the imperial vicar of Brescia, Moroello, Marquis of Malaspina.[50]

The story of the rebellion is quickly told. On the night of 14 December 1311, Moroello Malaspina imprisoned leaders of the pro-imperial faction. On the sixteenth, the insurgents, firmly in possession of the Communal Palace, rang the bells and assembled warriors. The standards of the Brusati were seen waving, and the cry "Death to the Ghibellines!" rang out in the great squares. Aided by exiles from neighboring cities, the rebels drove the Ghibellines from Brescia. But their victory was short-lived. A few days later the vicar of Bergamo, Bailardino of Nogarola (friend and relative of the Veronese *signore* and vicar Can Grande della Scala), arrived with a body of troops and took Brescia rapidly, as the city's walls and fortifications had been levelled by the Emperor-elect only shortly before.

The temporary rector appointed to rule Brescia at once instituted an inquest into the origins of the rebellion, but the majority of its instigators and their followers had already fled the city. From strongholds in the *contado* they undertook a serious harassing action that continued until after the Luxemburger's death.[51]

Henry's treatment of the rebel vicar deserves notice: while Theobald Brusati of Brescia (befriended by and a vassal of the Emperor-elect) and Sopramonte Amati of Cremona had received terrible deaths at his hands, the Luxemburger allowed the vicar Moroello Malaspina to go scot-free.[52] Once again the monarch displayed a disconcerting unpredictability in his justice —no asset in his relations with his Italian subjects.

The abortive rebellion of an already discontented Brescia was not the only sign of trouble to appear in northern Italy in the wake of the revolutions in Parma and Reggio. In Asti and Vercelli the Guelf factions again began to harass their Ghibelline opponents, although they did not openly turn against their temporal overlord at this time.[53] Yet it was an ominous sign that such disturbances could occur in Vercelli, one of the three cities entrusted to Philip of Savoy, royal councillor and nephew of Count Amadeus.

Vicenza, freed of Paduan overlordship, found that it had not achieved the complete liberty of action and lack of responsibility expected by many of its citizens.[54] But the malcontents' position was extremely delicate and precarious. They could turn for aid neither to Can Grande della Scala, imperial vicar and actual *signore* of neighboring Verona, who was eager to absorb Vicenza into his sphere of power, nor to Guelf Padua, which they had recently betrayed.

In Pavia, in western Lombardy, rebels struck a powerful blow against the imperial regime. Nominally subject to the vicar-general Philip of Savoy, Pavia was actually controlled once more by Count Philippone Langusco.[55] That Guelf royal councillor decided that he had no more to gain by remaining loyal to his feudal lord, the King of the Romans. Moreover, the renewed strength of the Ghibelline Matteo Visconti in Milan represented a positive threat to his position. Count Philippone grew increasingly bold in molesting his Pavian Ghibelline rivals during the fall and early winter of 1311–1312. After the successful revolutions in Parma and Reggio and the rapid formation of the Guelf League, Philippone openly cast his lot with the rebels. Shortly before 19 January 1312 he effected the insurrection of Pavia, and became *signore* of the city, as he had been before the arrival of Henry of Luxemburg. The nuptials of Count Philippone's daughter Helen with Ghiberto da Correggio served to consecrate the new state of affairs.

Since Antonio Fissiraga of Lodi had defected from the imperial cause several months earlier,[56] only one of the three Guelf *signori* who had sworn allegiance to the Emperor-elect and joined his council in Asti in the fall of 1310 was still apparently loyal—Simone degli Avvocati di Colobiano of Vercelli. These Guelf chieftains were moved by personal interests, which were stronger than feudal ties.

The Guelf League achieved one of its greatest successes at Cremona, most powerful city on the Po.[57] The Guelf factions of Cavalcabò and Amati had controlled that commune for more than forty years. The little sympathy that existed for the new imperial regime came principally from the followers of Jacopo Redenascho, a merchant rather than a warrior, born in exile and better known abroad than at home.[58] In October 1311 the Cremonese saw how few of their compatriots imprisoned by the King of the Romans the preceding April had survived their ordeal. Throughout the fall and winter of 1311–1312 Cremona suffered from the constant attacks of its Guelf exiles, led by William Cavalcabò.

The imperial regime imposed on Cremona must have appeared to its inhabitants to go from bad to worse. The vicars sent after the city's submission in April 1311 were, first, Richard Tizzone, long-exiled Vercelli Ghibelline, and then Geoffrey dei Vergiolesi, a combatant Pistoian exile. But the real ruler of Cremona remained Giovanni da Castiglione, Proctor-General of the Fisc in Lombardy and the March, and the city groaned under the exactions of this "most cruel" Luccan exile.[59]

Already the imperial sentence of the past spring had deprived Cremona of its *contado*. This situation was aggravated when Soncino, north of the city, was taken into the *camera imperii* during the first week of October.[60] On 3 January 1312 the Proctor of the Fisc struck a series of crippling blows against Cremona's economic life and military security by giving Passerino Bonacolsi, imperial vicar and *de facto signore* of Mantua, the fortress of Luzzara, a key point in Cremona's defense system.[61] At the same time the Ghibelline *signore* of Mantua received control of "the waters of the Po, and bridges and castles, and all the places of the entire Cremonese territory situated on the said bank[s] of the Po." These grants could not have been made to an enemy more desirous of seeing the ruin of Cremona.

All factors considered, Cremona was ready to welcome back its extreme Guelf faction. On 13 January 1312 followers of William Cavalcabò took advantage of the temporary absence of imperial forces to admit him into Cremona with a small band of followers. After brief but fierce combat the city fell to Cavalcabò—once more its *signore*. He wasted no time in approaching the newly formed Guelf League and requesting aid (from Bologna in particular) against Ghibelline and imperial attempts to retake the city. Henry of Luxemburg had lost "the key to the province of Lombardy." [62]

The Emperor-elect Reacts

The Emperor-elect took public recognition of the opposition developing against him in Italy as early as 20 November 1311. His first action was not to resort to force, but to initiate a series of legal investigations and court actions against the presumed offenders. The monarch wished to make clear to all that he acted not as a tyrant, but as a lawful ruler unjustly injured by his subjects.

Henry was determined, however, to take all necessary measures against the presumed culprits; for he was still definitely committed to restoring imperial rights and prestige and placing Italian cities within the framework of imperial administration. He gave no sign of seriously considering the alternative of allowing the city-states greater autonomy and practical independence within an imperial system that allowed for great individual variations and self-rule.

During the previous spring Dante had advised Henry of Luxemburg to seek the root of his troubles in Florence, and to crush that rebellious commune. On 20 November 1311 the King of the Romans officially cited Florence, accused it of the crime of lese majesty, and demanded that it send twelve proctors to Genoa by 4 December to excuse the city and promise obedience on the pain of an imperial sentence.[63] The Florentines "did not want to subject their necks to the mild yoke of imperial eminence," [64] said Henry, berating their "unbridled temerity and pride." [65]

When more than a month passed after the original citation with no response from Florence, Henry likened its citizens to "superbious sons of Lucifer." [66] He banned the city, deprived it of all rights of self-government, stripped it of imperial privileges, reclaimed the Florentine *contado* for the imperial fisc, and fined the city five thousand pounds of gold. From 24 January 1312 onwards all Florentines, whether of the city or its district, were declared rebels of the Empire and could be captured, though not slain, with impunity. The Emperor-elect included two financial clauses in his sentence of Florence in order to induce men to aid in its execution. He freed all debtors of Florentines from their obligations, and offered anyone who captured a Florentine and delivered him to an imperially controlled fort the prisoner's goods. The monarch specifically exempted members of his own immediate following (*familia*) and Florentines exiled for partisan reasons (*exules racione parcium*) from these penalties.

Five days later, 29 December, Henry turned to Parma and Reggio and ordered an investigation into their rebellions and in particular into the roles of Ghiberto da Correggio and two of his close associates. A Roman judge and the Florentine exile Palmieri degli Altoviti were to make the examinations "summarily and without the clamor and formality of a legal judgment." [67]

Only three months later, on 11 April 1312, did the Emperor-elect condemn Ghiberto da Correggio and his two companions to death for treason.[68] Parma, Reggio, Lucca, and Siena he sentenced much as he had Florence in December, except that they received lighter fines and from two to three weeks in which they could still return to imperial favor.[69] This grace period was explicitly denied Florence, whose sentence was reconfirmed. Once again Henry exempted members of his "family" and all political exiles from the consequences of the judgment.[70]

The King of the Romans filled more than a third of the published sentence with self-righteous recriminations against the rebels and elaborate descriptions of their crimes. Like the Florentines they were likened to "sons of perdition." [71] Henry explained at length his present conception of the conditions and needs of Italy upon his arrival, and of the good work that he had already done, and would continue to do if only evil men void of understanding and justice would not obstruct him. Because of the long absence of Kings of the Romans from Italy, he said, the *regalia* of the Empire had been usurped, cities torn by party strife and war and tyrannically ruled. Men had been unjustly forced into exile, their goods and property confiscated, and they themselves "compelled to beg in foreign cities." The Emperor-elect had brought peace to Lombardy, reconciling men of all parties. Now he wished to go into Tuscany where wars and animosities still raged, and grant to that province those same blessings of peace and justice that he had given Lombardy. In this document Henry sacrificed brute actualities to the noble-sounding phrases of empty rhetoric. Even so late as April 1312 he adhered to his claim to be above parties, and charged that the Florentine rebels were still acting in a partisan manner to the detriment of imperial Italy.

The monarch did not confine his reactions to threats and legal sentences. During January 1312 he strengthened his hold upon Lombardy, fortifying his most vigorous partisans in the March, the Ghibelline Bonacolsi and Scaligers, imperial vicars and *de facto signori* of Mantua and Verona. Early in the month Passerino Bonacolsi received a generous gift, in the hopes that he would be able to watch over and retain Cremona for the imperial cause. Next it was the Scaliger's turn. Already Can

Grande had urged that he be given the vicarship of Vicenza.
As this office fell vacant, Henry granted the Scaliger's wish
during the final days of January or the first week of February.[72]

The young Can Grande entered Vicenza on 11 February 1312.
He took over his new functions on the following day, installing
his cousin Frederick della Scala as communal podesta.[73] In less
than two weeks Can Grande exploited the fear of Paduan attacks to persuade the Major Council of Vicenza to grant him
extensive powers of *arbitrium,* similar to those he held as *signore*
of Verona. He received the right to punish criminals, including
political ones, and authority to appoint the commune's Council
of Wise Men for as long as he desired. This council and the new
vicar could "do and accomplish all things that they consider useful and good for the good state of the commune of Vicenza." [74]
The imperial vicarship had given the Scaliger the chance to
establish his personal rule in this city situated between his
stronghold of Verona and its powerful rival Padua—a position
that he had hitherto been unable to obtain.

The King of the Romans had taken a step in a new direction. Previously he had tended to grant a legal form of limited
authority, the imperial vicarship, to already existing Italian
signori in their home districts. Now that larger areas had to be
protected against immediate military threats and few competent
men were available for the job, Henry's solution was to increase the authority of *signori* whose loyalty and efficacy seemed
proven, extending their rule by grants of imperial jurisdiction
into areas that they had hitherto been unable to penetrate. The
concession to Passerino Bonacolsi in the Cremonese district and
that to Can Grande della Scala in Vicenza set the pattern for
similar moves to follow. The pacific-minded Emperor-elect found
himself compelled to cease paying that respect which he had
previously attempted to show for the sensibilities of many of his
Guelf subjects, at least in eastern Lombardy.

The rebellions and unrest in northern Italy called for a more
general remedy than extensions of power to native *signori*. The
office of Vicar-General of Lombardy, held by Count Amadeus of
Savoy, had failed as an instrument for maintaining the peace. It
had not been conceived of primarily as a military post, but
largely as an administrative office. Henry believed that the pres-

ent situation demanded that the rectorship of the province be principally a military assignment, handled by a professional warrior. His choice was Count Werner of Homburg, an experienced soldier from a small north German county.[75]

This new official who replaced the Vicar-General was designated the Captain General for Lombardy and appointed on 13 February 1312, two months after the rebellions of Parma and Reggio.[76] The Captain General was to maintain, defend, and govern imperial rights and honors in northern Italy, acting especially against the "rebels of the Empire." The Emperor-elect vested him with "all necessary power" to achieve this goal. To fulfill his mission Count Werner was immediately to form a league or confederation composed of the cities, states, towns, and generally of the "faithful of the Empire [*imperii fideles*]." Even during the aggravated conditions of early 1312 Henry of Luxemburg conscientiously avoided the use of the terms "Guelf" and "Ghibelline"—perhaps not wishing to appear to the Italians, the Pope, or even himself to be following in the footsteps of the ill-fated Hohenstaufen emperors.

Any who refused to join the Captain General's new confederation were to be punished. Count Werner was to receive counsel from imperial officials already in Lombardy, and the Proctor of the Fisc, Giovanni da Castiglione, was specifically designated to assist him.

The new Captain General promised to be vigorous. At Lodi he organized a meeting of representatives of cities obedient to the Empire. One of the Milanese delegates, the notary and chronicler Giovanni da Cermenate, has left an interesting account of the proceedings.[77] Exiles from every city in rebel hands argued that *their* commune could be retaken easily and urged the Captain General to recover it first. Men showed little interest in the general good or in the over-all necessities of the campaign, reports Cermenate, but each thought of his own personal advantage. The Milanese delegates soon persuaded the divided membership to agree upon the selection of a single chief to represent all the Lombard Ghibellines in deciding upon war plans with Werner of Homburg. The man chosen was Matteo Visconti, imperial vicar of Milan. Although he was now called vicar, and not *signore* or captain, Matteo effectively disposed of the forces of Milan, and the Empire's military need presented the opportunity to bring Milan's military, economic, and numerical superiority again to the fore.[78]

The Captain General showed himself to be an able fighter. In March 1312 he quelled an incipient rebellion in Lodi instigated by a vicar who had chosen to betray his trust.[79] The following month imperial forces regained Piacenza, which had been seized by Cremonese Guelfs in mid-February.[80] This represented a major gain, as Piacenza remained a central point in the fight against Cremona and Parma.

One important defection, however, even Count Werner could not prevent. Padua rebelled against imperial rule as soon as it learned that Henry had appointed its enemy Can Grande della Scala vicar of its former possession Vicenza. Imperial eagles were torn from municipal buildings and replaced by the emblems of the man whom Padua, along with the other Guelf rebels, desired as its nominal captain: Robert of Anjou. Following the Florentine example, Padua "caused the lord Emperor to be banned from the said city and its district." [81] Less than two days after the revolt Padua expressed its desire to join Bologna and the Guelf League.[82] Even the commune's vicar went over to the rebels and, renouncing his imperial office, accepted that of podesta of Padua.[83]

This rebel gain was partially offset by the death of two leading Guelf chieftains: the aged and ill Guido della Torre of Milan died a natural death early in 1313, while William Cavalcabò of Cremona was slain during an unsuccessful sortie against the fortress of Soncino 16 March.[84] These were costly losses since the Guelf rebels needed all the experienced warriors they could muster to counter the stratagems and attacks of such imperial vassals as Count Werner of Homburg, the Visconti, and the Luxemburger's Flemish cousins.

By early March 1312 the rebels nevertheless had cause for satisfaction. With Reggio, Parma, Pavia, Cremona, and Padua in open rebellion, imperial rule in all northern Italy was severely shaken. Henry of Luxemburg himself was tied down by plague and by administrative and diplomatic problems in Genoa. Pledged to continuing south, he had to leave the protection of imperial rights in the north to troops led by a German captain

and predominantly Ghibelline *signori,* communes, and exiles.
And as a new Guelfism came into being, the cause of "the faithful of the Empire" was rapidly becoming identical with that of
the Italian Ghibellines.

HENRY OF LUXEMBURG IN PISA

Only on 16 February 1312 could Henry of Luxemburg at last
leave Genoa and continue towards Rome and the imperial coronation.[85] His situation becomes clearer when we recall that this
departure occurred fourteen days after the original date fixed by
the Pope for the coronation, and so often lamented by Henry as
being too far in the future. Nor could the Emperor-elect travel
as he wished, for he had to take to the sea in order to avoid
forces stationed at the mountain passes by Florence and its allies.

The long-awaited King of the Romans reached Pisa on 6
March.[86] This commune which had already given Henry more
gold than any other Italian city now paid him the sixty thousand florins promised at Lausanne more than a year and a half
earlier.[87] Pisa presented the monarch with a splendid tent, be-
decked with jewels and surmounted by a golden imperial eagle.
His companions were regaled with gifts, and even common soldiers received new uniforms.

Pisa followed the Genoese example and renewed its fealty to
the King of the Romans. As in the case of Genoa, Henry took
this occasion to strengthen the clauses of the solemn oath, and
the Pisans now promised fealty "against all men" and obliged
themselves to aid the King in the recovery of even those things
he acquired in the future and then lost.[88]

Henry of Luxemburg demonstrated that the new wave of disturbances that threatened to destroy his hard-won control over
Lombardy had not damaged or radically altered his own conception of his position and rights. He removed the twelve
Ancients who had been chosen in the traditional manner to
guide Pisan affairs during March and April,[89] perhaps in order
to install a group of men of whose loyalty and attachment to his
cause he was certain.

But even the zealous Pisan followers of the Empire, confirmed
Ghibellines, did not want their customary political forms tam-

pered with or taken in hand by the King of the Romans, and
soon Henry's innovations produced rioting in the streets. The
monarch responded with only mild punishments and conceded
that the commune might enjoy its old laws and form of government.[90] Despite any political predilections, Henry could not
afford to alienate Pisa.

To Pisa came hordes of Ghibelline and White Guelf exiles,
eager to take up arms for the glory of the Empire and the destruction of their enemies. Prominent were Hildebrandinus,
Bishop of Arezzo and resolute opponent of Florence, Frederick
of Montefeltro, former podesta and captain of Pisa, Uguccione
della Faggiuola, excellent warrior and former podesta of Arezzo,
and Castruccio Castracani, militant Luccan exile who had been
living in Pisa for several years. The royal counsellor and familiar Simon Philip of Pistoia was still close to the King.[91] Reinforcements from north of the Alps included Duke Rudolf of
Bavaria, who had hitherto been actively campaigning with
Henry's son John in Bohemia.[92] The Florentine chronicler Villani estimated the Luxemburger's strength in Pisa at fifteen hundred foreign cavalry and numerous Italians.[93] With this force
the monarch planned to march directly to Rome.

The fighting in northern Italy did not end, however, merely
because the Emperor-elect wished to rest and reorganize his
forces in Pisa. At Quartesolo on 26 March Can Grande della
Scala showed his worth as vicar of Vicenza and soundly defeated
the Paduans and some Vicentines who had planned to retake
the city. He captured the leading plotters and dragged them
through Vicenza before publicly hanging them.[94]

Elsewhere the imperial cause did not fare so well. A Guelf
signore and imperial vicar of Treviso, Richard da Camino, was
assassinated on 5 April by a group of the city's leading Guelf
nobles. They had brought Richard and his family to power as
signori of the commune and supported him, even after he accepted an imperial vicarship. But once Padua, center of Guelfism
in the March, rebelled, then loyalty to the Empire meant alliance with a dangerous neighbor: Can Grande della Scala of
Verona. The Guelf lords ended this state of affairs by murdering
Richard da Camino. His brother and successor, Guecello, responded to the desires of the Trevisan nobles. Although he did

not enter the city into the Guelf League, he renewed its pact with Padua, which he aided militarily against Can Grande.[95]

In Piedmont worse was in store for the imperial cause. After sulking with many grievances, real and imagined, the nominally Guelf Solari in Asti rebelled, expelling their rivals and the imperial vicar on 6 April. This revolution contained a new element. To protect themselves against approaching imperial reinforcements commanded by Philip of Savoy, the Guelf rebels called into the city Hugh of Baux, seneschal of Robert of Anjou in Piedmont. On 17 April 1312 he accepted a limited signory of Asti in Robert's name. The commune was to divide its income with the Angevin and grant him limited military service. But unlike those cities adhering to the imperial cause, Asti retained the right to name its own vicar. Nor could Robert levy new taxes or ignore the communal statutes. Acceding to these terms, the Angevin absorbed into his sphere of power this commercially valuable Piedmontese city that for so many years had resisted his own advances and those of neighboring feudal lords, including the houses of Savoy. Yet by accepting the rule of a commune that had just now openly rebelled against the Empire, Robert committed an open breach of faith against the lord from whom he held the Counties of Piedmont, Provence, and Forcalquier in fief.[96]

This action in northern Italy did not, however, prevent Robert from continuing negotiations with Henry of Luxemburg for their long-projected marriage alliance. It was also advantageous to the Emperor-elect to attempt to reach an understanding, since Robert's brother already controlled much of Rome, where the imperial coronation had shortly to take place. In fact, Henry sent an embassy to Naples only four days after he arrived in Pisa.[97] A papal letter sent to Henry on 1 April must have further encouraged the Angevin-Luxemburg negotiations, as the Pope urged the King of the Romans to conclude the alliance with Robert as rapidly as possible.[98] Clement V laid special emphasis upon his own great and very special attachment to his liege vassal, Robert, and to the Kingdom of Sicily.

Several days before the dispatch of that papal letter an event occurred at the papal curia that had most serious consequences for Henry of Luxemburg's Italian expedition: the so-called betrayal of 28 March 1312. According to an Aragonese account written on 31 March,[99] Henry had sent letters to Pope Clement complaining that Angevin soldiery, led by Duke John of Gravina, was holding much of Rome and opposing the Luxemburger's entry into the city and his imperial coronation. The Pope and cardinals upon consideration of the situation had decided to assent to the requests of the Emperor-elect, and drew up letters for Duke John, ordering him to leave Rome. News of this decision reached the French court, and on 28 March, in a determined effort to prevent its implementation, three members of the royal family appeared before the Pope. Philip the Fair himself remained away only because of a high fever. After long discussions in which the French argued that the projected commands would seriously weaken the position of Robert of Anjou and involved great risks for the Church itself, the Supreme Pontiff was convinced. The letters for Duke John, already sealed, remained undispatched.

This papal action cannot be explained by concluding that a sick man, Clement V, had been unable to resist determined French opposition. The Pope could have ordered the letters sent after the French left, and, more important, he had already displayed an ability to resist serious pressure for a considerable length of time when he was convinced of the necessity for doing so—as in the case of the trial of Pope Boniface VIII for heresy.

The anti-imperial direction that the Avignon Pontiff was taking may have been influenced to some extent by the situations that had developed in Italy during the immediate past. But even granting that Clement was disturbed and unhappy about the wars that had been raging in Italy since December 1311 between the Emperor-elect and his Guelf subjects, would permitting a bloody battle in the streets of Rome improve conditions or promote a return of peace? [100]

A factor that at least the French court believed weighed strongly with the Pope was the security of his most important vassal in Italy, Robert of Anjou, King of Sicily and Rector of the Romagna. Already Clement had supported the Angevin's refusal to perform homage to the Emperor in person at the imperial coronation in Rome.[101]

When on 28 March the French argued that Robert was menaced by an alliance between his southern neighbor, Frederick of Trinacria, and the King of the Romans, although such a pact had not been concluded, their argument contained an element of truth. Frederick had sent envoys to Pisa in early March. During the second half of that month, perhaps tiring of Robert's procrastination and concerned over the presence of Angevin troops in Rome,[102] Henry of Luxemburg dispatched his first proctors to Frederick in order to conclude a military alliance, admittedly not specifically directed against Robert.[103]

Such an alliance between the Emperor-elect and the King of Trinacria was particularly distasteful to the Pope. Frederick was an enemy of the Papacy who held half of the papal fief of the Kingdom of Sicily against the wishes of the Holy See. He presented a definite threat to the security of Robert of Anjou, upon whom the Pope counted for strong support in regulating the affairs of Italy. Worst of all, a marriage alliance between Frederick and Henry once again brought to life the spectre of the unification of Sicily with the Empire, and the placing of papal Italy in the jaws of a gigantic pincers. Since the days of Innocent III the Papacy had labored assiduously to avoid this menace. Clement himself had shown great concern for the problem when in 1309 he made Robert of Anjou include in his oath of liege homage the solemn promise that neither he nor his successors would ever become King of the Romans or emperor.[104]

All of these immediate issues probably weighed in the papal decision not to assist the Emperor-elect; but also influential was Clement's general concern for the welfare and security of papal Italy, particularly in view of the presence close by of Ghibelline and imperial troops. Moreover, his clearly demonstrated double standard in judging Italian affairs (to wit, regarding the rebellions in imperial Brescia and papal Ferrara during the summer of 1311) made him more susceptible to French arguments and gave a greater cogency and strength to the other factors that went to make up his determination not to support Henry of Luxemburg.

Such was Henry's diplomatic position when, on 23 April 1312, six months after he had left the Lombard plains, he led his army out of Pisa. His hopes for success in maintaining any hold upon imperial Italy seemed to lie in settling his differences with Robert of Anjou (or at least in avoiding an open conflict), in future military victories, and in the increased prestige that he might derive from the imperial coronation. And that splendid ceremony was the next item on his agenda.

V

The Coronation—and After

Henry of Luxemburg's desire to acquire the imperial crown before commencing any other operations was complemented by the Florentine fear of risking a major military engagement, and thus the imperial expedition arrived safely at the Isola Farnese on the outskirts of Rome by 7 May 1312.[1]

Two envoys whom Henry had sent ahead to request Duke John of Gravina in Rome to prepare the city for his reception returned with their report.[2] Although they reached Rome on 30 April, Duke John had procrastinated several days before seeing them. During the interim they had witnessed heavy combat between the Ghibelline Colonna and the Guelf Orsini aided by Duke John's troops, particularly at the approaches to the Milvian Bridge—an important entrance to the city. When the imperial legates requested the Angevin duke to secure peace, or at least a truce, between the warring factions, he resorted to dilatory tactics and pleaded a lack of instructions from his brother Robert. The Roman noble Gentile Orsini gave the legates John's definitive answer. The Duke, he said, had originally been sent to Rome to honor Henry's coronation, but he had afterwards received orders from Robert not to permit the "King of Germany" to enter the Eternal City or be crowned in the Basilica

of St. Peter. He refused to make peace between the Orsini and
the Colonna because the latter were his enemies. John of Gravina
now officially renounced his allegiance and fealty [*diffidabat*] to
Henry of Luxemburg.

Gentile Orsini accompanied the legates to the Isola Farnese
where they were to await the imperial expedition. But even
Gentile, chieftain of the Roman Guelfs, was little satisfied with
the comportment of Robert of Anjou and his brother John, who
was already fighting against some of the vanguard of men loyal
to Henry, without having previously warned the Emperor-elect
of the Angevin renunciation of loyalty. Members of the French
royal house, declared Gentile, would never have acted that way.
Only the Orsini's "probity and legality" prevented Angevin
troops leaving the Isola Farnese from massacring the imperial
legates and their small escort.

This news took the King of the Romans unawares. Despite
many reports of Duke John's suspicious activities in Rome during the past months, he had expected no opposition, and according to the Bishop of Butrinto he approached the city "riding
unarmed." [3]

Henry quickly marshalled his forces in battle order and, refusing to cover his too brightly shining armor, crossed the Milvian Bridge at the head of his troops on Sunday 7 May. Angevin
troops firing down from a nearby tower inflicted only light
casualties on the advancing expedition.

The Emperor-elect did not intend to enter the Eternal City
furtively. Henry arrayed his army in a great procession and led
the parade through cheering crowds of the Roman populace.
The expedition proceeded to southeastern Rome and the sections
controlled by the Ghibelline Colonna. These included St. John
in Lateran and the Basilica of Santa Maria Maggiore, although
the enemy held the Colosseum. Unfortunately for the King of
the Romans, this was the very opposite end of the city from the
Basilica of St. Peter, where according to the papal directions the
coronation had to take place.

Bitter fighting became the order of the day as Ghibelline and
imperial troops desperately attempted to breach a way to St.
Peter's. But in vain. The enemy occupied almost all the Roman
strong points guarding the approaches to the sought-after basi-

lica, including the Torre della Milizia and Castel Sant' Angelo.

Henry ardently desired to be crowned in St. Peter's as soon as possible, and he was eager to use every means at his disposal to gain this objective. While directing military operations, he opened a series of negotiations with all who might further this end, including the Angevin Duke opposing him. On 10 May he officially requested aid from the cardinals whom the Pope had commissioned with carrying out the coronation ceremonies.[4] He asked them to intervene in person with Duke John and persuade him to cease his resistance. If their efforts proved ineffective, Henry petitioned that the cardinals crown him in St. John in Lateran. When lengthy discussions with Henry's enemies proved ineffective, however, the princes of the Church felt bound to refuse to crown the Emperor-elect other than in the place and manner explicitly commanded in their orders from the Pope.

Less than two weeks after his entry into Rome Henry's envoys returned from Naples and brought with them a series of startling proposals from the Angevin monarch.[5] Robert agreed to a marriage between his son, Charles of Calabria, and Henry's daughter upon conditions that would have greatly increased the Angevin's power and influence in Italy and denied the Luxemburger effective rule of Tuscany. The Emperor would be bound to aid Robert at sea (thus isolating Frederick of Trinacria) and pledge his friendship to the house of France. The promised bride, Beatrice of Luxemburg, was to be in Naples by the end of October. The Emperor and all his forces would have to leave Rome within four days after the coronation. In return Henry would have Robert's friendship and assistance, and receive a small annual payment and military service from the Tuscan Guelf communes. The lack of mention of the Kingdom of Arles in Robert's proposals may perhaps indicate the Angevin's awareness of the Pope's new policy for that imperial territory.

Robert's audacious conditions for permitting the peaceful coronation of his overlord for the counties of Piedmont, Provence, and Forcalquier, the King of the Romans, have aroused great scholarly interest.[6] Robert's biographer, Caggese, may be correct in saying that the proposals were not sent merely in order to be rejected. The Angevin had never sought open combat with Henry of Luxemburg and did not want it now. His propositions represented in part an effort to stall for time, and in part a serious attempt to establish firmly the hegemony of the house of Anjou in Italy upon a wider base than ever before.[7] Robert's terms came close to the goals formulated by the Guelf League in the winter of 1311–1312 and in points were almost identical with the last terms that Florence had considered satisfactory for a settlement with Henry. Florence had been unable to persuade its allies to agree to its most radical anti-imperial ideology, and quite possibly the Priory would still have settled for less than the death of the "King of Germany."

The Angevin's situation was difficult. If he acted contrary to Pope Clement's express orders, he risked losing papal support. He also knew that Frederick of Trinacria would seize the first opportunity for assaulting the Regno.[8] Moreover, Robert was troubled by a strong current of pro-imperial sentiment in his own kingdom.[9] In the Romagna, where he was papal Rector, his control was insecure, and in this very month of May rebellions and Ghibelline attacks shook that province.[10] On the other hand, Robert had allowed his Guelf allies to expect that he would personally lead a large contingent of troops from Naples to participate in the struggle against the Luxemburger in Rome. Florence, home of the Angevin's principal banking creditors, did not let him forget his obligation, and pressed Robert with embarrassingly frank and open letters reminding him of his alleged promises to aid it and urging him to hasten north.[11]

Angevin soldiers did set out from Naples and marched calmly towards Rome. But it appears that they had orders to stop short many miles south of that city. For a time they actually disappeared from sight. When anxious Florentine captains in Rome requested news from home concerning those expected Angevin reinforcements during the second week of June, the Priory had to confess its ignorance. It knew only of the many rumors in circulation—some placed the Angevin troops in Campania, some in Anagni, and others reported that they had never left Naples! On 17 June the Priory sent a scout south to search for them.[12]

Robert's very comprehensible unwillingness to commit himself fully and publicly on the side of his Guelf allies was strengthened by a factor much closer to home than considerations of the Papacy, Frederick of Trinacria, or conditions in the Romagna.

Robert knew that many in his own kingdom, particularly the masses of common people, were strongly pro-imperial.[13] When he requested his knights to do military service outside the Regno, the untamed southern barons did not hesitate to refuse absolutely.[14] Robert lacked the essential support necessary for a sustained major military campaign, and even risked possible disturbances and rebellions in his own lands.

By mid-June the Angevin found himself in real embarrassment and confusion, when copies of his negotiations with the Emperor-elect fell into Florentine hands.[15] The deceived and angry Priory immediately questioned Robert as to the verity and provenance of the incriminating documents, and requested him to cease any such dealings at once. Florence wisely left Robert a way for saving face by suggesting that he himself could not have performed such base acts, but rather they were the work of wicked enemies intent upon sowing dissension between the good king and his loyal Guelf allies.[16] Florence barraged Naples with letters and embassies containing a multitude of persuasive arguments and lightly veiled threats, intended to persuade Robert to stop treating with the "King of Germany," and give full, loyal, open support to the Black Guelf republic and its allies. The Priory feared greatly that when news of the Angevin's dealings reached Vienne it would have the disastrous effect of causing the Pope and the cardinals to turn against the Italian Guelfs. Robert was "supplicated" to write at once asking friendly cardinals to counter this expected reaction.[17]

The most complete and well-prepared summary of the Florentine arguments appears in a list of instructions dispatched to the commune's embassy in Naples.[18] Robert was to be reminded of his promises to send troops to oppose Henry in Rome and to appear there himself during the second week of June. He was accused of having been the very cause of the Tuscan communes' rebellion against the King of Germany, persuading them to such opposition![19] But these instructions too left the Angevin a way out, with the statement that the incriminating letters were not written by him, but by his enemies, most likely by Cardinal Luca Fieschi. The Angevin was not to listen to this prelate who had come to Naples for the express purpose of persuading him to make peace and ally with Henry of Luxemburg. Rather Robert

should come promptly to Rome to remove the suspicion and fear
that had been created in the minds of the masses in the Guelf
cities, common people who could not understand or reason too
well. The Angevin was bluntly asked whether even the Regno
would be secure if Ghibellines dominated Tuscany and Lombardy.

If Robert should deny his pacts with the Guelf League and side
with Henry, the Priory admitted that Florence and its allies
would be compelled to withdraw troops they had sent to Rome.
They would then mass in Tuscany and there oppose Henry and
all of his friends and accomplices—this last comment being a
not too subtle reference to Robert himself. On this note the
lengthy memorandum to the Florentine legates in Naples ended.

During the course of its correspondence with Robert, Florence
made explicit certain possibilities implicit in the Guelf program
of the past fall and winter. "If that enemy [the King of Germany]
should be killed, as might easily occur, there is no doubt . . . that
in the future no disturber of you or us will rise up in the name
of the Empire or will dare or presume to come to your lands or
ours," declared the Priory.[20] Another Florentine communication
to the Angevin expressed still more clearly the idea that the
present conflict with Henry of Luxemburg might mark the end
of the struggles between the German emperors and the Italian
communes: "This is the way and the path of truth and security,
and through it every hope for coming into Italy will be taken
from future Kings of Germany, if any are created." [21]

The Priory could not rest with theoretical statements. For
while the exposure of Robert's double-dealing and increased
Florentine diplomatic pressure made the Angevin promise that
he would be in Rome "personally and with all of his forces" by
29 June,[22] Robert continued to run with the hares and hunt with
the hounds. Indeed Duke John of Gravina battled on in Rome
until the Emperor's departure, but neither Robert nor his troops
ever made their long-heralded appearance in the city.

Florence was particularly disinclined to patience with its royal
ally because pledged Tuscan and Umbrian reinforcements arrived in Rome slowly and in insufficient numbers.[23] From May
to July Bologna discussed and projected plans for sending a contingent to Rome—soldiers that in the end it never dispatched.[24]

Florence displayed unflagging energy during this crisis, continually requesting increased support and sending large groups of its own soldiery into the fray. The Priory explained to Lucca that it considered the present fighting in Rome to be the most crucial phase in the entire campaign that had been conducted with ever-increasing intensity against Henry of Luxemburg.[25] While Ghibellines from all of Italy flocked to the Luxemburger, the battle was being waged "for the defense of the Guelf Party of all Italy." The conclusion: "If we destroy the pride [*superbiam*] of the King of Germany and of the Ghibellines in Rome we will win everywhere." This reasoning was backed by the biblical verse, "I shall smite the shepherd and the sheep of the flock will be dispersed." [26]

Fighting continued to rage unabated in the streets of Rome. To break the stalemate the Emperor-elect resorted to an ignoble ruse used by many before him. He called all the Roman nobles who had not come out decisively against him to a banquet, and there suddenly confronted them with the choice of loyal allegiance or opposition. Henry listened carefully and had all declarations, reservations, and conditions recorded. Then he demanded hostages or securities of many present and held some prisoners in person. In this manner he obtained control of most of the baronial strongholds in Rome, including the Colosseum and the Torre della Milizia.[27]

When this coup did not open the road to St. Peter's, the Emperor-elect even promised not to molest or retaliate in any way against Duke John of Gravina and his Guelf allies if they would allow him to be crowned in the designated basilica. This humiliating offer was rejected.[28] Even a threatened assault upon the Guelfs by the mass of the Roman populace, tired of seeing the city destroyed and kept in turmoil, had no effect.

Diplomacy, pleas, and threats had not succeeded. The only chance remaining was a decisive test of arms. This took place on Wednesday, 26 May 1312, and was one of the greatest battles fought in Rome during the Middle Ages. Henry's northern knights were the best-trained participants, but the advantage lay with the defenders in those narrow, twisted streets leading to the Tiber. After hours of fierce combat the imperial forces retired in defeat. The decisive assault had failed. The Emperor-elect suffered grave losses. Together with an uncounted number of common soldiers, at least one hundred fifty important imperial vassals died in battle or as a result of wounds. Among the casualties were Henry's cousin and councillor, Theobald of Bar, Bishop of Liège, and Peter of Savoy. Robert of Flanders, another of the monarch's cousins, lay seriously injured, along with the Roman Stephen Colonna. Soon Florence triumphantly paraded the captured standards of the King of the Romans and the Counts of Savoy and Flanders.

Despite the victory on 26 May, the Tuscan Guelfs had not comported themselves well during the battle. Their troops in Rome were thoroughly weary. Discouraged by Robert's failure to appear, many began to drift homewards without permission after the great fight.[29]

Unfortunately for the Emperor-elect, his own soldiers showed the same inclination, and contingents from the Umbrian cities along with isolated groups of Italian Ghibellines were seen leaving the city.[30] Gradually the opposing sides tended to approach equal strength. By 27 June the entire affair seemed reduced to only a question of money—needed to purchase the services of mercenaries. On that date the astute observer Christian Spinola wrote to James II of Aragon from Genoa that Robert intended to exhaust the Emperor.[31] And "King Bertha," as his disgusted allies now began to dub the Angevin,[32] could count upon the immense resources of the Florentine banking houses.

The weeks of fighting in Rome had brought relief to none, and as the day appointed for the coronation approached, the perplexed cardinals accompanying the imperial expedition became increasingly certain that the Emperor-elect would be unable to obtain St. Peter's by 29 June. Since no messenger had returned from the papal curia with an answer to the request that Henry of Luxemburg be crowned in St. John in Lateran, the cardinals faced a serious dilemma. On the one hand, they wished to crown Henry as soon as possible and put an end to the destructive fighting in the Eternal City. On the other, they had grave doubts as to their authority to perform the ceremonies in any place other than the traditional one named in the coronation *Ordo* and decreed in their commission from Pope Clement. Was there not the peril, for example, that the oath to be the protector and defender of the Pope and the Church which Henry VII had to swear in the Chapel of S. Maria de Turribus would lose its efficacy if sworn elsewhere? [33]

At last the cardinals were forced to act. Niccolo de' Buonsignori of Siena, formerly vicar of Asti and then of Milan, now vicar of the Roman Senator Louis of Savoy, harangued a large group of battle-weary Romans. The mob then marched upon the cardinals and demanded that they crown Henry in St. John's. To have refused might have precipitated the Romans into acts of exceptional violence. "We greatly feared those insane rustics," explained the Bishop of Butrinto. The cardinals acquiesced to the demands of the mob—and of Henry and his court.[34]

On 29 June 1312 Henry of Luxemburg became Emperor Henry VII in the Basilica of St. John in Lateran. Three times he brandished a drawn sword before placing it in its gold scabbard on the high altar in sign of service to the Church. The Roman populace chanted loud the ancient acclamation "To the mighty Emperor Henry, always Augustus, life and victory!"

Even this unique and festive day could not pass in perfection before the brute realities of Henry's position reasserted themselves. While the august company partook of the coronation banquet, it was forced to interrupt its feasting and seek cover as a shower of missles unexpectedly burst through the windows— a not too auspicious beginning for the reign of the Emperor Henry VII.[35]

The monarch did not allow that untoward event completely to dampen his spirit. On the very day of his coronation Henry VII promulgated a *Constitutio contra haereticos et sacrilegos* and dispatched encyclicals announcing his new dignity.[36] These documents offer interesting indications as to some conceptions which the Emperor now had of his new role. He claimed that his imperial diadem and his government of the Empire were direct gifts from God, and thus made no actual acknowledgment of a papal control over the *imperium*.[37] Henry VII likened earthly government to the celestial hierarchy and declared that all men and kingdoms ought to be subject to the Emperor.[38] Rome, he noted, had been the site of the imperial throne before it housed the Apostolic See.[39] But if Henry supported the Gela-

sian conception, he made it clear that the pre-eminence and rule
of the Church existed *"in spiritualibus."* [40] While the Emperor's
phrases and images will win no laurels for originality, and may
even have been composed for him by attendant notaries, they
perhaps still offer hints as to the general framework within
which he viewed his new role, his rights and prerogatives.

The reactions to his coronation encyclicals could not have
made Henry VII happy.[41] Philip the Fair quickly responded to
his "dearest friend" the Emperor, but after a brief congratulatory
paragraph the tone of the French king's letter changed abruptly.
Philip expressly denied that the Emperor had any authority over
France, and declared that

> it is well known and generally proclaimed by all and every-
> where, that from the time of Christ onwards the Kingdom of
> France had only its own king, under the same Jesus Christ,
> King of Kings, and Lord of Lords, and Ruler of every crea-
> ture, recognizing or having no temporal superior, whoever
> was the reigning Emperor.[42]

Philip IV challenged the Emperor's right to have sent a copy of
his coronation encyclical to Lyon, and claimed that that city
(which he had seized only in the summer of 1310) was well
known always to have pertained to the Kingdom of France and
had never done homage to the Empire. The monarch who had
overcome the mighty Pope Boniface VIII was not about to see
his pretensions shaken by a Count of Luxemburg become Emperor.

If this French reaction displeased the Emperor, that of Clement V must have disturbed him even more. It appears that for
more than six months after the coronation of 29 June the Pontiff
did not officially address as "Emperor" the man whose journey
to Italy he had publicly sponsored.[43] Rather, ten days before the
coronation Clement had dispatched letters demanding a one-
year truce between Henry and Robert, and asking the Luxemburger to send proctors to the papal curia to place all questions
between the two monarchs in the Pope's hands for arbitration.
Clement sent specific orders to Rome forbidding Henry to invade Robert's Kingdom of Sicily, and demanding that he swear
a solemn oath not to do so. The Pope feared too that the Em-

peror might threaten the validity of the papal possession of Rome and commanded Henry to leave Rome on the very day of the coronation, prohibiting him from returning to Church lands.[44]

The Pope himself could not daunt Henry VII, so sure was the new Emperor of his own position. Robert was now one of his declared enemies, and although he did not intend to proceed immediately against the Angevin, the Emperor wished to make it clear that he was within his rights to plan such operations. During the first week of August he sent official protests to the Pope, and refused to swear the demanded oath not to invade the Regno.[45] He contested Clement's right to impose a truce between the Emperor and one of his vassals. Henry complained against the imposition of a truce without first consulting the interested parties, and protested that he was not even at war with Robert, despite the Angevin's having committed numerous acts of aggression and illegally occupied portions of imperial Italy.[46]

Henry also answered a serious assertion made by Pope Clement in his most recent correspondence. He boldly rejected the claim that the Emperor was bound to the Papacy by an oath of fealty and stated that neither he nor his predecessors had ever done such fealty.[47] Regardless of his urgent need for papal support in Italy, Henry did not hesitate to assert his position openly and to speak out once more in defense of the rights of the Empire.

The Emperor had determined upon a course of action. Immediately after his coronation he sent Simon Philip of Pistoia, now his chamberlain, with several other knights to Sicily. Less than a week later they concluded a series of pacts and treaties with Frederick of Trinacria.[48] Opposed by Robert and the Italian Guelfs, conspired against by Philip the Fair, and deserted by the Pope, the Emperor turned to the one military power willing and able to aid him.

Henry promised his daughter, Beatrice (subject of three years of negotiations with Robert of Anjou), to Frederick's son Peter. The two monarchs concluded a military alliance valid against all except the Pope and the Church.[49] Frederick became Admiral of the Empire, with command over all naval operations; and the cities of Venice, Genoa, and Pisa were notified of this commission and ordered to obey him.[50] The Aragonese, however, did not receive his new post at the Emperor's side as an outright gift. Frederick promised to pay Henry VII the sizeable sum of one hundred thousand florins and to contribute fifty thousand florins a year to the imperial treasury for the duration of hostilities in Italy.

The new admiral and imperial ally was informed of Robert's many crimes and told that the Emperor would shortly declare the King of Sicily guilty of lese majesty. For the present Frederick was to wage war on sea and land against Florence, Lucca, and Siena, rebels of the Empire "set aflame by the spirit of Satan" [51] whom Henry had already legally condemned.

The appointment of an admiral did not free the Emperor to dash northward and humble the Tuscan rebels. In Rome itself many details remained to be attended to. Not the least of these was the reception of a gift of money from the Eternal City large enough to provide pay for the imperial troops. On 21 July Henry sought relief from the pestilential Roman heat and moved his camp to the little town of Tivoli—a summer haven for the Roman nobility since the time of the Republic. There the Emperor complied with papal wishes and released the prisoners taken during the recent fighting,[52] and restored to the various cardinals the buildings and fortifications that he held in Rome. In practice the Emperor did not challenge papal claims to the Eternal City.

On 19 August the Emperor Henry VII once more returned to Rome, and on the following day he passed through its gates for the last time.[53] His objective was Tuscany, and the great struggle with Florence, the heart and nerve center of Italian Guelfism and rebellion.

THE EMPEROR DOES BATTLE

After his imperial coronation Henry of Luxemburg projected a decisive campaign against Florence and its Tuscan allies. But although this would require large quantities of men and money, Henry, as usual, lacked funds.[54] His difficulties were compounded by the inescapable need to distribute many gifts among northerners and Italians, prelates and laymen, to reward them for past assistance and—more important—to secure their future service. Germans given money fiefs did not ordinarily receive cash, but the right to collect tolls or other exactions from cities and castles north of the Alps. Nor did the Emperor conceal his poor financial situation. In a grant made only nine days after the coronation he plainly stated that a count was to receive one hundred and twenty-five silver marks in the form of toll rights in Switzerland, "because we do not have the money at hand." [55]

No desires for economizing could interfere with the necessity for rewarding certain important persons. The pro-imperial Nicolas of Prato, Cardinal Bishop of Ostia and Velletri, had done yeoman service since his arrival at Brescia a year before. In the grant of an annual fief of five hundred silver marks to Nicolas, Henry specifically recorded that this spontaneous gift was made in the hopes that the cardinal would continue to aid the Emperor, and "especially that he should promote the business of the Empire at the Apostolic See." [56]

Even generous rewards, however, could not prevent the loss of a sizeable portion of Henry's army after the imperial coronation. Many northern nobles had simply tired of the long and seemingly fruitless Italian campaigning. Their feudal obligations acquitted once Henry was crowned, they desired to return home as quickly as possible. The movement northward took on dangerous proportions during the expedition's stay in Tivoli (21 July–19 August), with the departure of Duke Rudolf of Bavaria, Counts Guy and Hugh of Vienne, and Rudolf of Nidau, and Frederick, Burgrave of Nuremberg. Louis of Savoy, nephew of Count Amadeus, returned home after having been burdened with the senatorship of Rome for two trying years. Some men could not even be tempted to stay by substantial cash offers. The Colonna, for example, refused to accept a fief of three thousand florins. Numerous soldiers left the imperial camp without permission, and Henry VII probably lost four hundred cavalry alone.[57]

The exodus of troops from Rome and vicinity was not one-sided, but the Italian Guelf partisans could return to the scene of battle with far greater facility than Henry's French, Germans, and Lowlanders. In fact, on hearing of the impending siege of Florence, huge numbers of cavalry and infantry poured into that city from Guelf communities in Tuscany, Umbria, and the Romagna. Bologna prepared to send "the entire militia and the whole people of the city," if it should prove necessary.[58]

The Emperor could not replace lost northern soldiery with reserves from Lombardy, for during the summer fighting in that region increased in intensity. The Captain General, Werner of Homburg, reported serious losses—in the west Casale and Valenza had fallen to Robert's seneschal in June. Bologna had set out to reduce Modena, the only remaining imperial stronghold in Emilia. Aided by Modenese exiles and some Guelfs still within Modena, Bologna scored an impressive victory at the battle of Baggiovara on 8 July—even the imperial vicar (and *de facto signore*) of Modena, Francesco della Mirandola, fell prisoner. Only assistance from Verona and Mantua checked the powerful Bolognese offensive on 27 July.[59]

This campaign had a sequel worth noting. The Modenese saw only one way of escaping sure destruction and sent messengers to offer the rule of their city to the Bonacolsi of Mantua. These "accepted benignly," and on 5 October Passerino Bonacolsi entered Modena and officially assumed its regime. Two days later he concluded a five-year truce between Modena and Reggio, a city in rebellion against the Empire. And all this took place as if the Empire and Henry VII were nonexistent. Only seven months later did the Modenese think to request formally that the Bonacolsi be given the vicarship of their city. A Lombard Ghibelline *signore* had expanded his domains. But the *signore* was also an imperial official, taking over an imperial city and dealing with enemies of the Empire. Dynastic and personal interests here had precedence over all others.[60]

Almost simultaneous with the Modenese campaign another significant drama unfolded in Vercelli.[61] When in July 1312 fighting broke out between the Ghibelline Tizzoni and the Guelf Avvocati, Philip of Savoy, vicar-general of Pavia, Novara, and Vercelli rapidly appeared on the scene. The Tizzoni called in Werner of Homburg, Captain General of Lombardy. A quarrel flared up between the two men, perhaps provoked by Count Werner. Both participants suffered slight injuries and retired, Philip to the houses of the Avvocati and Werner to those of the Tizzoni. The city's warring factions agreed to a new peace arbitration, largely through the intercession of Mary of Brabant, wife of Count Amadeus V of Savoy. This could not mask the fact, however, that a dangerous split had occurred in the leadership of the imperialists which gravely injured the Emperor's position in the north.

The imperial weakness did not escape the enemy's notice. Less than a fortnight later the rebel Count Philippone Langusco of Pavia seized Vercelli and, aided by the Avvocati, burned the quarters of the Tizzoni. Now Simone degli Avvocati di Colo-biano—the last of Henry VII's three Guelf *signori* councillors—renounced his imperial allegiance.

Asti and Pavia were already in enemy hands, and the loss of Vercelli was a serious setback for the Emperor. In September 1312 the three cities united even more closely, as both Pavia and Vercelli followed the example set by Asti and gave themselves to Robert's seneschal.[62]

Only Novara remained of the three cities entrusted by Henry of Luxemburg to Philip of Savoy, and that vicar-general became the object of grave accusations by his predominantly Ghibelline opponents. But although Philip had not been overly zealous in his custody, it was to his private interests that he not lose control over Pavia and Vercelli, which bordered on his own territories. Henry VII did not believe the charges of treason made against this Savoyard and initiated no proceedings against him. Yet the lack of harmony between the powerful Piedmontese and the German Captain General of Lombardy continued to damage the effectiveness of the embattled imperial forces in northern Italy.[63]

Important as these events were, Henry VII had little time to devote to Lombardy as he hastened to do battle with Florence, "the viper turned upon the entrails of its mother." At long last Dante's advice was to be heeded, but was the *alto Arrigo* in time?

The Emperor left Rome on 20 August and turned north toward Sutri, Viterbo, and Todi. In early September he reached the hostile Perugian *contado*, which his soldiers pillaged and burned.[64] After a two-day pause in Cortona, on 7 September the army reached the Ghibelline stronghold of Arezzo—the final stopping place and assembly point for the assault against Florence.

In Arezzo Henry attended to several matters that he wished to settle before the campaign. On 12 September an official citation was publicly promulgated against Robert of Anjou and affixed ceremoniously to the door of the city cathedral. The Angevin was informed of his crimes and given three months within which he could answer for them in person before the Emperor. This was the first step in the legal trial and punishment of a rebellious vassal. Henry VII was definitely going to ignore the papal command not to wage war against the Angevin.[65]

The imperial troops left Arezzo on 12 September and crossed into the Florentine *contado*. The siege began the following week. The Emperor was greatly outnumbered and only disposed of about two thousand cavalry, half Italian and half northern, and fifteen thousand infantry. Inside Florence there were four thousand cavalry and approximately sixty thousand foot soldiers.[66] So great was the disproportion that the besiegers could never encircle the city! In vain some of Henry's best Italian captains advised against even undertaking the siege.[67] But as Bishop Nicolas of Butrinto relates, Henry of Luxemburg often did as he pleased and did not always follow the advice of his counsellors when it ran counter to his own ideas.[68]

The actual siege of Florence lasted exactly six weeks. The imperial army ravaged the countryside, took many prisoners, and captured important forts—but it could not penetrate the city itself. At almost the outset of the campaign the Emperor fell ill with malaria, but thanks to his doctors he was nearly well when his soldiers withdrew from the walls of Florence.[69]

Although the unsuccessful siege ended 31 October, the imperial forces battled in the Florentine *contado* for another four months. Throughout the fighting the Emperor demonstrated a mercy and nobility that must have surprised those who had seen him before the walls of Brescia in 1311. In little more than two years in Italy he had lost his wife and a brother. It might have been reasonably expected that the disappointed and ailing monarch would vent all his wrath and vindictiveness upon the Florentines, the fountainhead of opposition. Yet the Emperor treated prisoners generously. Once he refused to use a large group of captured Florentine families as hostages against their city. He ignored the advice of many Tuscan Ghibellines and ordered the immediate release of the innocent noncombatants.[70]

On another occasion some fifty Catalan nobles, Florentine mercenaries, fell prisoner. Many advised Henry to punish them with death by hanging (as decreed in one of his own edicts) in order to discourage other Catalans from remaining in the rebel service. Henry VII would not hear of this, but heeded the pleas for mercy made by several prelates in his following and freed the prisoners at Christmas.[71]

An episode involving a wealthy young Florentine noble captured by imperial soldiers reveals that the Emperor combined a little political innocence with his mercy and nobility.[72] Numerous Florentine Ghibellines demanded the captive's life; however Henry not only spared the young man and his companions, but sent him into Florence with the request that he negotiate a peace. It is no great surprise that this diplomatic stroke came to nought.

The Emperor was not alone, nevertheless, in wanting to find a peaceful solution to this war with the Tuscan Guelfs. Attempts of its subjects and allies to deal with the enemy kept Florence quite busy. Siena lived up to the striking description given it by Dino Compagni and sent several monks to open secret peace negotiations with Henry VII. The Emperor would not countenance this. He declared that it would be beneath his honor not to contract openly, and so discarded a possibility for undermining the Florentine cause through a commune that had once been the greatest Ghibelline stronghold in Tuscany.[73]

Henry VII did achieve victories in battle. He captured a large part of the Florentine *contado* and installed his vicars in conquered communes and towns. Literally dozens of communities recognized his authority.[74] But these victories were ephemeral, and once Henry turned north nearly all the towns returned to Florentine control.[75]

More interesting than the fact that communities seized by the imperial forces swore allegiance to the Emperor are the forms of the oaths that they swore. These differ greatly from any taken previously to the northern monarch, even by his most enthusiastic followers. They are the insincere promises of men who have been taken by force and are willing and eager to swear to anything that may be demanded of them, or that they think will please their new master. The men of one town promised to ap-

pear "twice and more and as many times as might be necessary" before "the lord Emperor of the Christians." [76] Some promised "perpetual" allegiance.[77] Others swore to do "each and
every thing that will be imposed upon them." [78] The host of
splendid titles given Henry by these Florentine towns would
have been a tribute to him had they been meant sincerely. One
community acclaimed him as "the most serene and glorious
prince, lord Henry, King of the Romans and always most worthy
august Emperor." [79] So spoke men who were prepared to desert
Henry VII the day he left their district.

The Emperor's troubles during his months in Tuscany were
not limited to battling the enemy and surveying a host of newly
acquired towns that could be little trusted.[80] Even loyal cities,
such as Cortona, failed to support him.[81] Faithful Pisa, strained
to the limit, began to send him large numbers of untrained rustics instead of citizens as soldiers. Those peasants were soon far
in arrears in their pay and took the first opportunity to desert
the army and return home.[82]

The situation in Lombardy too offered the Emperor little
cheer. True, in November 1312 the Guelf Rossi of Parma joined
with Ghibellines and imperial troops against their old enemy
Ghiberto da Correggio, and retook Borgo San Donnino, midway
point on the Emilian Way between Parma and Piacenza. The
victorious soldiers, notes a chronicler, bore not only the imperial standards, but also those of Matteo Visconti.[83]

Padua too had experienced a thrill of fear when an ambitious
noble, Nicolo da Lozzo, secretly gave his *contado* fortresses to
Can Grande della Scala of Verona.[84]

These incidents could not erase the fact that in northern Italy,
as in Tuscany, imperial losses far outbalanced successes. In the
east the Guelfs gained strength when in December 1312 an internal revolution in Treviso re-established republican government and assured Henry VII's enemies of that city's support.[85]
In the west Robert's seneschal received Vercelli and Pavia in
September, and then joined forces with the Torriani, Guelf
exiles from Milan.[86] Fortunately for the Emperor, most of Robert's activity in imperial Italy was confined to receiving cities
and forts that had *already* rebelled from the Empire, and to aiding his Tuscan allies. Robert of Anjou was too busy preparing

to defend his own Kingdom of Sicily against the Emperor's expected attack to commit his own forces heavily in the north.[87]

In January 1313 Robert received new support and encouragement as the Pope included Ferrara within his jurisdiction as Rector of the Romagna.[88] Although the Pope may have acted largely in response to a local Ferrarese danger, Henry VII could hardly have failed to notice this sign of papal approval of a man who even now was under citation as a rebel of the Empire.

Whatever his wishes, the Emperor could not settle accounts at once with the King of Sicily. Four months of fighting in Tuscany had taken a terrible toll of men. Henry's cousin, Robert of Flanders, seriously wounded in Rome, had his fill early. He left the imperial camp in November 1312 despite the Emperor's refusal to release him. Other soldiers, Italians as well as northerners, followed suit throughout the winter.[89]

Henry's imperial coronation had brought him little of the increased prestige and power that he apparently had expected. Deserted by the Pope, conspired against by the King of France, openly opposed by the Italian Guelfs and Robert of Anjou, Henry had seen no great popular flocking to his standard after the coronation. In early March 1313 the Emperor gave up the futile campaign in the Florentine *contado* and marched north towards the haven of Pisa, there to gather strength for the next, and decisive, phase of his war against the Italian rebels. Henry VII would require all of his diplomacy, military skill, finances, health—and luck—for the coming test.

VI

The Final Crisis

On Saturday 10 March 1313 Henry of Luxemburg entered Pisa a second time. He had decided upon a simple and direct course of action. Thoughts of peace and tranquil rule over a grateful people were forgotten as an offended monarch prepared to subdue his rebellious subjects with naked force. The immediate target was Robert of Anjou. Imperial troops would advance directly to his principal base of power and conquer him in the Kingdom of Sicily.

This program was far simpler to formulate than to execute. Henry VII knew that the Pope completely opposed such action, and had menaced any invader of the Regno—including the Emperor—with excommunication.[1] Henry therefore dispatched an embassy to the papal curia late in July 1313, charged with solemnly protesting Clement V's actions in favor of Robert "who formerly called himself King of Sicily," and with presenting the imperial case in such a manner as to regain papal support. The Emperor explained that the Supreme Pontiff had been badly misinformed as to the issues at stake, and requested that he cancel the prohibition against the invasion of the Regno and act against "the ex-King of Sicily." Henry argued that Clement should depose Robert as Rector of the Romagna, and should order Provence to obey the Emperor. The Luxemburger even sought new papal favors in the form of the tithes and fruits of vacant churches, similar to those granted the kings of France and England.[2]

Henry VII was determined to carry out his plans even if papal opposition continued. He expressed himself concisely to the worried Bishop of Butrinto in tones that harked back to the righteous defiance of a Henry IV or a Barbarossa: "If God is with us neither the lord Pope nor the Church will destroy us, and God we have not offended." [3]

Robert of Anjou realized his danger and sought support wherever it was to be found. Reluctant though he was to come to grips with Henry VII, he strengthened his alliance with the Tuscan Guelf communes. In mid-February 1313 Robert at last accepted the captainship of the Guelf League, after three years of procrastination, and he agreed to send north as its war commander his brother Peter, Count of Eboli.[4] Yet even this did not mark a new aggressive stand, for as late as 19 June Florence complained that the promised commander and his soldiers had not arrived.[5] Robert held his army in reserve for the defense of his own kingdom.

While the imperial troops regained their strength in Pisa, Robert did solidify his bonds with the rebel Italian cities in another fashion: a host of communes and Guelf exile bands rushed to deliver themselves into the signory and protection of the Angevin ruler. In March Robert received Parma, Cremona, and the exiles of Lodi, Brescia, Bergamo, and Crema,[6] while Asti and Vercelli renewed their homage to his seneschal.[7] These acquisitions, combined with control over large portions of western Lombardy (including Pavia, Casale, and Valenza), gave Robert considerable power in northern Italy.[8]

The acceptance of new signories, however, did not signify that Robert's *personal* authority was greatly augmented in northern Italy. Particularly in the east where his seneschal could not penetrate, the Guelf rebels were left much to their own devices. The Angevin did not install one of his vassals or officials from the Regno as military commander in eastern Lombardy, but limited himself to naming Ghiberto da Correggio "Captain General of the City of Parma and of Cremona and of the whole

Guelf Party of Lombardy." [9] The opportunist *signore* seemed to have changed sides wisely.

North Italian Guelfs were not alone in seeking Angevin aid. In late April the Priory offered Robert the signory of Florence for five years, upon the condition that he not alienate any of the commune's castles, towns, or persons, nor grant amnesty to exiles. Prato, Pistoia, and many smaller Tuscan cities soon followed the Florentine example. [10]

Robert of Anjou had become the figurehead uniting all the powers in the peninsula that fought against the Luxemburg Emperor.

The Emperor did not wish to launch his great military campaign without first clarifying the legal situation of Robert and all others in Italy who contumaciously defied their lawful ruler. He called upon his jurists and notaries to study carefully the crimes against the Empire committed by each offender, and to legally process and sentence him. Three weeks before his arrival in Pisa Henry VII pronounced elaborate sentences against the Tuscan rebels. The first of these actions comprehended generally all clerics and other vassals who had been called before Henry's council and had failed to appear. These men were deprived of their imperial privileges, rights, and fiefs. [11]

A second sentence condemned four Tuscan communes not previously judged, five castles, and individuals from six cities, including Pisa. [12] The document cited by name more than five hundred inhabitants of Florence and almost one hundred men from the Florentine *contado*.

The condemned communities lost their imperial privileges and jurisdictions, autonomy, and rights of self-rule, were fined, and had their *contadi* confiscated by the imperial fisc. All this accorded with Henry's previous judgments against Italian rebels. But this sentence of 23 February 1313 contained several innovations. The Emperor commanded that citizens of the condemned places be captured and hanged and their goods confiscated by the fisc. Hitherto the death sentence had been reserved for special traitors, such as Ghiberto da Correggio, not applied indiscriminately to all citizens of a rebel city. The rebels' obstinacy appears to have decided the monarch upon more desperate measures.

Exemptions from this sentence, however, were more general than earlier ones (reserved to members of Henry's "family" and political exiles), and now included all persons exiled from the condemned communities for any reason whatsoever. The Emperor needed support from every quarter possible.

Of interest are several clauses relating to finances—an item close to the heart of the needy sovereign. In the sentence of December 1311 against Florence all debtors of Florentines were freed of their debts, and the captor of a Florentine could keep his prisoner's goods. The sentence of February 1313 stipulated instead that debtors of rebels became debtors of the imperial fisc, to pay it "without the clamor or formality of a legal judgment." The captor of a rebel could retain only one third of his prisoner's goods. While such measures were designed to help fill the imperial coffers, they may have removed some of the inducement for heroic enterprise among the faithful of the Empire.

The Emperor's financial need led him to enact another measure—one so desperate that even Italians who sided with him deplored it: he ordered that the most valuable and stable gold currency in western Europe, the florin, be imitated in imperial mints. Through this command for legalized counterfeiting Henry VII tacitly confessed the failure of the new coinage in which he had placed such hope a year and a half earlier.[13]

On 2 April 1313 the Emperor supplemented the sentences passed against various individuals and communities with proclamations intended to establish generally criteria for distinguishing and dealing with rebels of the Empire. These he published in two separate documents, each issued in both Latin and French. They received the appellation "the Pisan Constitutions," and became a permanent part of imperial law.[14]

In the first of these documents, the *Edict on the Crime of Lese Majesty*, Henry boldly applied to the Emperor the famous final definition of *Unam Sanctam*, and declared that human and divine precepts commanded that "every human spirit must be subject to the Roman prince."[15] Once again, as in the summer of 1312, Henry VII tacitly denied the validity of the Donation of Constantine. Summary inquisitions could be conducted against those suspected of lese majesty "without the clamor and formality of a legal judgment," continued the Constitution. If the accused failed to appear to answer the charges within a fixed time, he was to be sentenced, notwithstanding any laws or customs to the contrary.

The second document, the *Declaration Who Is a Rebel,* was issued, Henry explained in the introduction, because some subjects of the Empire in Lombardy and elsewhere had doubts about the matter. The Emperor decreed that all were to be considered rebels who openly or secretly committed any act of rebellion or machinated against the Emperor or his officials. All such persons were henceforth subject to imperial displeasure and the substantial fine of one thousand pounds of gold.

These general edicts did not substitute for individual sentences. We have scattered chronicle references to the condemnation of Pavia, Asti, Vercelli, Alba, Alessandria, Casale, and Valenza (all in the hands of Robert of Anjou), and the sentencing of the former royal counsellors Count Philippone Langusco of Pavia and Simone degli Avvocati di Colobiano of Vercelli, and others.[16] On 16 May 1313 Henry VII sentenced Padua to a punishment similar to that assigned the Tuscan rebels in February. Its citizens too were condemned to death by hanging, and its debtors became debtors of the imperial fisc. But no financial inducement was offered for the capture of Paduans. The only concession made Padua was the promise of amnesty for those who came to the Emperor within two months—for Henry needed soldiers and wanted to weaken his enemies militarily.[17]

These condemnations of Italian communes and individuals might appear merely the empty threats of an enraged and disappointed Emperor. The rebels continued to resist with arms as fiercely as ever. The sentences were ignored at the time of their publication. Had not Florence and Padua gone so far as to ban the Emperor himself from their territories?

In reality the rebels were not completely at ease. The practical need of winning and keeping allies forced the Guelfs to stand by the claim that they were fighting a just war and were not simply rebels against legitimate authority. But long after the death of Henry VII many educated men still believed that only the Emperor had the right of sovereignty or God-given rule in Lombardy and Tuscany. Even so-called Guelf cities and lords felt a need to exercise a legitimate rule and to hold their possessions by valid imperial privileges. This phenomenon passes beyond the limits of purely juridical interest when we consider that hardheaded business men willingly paid enormous sums of money for this legitimization. And the payments did not result from momentary whims. For many years communes condemned by Henry VII expressed the desire to procure the cancellation of their sentences. Thus in the mid-fourteenth century communes and lords alike gave the Emperor Charles IV huge sums in order to obtain the invalidation of the sentences levied against them by his grandfather, Henry VII. Florence alone paid one hundred thousand florins, and Padua too bought a cancellation of the sentence pronounced against it by the Emperor it had banned.[18]

Henry VII did not limit his sentences to entities almost universally acknowledged as within his jurisdiction. He was so thoroughly angered that he sought to process and condemn even the commune of Bologna and many inhabitants of the papal territory of the Romagna. He put the problem to Milanzo, an exiled Bolognese Ghibelline jurist. Milanzo presented the Emperor with a series of arguments intended to demonstrate that Bologna and the Romagna could be considered as not pertaining to the Church, but as being imperial, at least while Robert of Anjou administered them. Hence as they were actually comprehended among the Angevin's lands, they were already legally confiscated into the imperial fisc.[19] It is of relatively secondary interest that in his desire to satisfy his master and to see his enemies at home humbled, the Bolognese exile adopted certain arguments that he must have known to be specious. The fact is that this decision satisfied Henry VII. He ordered that Bologna and over five hundred of its specified citizens be cited to answer charges against them within a fixed time. If they failed to respond, they would be condemned as rebels of the Empire. On 8 May 1313 the citation was read and published in a Bolognese square. There is no known trace of a subsequent sentence, and possibly none was pronounced before the Emperor's death.

Although an imperial jurist had discovered arguments to sustain the contention that Bologna and the Romagna were not possessions of the Church, and hence could be punished, the Emperor had acted audaciously. He himself had sworn at Lausanne in 1310, and again after his imperial coronation, that those lands were Church property. In the winter of 1310–1311 Clement V had denied him permission even to cross Bolognese territory. How palatable would the Pontiff find the excuse that those territories did not really belong to the Holy See?

The Emperor seemed to give little heed to such considerations. Set on crushing all who opposed him, Henry VII threw caution to the winds.

On 26 April 1313 the Emperor condemned Robert of Anjou, who now obviously enjoyed papal protection and favor.[20] After recounting God's just judgment of the rebellious Satan, Henry VII declared Robert, *"perditionis alumpnus,"* guilty of lese majesty and a rebel of the Empire. All persons and communities were to sever their relations with him, and their obligations towards him were officially cancelled. His subjects had two months within which to leave him without incurring any penalties. All his lands and goods were confiscated by the imperial fisc—the sentence did not specifically mention, or except, the Kingdom of Sicily or the Angevin's Sicilian vassals. Robert, "who entitles himself King of Sicily," was condemned to death by decapitation. Such punishment, said the Emperor to the Bishop of Butrinto, should please the Pope.[21] This assertion recalls the brazen proclamations made many times in the past by Florence, which claimed to act for the good of the Church when it offended the imperial candidate openly sponsored by the Papacy.

The imperial condemnation of Robert drew a sharp response. Philip the Fair publicly championed his Angevin cousin and opposed the Emperor. In a letter that played upon the Pope's desire for a crusade, Philip requested that the endangered King of Sicily be placed under special papal protection. He strongly implied a threat against the Emperor, stating that "we cannot easily endure the disinheritance of the said King of Sicily, who draws his origin from our family and descends from our royal house." [22]

The menaced king himself broadcast a scornful rejection of

the imperial sentence. He denounced Henry as an enemy of the Church and of peace who had obtained the Empire fraudulently in order to ruin the true followers of the Church. Robert cried that he cared not at all for "the fatuous verbosity" of Henry's sentences, "the garrulity of an effeminate senescence," and challenged the Luxemburger's right to judge him.[23] The Angevin wisely emphasized the fact that he held his kingdom directly from the Papacy, for it was to his advantage to keep the Pope fearful of losing the Regno through an imperial invasion.

Henry and Robert appealed to European opinion for justification and support, and employed jurists, lawyers, and theologians in a war of polemic. The Emperor had perhaps first seriously considered his theoretical and legal rights and the foundations of his authority during the first week of August when he was confronted with papal claims severely challenging his freedom of action. After consultation with his jurists, Henry VII had strongly rejected Clement's attempt to impose a truce between him and Robert and to prohibit an attack on the Kingdom of Sicily, and he had denied the papal assertion that he had sworn an oath of fealty to the Pope.[24]

Three months later, on 14 November 1312, the Pavian jurist Johannes Branchazolus offered Henry VII an opinion "On the beginning and origin and power (*potencia*) of the Emperor and the Pope." [25] He allowed the Papacy authority only in the spiritual realm, and argued that both imperial and papal power were of divine origin—both admittedly unoriginal statements, but indicative of the atmosphere within which Henry VII thought and acted. Branchazolus asserted that an elected Emperor did not need to be crowned by the Pope, for "as he was crowned before the advent of Christ, so he is still crowned today, since Christ made no innovations concerning [imperial coronation]. . . . Those who have the power to elect have the right to crown . . . and coronation by the Pope adds nothing substantially to the Emperor's power." [26]

More interesting are the jurist's observations on the relationship between imperial and papal rule:

as the virtues of the soul [*anime*] follow the constitution [*complexiones*] of the body, and as the body dominates the soul, although . . . the soul be worthier than the body, so the Pope [*apostolicus*] follows the Emperor, albeit giving him perfection, so that he may potentially act and live, and the Emperor dominates the Pope, although he whose office it specifically is to govern souls and spiritual things [*spiritualia*] can be said to be worthier than the Emperor.[27]

Thus by relying largely upon the Aristotelian treatment of soul and body, the Pavian jurist arrived at a more extreme imperialist position that Henry VII had hitherto taken, and one which he must eschew if he were not to follow in the footsteps of the great Salian and Hohenstaufen emperors and to court openly papal wrath.

A treatise that appeared in the Sicilian court of Frederick of Trinacria did nothing to allay papal fears.[28] This treatise proffered the traditional arguments that the Emperor was superior to the Pope in all temporal matters, left the Pope supremacy only in the spiritual realm, and denied that an Emperor need be crowned by the Pope. But the Sicilian polemist applied his theories to many topical issues and carried his argument into new realms. He adduced imperial superiority in *temporalia* to prove that Clement V had no right to order a truce between Henry VII and Robert of Anjou, and thus the threatened papal excommunication had no serious foundation.[29] The tractate further stated that the oath sworn by the Emperor at his coronation to the Pope signified not vassalage, but Christian reverence and devotion.[30] The jurist challenged the papal ownership of Rome, *"caput imperii,"* which Henry VII had tacitly accepted in his protests of August 1312. The Sicilian denied the validity of the Donation of Constantine, noting that both Justinian and Charlemagne had claimed to rule the Romans.[31] He then combined extreme Ghibelline theory with a "nationalist" attack upon Robert of Anjou, enemy of Frederick of Trinacria:

The Kingdom of Sicily and especially the island of Sicily pertains to the Empire like other provinces . . . . for the whole world is the Emperor's [*totus enim mundus imperatoris est*] . . . . the Emperor is lord of the world [*imperator est dominus mundi*].[32]

Henry VII had carefully avoided any allusion to the ownership of Sicily in explaining his treatment of Robert to the Pope. The Sicilian treatise opened old wounds, and revived the spectre of the unification of Sicily with the Empire. And what pontiff could long tolerate an emperor who claimed to rule Sicily and threatened to place the Papal States in a mighty pincers?

One pro-imperial tractate probably appeared between the spring of 1312 and 14 March 1314: Dante's *Monarchy*. The author stated at the outset that he would resolve three questions concerning the "temporal Monarchy":

> whether it is necessary for the well-being of the world . . . . whether the Roman people by right assumed for itself the office of the Monarchy, and third, whether the authority of the Monarchy depends upon God immediately or upon some minister or vicar of God.[33]

One may agree with A. P. D'Entrèves that the *Monarchy* is primarily a work of political philosophy whose greatest novelty lies in "the notion of *humana civilitas* . . . used as the keystone in demonstrating the function and necessity of the universal Empire" (p. 47), and still recognize M. Maccarrone's demonstration that, in Book III at least, Dante supported the immediate God-given independence of imperial authority with arguments based upon both contemporary polemic of theologians and formulae of imperial jurists.

Certain documents from the chancellery of Henry VII may have influenced the *Monarchy*, as in the case of the imperial encyclical of 29 June 1312 which stressed the God-designed parallel between heavenly and earthly monarchy to glorify the peace and unity which the Emperor brought to man.[34] Passages in the *Monarchy* may have been directed against specific claims of the polemists who opposed Henry VII,[35] although it is often impossible to ascertain whether Dante was contending with the extant juristic and theological tractates, or with similar ones, and whether his arguments were initial attacks or rebuttals. Nevertheless, Dante, "the first anti-hierocratic theologian who directly and amply defends the Empire," [36] provided impassioned arguments for the defenders of the *alto Arrigo,* in whom the poet saw the one possibility for the realization of the goals of mankind on earth.

The very treatise which Dante dedicated to the defense of the Empire is significant in that it reveals secular patterns of thought that appear to jibe poorly with the universal medieval Empire captained by Henry of Luxemburg. In a recent study E. H. Kantorowicz suggests that

> In order to prove that his universal Monarch was free from papal jurisdiction, Dante had to build up a whole sector of the world which was independent not only of the pope, but also of the Church, and, virtually, even of the Christian religion—a world sector actualized in the symbol of the "terrestrial paradise," which . . . . had its own autonomous and independent functions in juxtaposition with the celestial paradise. . . .
>
> It was . . . the major premise of the whole scheme of the *Monarchy* that Dante, inspired by Aristotle, attributed to the human community a moral-ethical goal which was "goal in itself," was para-ecclesiastical, and therefore independent of a Church which had its own goal. . . .
>
> Dante's metaphysical surgery exceeded that of others who before him had separated the empire from the embrace of the Church . . . by appropriating, as it were, the intellect for the state and leaving the care of the soul to the Church. Dante did not turn *humanitas* against *Christianitas,* but thoroughly separated the one from the other; he took the "human" out of the Christian compound and isolated it as a value in its own right.[37]

Kantorowicz rightly notes that the duality of goals which Dante ascribed to the Pope and the Emperor did not necessarily imply a conflict of loyalties or an antithesis. Yet by so strongly emphasizing earthly goals and elevating them to an independent position, Dante seems to point the way to a new form of state and a new secular age that could better accommodate the nascent nation-state of Philip IV or the dynastic state of Robert of Anjou than the medieval Christian Empire of Henry VII.

Despite Dante's fervor and eloquence, pro-imperial polemic

battled a far weightier mass of juristic, theological, and philosophic opposition from supporters of both Anjou and Avignon. Angevin and papal partisans attacked the Emperor from many positions and on a host of specific issues, including the nature of the Emperor's coronation oath to the Pope, the papal authority to impose a truce between Henry and Robert and to demand an oath not to invade the Regno, and the papal right to withhold from Henry aid against the Tuscan rebels.

An unknown theologian absolutely rejected the principal thesis of Book III of the *Monarchy* and argued the extreme hierocratic claim that imperial power comes indirectly from God through papal mediation. The Pope or Vicar of Christ possesses *plenitudo potestatis* and is the judge of both spiritual and temporal affairs, only committing the execution of temporal power to the Emperor.[38] As Vicar and Shepherd of Christ the Pope must prevent transgression of divine precepts and hence can order the Emperor to swear not to invade the papal Kingdom of Sicily.[39] The hierocratic theologian directly challenged the Emperor's lawmaking power:

> if emperors or kings establish any laws, it is for the Vicar of Christ as a superior judge to approve or reject those laws; nor should they seem to bind the people unless they have been approved by the Vicar of Christ.[40]

Jurists too entered the lists, and used the Roman Law itself to assail the imperial position. A lawyer cited the *Digest* to argue that Henry VII could not pursue Robert into "foreign provinces," but must seek satisfaction from the ruler of those provinces, the Pope. He adopted the same source to prove that "the Roman Empire has boundaries and limits." The Constantinian Donation was cited against the *Digest* allegation, "*Roma communis est patria.*" [41] The same legal treatise defended the right of kings to secede from the Empire with the familiar Augustinian argument that since it had grown through violence and occupation, the Empire could be dissolved by the same cause. As to the Tuscan rebels, Henry VII had no right to expect that Clement V would excommunicate them and place their lands under interdict, as the Pope had first to hear them and judge the validity of the Emperor's charges. Hence papal rejection of the imperial request did not free Henry from his obligations and fealty to the Supreme Pontiff.[42]

Another legal tractate still further assailed imperial authority with the claim that the Emperor could not condemn *any* defendant of lese majesty.[43] The *Lex Julia* dealing with lese majesty comprehended acts directed against the *res publica,* which was stated to be the city of Rome. Since the emperors had lost Rome through the Constantinian Donation the Empire was no longer a *res publica.* Against those who claimed that the Emperor *ought* to rule the whole world, this treatise argued the mutability of all human institutions, the fact that the Empire rested upon violent acquisition, and the right of prescription. Henry VII's own actions were cited against him to prove that he recognized the papal jurisdiction over Rome.

Robert of Anjou himself sent the Pope two petitions. Although these drew upon arguments of anti-imperial jurists and theologians, they were political and pragmatic in approach. In the first, Robert attempted to enlist the Pontiff's sympathy by portraying his family as papal champions in Italy who were being attacked for their devotion to the Church.[44] Robert expatiated upon Hohenstaufen violence and Ghibelline rebellion against the Church in Italy. He claimed that after the Papacy called upon the Angevins as its protectors, Germans and Ghibellines conceived a mortal hatred against them. Robert then argued that his own relations with Henry of Luxemburg had always been correct, and cited his attempts to negotiate a marriage alliance as a proof of his friendly intentions. He defended the presence of his brother's troops in Rome with the explanation that they had come to honor the imperial coronation and to defend the Regno against an expected invasion by Robert's old enemies. Robert, quite sensibly, laid great stress upon the fact that the invasion of his kingdom by the Emperor would greatly harm and offend the Church. The Angevin staunchly defended Clement's right to bind Henry not to invade the Regno, and noted that the Pope could confirm an emperor in office, demand an oath of fealty from him, and administer the Empire when it was vacant. Robert then urged that Clement V nullify Henry's imperial coronation, since it had not been carried out in accordance with protocol.

Robert's second petition, composed after the death of Henry VII, is even more interesting reading.[45] The Angevin advised the Pope to be very cautious in approving future Kings of the Romans and emperors, considering the evils that they bring to Italy and the Church.[46] Robert supported his contention by offering examples of emperors who had harmed the Church— among them Nero, Domitian, Trajan, Frederick II, and Henry VII. The Angevin papal vassal, cousin of the King of France, then presented an instructive, if biased, description of the course generally followed by recent emperors.[47] The root of the evil, claimed Robert, is that an emperor "wants no consort in power." As soon as he is elected, a "King of Germany" turns against the King of France on the pretext that he has occupied imperial lands. He then comes to Italy where at once Ghibellines persuade him that he will not have his full *dominium* until he holds Sicily, as did Frederick. Thus it was with Henry VII, whom the Ghibellines fatuously told he was "lord of the world," and should "rule the Roman Church." With some truth perhaps, Robert complained that Frederick of Trinacria and his Sicilians had taught their ally Henry that he should rule all nations and that the Pope's power was strictly limited to *spiritualia*. Henry's election had ruined "all Italy," harmed Robert himself, Philip the Fair, and other princes. Robert lamented that

> the Kings of the Romans are accustomed commonly and generally to be elected from among men of the German tongue, which [language] usually produces a bitter and intractable people who adhere rather to barbaric ferocity than to the profession of Christianity . . . . Care must be taken . . . that Germanic ferocity does not produce strife among so many kings and nations and does not convert the sweetness of Italy into bitterness.[48]

The Angevin monarch climaxed his arguments by developing a theme suggested in Florentine correspondence during the fight for Rome: He requested the Pope to elect and confirm no future "King of Germany," and, particularly, to make certain that no imperial candidate ever again venture into Italy. The course of experience and polemic at last brought Robert of Anjou to demand the destruction of the Holy Roman Empire.[49]

The strife and polemic of course reached the papal court, where it had a profound effect. On 14 March 1314, six months after Henry's death, Clement V directly and openly established the papal position in public law. His bull *Romani principes* reviewed Henry VII's oaths and promises, and declared that the Emperor had sworn fealty to the Papacy and bound himself as a vassal of the Church. *Pastoralis cura,* issued the same day, justified Robert of Anjou and cancelled the imperial sentence against him in terms which announced papal adherence to a definitely hierocratic program. Clement revoked Henry's judgment

> as much from the superiority which there can be no doubt that we have over the Emperor, as from the power by which we succeed to an Emperor *vacante imperio,* and not less from that plenitude of power which Christ . . . conceded to us.[50]

THE EMPEROR PREPARES FOR WAR

While polemists exchanged piercing arguments and challenges, Henry VII prepared for mortal combat in the late winter of 1313. Pisa was his base of operations.[51] This Ghibelline commune burned for revenge against its enemy Florence, and strained every nerve in an effort to support the Emperor. Battling constantly with Lucca to the north, Pisa had still sent Henry many men and large amounts of matériel during the months of warfare in the Florentine *contado.* The city whose naval power had been crippled at Meloria in 1284 had supported Henry at Rome with a fleet of seven galleys—a fleet lost to Robert's admiral, the Genoese Guelf, Rainerio Grimaldi.[52] Expenditures for the Emperor had exhausted Pisan finances; [53] and still in December 1312 the commune had promised Henry VII the enormous gift of two hundred thousand florins,[54] of which one hundred twenty thousand were to be paid within three months. The import of these staggering sums becomes clearer when we recall that Pisa's total income during a single year in this period appears to have been less than two hundred forty thousand florins.[55] As early as June 1312 a competent observer had written, "The Pisans are placed under great debt because of the Emperor, and they seem to be stupefied." [56] A week and a half before Henry's second entry into the city that same observer reported, "The Pisans really are now in a worse state and condition than they have been for a long time, for the Emperor is eating them up daily." [57]

Henry VII tried to reorganize Pisan affairs so that the commune might better serve him during the coming war. He set new tax rates and terms of military service. Taxes ordinarily paid into the communal treasury were assumed completely and directly into the imperial coffers.[58] The Emperor called for more Pisan ships and soldiers, and offered exiles amnesty if they would fight for the Empire.[59] Throughout the spring and summer of 1313 Pisa bore the brunt of the campaign intended to clear the passes from northern Lombardy and Liguria.[60]

Pisa alone could not supply the force needed to conquer the Kingdom of Sicily. One of the Emperor's first thoughts was to create a fleet powerful enough to transport a large army and to crush the Angevin at sea. The imperial admiral, Frederick of Trinacria, would provide some of this sea power. Henry requested him to serve with a dozen ships in Sicilian waters for a month and a half, and to send at least a half dozen completely outfitted galleys to Pisa for three months' service under the command of a competent admiral.[61] In addition the Emperor sent an embassy to Genoa on 6 April, seeking the use of twenty-five galleys (to be ready by mid-May) at the commune's expense. If Genoa proved reluctant the embassy could accept as few as fifteen ships.[62]

This concession proved unnecessary, for the imperial vicar Uguccione della Faggiuola and Opizzino Spinola handled the matter astutely in Genoa. Opizzino guided the imperial proposal through a series of councils and commissions, making sure that the boards that considered it were composed of men favorable to the Empire. Climaxing this maneuvering with a public announcement of imperial privileges granted Genoa on 27 March, Opizzino achieved the desired results.[63]

Henry VII even requested Venice, which his own jurists recognized as "never having been subject to the Empire," [64] to contribute fifteen, or at least ten, armed galleys to the Emperor by mid-May.[65] Henry tried to tempt the Venetians into joining the

war. Milanzo, the exiled Ghibelline Bolognese jurist, suggested
that he offer Venice much of the Paduan *contado,* localities in
the Romagna, and a share of the money that it was thought to
be holding in safekeeping for Padua, Treviso, and other rebel
cities. Although Henry sent Milanzo and three other legates (two
of them prominent Guelf exiles) to Venice with these proposals
at the end of May,[66] the Venetians preferred to remain out of
the uncertain conflict that could drain their resources and place
their city and fleets in dire peril.

Troops as well as ships were needed to conquer Robert of
Anjou and his allies. Henry's failure even to encircle Florence
during the past fall had underlined his military inadequacy. In
December and January he sent letters and messengers to the
principal imperial vassals in Vienne, Burgundy, Provence, Germany, and the Lowlands, asking them to be in Pisa with decent
followings of soldiers by 1 May 1313. In early January Henry's
son, King John of Bohemia, held an imperial diet in Nuremberg and ordered all Germans to send the Emperor military aid
at once.

But not all men were ready or eager to leave their affairs and
dash south. Cities sent Henry VII letters embellished with
phrases expressing eternal love for the Empire, and communicated their deepest regret at their inability to dispatch aid at
this time. Imperial messengers found themselves forced to postpone the planned assembly in Pisa by twenty days—and still
reinforcements did not arrive in sufficient number. Sizeable contingents left for Italy only in mid-August.[67]

Henry VII sought reinforcement from all quarters. On the
very day that legates set out to seek ships from Genoa and
Venice, 6 April 1313, other embassies went to every important
city and lord in imperial Italy, requesting that sufficient numbers of troops be sent to Pisa by mid-May, the same time the
naval squadrons and German contingents were due. The Emperor demanded financial contributions from those communes
and vicars that had fallen behind in their payments to the treasury.[68] In Lombardy imperial ambassadors were to confer with
Count Werner of Homburg, Captain General, and Giovanni da
Castiglione, Proctor-General of the Fisc, and together determine

the quota that could justly be expected from each person and place assessed.

The Emperor called upon some of the most powerful men in Italy to appear personally in Pisa and participate in the coming campaigns in Tuscany and the Kingdom of Sicily.[69] If the situation in his sphere of operations did not deteriorate, Werner of Homburg himself was to come to Pisa. Henry VII specifically ordered that all Tuscan exiles from rebel communes who were dwelling in the north come to Pisa or pay the treasury large sums of money. If the Luxemburger had his way, the coming war in the south would be one of the greatest military campaigns ever conducted in Italy.[70]

The Emperor received a decidedly unenthusiastic response to this recruitment drive.[71] Brescia, surrounded by hostile exiles, and Modena, fighting off Bologna, Parma, Reggio, Cremona, and various Romagnols, sent lengthy apologies and protestations of loyalty and explained that they could furnish neither troops nor money. Matteo Visconti in Milan requested an outright cancellation of his annual debt to the treasury until the cessation of hostilities.[72] Only the Scaligers and Bonacolsi sent the Emperor a sizeable contingent of troops; but their detachment of two hundred cavalry and accompanying infantry was cut to pieces almost as soon as it arrived in the Lunigiana.[73] In mid-May 1313, more than two months after his arrival in Pisa, Henry VII still did not have enough soldiers to launch his great offensive.

Since the Emperor had not only to secure new troops, but to retain those already in service, he was constrained to grant gifts in larger number and of greater value than before. This process continued at an unabated pace through the spring and summer of 1313. According to the Bishop of Butrinto, almost all non-Italians except the Germans received sums varying from three hundred to two thousand florins, while many were also assigned castles. As the monarch did not hold as many castles in Italy as he had knights to reward, he frequently granted annual stipends to be paid by the imperial fisc until lands could be found. The recipients were required to do military service, beginning with the coming campaigns.[74] Italians received fiefs in the peninsula, although often with the reservation that they were to be held at the royal pleasure—a precaution meant to insure continued good conduct.[75] Almost all Germans, according to the same source, obtained fiefs and offices in Germany.[76]

Despite the strain upon the imperial resources, most new grants of the spring and summer of 1313 were larger than earlier ones, an indication of the Emperor's increased need. Thus Nicolas of Prato, Cardinal Bishop of Ostia and Velletri, who had received an annual fief of five hundred silver marks in August 1312, was granted over two thousand gold florins a year on 17 March 1313.[77] Count Werner of Homburg, Captain General in Lombardy, obtained a fief of three thousand florins on 16 May 1313, although he had received another of one thousand silver marks less than four months earlier.[78]

Soon increasing indebtedness and an inadequate income made Henry resort to dubious expedients.[79] He now granted in fief even communes and castles that he himself had rescued from the molestations of their more powerful neighbors and placed in the protection of the "chamber of the Empire." This spoilation of the imperial patrimony was not a measure adapted to retaining the loyalty and support of many small communities. If they could be given in fief to a lord and deprived of their customary liberties and autonomy, why aid the Emperor's war effort? [80]

Henry also tried to reward his followers with places which he did not possess, as they actually were in rebel hands. While he may have hoped that the recipients would attempt their recapture, this was probably not his motive in all cases. Non-Italians battling in Tuscany, for example, received enemy-held cities in northern Italy. Although Henry had tried a similar expedient in February 1312,[81] the granting of places held by the enemy became a general policy only in 1313. In February of that year Count Amadeus of Savoy received Asti and its *contado*,[82] and in May Alba was donated to the Marquis of Saluzzo,[83] and Lodi to the Marshal, Henry of Flanders.[84]

A measure which the Emperor adopted in May 1313 in order to weaken his enemies actually highlights his troubles. He offered complete amnesty and the opportunity to serve him upon very favorable terms to Robert's admiral, Conrad Spinola, and to certain other Genoese.[85] Henry subordinated any thoughts of absolute justice and right to an absolute concentration upon winning the coming war.

As if it were not difficult enough to procure sufficient men, money, and supplies, numerous other problems beset Henry VII. From every corner of imperial Italy he received petitions for added concessions of authority, territory, and money from men who capitalized upon his dire need for their support to increase their pretensions markedly.

The Marquis of Monferrat, for example, requested the vicar-ships of Tortona, Ivrea, Canavese, St. Vas, Casale, and Valenza. He received the support of his father-in-law, Opizzino Spinola, and of Richard Tizzone of Vercelli, and within a short time obtained at least four of the desired vicarships.[86]

Even Philip of Savoy, under grave suspicion because he had lost Pavia and Vercelli, did not hesitate to present the Emperor with a new group of demands.[87] He protested his innocence and asked Henry to help him procure money owed him for those vicarships, and to give him money promised earlier for his renunciation of the title to the Principate of Achaia. He further sought eight thousand florins for his services at the siege of Brescia in 1311 and elsewhere in Lombardy.

Matteo Visconti, vicar-general of Milan, made far more serious demands, which he often included in lengthy reports on the state of Milan, and of neighboring cities such as Pavia, Vercelli, Bergamo, Crema, and Tortona.[88] These same cities had been within the Milanese orbit when Guido della Torre ruled the city in 1310. Guelf or Ghibelline, *signore* or vicar, the metropolis enjoyed approximately the same sphere of influence.

Matteo's requests often aimed at diminishing his own dependence and that of Milan upon the Emperor, for while governing as imperial vicar he busily sought to re-establish his own authority and become the *signore* he had been before 1302.[89] Matteo repeatedly requested that Milan be given complete control of its entire *contado,* and that vicars in the *contado* be subject to the vicar of Milan, rather than answerable directly to the Emperor. He specifically asked that Milan once more dominate Monza and Treviglio, although Henry of Luxemburg himself had freed and exempted them from the Visconti's vicarial jurisdiction. Matteo

tried to gain even that portion of imperial income expressly
denied him in 1311, and asked that Milan have the right to keep
all captured rebel territories and goods. He insistently asked to
be excused from paying the twenty-five thousand florins a year
that he owed the imperial treasury in return for the imperial
income of Milan, and sought authority to readmit rebels to grace
—a source of income and a means for strengthening his personal
power.

Galeazzo, Matteo's oldest son, sent the Emperor his own requests. He particularly desired various *contado* lands of the late
rebel chief Guido della Torre in perpetual fief. Thus, while
technically remaining a part of imperial territory, they would
really increase the personal patrimony of the Visconti.[90]

If the Emperor granted these petitions he would renounce all
practical control over the most important city in northern Italy.
Despite his urgent deed for Visconti support, Henry refused them
until his death. Perhaps he realized that the Visconti would still
fight earnestly for the imperial cause in Lombardy because it was
to their interest to ruin the Guelf Torriani and their allies and
to expand the area of Milanese predominance.

In fact, though Henry VII did not satisfy his requests, Matteo
Visconti rapidly increased his power through his adherence to
the Empire. In March 1313 one of his closest friends became
vicar of Novara. This actually formed a steppingstone to Visconti
control, for in July Matteo's second son succeeded to that vicarship.[91]

The Visconti achieved a similar success in Piacenza.[92] On
21 April 1313 Baldwin of Trier paused in his journey north to
decree a peace pact between two warring imperial factions in
that city, a pact which named Galeazzo Visconti as sole vicar of
Piacenza. Unlike the peace pacts that his brother had concluded
for most Lombard communes during the winter of 1310–1311,
Baldwin's arbitation made specific provision for many matters
that could become the subject of dispute, and contained orders
concerning duties, rights, and salary of the vicar, the composition
of the communal councils, and the custody of forts and castles.
Real power over Piacenza was given to Matteo and Galeazzo
Visconti, who were to have complete authority to supervise the

arbitration and to make any changes they felt necessary in the Archbishop's absence.

The Visconti profited too from other peace arbitrations which Baldwin pronounced for the divided imperial parties of nearby Bobbio and Lodi.[93] Matteo was to supervise the Bobbio pact, and to hold various forts in Lodi in the Emperor's name, receiving twenty thousand silver marks as security for the good behavior of returning Lodi exiles.

Baldwin of Trier had not concerned himself with communal liberties and autonomy. His prime interest was to assure a stable regime and order in these imperial outposts. He reconciled quarrelling factions to prevent the cities from falling into enemy hands and to make them serviceable as military bases. To this end he called upon the strongest individual in the region, the imperial vicar of Milan, to watch over and control these trouble spots. That in so doing he helped Matteo Visconti gain a foothold in three more communities does not appear to have interested the Luxemburg prelate as he hastened north to procure aid for his brother, Henry VII.

Southeast of Milan, on the Ligurian coast, the Genoese sought to profit from the Emperor's military need. Genoa was dissatisfied with the general privilege that the monarch had belatedly and grudgingly granted it 27 March 1313.[94] That document was too limiting, with its annoying clause, "save every right of the Empire." Mention of the Emperor's twenty-year rule over Genoa too openly reminded the city of its subjection.

New petitions to Henry VII and his council represented an attempt to shake loose imperial control, regain a large measure of self-government and autonomy, and augment Genoa's authority in the Riviera.[95] It was requested that the vicar's salary be decreased and that he be bound to the Council of Ancients in many matters. The Genoese wished their Riviera to extend so far south as to include the Gulf of La Spezia. The city wanted complete control over the appointment of vicars for the Riviera, and criminal jurisdiction in that region. Genoa even sought the right to purchase or justly acquire in any way whatever lands or jurisdictions it could, regardless of feudal customs or privileges to the contrary. Within the city itself the Genoese requested that all cases—civil and criminal—be tried according to communal law, without any possibility of appeal. The city wanted authority to decide upon war or peace within its sphere of influence, and to grant and use reprisals at its own discretion.

Henry VII rejected these extraordinary demands whose concession would have made Genoa almost an independent power, somewhat like Venice. He probably assumed that Genoa would continue to assist him despite this refusal, much as it had during the year preceding the general privilege of 27 March.

Such were only a few of the most important of the many cities and individuals who petitioned the Emperor for new privileges and rights during the spring and summer of 1313.[96] To whom and to how many could Henry say no, and still receive the support necessary for the coming war?

Still another major problem demanded attention before the Emperor could begin his long-planned campaign: animosities and dissension rent his own camp. Some cities engaged in disputes with their neighbors, and groups of pro-imperial nobles fought among each other. If Henry VII was to receive effective aid from his Italian subjects, he had first to re-establish peace, internal order, and cohesion among them.

Examples of this lack of harmony abound, and we need select only a few of the more prominent ones for illustration. Already we have noted how the confusion in some cities near Milan led Baldwin of Trier to increase Visconti power in an effort to attain stability. Genoa too was divided against itself, torn by the jealousies of the Ghibelline factions of Doria and Spinola, as it had been for decades before Henry's arrival. Each wished to possess the majority of city offices, vicarships, and control over the Riviera. Despite the vicar-general's efforts to maintain order, murders were wantonly committed. In the Riviera bands of soldiers attached to the opposing factions fought each other in the names of various local vicars, who in turn were members or followers of the contending families. Local feuds aggravated the situation and kept the Riviera in violent disorder.[97] In vain Henry ordered that offices be equally divided among the Doria and the Spinola, and that local vicars be carefully supervised by the vicar of Genoa.[98] Men concentrated more upon winning battles at home than upon aiding the Emperor.

The lands east of Genoa and north of Tuscany presented much the same picture. The great troublemakers in Versilia, Garfagnana, and the Lunigiana were those warring nobles, the Marquises of Malaspina.[99] The very branch of the family that supported the imperial cause was divided, and several Malaspina demanded redress against kinsmen who had seized their lands. Imperial efforts to restore harmony met only with vociferous protests of innocence and attempts at evasion.[100] Meanwhile other Malaspina warred with Opizzino Spinola of Genoa and to the north carried on bitter disputes with Tortona.[101] The Malaspina had lost some of their interest in the great war to recover imperial rights in Italy and concentrated upon improving their dynastic position.

Not even Amadeus of Savoy, Henry's brother-in-law and one of his closest advisers, could devote himself completely to the Emperor's service, since another imperial vassal, Count John of Vienne, was assaulting his home territories. In June 1313 Amadeus requested permission to leave the imperial court and direct the defense of his own possessions. In order to avoid this loss, on 27 June the Emperor ordered John to cease hostilities against the Count of Savoy upon pain of losing all his imperial fiefs and privileges and having his vassals freed of their obligations to him.[102]

Another form of internal dissension menaced the Emperor at least as much as his Italian subjects' internecine quarrels: rumors and reports of corruption and high treason filtered into Pisa. Already Philip of Savoy was suspected of favoring the Guelfs and permitting, or even aiding, the rebellions of Vercelli and Pavia. Called to Pisa, ordered to bring his hostages from those rebel cities to Henry VII, commanded to turn over forts in the Asti *contado* to his uncle Amadeus, Philip did not help his case by ignoring the Emperor's instructions.[103]

The monarch received still other disturbing news from Genoa: many in that seaport community openly trafficked with the enemy, contrary to express imperial commands. Robert of Anjou, who had granted lavish gifts to divers Genoese as early as October 1312, had succeeded in sending large sums of money into the city to purchase the services of its citizens against their lord and Emperor. The Angevin's Genoese admiral openly flaunted imperial authority, visiting and remaining in the port with impunity.[104]

Alarming accounts of mismanagement, maladministration, extortion, and collusion with the enemy moved Henry VII to order a secret investigation of two of the most powerful officials in Italy, Count Werner of Homburg, Captain General in Lombardy, and Giovanni da Castiglione, Proctor of the Fisc in Lombardy. In Brescia, Modena, Verona, and Mantua more than two dozen witnesses testified before the legates assigned to this inquest during their two-month tour. The tenor of the evidence seems to show that the two officials were doing well in their main task of fighting rebels and protecting communities loyal to the Empire. At times they ignored or acted contrary to the desires of individual cities or groups of Ghibelline exiles. But this was relatively unimportant to Henry, as were bits of evidence indicating that in the past they (and especially Da Castiglione) had run roughshod over the traditions and even the rights of certain communes entrusted to their care.[105]

The Emperor was far more perturbed by rumors concerning the second most powerful imperial official and soldier in eastern Lombardy and Emilia. Passerino Bonacolsi, imperial vicar and actual Ghibelline *signore* of Mantua and Modena, was accused of treason—

> of conducting secret dealings and discussions with Ghiberto da Correggio, with those of Cremona, Parma, and Reggio, and with the Brescian exiles, traitors and rebels of the lord [Emperor] and of the Empire; of favoring, receiving, and nourishing them in the lands and places of the Empire that are under his regime, sending many of them victuals and other necessities, and in many other ways giving them aid, counsel, and favor.[106]

On 27 May 1313 Henry dispatched an embassy to investigate this situation. If Can Grande della Scala condemned Bonacolsi, he was to be removed immediately from his vicarships and Modena was to be restored to Francesco della Mirandola. One of the legates was to act as vicar of Mantua until a new one could be appointed. On the other hand, should Can Grande absolve Passerino, then the latter was to be assured that Henry

VII honored him and did not believe the stories circulating against him.[107]

Although the young Scaliger absolved his Mantuan ally and friend of many years, extant evidence indicates that Bonacolsi was not completely innocent of the charges levelled against him.[108] He had assumed the government of Modena and made peace treaties between that commune and the rebel city of Reggio without consulting the Emperor. He had concluded at least one truce between Reggio and his own city of Mantua. A Guelf chronicler even claims that he secretly favored the Guelfs in his own lands. It seems fair to say that Passerino made arrangements with the enemy that helped create periods of peace in the territories under his control in order to prevent war-weary populations from turning against his rule. Nonetheless he carried on the fight against rebels of the Empire in many places in order to prevent his own defeat and the loss of his lands—particularly those that the Emperor had given him recently, such as parts of the Cremonese *contado*.

Suspicions and evidences of corruption and dissension within the imperial ranks, the difficulty of gathering and paying for troops and ships, and constant fighting with large Angevin and Italian Guelf forces in northern Italy, all increased the difficulty of Henry VII's self-appointed mission of crushing and punishing first Robert of Anjou and then the Tuscan rebels.

THE DEATH OF AN EMPEROR

On 8 August 1313 Henry VII believed that his army was at last ready for the decisive campaign, and led it out of Pisa after a stay of almost four months.[109] According to Villani, he commanded twenty-five hundred northern cavalry and fifteen hundred mounted Italians. His first goal was Rome, and from there he would march directly to the Kingdom of Sicily. By 1 September the imperial fleet would complement this land action with a naval assault upon the Regno.[110]

Four days out of Pisa the army approached rebel Siena. Rumor had it that many Sienese planned to deliver the city treacherously to the Emperor. The Sienese Ghibelline banker Niccolo de' Buonsignori advised Henry that a civil conflict between the *popolo* and the nobility would soon tear the city asunder. But when the commune's Guelf government speedily stifled an attempted insurrection, Henry VII found himself facing locked gates and a city that could be taken only by a long siege.[111]

Whatever hopes or expectations the Emperor may have nourished remained unsatisfied. As in the siege camp before Florence, he fell ill with a high malarial fever. Physicians' desperate efforts did not prevent him from growing steadily weaker. On 22 August he was carried to the town of Buonconvento. There he died two days later.[112]

The imperial army returned to Pisa in mourning. On Sunday, 2 September 1313 the remains of Henry VII were laid to rest with great pomp and ceremony in a splendid stone sarcophagus in the cathedral.

The Emperor's northern followers lamented loudly when they learned of his death. Ghibelline and White Guelf exiles rent the air with their cries, as did cities that had counted greatly upon the Emperor for their future prosperity and supported him to the end. Among the saddest was Pisa. As the chronicler Sardo later explained, "Never was so great grieving and crying done by the Pisans as at that time, for they had spent two million florins—which they had never before done for anyone—and they remained in great trouble, without money or any aid." [113]

Italian Guelfs understandably reacted diversely. Florence published a joyous encyclical on 27 August, announcing the demise of "the tyrant, that most savage Henry, former Count of Luxemburg, whom the rebels and ancient persecutors of the . . . Mother Church, namely the Ghibellines, called King of the Romans and Emperor of Germany." [114] Even in death Florence denied the Luxemburger his due title.

When the news reached Parma, the elation and happy abandon surpassed anything seen in the lifetimes of its oldest inhabitants:

> At once wild rioting broke out, and in the evening fires were lit on every tower in the city and on top of every house and palace, on the Baptistry, the Cathedral Tower, and St. John's. At every gate, in every boulevard and street, fires of wood and

dried brush blazed until the light of dawn, and the bells did not cease pealing for joy. And such festivities lasted for eight days and more.[115]

Aftermath—and Conclusions

After the Emperor's death the forces that he had assembled with such great fatigue dispersed rapidly.[116] Tuscan Ghibelline and White Guelf exiles sought refuge in Pisa and Arezzo. Most of the non-Italian troops quickly set out for home.[117]

In northern Italy, although a few of the most divided and war-torn communes such as Cremona and Brescia made peace pacts with their exiles,[118] fighting continued between the pro-imperial cities and Ghibelline exiles and their enemies, the forces of Ghiberto da Correggio in the east and of Robert of Anjou's seneschal in the west.

The Visconti bore the major burden of the fighting for the Ghibellines in central Lombardy; and a lack of funds to pay for troops complicated their task.[119] Nevertheless Matteo Visconti consolidated his hold upon Milan, using the imperial vicarship as a legal basis for his authority. He stubbornly clung to this title until 1317, when he relinquished it upon the threat of papal excommunication. The vicarship served him not only at home, but in gathering allies for his struggles with neighboring Guelf communes and exile bands.[120]

Matteo Visconti and his son Galeazzo, imperial vicar of Piacenza, did not base their authority for government solely upon their vicarships. They tried to reinforce the validity of their rule with concessions of authority from their subjects as most north Italian *signori* had done before them. On 10 September 1313 Galeazzo was appointed *"dominus perpetuus"* of Piacenza.[121] When the General Council of Milan nominated Matteo Visconti *"dominus et rector generalis,"* having *"merum et mixtum imperium"* ten days later, it clearly stated that the action was taken because grave doubts had arisen as to the validity of his jurisdiction over Milan after the death of the Emperor who had made him vicar.[122]

Matteo soon gained two advantages that Henry VII had steadfastly refused him: control over the Milanese *contado* and direct access to the goods and lands of rebels. By the end of 1313 Milan again controlled Monza, a city freed and protected by Henry. In 1314 Matteo had already established a court to dispose of rebel lands.[123]

Outside of Milan, Visconti arms and diplomacy achieved remarkable successes. By the end of 1313 the Visconti controlled Piacenza, Lodi, Bobbio, and Novara—and they had gained their first foothold in each through imperial vicarships or supervisory rights. A year later their sphere of power included Como, Bergamo, and Tortona. In 1315 they captured Pavia and Cremona, while Alessandria submitted to them voluntarily in order to escape Angevin rule. During 1316 Parma and Vercelli joined the Visconti fold. All the satellite cities had Visconti vicars or podestas and were under Milanese tutelage.[124] A much more powerful Visconti overlordship had replaced the short-lived Torriani signory in Milan and hegemony in central Lombardy. And that overlordship owed its start, both militarily and legally, to Henry of Luxemburg.

East of Milan after the Emperor's death two Ghibelline *signori* and imperial vicars continued to war against allied Guelf forces led by Padua and Ghiberto da Correggio, Captain General in Lombardy for Robert of Anjou. Although the Scaliger and Bonacolsi already controlled Verona and Mantua when Henry of Luxemburg arrived in Italy, they clung tenaciously to the vicarships he had granted them.[125] The Bonacolsi owed him the legitimization of their rule over Modena, while the Scaligers were indebted to him for Vicenza—liberated by Henry after four decades of Paduan custody. The Scaligers also could thank the late Emperor for the opportunity he had given them to challenge the formerly undisputed hegemony of Padua. A war that began in 1312 for the possession of Vicenza expanded, and became a decisive struggle for rule of the Trevisan March.

Padua, on the other hand, intensified its Guelfism and its anti-imperial attitude after the death of Henry VII. On 1 November 1313 it branded all Ghibellines in the city and *contado* as traitors and adopted a new constitution. Henceforth Guelfs would rule alone in the proud republic.[126]

To the south, in Emilia and the bordering area of the Romagna, the Emperor's death brought no relief in the bitter warfare. Bologna, under the jurisdiction of Robert of Anjou, still fought Modena, and Guelf Parma and Reggio battled their old enemies.

When Henry VII suddenly died, it appeared that Florence and its allies would have no trouble in overcoming their dispersed and demoralized opponents and winning the lasting hegemony of Tuscany. But Pisa threw all of its energies and resources into the unequal conflict, and found a *signore* in the warrior Uguccione della Faggiuola, Henry VII's last vicar for Genoa. He hired one thousand Lowland cavalry, many of them remnants of the Luxemburger's army, and took the offensive. In the spring of 1314 he conquered Lucca. At Montecatini 29 August 1315 Uguccione, aided by troops of Matteo Visconti, the Bonacolsi, and the Bishop of Arezzo, inflicted upon Florence one of the greatest defeats that commune ever suffered. But even the death of two Angevin princes that day did not prevent the nominal *signore* of Florence, Robert of Anjou, from continuing political discussions and negotiations which led to the establishment of relative peace in Tuscany in the spring of 1317.[127]

The fact that military alliances formed under the impetus of Henry VII's expedition tended to continue did not mean the perpetual unity of the Guelf League. New situations produced changed political programs. In the 1330's, for example, men saw Guelf Florence allied with Ghibelline Visconti Milan against a son of Henry VII and a papal legate. And although some Guelfs might argue against the creation of future emperors, many quickly sought all possible advantages from the Empire. The very communes that had attacked the imperial vicarships when these were held by appointees of Henry VII later tried to gain those offices for themselves in order to reinforce their legal position.[128]

A casual observer might have marked Florence's reluctant ally and temporary *signore*, Robert of Anjou, as the great winner among the Italian opponents of the late Emperor. In the summer of 1313 he possessed the signory of numerous Lombard and Tuscan cities. These lordships were not based upon a real desire for Angevin rule, however, and had only been motivated by fear of conquest and loss of autonomy to a more dangerous power.

The Regno was too weak and disturbed to provide Robert with the soldiers and money necessary to consolidate and make effective his hold upon the many Italian communes he "possessed." With the exception of those in Piedmont, close to his county of Provence, most of his Italian signories ended within a few years. Even in Piedmont he lost ground to the forces arrayed against him—Amadeus V and Philip of Savoy, Manfred IV of Saluzzo, Theodore of Monferrat, and the Visconti.[129] Robert's hopes outreached his economic and military potential and, after certain fluctuations, he watched his power recede until it resembled its original limits.

That Robert's overextension was at its peak during the first year after the death of Henry VII was in large measure due to new grants of authority from Pope Clement V. In the fall of 1313 he appointed Robert Senator of Rome. On 14 March 1314, the very day he defended the Angevin and attacked the late Emperor in *Romani principes* and *Pastoralis cura,* the Supreme Pontiff exercised the claimed papal right to fill imperial offices in the absence of an emperor. He named Robert "Vicar of the Empire in the parts of Italy subject to the Empire," and commanded him to administer imperial Italy independently of his various papal offices, such as the rectorship of the Romagna and the kingship of Sicily.[130] Less than four years after he had solemnly sworn to Clement V that he would never accept office in any other papal possession or become King of the Romans or emperor, Robert of Anjou held two of the most important papal offices in Italy and was allegedly the nominal representative of the Holy Roman Empire in the peninsula.

The Pope's support of the Angevin, however, and the fortuitous death of Henry VII did not represent any real gain over the papal position at the time of the Luxemburger's election. True, Clement had prevented the union of Sicily with the Empire, which would have placed the states of the Church in the jaws of a great pincers. Yet despite Robert's guardianship, papal possessions in Italy were no more secure than they had been in 1310. Roman nobles once more engaged in fratricidal warfare, discord and rebellion racked the Romagna, and the remaining

Papal States seethed with the strife of many communes and lords. And did Clement take no risks in giving one man, Robert of Anjou, legal rule of an area closely resembling the modern state of Italy? While siding against the Empire, had not Clement lost in Henry VII one of the few men upon whom he could count for support in his differences with the overbearing Philip the Fair? Even the Pope ought not to have accounted the death of the Emperor Henry VII on 24 August 1313 an unmixed blessing.

Henry of Luxemburg's arrival in Italy had occasioned popular enthusiasm. To many his coming presaged a return of peace and tranquility to the strife-torn land. Although the northern monarch was unfamiliar with Italian political, economic, and social conditions, he rapidly developed a program of pacification and imperial reorganization. By dispensing impartial judgments and peace arbitrations, he sought to end discord. He quickly instituted a regime of city vicarships throughout Lombardy and replaced both communal magistrates and ruling *signori* with imperial rectors responsible for government and the maintenance of peace. Henry made a determined effort to discover and reclaim usurped imperial lands, rights, and jurisdictions—even when such action threatened the prosperity of the most flourishing cities in northern Italy.

Powerful cities did not wish to relinquish their local autonomy and their gains in the struggle for regional hegemony, however, and no community welcomed inquiries into the legal basis for control over its *contado*. Henry's attempts to reassert the rights and jurisdictions of the Holy Roman Empire met determined resistance. In Lombardy dominant *signori* who feared for their positions began the rebellion. In Tuscany, where city republics enjoyed considerable popular support and freedom from external control, Florence became the physical and ideological center for resistance against efforts to alter the existing situation to the detriment of ruling parties and cities. The Priory successfully revived Guelfism and made it the rallying point round which to gather allies in the fight against imperial pretensions. And as Henry sought to establish his rule securely, even cities which stood to gain much from his success chafed under imperial government and desired their lost political autonomy and economic freedom.

Henry's situation was complicated by the fact that he was not left alone to deal with his Italian subjects. The late medieval Empire was not matched directly against the city-state. The nascent kingdom of France entered the struggle, as Philip the Fair used his proven diplomatic skill to frustrate the Emperor's designs. The Capetian was aided by his Angevin cousin of Naples, intent upon maintaining, and if possible improving, the position of his dynasty in the Italian peninsula. Nor could the Emperor ignore the desires of the first Avignon Pope. Public papal support was essential for any successful *Romzug*. It was Henry's misfortune that the security of the Papal States was one of Clement V's major concerns, and that the Pontiff recognized the danger of opposing Philip IV.

In the early fourteenth century the Empire proved unable to overcome the combined interests of city-states, kingdoms, and a secularly oriented Papacy. Perhaps Henry's only realistic solution would have been to come to terms with Florence and its allies early in 1310, and to recognize the autonomy and practical independence of the Italian city-states. He might thus have avoided a mortal conflict. But Henry VII took his role seriously. His very attachment to a medieval Christian imperial tradition and to the cause of justice and peace prevented his considering this possible reconciliation between Empire and city-state.

From 1310 to 1313 Italy was the scene of a great tragedy as the monarch who had come to end partisan conflict and warfare became embroiled in it. Against his own will Henry VII assumed the role of Ghibelline party chief, intensified factionalism, and seemed to bring Europe to the brink of another cataclysmic struggle.

The failure of the Empire as a governing force in Italy did not mean that Henry's enemies had discovered a novel and more effective solution to the difficulties that plagued the peninsula. The Italian expedition rather accentuated and reinforced existing tendencies, crystallizing and giving them added strength and direction.

Henry VII aided the development of the signory by offering it apparent legitimacy in the form of imperial vicarships and by granting *signori* authority over new lands. Military and political exigencies of Henry's expedition encouraged the signory to spread from its favorite breedings grounds in northern Italy and the Romagna into Tuscany, heart and nerve center of the independent commune.

Henry's arrival forced the Italian cities and lords to work together in networks of supraregional alliances in order to defend or oppose his program. After the Emperor's death, Italian political problems continued as peninsula-wide issues. Interests and activities of one city could not remain localized or isolated. Men were gradually creating that *Staatensystem* which was to be so critical a factor in the following century.

The expedition of Henry VII definitively discredited the medieval imperial solution to Italy's problems. It marked the end of a major chapter in Italian political history—as the victory of the city-state, western kingdoms, and Avignon Papacy hastened the approaching Renaissance.

Abbreviations

ASI: Archivio Storico Italiano.

Bonaini, *Acta:* F. Bonaini, ed., *Acta Henrici VII.,* 2 vols. (Florence, 1877).

Butrinto: *Nicolai episcopi Botrontinensis Relatio de Itinere Italico Henrici VII Imperatoris ad Clementem V Papam,* in vol. III, Stephanus Baluzius, *Vitae Paparum Avenionensium,* ed. G. Mollat (Paris, 1921), 491-561.

Caggese, *Roberto:* R. Caggese, *Roberto d'Angiò e i suoi tempi,* 2 vols. (Florence, 1921-1930).

Cermenate: *Historia Iohannis de Cermenate notarii mediolanensis de situ ambrosiane urbis . . . ab initio at per tempora successive et gestis imp. Henrici VII,* ed. L. A. Ferrai (Fonti per la storia d'Italia, II; Rome, 1889).

Chron. Parmense: Chronicon Parmense, ed. G. Bonazzi, *RR.II.SS.,* n.s., IX, Pt. 9 (Città di Castello, 1902).

Davidsohn, *Geschichte:* R. Davidsohn, *Geschichte von Florenz,* 4 vols. (Berlin, 1896-1927).

Dino Compagni: *La Cronica di Dino Compagni,* ed. I. del Lungo, *RR.II.SS.,* n.s., IX, Pt. 2 (Città di Castello, 1916).

Dönniges, *Acta:* W. Dönniges, ed., *Acta Henrici VII,* 2 vols. (Berlin, 1839).

Ferreto: Ferreto de' Ferreti, *Historia rerum in Italia gestarum,* ed. C. Cipolla, 3 vols. (Fonti per la storia d'Italia, XLII-XLIII; Rome, 1908-1920).

MGH: Monumenta Germaniae Historica. When cited alone, this abbreviation indicates *MGH, Const.,* IV, 4, J. Schwalm, ed. (Hannover-Leipzig, 1906-1911).

Mommsen, *Ital. Analekten:* T. E. Mommsen, ed., *Italienische Analekten zur Reichsgeschichte des XIV. Jahrhunderts (1310-1378)* Schriften der *MGH,* XI; Stuttgart, 1952).

Mussato: *Albertini Mussati Historia Augusta,* ed. L. A. Muratori, *RR.II.SS.,* X (Milan, 1727).

RR.II.SS.: Rerum Italicarum Scriptores, ed. L. A. Muratori, 25 vols. in 28 (Milan, 1723-1751).

RR.II.SS., n.s.: *Rerum Italicarum Scriptores,* new edition, eds. V. Fiorini and
G. Carducci (1900—, Città di Castello, and later Bologna).

Schneider, *H. VII:* Friedrich Schneider, *Kaiser Heinrich VII.* (3 Hefte, continuously paged; Greiz-Leipzig, 1924-1928).

Ventura: *Memoriale Guilielmi Venturae civis astensis,* ed. C. Coelestinus,
in *Monumenta Historiae Patriae,* V (*Scriptores,* III) (Turin, 1848).

Villani: *Cronica di Giovanni Villani a miglior lezione ridotta,* 4 vols. (Florence [Magheri], 1823-1825).

Notes

NOTES: PROLOGUE. ITALY.

1. For a brief introduction to the ideological attacks made upon the Empire in the thirteenth and early fourteenth centuries, see W. Ullmann, "The Development of the Medieval Idea of Sovereignty," *English Historical Review*, LXIV (1949), 1ff.

2. *Regestum Clementis V Papae*, vol. IV (Rome, 1886), No. 4782, pp. 316ff. For similar papal-Angevin negotiations in 1263 and 1264, see S. Runciman, *The Sicilian Vespers* (Cambridge, 1958), 70, 78f.

3. See R. Caggese, *Roberto d'Angiò e i suoi tempi*, 2 vols. (Florence, 1921-1930); G. M. Monti, *La dominazione angoina in Piemonte* (Biblioteca della Società Storica Subalpina, CXVI; Turin, 1930); E. G. Léonard, *Les angevins de Naples* (Paris, 1954).

4. Butrinto (*Nicolai Episcopi Botrontinensis Relatio de Itinere Italico Henrici VII Imperatoris ad Clementem V Papam*, in vol. 3, Stephanus Baluzius, *Vitae Paparum Avenionensium*, ed. G. Mollat [Paris, 1921]), p. 503. For Venice see H. Kretschmayr, *Geschichte von Venedig*, 3 vols. (Gotha, 1905-1934); R. Cessi, *Storia della Repubblica di Venezia*, 2 vols. (Milan-Messina, 1944-46).

5. Extreme hierocrats would argue of course that the Emperor exercised his jurisdiction only as a delegate of papal authority, while the extreme imperialists held that the Emperor was the supreme temporal ruler in all lands, even in the so-called States of the Church.

6. It was only in the spring of 1310 that Venice reluctantly prepared to come to terms with Clement V, after warring bitterly against him for over two years for the possession of Ferrara. (See G. Soranzo, *La guerra fra Venezia e la S. Sede per Ferrara* [Padua, 1905].) For papal Italy under Clement V, see A. Eitel, *Der Kirchenstaat unter Klemens V.* (Abhandlungen zur mittleren und neueren Geschichte, I; Berlin-Leipzig, 1907); cf. G. Mollat, *Les papes d'Avignon (1305-1377)* (9th ed.; Paris,

1949); G. Ermini, *Stato e chiesa nella monarchia pontificia dei secoli XIII e XIV* (Bologna, 1932); E. Duprè Theseider, *Roma dal comune di popolo alla signoria pontificia (1252-1377)* (Storia di Roma, XI; Bologna, 1952).

7. On the Kingdom of Italy, see B. H. Sumner, "Dante and the *regnum italicum*," *Medium Aevum*, I (1932), 1ff. As there is no modern monograph devoted exclusively to imperial Italy in this period, the reader is referred to Valeri, N. *et al., Storia d'Italia*, I: *Il Medioevo* (Turin, 1959); L. Salvatorelli, *L'Italia comunale dal secolo XI alla metà del secolo XIV* (Milan, 1940); R. Caggese, *Dal concordato di Worms alla prigionia di Avignone (1122-1377)* (Turin, 1939); to older studies such as W. F. Butler, *The Lombard Communes* (London-New York, 1906); and to the works on individual Italian cities cited below.

8. For Guelfism in the early fourteenth century, see W. Bowsky, "Florence and Henry of Luxemburg, King of the Romans: The Rebirth of Guelfism," *Speculum*, XXXIII (1958), 177ff. Even the Guelf families and factions which had dominated Cremona and Padua for decades were interested primarily in maintaining their own positions and the advantages of their cities, rather than in dogmatically denyng the rights of the Empire or vindicating those of the Papacy. Cf. W. Bowsky, *op. cit.*, 180.

9. Cermenate (*Iohannis de Cermenate notarii mediolanensis de situ ambrosiane urbis . . . ab initio at per tempora successive et gestis imp. Henrici VII*, ed. L. A. Ferrai [Fonti per la storia d'Italia, II; Rome, 1889]), Ch. 16, p. 40.

10. See, e.g., G. Salvemini, *Magnati e popolani in Firenze dal 1280 al 1295* (Florence, 1899); R. Davidsohn, *Geschichte von Florenz*, 4 vols. (Berlin, 1896-1927), esp. III (1912), and *Forschungen zur Geschichte von Florenz*, 4 vols. (Berlin, 1896-1908); P. Villari, *The First Two Centuries of Florentine History*, trans. L. Villari (London, 1908; from 2nd Italian ed., Florence, 1905).

11. See N. Ottokar, *Il comune di Firenze alla fine del dugento* (Florence, 1926), pp. 48, 54f., 130, 149ff.

12. A large body of literature is devoted to the problem of the signory in thirteenth- to fifteenth-century Italy. Still useful is E. Salzer, *Ueber die Anfänge der Signorie in Oberitalien* (Berlin, 1900). See L. Simeoni, *Le Signorie*, 2 vols. (Storia politica d'Italia; Milan, 1950), with review by H. Baron, in *Historische Zeitschrift*, CLXXIV (1952), 31ff. See also L. Simeoni, "Signorie e principati," *Questioni di storia medioevale*, ed. E. Rota (Como-Milan, 1946), 413ff. A perceptive general study is G. B. Picotti, "Qualche osservazione sui caratterri delle signorie italiane," *Rivista Storica Italiana*, X (1926), 6ff. F. Ercole, *Dal comune al principato* (Florence, 1929), a series of essays done earlier in the century, must be used with caution despite its erudition and many flashes of insight.

13. For the presence of podestas in Lombard cities controlled by *signori* in the summer and fall of 1310, see *Monumenta Germaniae Historica, Const.*, IV, 4, ed. J. Schwalm (Hanover-Leipzig, 1906-1911) (*MGH*), No. 366, p. 314 (Milan); No. 372, p. 319 (Piacenza), No. 379, p. 320 (Cremona); Nos. 370, 371, pp. 317, 318 (Crema and Lodi); No. 379, p. 326 (Vercelli). See also G. B. Picotti, *I caminesi e la loro signoria in Treviso dal 1283 al 1312* (Livorno, 1905), 327 (Treviso); F. Bonaini,

ed., *Acta Henrici VII*, 2 vols. (Florence, 1877), I, No. 47, p. 60 (Verona); No. 77, p. 108 (Parma); W. Dönniges, ed. *Acta Henrici VII*, 2 vols. (Berlin, 1839), I, No. 7, p. 9 (Modena); No. 8, p. 10 (Mantua).

14. See G. de Vergottini, "Vicariato imperiale e signoria," *Studi di storia e diritto in onore di A. Solmi* (Milan, 1941), I, 43ff.

15. The entire problem of city-*contado* relations in thirteenth- and four-teenth-century Italy has not been sufficiently studied and merits further scholarly consideration. See E. Fiumi, "Sui rapporti economici tra città e contado nell' età comunale," *ASI*, an. 114 (1956), 18-68; G. De Vergottini, "Origini e sviluppo storico della comitatinanza," *Studi Senesi*, XLIII (1929), 347-481.

16. H. Finke, ed., *Acta Aragonensia*, 3 vols. (Berlin-Leipzig, 1908-1922) provides ample documentation of Aragonese activity in Italy.

17. For the early history of French expansion, see F. Kern, *Die Anfänge der französischen Ausdehnungspolitik* (Tübingen, 1910).

NOTES: CHAPTER I. PLANNING AN EXPEDITION

1. For Henry's family background and a general account of his rule of Luxemburg, see H. Brosien, "Heinrich VII. als Graf von Luxemburg," *Forschungen zur Deutschen Geschichte*, XV (1875), 475ff.; F. Schneider, *Kaiser Heinrich VII.* (*H. VII*), 5-10, 34-43, 342-350. Scholarly estimates place Henry's birth between 1269 and 1279, and Schneider settles upon 1274-75.

2. Henry III of Luxemburg was defeated and slain at the battle of Wor-ringen in 1288, which he had fought against John I of Brabant for the possession of Limburg. He was survived by his wife, Beatrice of Avesnes, his sons Henry, Walram, and Baldwin, and two daughters, one of whom became a nun, while the other married the Lord of Herstal and Montcornet in 1298. Henry IV also made peace with his father's other enemies, including the Counts of Chiny and Jülich.

3. For an exception, see F. Kern, ed., *Acta Imperii, Angliae et Franciae* (Tübingen, 1911), No. 92 (12 Nov. 1294), p. 66.

4. For Clement V, the papal curia and the election of 1308, see E. E. Stengel, *Avignon und Rhens* (Weimar, 1930), 1-35; F. Kern, *Die Anfänge*, 298-314; F. Kern, ed., *Acta Imperii*, Nos. 179, 180, p. 119.

5. Peter of Aspelt had studied in Bologna, Padua, and Paris, and held a high position in the court of Wenzel II, King of Bohemia and Poland. In 1297 Boniface VIII appointed him Bishop of Basel, and in 1306 Clement V promoted him to the Archbishopric of Mainz where he remained until his death in 1320. See J. Heidemann, *Peter von Aspelt als Kirchenfürst und Staatsmann* (Berlin, 1875).

6. See *MGH*, Nos. 237-238 (11, 12 May 1308), pp. 200ff. With Henry at Nivelles were the Duke of Brabant, and the Counts of Hainault, Namur, Jülich, and Looz.

7. *MGH*, No. 262, pp. 228f.; section quoted is on p. 229. For the promises Henry made before his election see *MGH*, Nos. 257-259, pp. 218ff.; Schneider, *H. VII*, pp. 22f.

8. See Figures 1, 2.

9. Albertino Mussato, *Historia Augusta*, ed. L. A. Muratori, *RR.II.SS.*, X (Milan, 1727) (Mussato), Bk. I, Rub. 13; *La Cronica di Dino Compagni*, ed. I. del Lungo, *RR.II.SS.*, n.s., IX, Pt. 2 (Città di

Castello, 1916), Bk. III, Ch. 23, p. 221. See also Henry's funeral monu-
ment, now in the Cathedral of Pisa, e.g., in G. Irmer, *Die Romfahrt
Kaiser Heinrich's VII. im Bildercyclus des Codex Balduini Trevirensis*
(Berlin, 1881), preceding p. 105.

10. L. von Ranke, *Weltgeschichte*, IV (Leipzig, 1896), 364; R. Davidsohn,
     Geschichte, III, 346. A minnesinger from Lorraine accompanied Henry
     to Italy, *MGH*, No. 929, p. 953. Henry personally ordered that the
     "Liber propositorum et expeditorum in consilio Henrici VII im-
     peratoris" be prepared "in lingua Guallica sive Romana pro com-
     moditatis ipsius domini, ut ipse facilius intelligere possit ea que coram
     eo et dicto consilio proposita fuerint et etiam expedita" (*MGH*, No.
     933, p. 969, 6 April 1313).

11. Giovanni Villani, *Cronica* (Florence [Magheri], 1823), Bk. IX, Ch. 1.
     The Guelf chronicler Ferreto de' Ferreti observed, "Nec quidem, ut
     aiunt, quispiam eo [Henrico] iustior clementiorve aut prudentia maior
     inter Germanorum ducum apices tunc inventus est, qui, si perfidiam
     Ytalorum inexpertus agnovisset, dolosque vitasset, merito labentes
     imperii partes depressosque tyrannide populos in salubrem stationis
     libertatem reformasset" (*Historia rerum in Italia gestarum*, ed. C.
     Cipolla, 3 vols. [Fonti per la storia d'Italia, XLII, XLIII], Rome, 1908-
     1920, I, 293).

12. *Iohannis Abbatis Victoriensis liber certarum historiarum* [John of
     Victring], ed. Fedor Schneider, 2 vols. (SSRG in usum scholarum, LV,
     LVI; Hannover-Leipzig, 1909-1910), II, p. 26 (Lib. IV, Rec. A, Ch. 11);
     Die Chronik Johanns von Winterthur, ed. F. Baethgen and C. Brun
     (SSRG, n.s., III; Berlin, 1924), 60, 65; *Cronica Aulae Regiae*, I, Ch. 113,
     in *Die Königsaaler Geschichtsquellen*, ed. J. Loserth (*Fontes Rerum
     Austriararum, SS.*, VIII; Vienna, 1875) 334f. Cf. Villani, Bk. IX, Ch. 1.

13. For grants to Baldwin of Trier, see *MGH*, Nos. 274-276 (17 Jan.-6 Feb.
     1309), pp. 239ff.; cf. *MGH*, Nos. 331-332 (28 Sept.-31 Dec. 1309), pp.
     286f. Henry's cousin John of Namur received the administration of
     the County of Cambrai, *MGH*, Nos. 290-292 (30 May-5 Nov. 1309),
     pp. 252ff.; cf. Nos. 337-340 (25 Nov. 1309-10 Sept. 1310), pp. 290ff.
     See also *MGH*, Nos. 270-272 (14 Jan.-8 June 1309), pp. 237f (conces-
     sions to the Archbishop of Mainz); No. 273 (14 Jan. 1309), pp. 238f.
     (a promise to the Counts Palatine of the Rhine, Dukes of Bavaria);
     Nos. 279-280 (7 Feb. 1309), pp. 242f. (grants to the Archbishop of
     Cologne; cf. Nos. 327-330, 26-28 Sept. 1309, pp. 284ff.).

14. *MGH*, Nos. 277-278 (30 Jan. 1309), pp. 241f. The Duke of Brabant
     and Henry's cousin John of Flanders led the embassy to Paris.

15. For the Diet of Spires see *MGH*, Nos. 309-326 (26 Aug.-10 Oct. 1309),
     pp. 273ff.

16. In the summer of 1309 Henry's embassy asked the Pope, "quatinus sibi
     [Henrico] inunctionem, consecracionem et coronam cicius quam po-
     teritis dignemini impertire" (*MGH*, No. 294, 26 July 1309, p. 257).

17. *MGH*, No. 466 (Nov. 1310), p. 411 lines 32f.

18. Cf. Davidsohn, *Geschichte*, III, 347; Schneider, *H. VII*, 55, 234.

19. See *MGH*, No. 306 (24 June 1309), p. 271 lines 12ff., a letter of recog-
     nition for Henry's three legates issued at Nuremberg and addressed to
     Mantua. The legates were: (1) Henry of Geldern, jurisprudent. He was
     later one of four royal proctors sent to conclude a treaty with Philip
     IV in the spring of 1310 (see *MGH*, No. 351, 26 April 1310, p. 298).
     (2) Henry of Beaufort, Dapifer of Luxemburg. Although called a

"familiar" of the Emperor in 1313, his name appears on only one other document in which he is named as one of three couriers sent to Germany for reinforcements (*MGH*, No. 907, 1 Jan. 1313, p. 920). (3) Henry of Ralvengo, citizen of Asti. For other citations of these legates see *MGH* (index), pp. 1480, col. 3, 1481, cols. 1, 2.

20. Rudolf of Habsburg sent a lengthy encyclical to Italy, 9 July 1275, announcing the arrival of the imperial archchancellor and others who would pave the way for his trip to Italy and collect subsidies for him (*MGH, Const.,* IV, 3. No. 85, pp. 73ff.). Rudolf's legates bore with them a standard form for an oath of fealty that was to be taken by his Italian subjects (*ibid.,* No. 86, 9 July 1275, pp. 77ff.). For Rudolf's other missions to Italy, see the citations in F. Ercole, *Dal comune al principato*, 136, n. 2. For Adolf of Nassau's encyclical, *MGH, Const.* IV, 3, No. 505, (21 March 1294) pp. 486f. On the same day Adolf named Matteo Visconti imperial vicar in Lombardy, and on 19 Feb. 1294 he confirmed all Milanese imperial privileges (J. F. Böhmer, ed., *Regesta Imperii, 1246-1313,* Stuttgart, 1844-57, No. 189, p. 173, No. 246, p. 179). Of Henry's three immediate predecessors, Rudolf had shown the greatest interest in Italian affairs and Albert the least, but all had either appointed or confirmed Italians and northerners to vicarships of diverse regions in Italy. See citations in Ercole, *op. cit.,* 137, n. 1.

21. See the documents concerning this embassy in *MGH*, Nos. 292f. (2 June-11 Aug. 1309), pp. 254-269.

22. The embassy to Avignon was led by Henry's brother-in-law, Count Amadeus V of Savoy, his cousin Count Guy of Flanders, John Dauphin Count of Vienne, Count John of Saarbrücken, Simon of Marville (jurisprudent, papal chaplain and treasurer of Metz Cathedral), Sigfried of Gelnhausen (Bishop of Chur), and Otto of Granson—Bishop of Basel and close friend of Amadeus V.

23. See *MGH*, No. 294 (26 July 1309), p. 257. Peter of Zittau, author of *Cron. Aulae Regiae,* states that almost from the time of his election Henry was convinced that it was his mission to recover the Holy Land as soon as he became Emperor (Bk. I, Ch. 114, *ed. cit.,* pp. 338f.). Against this, compare Henry's own statement to the Pope in the fall of 1310 that he planned a long stay in Germany as soon as he could settle Italian affairs (*MGH*, No. 466, p. 411, lines 24f.). The Emperor's early death makes an absolute judgment on this matter difficult.

24. *MGH*, No. 299, p. 264, esp. lines 15f. The encyclical even recalled (p. 264, lines 6ff.) the roles of *sacerdotium* and *imperium* as defined in that favorite imperialist text, Justinian's *Nov.,* VI, Praef. Cf. *MGH*, No. 298 (26 July 1309), p. 261, lines 28f., 38f. (Clement's letter to Henry). See M. Maccarone, "Il terzo Libro della '*Monarchia*,'" *Studi Danteschi,* XXXIII (1955), 21, 133.

25. For the material in this paragraph, see esp. C. Wenck, *Clemens V. und Henrich VII.* (Halle, 1882), 132-140, esp. 137, n. 1.

26. For the plan proposed by Nicolas III, and seriously considered from 1277 until the Sicilian Vespers (1282), see P. Fournier, *Le royaume d'Arles et de Vienne 1138-1378* (Paris, 1891), 231ff.; S. Runciman, *The Sicilian Vespers,* 184f.; J. F. Böhmer, ed., *Regesta Imperii* (Innsbruck, 1898), new ed., vol. VI, Pt. 1, ed. O. Redlich, No. 1156a, pp. 290f.

27. The plan of 1309 was first proposed not by Clement V himself, but by Cardinal Jacob Stefaneschi, called Gaetani. The son of a former Roman Senator, he was not related to Boniface VIII, who made him a

cardinal in 1296. Stefaneschi opposed the persecution of Boniface's memory, and favored good relations between the papal curia and the Empire. For the marriage alliance proposals of 1309, see C. Wenck, *Clemens V.*, 142ff.

28. See *MGH*, No. 514 (24 Dec. 1310), p. 473 lines 35f. This is a report to Philip IV from his embassy at the papal curia.

29. Cf. P. Fournier, *Le royaume d'Arles*, 235. For the encroachment on imperial lands and jurisdictions by Philip IV and his predecessors, see esp. F. Kern, *Die Anfänge der französischen Ausdehnungspolitik, passim*. Note particularly Philip's designs upon Lyon, climaxed by a successful attack upon the city in the summer of 1310. Henry of Luxemburg protested this action, but without positive results. Kern, *op. cit.*, 227ff., 259, 263ff.; F. Kern, ed., *Acta Imperii*, No. 193, s.d., p. 130.

30. The meeting at Spires in 1309 is ignored by most chroniclers, both northern and Italian. Mussato, Bk. I, Rub. 8, e.g., discusses only the second Council of Spires in 1310. Only Dino Compagni seems clearly to refer to the meeting of 1309 (Bk. III, Ch. 24, p. 223): "Nel primo consiglio fu [Arrigo] offeso da' Fiorentini, perchè a' preghi loro l'arcivescovo di Maganza lo consigliava che non passasse, e che li bastava esser re della Magna, mettendoli in gran dubbio e pericoli il passare in Italia." On the two diets at Spires see G. Sommerfeldt, *Die Romfahrt Kaiser Heinrichs VII. (1310-1313)*, Teil I. (all published) (diss.; Königsberg, 1888), 54ff.

31. Unfortunately Compagni's assertion that Peter of Aspelt gave his advice at the request of the Florentines is not confirmed elsewhere, and the Archbishop's background was such that he could have reached his conclusions independently.

32. John, son of Henry of Luxemburg, was betrothed to Elisabeth, an heiress to Bohemia. For details, see Schneider, *H. VII*, pp. 50ff.

33. *MGH*, No. 319, pp. 279ff.

34. See Bonaini, *Acta*, I, No. 180, pp. 279ff., No. 4 (20 Dec. 1309), p. 8.

35. On Henry of Ralvengo, cf. above, Ch. I, n. 19. For De' Guaschi, one of the legates sent by Henry to Mantua 1 September 1309 (*MGH*, No. 312, pp. 274f.), cf. Schneider, *H. VII*, p. 88 and A de Gerbaix de Sonnaz, *Amè V de Savoie et les savoyards à l'expedition de l'empereur Henri VII de Luxembourg à Rome, 1308-1313* (Thonon-les-Bains, 1903), 29.

36. Davidsohn, *Geschichte*, III, 416, n. 4.

37. Cf. *MGH*, Nos. 117, 200 and Davidsohn, *Geschichte*, III, 238, 296f. Davidsohn states (*ibid.*, 348, 414f.) that at approximately this time the Florentine banker Guido di Filippo dell'Antella was sent to Germany by the city's Ghibellines and White Guelfs, adding that he became a member of Henry's royal council in Italy and was present at the siege of Brescia in 1311. The evidence for these assertions, however, is rather incomplete. Guido does not appear in the indices of *MGH* or Bonaini, *Acta*, and there is no indication of a journey north or service with Henry in Italy in the "*Ricordi*" of Guido's life, pub. in *ASI*, ser. I, vol. IV, pt. I (1843), pp. 3ff. This author has been unable to see the Ghibelline Register of 1377 cited by Davidsohn, pub. in *Giotto. Bollettino storico, letterario, artistico del Mugello* (Borgo San Lorenzo, 1902, 1903). It is not clear from the extant evidence whether the exiled

Pistoian knight, Simon Philip de Realibus, a *spenditore* in Henry's embassy to Tuscany during the summer of 1310, was appointed by the Emperor-elect before the embassy set out from Germany, or was added to the embassy during its travels in Italy. See Davidsohn, *Geschichte*, III, 380f.; Villani, Bk. VIII, Ch. 120; cf. *Cronaca Pisana di Ranieri Sardo dal anno 962 sino al 1400*, ed. F. Bonaini, *ASI*, ser. I, vol. IV. pt. 2 (1845), p. 93, and *MGH*, Nos. 715 (p. 698), 716 (p. 701).

38. Clement granted the Romans permission to choose their own chief magistrate on 14 March 1310, *Regestum Clementis Papae V* (Rome, 1887), V, No. 6280, pp. 390f. Duprè Theseider *(Roma dal comune di popolo*, 398f.) is probably correct in his conjecture that Louis' election was more a solution of convenience in the light of the coming imperial coronation than a sign that Ghibellinism prevailed in Rome. The Senator selected as one of his judges Dante's friend, the famous jurist Cino da Pistoia.

39. *MGH*, Nos. 362, 363, 364, pp. 309f., 311, 312.

40. The principal sources for this embassy are published in *MGH*, No. 361 (10 May 1310), pp. 308f., the legates' letters of credentials; Nos. 362-378 (26 May-4 Aug. 1310), pp. 309-325, responses given the embassy by Ivrea, Casale, Valenza, Tortona, Milan, Vigevano, Novara, Monza, Crema, Lodi, Piacenza, Cremona, Brescia, Borgo S. Donnino, the Patriarch of Aquileja, special proposals for Venice, and responses of the Venetian Doge. No. 379 (post 4 August 1310), pp. 325-331, is a summary in French of the embassy's report to the King. It contains information about cities and persons not included in the preceding group of surviving official documents, together with details concerning the treatment received by the legates in their travels. Useful chronicle sources for the embassy are Cermenate, Chs. X-XV, pp. 20-25; Ferreto, I, pp. 277-281; *Chronicon Parmense*, ed. G. Bonazzi, *RR.II.SS.*, n.s., IX, Pt. 9 (Città di Castello, 1902), 117; Bonifazio da Morano, *Chronicon Mutinense*, ed. L. A. Muratori, *RR.II.SS.*, XI (Milan, 1727), col. 96. See Bonincontro Morigia, *Bonincontri Morigiae Chronicon Modoetiense*, ed. L. A. Muratori, *RR.II.SS.*, X (Milan, 1727), cols. 1095f. as a supplement to Cermenate. (For the value of *Chron. Modoet.*, see W. Dönniges, *Geschichte der deutschen Kaisertums im vierzehnten Jahrhundert*, I: *Kritik der Quellen für die Geschichte Heinrichs des VII des Luxemburgers* [Berlin, 1841], 100f.)

41. Ferreto, I, 279.

42. See, e.g., below, Ch. I, nn. 59, 61ff., 76, 78-81, 84, 101, 107f., Ch. II, nn. 95ff. ("liberty"). Cf. the encomium of Henry in Dino Compagni, Bk. III, Ch. 24.

43. *MGH*, No. 379, p. 331.

44. The embassy addressed Venice as almost a sovereign power, cf. *MGH*, No. 376, pp. 323f. The nearby Patriarch of Aquileja also paid the legates' expenses, and he recognized Henry as his lord "in temporal things."

45. *MGH*, No. 379, p. 327.

46. Cf. *MGH*, Nos. 540-541 (6 March-2 April 1310), pp. 495, 496; W. Dönniges, *Acta*, II, No. 11 (10 Jan. 1311), p. 130. For the Langusco political tradition, see G. Bascapè, "I conti palatini del regno italico e la città di Pavia dal comune alla signoria," *Archivio Storico Lombardo*, ser. 7, LXII (1935) (printed 1936), pt. 2, 281ff., 330f., 346, 350, 362f.

For Philippone's attitude during the summer of 1310, see Cermenate, Chs. XII, XIV-XV, pp. 22f., 25; Ferreto, I, 278, 280. The Beccaria, the leading Ghibellines of Pavia, had originally been Guelfs, probably of bourgeois origin, and tried to pose as the champions of threatened communal autonomy.

47. For the embassy in Piacenza, see *MGH*, No. 372, p. 319, No. 379, p. 328.

48. *MGH*, No. 379, p. 330; *Chron. Parmense*, 117. For Ghiberto see esp. M. Melchiorri, "Vicende della signoria di Ghiberto da Correggio in Parma," *Archivio Storico per le Provincie Parmensi*, n.s., VI (1906 [1907]), 1-201 (159ff.: 43 docs.).

49. *MGH*, No. 379, p. 329. For Da Camino and the Visconti, see G. B. Picotti, *I caminesi e la loro signoria in Treviso dal 1283 al 1312* (Livorno, 1905), 196, 337.

50. *MGH*, No. 379, p. 330.

51. Alberto di Bezano, *Alberti de Bezanis abbatis S. Laurentii Cremonensis cronica pontifica et imperatorum*, ed. O. Holder-Egger (SSRG in usum scholarum, LII; Hannover-Leipzig, 1908), 73. Cortusiis does not agree with Alberto that the Paduans feared Henry's advent, *Guillelmi de Cortusiis Chronica de Novitatibus Padue et Lombardie*, ed. B. Pagnin, *RR.II.SS.*, n.s., XII, Pt. 5 (Bologna, s.d. [*c.* 1941]), p. 12.

52. *MGH*, No. 379, p. 329; Ferreto, I, 279.

53. *MGH*, Nos. 367, 379, pp. 315, 327. Vigevano gave the legates gifts. For Vigevano's relation to the Empire, see P. Darmstädter, *Das Reichsgut in der Lombardei und Piemont (528 bis 1250)* (Strassburg, 1895), 195.

54. *MGH*, No. 369, pp. 316f. For Monza's relation to the Empire, see P. Darmstädter, *Das Reichsgut*, 179. For Monza's claim to being a coronation site, see B. H. Sumner, "Dante and the *regnum italicum*," *Medium Aevum*, I (1932), 21f.; R. Elze, "Die 'Eiserne Krone' in Monza," Ch. 19 of P. E. Schramm, *Herrschaftszeichen und Staatssymbolik* (Schriften der *MGH*, X, Pt. 2; Stuttgart, 1955), II, 450ff.; K. Haase, *Die Königskrönungen in Oberitalien und die eiserne Krone* (Strassburg, 1901).

55. Unfortunately reports do not indicate that the embassy visited Treviglio, subject to Milan despite its right to enjoy only direct imperial jurisdiction; cf. P. Darmstädter, *Das Reichsgut*, 72; and the pact of 7 March 1309 between Treviglio and Guido della Torre, publ. by G. Barelli in *ASI*, ser. 5, XXX (1902), 46ff. Borgo S. Donnino, on the Emilian Way between Piacenza and Parma, harassed by both and by Cremona, also told the embassy that it pertained to the *camera imperii* (*MGH*, No. 379, p. 330). The legates had their expenses paid by two other cities: Bergamo, whose rival factions at the moment lived together in uneasy peace, and Brescia, ruled by the nominally Ghibelline Maggi who constantly feared antagonizing the Della Torre and being expelled from their position. For Bergamo: *MGH*, No. 379, p. 328; cf. Ferreto, I, 275, and B. Belotti, *Storia di Bergamo e dei Bergamaschi* (Milan, 1940), I, 408f. For Brescia, *MGH*, Nos. 374, 379, pp. 320f., 328f. For the Maggi political allegiance, cf. R. Davidsohn, *Forschungen*, IV, pp. 539 (5 Oct. 1271), 540 (2 Jan. 1281), 541 (9 May 1295), 553 (23 Oct. 1294).

56. For events in Milan, *MGH*, Nos. 366, 379, pp. 313ff., 327; cf. Cermenate, Chs. X-XII, pp. 20ff.

57. *MGH*, Nos. 368, 379, pp. 315f., 327f.

58. *MGH*, No. 371, p. 318, lines 33ff.

59. See Cermenate, Chs. XII-XV, pp. 22ff.; Ferreto, I, 278ff.

60. Ferreto, I, 281.
61. See *MGH*, No. 438, p. 383, lines 27ff.; No. 441, p. 387, lines 27ff.
62. *MGH*, No. 366 (22 June 1310), p. 314.
63. These two communes were Crema and Como. See *MGH*, Nos. 370, 379, pp. 317f., 328.
64. See *MGH*, Nos. 374, 379, pp. 320f., 328f. (Brescia); cf. No. 379, p. 329 (Treviso).
65. *MGH*, No. 373, p. 320. For Cremona and the Cavalcabò, see U. Gualaz-zini, *Il "populus" di Cremona e l'autonomia del comune* (Biblioteca della Rivista di Storia del Diritto Italiano, XIV; Bologna, 1940); A. Cavalcabò, *Le ultime lotte del comune di Cremona per l'autonomia* (Cremona, 1937), a work to be used with caution as its scholarly technique is at times questionable—see the review by E. Duprè Theseider, *Rivista Storica Italiana*, ser. 5, IV (1939), 441ff.
66. Only the Bishop of Vercelli displayed a positively hostile attitude towards the embassy, and refused to answer certain questions. *MGH*, No. 379, p. 326; cf. G. C. Bascapè, "I conti palatini del regno italico," (cited above, Ch. I, n. 46), 354, n. 5.
67. *MGH*, No. 359, pp. 306f. Tizzone offered to meet Henry in Ivrea or Susa with 100 knights, and promised that as soon as he and his followers were restored to Vercelli he would see to it that the city served the imperial expedition and obeyed Henry's every wish.
68. Our knowledge of the embassy's stay in Asti is based upon the chronicle of Guilielmus Ventura, a possible eyewitness, *Memoriale Guilielmi Venturae civis astensis*, ed. C. Coelestinus, *Monumenta Historiae Patriae*, V *(Scriptores, III)* (Turin, 1848), col. 771. Ventura places the embassy in Asti in the period of Robert of Anjou's stay in Alba, but before the conclusion of his pact with Asti, which would be post 11 July—in 28 July. (See Caggese, *Roberto*, I, 115; G. M. Monti, *La dominazione angoina*, 120, 121.) Ventura's chronology is contradicted by stronger evidence that the embassy was in Pisa during the latter part of June, and arrived at Florence on 3 July.
69. Although Asti concluded a treaty with Robert on 28 July 1310, this was a military alliance and not an act of homage. For the text of that treaty see G. M. Monti, *La dominazione angoina*, 351-357. See also below, Ch. I, n. 116, Ch. II, nn. 33ff. Robert only succeeded in becoming lord of Asti (with limitations upon his rule) in the spring of 1312 because the city was on the verge of falling to hated enemies.
70. For the embassy in Pisa, see Davidsohn, *Geschichte*, III, 383; cf. *Cronaca Pisana di Ranieri Sardo, ASI*, ser. I, vol. VI, pt. 2 (1845), Ch. 51, p. 93. For Pisa in this period see D. Herlihy, *Pisa in the Early Renaissance* (New Haven, 1958), G. Volpe, "Pisa, Firenze, Impero al principio del 1300 e gli inizi della signoria civile a Pisa," *Studi Storici*, XI (1902), 177-203, 293-337.
71. Giovanni was the son of Cerchio de' Cerchi, first leader of the White Guelfs in Florence, and had been sentenced to death by his native city. Davidsohn, *Geschichte*, III, 383, 414.
72. *MGH*, No. 1273 (30 June 1310), pp. 1407f.
73. See above, Ch. I, nn. 30f.
74. The best single collection of sources on the formation and early meetings of the league during the spring and summer of 1310 is T. E. Mommsen, ed., *Italienische Analekten zur Reichsgeschichte des XIV.*

Jahrhunderts (1310-1378) (Schriften der MGH, XI; Stuttgart, 1952),
Nos. 1-6, pp. 21-24, Nos. 9-10, p. 25; the treaty of mid-March is sum-
marized in No. 1, pp. 21f. See also Caggese, *Roberto*, I, 117; Davidsohn,
Geschichte, III, 383; G. Fasoli, "Bologna e la Romagna durante la
spedizione di Enrico VII," *R. Deputazione di Storia Patria per l'Emilia
e la Romagna, Atti e Memorie*, IV (1938-1939), 18f.; V. Vitale, *Il
dominio della parte guelfa in Bologna (1280-1327)* (Bologna, 1901),
124ff.

75. See C. Wenck, *Clemens V.*, 133ff.
76. Mommsen, *Ital. Analekten*, No. 6 (26 June 1310), p. 24. For the decision
    to deliver a common response to Henry's legates, cf. Davidsohn,
    Forschungen, II (Berlin, 1900), p. 273, No. 2110 (23 July 1310), stating
    that it had been agreed at Bologna to hold a conference for preparing
    such an answer. On 24 July the Defense Council of Volterra submitted
    to the commune's General Council consideration of a Florentine request
    that Volterra choose representatives to attend a meeting of the Tuscan
    league (1 August) to decide upon a common answer to the "magnifico
    domino regi Romanorum." Mommsen, *Ital. Analekten*, No. 10, p. 25.
77. Mommsen, *Ital. Analekten*, No. 7 (10-11 July, 1310), p. 24 (Prato);
    No. 9 (14 July 1310), p. 25 (Volterra); Dino Compagni, Bk. III, Ch. 34,
    p. 252 (Prato); Davidsohn, *Geschichte*, III, 384 (Siena, Volterra, Prato,
    Lucca, Florence).
78. Villani, Bk. VIII, Rub. 120.
79. Dino Compagni, Bk. III, Ch. 35, p. 255.
80. *Ibid.*, Bk. III, Ch. 34, p. 252.
81. Bonaini, *Acta*, II, No. 4 (10 Nov. 1310), pp. 3f.
82. Cf. above Ch. I, n. 81; Bonaini, *Acta*, II, No. 5 (18 Nov. 1310), p. 4; No.
    7 (18 Nov. 1310), pp. 5f.; No. 9 (2 Dec. 1310), p. 6; No. 10 (26 Dec.
    1310), p. 7. On the distinctions between the rights of the King of the
    Romans–Emperor-elect and those of the Emperor, cf. F. Kern, "Die
    Reichsgewalt des deutschen Königs nach dem Interregnum," *Historische
    Zeitschrift*, CVI (1911), 39-95; and E. H. Kantorowicz, *The King's Two
    Bodies* (Princeton, 1957), 317ff.
83. Even Guido della Torre, Captain of Milan, was enmeshed in a bitter
    struggle with his cousin, Cassone, Archbishop of Milan. Cermenate,
    Ch. XV, pp. 26f.; *Annales Mediolanenses*, ed. L. A. Muratori, *RR.II.SS.*
    XVI (Milan, 1730), col. 690.
84. For the popular enthusiasm which greeted Henry's arrival, cf. *infra*,
    Ch. I, nn. 41, 107ff., 115.
85. For the Diet of Frankfort, cf. *MGH*, Nos. 396-406, pp. 348ff.; for the
    Diet of Spires, cf. *MGH*, Nos. 412-434, pp. 361ff.
86. Mussato, I, Rub. 8; John of Victring (cited above Ch. I, n. 12), p. 57,
    n. 40.
87. For the organization of the three military expeditions at Spires, and
    lists of some of the more important participants in each, see *Cronica
    Aulae Regiae* (cited above Ch. I, n. 12), I, Ch. 103, pp. 276f., Ch. 108,
    p. 305.
88. Ferreto, I, 287-288. Eight documents dealing with promises made before
    Henry's arrival in Italy by non-Italians for military service in Italy are
    printed in *MGH:* (1) 17 Sept. 1309 (No. 319, pp. 279f.), Leopold of
    Austria, to serve for six months with 100 heavy cavalry and 100 knights
    armed with bows. (2) 8 June 1310 (No. 383, pp. 332f.), two nobles

of Weissenburg, to serve with eight heavy cavalry, two archers, arms and horses, for one year. Henry promised them 184 silver marks, but as he lacked money they were to receive the fruits of an imperial valley for one year (valued at 60 marks) with the remainder to be paid by 24 Feb. 1311. (3) 30 Aug. 1310 (No. 383, p. 333), Dauphin Guy of Vienne, Lord of Montaubin, to serve with 400 heavy cavalry for a year. In return he received rights to certain tolls in the areas of two of his castles. (4) 17 Oct. 1310 (No. 453, p. 394), Dauphin Hugh of Vienne, Lord of Faucigny, to serve with ten knights and 30 heavy cavalry for one year, in exchange for 130 silver marks and £2,400 in Genevran denarii. (5) 1 Sept. 1310 (No. 1275, pp. 1409f.), Dauphin John of Vienne, to serve with 100 troops for six months, under the same conditions of payment as granted Guy. (John II, Lord of Vienne, did not serve in Italy, although his brothers Guy and Hugh did.) (6) 18 Sept. 1310 (No. 385, p. 334), Werner of Randecke, to serve with Walram of Luxemburg with eight cavalry for six months. (7) 20 Sept. 1310 (No. 386, pp. 334f.), a contingent of nobles and burghers from Spires to serve in Italy. (8) 12 Oct. 1310 (No. 451, p. 393), [while Henry was in Geneva] Bishop Aimo of Geneva, to serve with 14 heavy cavalry for one year. Henry had already given Aimo 130 silver marks, and was to pay his troops the stipulated wages regardless of any money Aimo might receive from various nobles while in Italy. See also promises made after Henry's arrival in Italy, from two Italians: 3 Nov. 1310 (No. 462, p. 407), Philip of Savoy, to serve with 100 cavalry for one year; 25 Nov. 1310 (Nos. 483, 1308, pp. 1447, 438f.) Marquis Theodore of Monferrat, to serve with 100 cavalry for a year at his own expense. Cf. also Davidsohn, *Geschichte*, III, 402; Schneider, *H.VII*, 83.

89. *MGH*, No. 395, pp. 347f.

90. For the embassy dispatched to Paris 26 April 1310, see *MGH*, Nos. 351-354, pp. 298ff.

91. For the meeting of 22 Aug. 1310, cf. *MGH*, No. 394, p. 347, lines 3ff. For the seizure of Lyon, see above, Ch. I, n. 29.

92. For this embassy and its aftermath, see esp. *MGH*, Nos. 390-394 (27 June-30 Aug. 1310), pp. 338ff.; Nos. 435-441 (1 Sept.-8 Oct. 1310), pp. 375ff.; Nos. 454-455 (11 Oct.-ex 11 Oct. 1310), pp. 395ff.

93. See *MGH*, No. 390 (27 June 1310), pp. 338f. The Pope agreed to appoint a papal *legatus a latere* to aid Henry in Italy, naming for the post Cardinal Arnald Pellagru—Clement's nephew and a very close friend of the Florentine Priory. The Pope also declared his willingness to appoint a legate for Germany if the King still so desired, and he reminded Henry that the petition that Henry of Villers be made Bishop of Trent had already been granted.

94. For the election of Louis of Savoy, see above, Ch. I, n. 37. For the 15 ecclesiastical posts, see E. E. Stengel, ed., *Nova Alamanniae* (Berlin, 1921), I, Pt. 1, No. 74 (5 July 1310); and *MGH*, No. 449 (24 Sept. 1310), p. 392 line 10; cf. *MGH*, No. 581 (24 Feb. 1311), pp. 537f.

95. See *MGH*, No. 435, p. 377 lines 31f.; No. 436, p. 380 lines 8f.; No. 440, p. 385 line 41–p. 386 line 10.

96. See *MGH*, No. 391, pp. 340-342, the form submitted to Henry by the Pope; No. 393, pp. 343-346, the promises actually made by Henry at Hagenau, 17 Aug. 1310; No. 454, pp. 395-398, the second form of the promises, as sworn by Henry at Lausanne, 11 Oct. 1310; No. 455, pp.

398-401, an explanatory letter sent to Henry by Clement after receiving the promise of Lausanne.

97. See the *"Privilegium Regium Secundum,"* 14 Feb. 1279, *MGH, Const.* IV, 3, No. 223, esp. p. 210.
98. *MGH*, No. 438 (16 Sept. 1310), pp. 282ff.
99. *MGH*, No. 391, p. 342 lines 12f.
100. *MGH*, No. 455, p. 401 lines 32f.
101. See *MGH*, No. 441 (8 Oct. 1310), p. 387 line 27–p. 388 line 6; cf. No. 438 (16 Sept. 1310), p. 383 line 27–p. 384 line 4.
102. *MGH*, Nos. 435-436 (1 Sept. 1310), pp. 375-381.
103. *MGH*, No. 435, p. 377 lines 31ff.; No. 440, p. 385 lines 41ff., 386 lines 24f., 37f.
104. *Regestum Clementis Papae V* (Rome, 1888), IX, No. 10347, pp. 122f.
105. Cf. G. Fasoli, "Bologna e la Romagna" (cited above, Ch. I, n. 74), 23.
106. *MGH*, No. 444, pp. 389f.
107. Dante, *Letter* V, probably written at Forli, Sept.-Oct. 1310.
108. Dante, *Convivio*, IV, iv, ix, quotes from IV, iv, 7, ix, 10. Cf. A. P. D'Entrèves, *Dante as a Political Thinker* (Oxford, 1952), 34f.
109. Dönniges, *Acta*, II, No. 3, p. 122.
110. Mussato, Bk. I, Rub. 6, col. 328. At Spires too Henry probably met the representatives of Leo Lambertenghi, Bishop of Como, who had not resided in his bishopric since 1303 because of his pronounced Ghibelline sympathies. Ferreto, I, 292. Cf. G. Biscaro, "Benzo da Alessandria e i giudizi contro i ribelli a Milano nel 1311," *Archivio Storico Lombardo*, ser. 4, VII (an. 34) (1907), p. 311.
111. Cermenate, Ch. XVI, pp. 30f.; *Chron. Modoet.*, col. 1096.
112. The only source for the appearance of Brusati or his envoys at Spires is Mathias of Neuenberg, *Chronica*, ed. A. Hofmeister (*MGH, SS*, n.s., IV; Berlin, 1924-40), 81. Later official documents only mention Brusati as first appearing before Henry at Asti in the fall of 1310 (cf. *MGH*, No. 653, p. 622). Also against the accuracy of Mathias' account, see Hofmeister's arguments, *loc. cit.*
113. Mommsen, *Ital. Analekten*, No. 2 (8 May 1310), pp. 22f.; a Bolognese decision to pay £6 to a returning scout, sent to Germany in March. Davidsohn, *Forschungen*, II, No. 2112 (July 1310), p. 273 (San Gimignano).
114. Butrinto, 492f.; cf. Cermenate, Ch. XVI, pp. 25f., and G. Flamma, *Manipulus Florum*, ed. L. A. Muratori, *RR.II.SS.*, XI (Milan, 1727), col. 719.
115. Butrinto, 496, 499; Cermenate Ch. XI, p. 22. Guillelmus de Pusterla, son-in-law of Matteo Visconti and a leading Milanese noble, was placed under special surveillance and prevented from leaving the city.
116. See Caggese, *Roberto*, I, 115ff.; G. M. Monti, *La dominazione angoina*, 120ff.; for Robert's reception and activities in Florence (late Sept.-early Oct. 1310), see Davidsohn, *Geschichte*, III, 388ff.

NOTES: CHAPTER II. "THE EMPEROR HENRY'S MOST AUSPICIOUS ENTRY INTO ITALY."

1. Dante, closing lines of *Letters* VI, VII.
2. See C. Cipolla ed. of Ferreto, I, 284, n. 4; *Chronicon Parvum Ripaltae*, ed. F. Gabotto, *RR.II.SS.*, n.s. XVII, Pt. 3 (Città di Castello, 1912),

2of. The best chronology is still F. Ludwig, *Untersuchungen über Reise- und Marschgeschwindigkeit im XII. und XIII. Jahrhundert* (Berlin, 1897), 74f. Henry arrived at Bern in Swiss Savoy on 29 September 1310, and remained ten days. On 8 or 9 October he reached Murten, on the 9th or 10th he came to Lausanne, which he left on the 11th, arriving at Nyon the same day. On 12 October he reached Geneva, and set out across Mt. Cenis on the 13th. On 23 October the expedition reached Susa in Piedmont, and remained for six days. It arrived at Avigliana on the 29th, and Turin the 30th. Henry went from Turin to Chieri on 6 November, and reached Asti on 11 November, remaining for one month.

3. For the Pisan embassy (led by Giovanni Ronconte, jurisprudent, and Giovanni [Vanni] Zeno dei Lanfranchi), see *MGH*, No. 456, p. 402; Davidsohn, *Geschichte*, III, 384f.

4. The Roman embassy had only reached Modena on 15 October 1310, Bonifazio da Morano, *Chron. Mutinense, RR.II.SS.*, XI, col. 97. (For its arrival in Turin, 31 October, see Butrinto, 492; *Chron. Parvum Ripaltae, RR.II.SS.*, n.s., XVII, Pt. 3, p. 21.)

5. The major Tuscan chronicles, and Dino Compagni, usually a careful observer, do not mention Florentine preparations to meet Henry before he crossed the Alps. The three documents cited by Davidsohn, *Geschichte*, III, 384, n. 6, are not to this point (that from Archivio di Stato, Volterra, is now published in Mommsen, *Ital. Analekten*, No. 10). There *is* evidence that the Florentine League discussed sending envoys to Henry in November, and a Florentine embassy was only formed during the last week of that month—and then not sent. Perhaps Villani, who wrongly claims that Henry remained for several months in Lausanne "waiting for his forces and the embassies of the Italian cities" (IX, 7), referred to this November project. See Bonaini, *Acta*, II, Nos. 4, 5, 7 (10, 18, 23 Nov. 1310), pp. 3ff. For terms Florence desired of the Emperor-elect (10 Nov. 1310), see above, Ch. I, n. 81. Bologna considered sending an embassy to Henry, in the company of the Cardinal Legate Arnald Pellagru, as early as 21 Oct. 1310. Mommsen, *Ital. Analekten*, No. 12, p. 26.

6. Cf. *MGH*, Nos. 457-458 (inter 24-29 Oct.), pp. 402f.

7. *MGH*, No. 463 (in 9 Nov. 1310), pp. 407f.

8. For Henry's lack of funds, see Cermenate, Ch. XX, p. 44; Villani, Bk. IX, Ch. 7. For the size and composition of Henry's army, and his financial situation, see above, Ch. I, nn. 88f.; cf. Schneider, *H.VII*, 82ff. Mussato (Bk. I, Rub. 9) estimates Henry's cavalry at "almost 300," Cermenate (Ch. XVI, p. 33), at 500, Butrinto (492), describes Henry's troops as "few." For an illustration of the treasure wagon, see Figure 3. For the Lombard Guelf cavalry escort, Butrinto, 493.

9. *MGH*, No. 460 (3 Nov. 1310), pp. 404f.

10. Many extant oaths of fealty to Henry of Luxemburg exist only in abbreviated imbreviatures. The following complete forms (publ. in *MGH*) contain the promise to recover things acquired in the future and then lost: Casale Monferrat (p. 408), Novara (p. 455), Milan (p. 466), Bergamo (p. 477), Cremona (p. 490), Lodi, second oath (p. 474), and the oath sworn by the royal councillors in Asti, 29 Nov. 1310 (p. 443).

11. The following promised to recover the *regalia* and rights of the Empire

(MGH): Asti (p. 417), Amadeus of Savoy (p. 434), Theodore of Monferrat (p. 437), Vercelli (p. 447), Guillelmus de Pusterla (p. 482), Milan, second oath (p. 535), Padua (p. 587). Two of Henry's strongest supporters in Italy, Genoa (p. 526) and Pisa (p. 561), promised at first only to defend and retain the rights of the Empire, not to recover them.

12. J. F. Böhmer, ed., *Acta Imperii Selecta* (Innsbruck, 1870), No. 1002, p. 73, an oath sworn by the Bishop of Arezzo, *c.* 1081; cf. *MGH, Const.* IV, 3, No. 86 (9 July 1275), pp. 77f., the standard oath of fealty to be taken by all imperial subjects in Italy to Rudolf of Habsburg. This is longer and more detailed than any recorded oath to Henry VII, and includes a promise to give the King's couriers good treatment. For the "New Form" oath, see a so-called standard form for fealty to Henry of Luxemburg (never applied universally, however), E. E. Stengel, ed., *Nova Alamanniae,* I, Pt. 1 (Berlin, 1921), No. 80, pp. 37f., s.d.

13. At Turin, Philip of Savoy joined his uncle Amadeus at the royal court.

14. *MGH,* No. 460, p. 405. Palmieri degli Altoviti had assisted Giano della Bella in drawing up the famous Florentine Ordinances of Justice (1293), and then turned against him. Palmieri was sentenced to death for fighting against his native city (Davidsohn, *Geschichte,* III, 414). For his service to Henry of Luxemburg, cf. *MGH,* Nos. 716, 721, pp. 705, 710.

15. Botrinto, 493. For Richard's promise to serve with 100 knights, see above, Ch. I, n. 67.

16. See, e.g., above, Ch. I, n. 110; cf. F. Cognasso, "L'unificazione di Lombardia sotto Milano," in *Storia di Milano,* ed. G. Treccani degli Alfieri, V (Milan, 1955), 21f.

17. Cermenate, Ch. XVI, p. 32; Butrinto, 493f. (an eyewitness), *q.v.* for events during the remainder of Henry's stay in Turin.

18. When the Guelf Marquis, Theodore of Monferrat, son-in-law of the Genoese Ghibelline exile Opizzino Spinola, appeared in Turin with 200 cavalry and asked to be enfeoffed with the marquisate, Henry refused temporarily, since the rightful possession of the territory was in dispute.

19. For the dispute over Chieri, see Butrinto, 494f.; *Chron. Parvum Ripaltae, RR.II.SS.,* n.s. XVII, Pt. 3, p. 20, n. 7; cf. P. Darmstädter, *Das Reichsgut in der Lombardei,* 217f.

20. Possibly Count Amadeus seconded the advice of the Guelf counsellors. On this incident, see Butrinto, 493, 494; Cermenate, Ch. XXIX, p. 66.

21. For the introduction of a vicar into Chieri, see Butrinto, 494; *Chron. Parvum Ripaltae, RR.II.SS.,* n.s., XVII, Pt. 3, p. 21. Cf. the communal statutes prepared during the spring of 1311, *Statuti civili del comune di Chieri, 1313,* ed. F. Cognasso (Biblioteca della Società Storica Subalpina, LXXVI, pt. 2; Pinerolo, 1913), Rub. 1, pp. 1f.

22. *Statuti civili . . . di Chieri,* Rub. 3, p. 3. For the salary of the podesta see L. Cibrario, *Delle Storie di Chieri libri quattro con documenti,* I (Turin, 1827), 298. At the time of Henry's entry, Chieri had no captain of the people or similar official, and no society of the people existed during the imperial vicarship; cf. *Statuti civili,* Rub. 318, p. 102; Cibrario, I, 287.

23. *Statuti civili . . . di Chieri,* Rub. 314, pp. 100f.; cf. Rub. 230, pp. 74f., Rub. 301, pp. 94f.

24. See Figure 5. For events in Asti, see (in addition to the documents cited

below from *MGH* and Bonaini, *Acta)* Butrinto, 495f., Cermenate, Ch. XVI, pp. 33ff.; Ventura *(ed. cit.* above, Ch. I, n. 68), col. 777. For events from this point on there exist numerous official documents, originals and copies in local archives, and a series of imbreviaturas intended to serve as reminders and guides for Henry and his court. The two notaries who bore the brunt of this secretarial task throughout the expedition were placed on the royal council and were privy to its weightiest decisions. One of them, John of Diest, called de Cruce, a clerk of Liège, was probably a servant of Henry's cousin, Theobald of Bar, Bishop of Liège. The other, Bernard de Mercato from Yenna in Savoy, had previously worked for Count Amadeus, to whose service he returned after the expedition. Although there was no clear-cut division of work among the notaries, most documents concerning Savoy, as well as the journal of business transacted in the council (begun in the spring of 1313), seems to have been entrusted to Bernard de Mercato. The chancellery in Italy was headed by Henry, Bishop of Trent (former Abbot of Villers), appointed vicar by the imperial chancellor in Italy, Archbishop Henry of Cologne. On the chancellery in Italy under Henry VII, see Schneider, *H.VII,* 322f.; H. Kampf, "Zu einem Imbreviaturenbuch und einem Register Bernards de Mercato," *Mitteilungen des Instituts für oesterreichische Geschichtsforschung, Erg. Bd.,* XIV (1939), 391ff.; V. Samanek, "Die verfassungsrechtliche Stellung Genuas, 1311-1313," *Mitteilungen des Inst. f. oesterr. Geschichtsforschung,* XXVII (1906), 237ff.

25. Bonaini, *Acta,* I, No. 40 (23 Oct.-13 Nov. 1310), pp. 50ff.
26. Bonaini, *Acta,* I, No. 48 (15 Nov. 1310), pp. 61ff.
27. *MGH,* No. 468 (15 Nov. 1310), pp. 415ff.
28. *MGH,* No. 469 (15 Nov. 1310), pp. 417f.
29. *MGH,* No. 470 (16 Nov. 1310), p. 418. One of the men presenting Henry's demand was the Pistoian exile Simon Philip de Realibus (see above, Ch. I, n. 37), who was now designated as a "familiar" of the King. He had firmly established his position at the court, and less than two months later was serving as treasurer for the entire expedition, immediately responsible to the chancellor for the receipt and expenditure of thousands of florins (*MGH,* No. 1149, Dec. 1310-July 1311, pp. 1144ff.). The other bearer of the royal request of 16 Nov. 1310 was Henry's young cousin, Henry of Flanders, already designated as Marshal of the imperial forces in Italy; cf. V. Samanek, "Der Marschall des Kaisers in nachstaufischen Reichsitalien," *Quellen und Forschungen aus italienischen Archiven und Bibliotheken,* XIV (1911), 38ff.
30. *MGH,* No. 471 (18 Nov. 1310), pp. 419f.
31. For Niccolo de' Buonsignori, cf. Davidsohn, *Geschichte,* III, 413f.
32. Ventura (col. 777) casts doubt upon the voluntary nature of this cession of authority, but his account is confused and seems to telescope the most dramatic features of two meetings and add a large element of his own anger.
33. Ventura, col. 777.
34. On the burning of Asti's treaties with Robert of Anjou, see, in addition to Butrinto, 495 and Ventura, col. 777, *MGH,* No. 1288 (31 March 1312), pp. 1424 lines 30f., 1425 lines 1f. (first publ. by H. Finke, ed., *Acta Aragonensia,* I, No. 201, pp. 285ff.). This was not to be the last time that Robert was tactfully afforded a convenient escape from the

responsibilities of his own conduct. Cf. Bonaini, *Acta*, II, No. 132 (17 June 1312), p. 106; a letter to Robert from the Florentine Priory. (See below, Ch. V, n. 16.)

35. For the Florentine spy, cf. Bonaini, *Acta*, II, Nos. 1-2, 14 Oct. 1310, pp. 1f. For the terms of 10 Nov. 1310, see above, Ch. I, n. 81.
36. *MGH*, No. 472, pp. 421ff.
37. *MGH*, No. 473 (25 Nov. 1310), p. 425.
38. *MGH*, No. 474 (3-4 Dec. 1310), pp. 425f.
39. Ventura, col. 777; cf. Mussato, Bk. I, Rub. 10.
40. *MGH*, No. 574, pp. 427ff.
41. See, e.g., *MGH*, No. 512 (2 Jan. 1311), p. 466 lines 40ff.; No. 545 (14 Jan. 1311), p. 501 lines 2ff.; W. Dönniges, *Acta*, I, No. 43a, p. 29; No. 44, p. 30; No. 33, p. 26, No. 56, p. 33.
42. *MGH*, No. 476 (8 Dec. 1310), pp. 429f.
43. *MGH*, No. 472, p. 423, esp. line 36, and G. M. Monti, *La dominazione angoina*, Doc. XVII, esp. p. 351.
44. Cf. P. Torelli, "Capitanato del popolo e vicariato imperiale come elementi costitutivi della signoria bonacolsiana," *R. Accademia Virgiliana di Mantova, Atti e Memorie*, n.s., XIV-XVI (1923), 120.
45. *MGH*, pp. 422 lines 45ff., 427 line 13, 428 lines 2, 33ff., 430 lines 1f.
46. *MGH*, pp. 424 line 44, 429 lines 18f.
47. *MGH*, No. 464, p. 408f. Cf. above, Ch. II, n. 7.
48. See Dönniges, *Acta*, I, No. 7, pp. 9f. (Modena), No. 8, pp. 10f. (Mantua), No. 6, pp. 7f. (Verona). The proctors were appointed respectively on 13, 16, 15 Nov. (The doc. of appointment for the Veronese proctor is also in Bonaini, *Acta*, I, No. 47, pp. 6of.) The exiles from Modena and Verona appointed proctors to appear before Henry, swear an oath of fealty to him, and grant him power to arbitrate their disputes on 30 Dec. 1310 (Bonaini, *Acta*, I, No. 133, pp. 211ff.) and 19 Jan. 1311 (*ibid.*, No. 90, pp. 131ff.) The document for the Mantuan exiles is not extant, but their proctors appeared before the Emperor-elect in Milan on 13 Jan. 1311 (Dönniges, *Acta*, I, No. 53, p. 32). See P. Torelli, "Il capitanato del popolo" (cited above, Ch. II, n. 44), 126, for a request made in Asti by the Mantuan embassy for a fief for Passerino (Raynaldo) Bonacolsi.
49. *MGH*, No. 477, pp. 430f.
50. For Matteo Visconti's arrival in Asti, and his activities there, see F. Cognasso, in *Storia di Milano*, ed. G. Treccani degli Alfieri, V, 25-30.
51. Cermenate, Ch. XVI, p. 36. On 4 Dec. 1310, in Asti, Matteo Visconti signed a treaty with Cassone della Torre, Archbishop of Milan, that seemed to favor the latter. (G. Merula, *Antiquitatis Vicecomitum*, in J. G. Graevius, *Thesaurus antiquitatum et historiarum Italiae*, III, Pt. 1 [Leyden, 1704], cols. 150f.) Matteo pledged not to act against Milan, its *contado*, and the communes of Bergamo, Lodi, Crema, Novara, Vercelli, Tortona, and Cremona, without Cassone's approval. He promised to aid the archbishop and never to govern lands pertaining to his see. When we recall that Cassone was at the time battling his cousin Guido della Torre, this pact seems less an attempt by Matteo to impress the King with his peacefulness than a combination of two rivals against a third for control in Milan.
52. Pellagru had led the papal crusade against Venice for Ferrara, and before returning home spent two months in Florence. He was feted and

given cash presents there, and probably was not unaware of the plans being made for active resistance against the Emperor-elect when he left the Black Guelf commune early in November. Pellagru served as the instrument for the introduction of Bolognese spies into the imperial court at Asti (Mommsen, *Ital. Analekten*, No. 12, 21 Oct. 1310, p. 26). Pellagru may himself have requested that he be relieved of the mission of assisting the King of the Romans. He stayed only briefly in Asti, and then continued to Avignon. Cardinal Legate Thomas of Santa Sabina left Avignon for Italy 28 Sept. 1310, but fell ill and died at Grenoble 13 Dec. 1310. (Cf. *MGH*, No. 440, pp. 384ff.) Other cardinals were sent to Henry in the summer of 1311.

53. Cardinal Pellagru dispatched the papal chaplain Master Galasso of the Counts of Mangona to the Church of St. Ambrose in Milan to inquire into the whereabouts of the iron crown and details of the Lombard coronation. Galasso, once placed in charge of White Guelf Pistoia by Cardinal Nicolas of Prato, was already a counsellor and familiar at Henry's court. *MGH*, No. 484 (25 Nov. 1310), p. 439; cf. Davidsohn, *Geschichte*, III, 413.

54. For the embassy sent by Henry to the Pope, 19 Nov. 1310, see E. E. Stengel, ed., *Nova Alamanniae*, I, Pt. 1, No. 79, pp. 36f.; *MGH*, No. 466, pp. 411ff. (the list of arguments presented to the Pope); Butrinto, 497; cf. *MGH*, No. 467 (9 Dec. 1310), pars. 3f., pp. 413f., and No. 1149, p. 1146 lines 46ff. On Henry's desire for a rapid departure for Rome and an early coronation, cf. Ferreto, I, 296f.; *MGH*, No. 517, pp. 478f.

55. *MGH*, No. 467 (par. 7), pp. 414f.

56. On 24 Nov. 1310 Henry had accepted the homage of his brother-in-law, Count Amadeus V of Savoy, a man generally friendly to Guelfs, and invested him with all his imperial fiefs (*MGH*, No. 479, pp. 432ff.). See also *MGH*, Nos. 481-482 (25 Nov. 1310), pp. 435ff. (investiture of the Marquis of Monferrat, and the marquis' oath of fealty). *MGH*, No. 1308, p. 1447 (original) and No. 483, p. 438 (imbreviature): the marquis' pledge of military service. In this case where we can compare the imbreviature with the complete form, it should serve as a warning to note that the abbreviated form omits a clause to the effect that the marquis was bound to serve with only 50 knights, not 100, from the date of Henry's departure from Asti until 1 Jan. 1311. One cannot assume the absence of essential clauses from a particular act by reason of its absence in the imbreviature.

57. *MGH*, No. 487 (29 Nov. 1310), pp. 442ff.

58. Cermenate, Ch. XVI, p. 37; *Chron. Modoet.*, col. 1097; Dino Compagni, Bk. III, Ch. 25, pp. 224f.

59. Cf. Cermenate, Ch. XVI, p. 32.

60. On 12 Dec. 1310, Casale renewed its fealty to Henry, *MGH*, No. 464, p. 409; cf. above, Ch. II, n. 7. The town did not long enjoy its independence, as Henry gave it in fief to Count Philippone Langusco of Pavia two months later. Butrinto, 507; *MGH*, No. 579, p. 534 line 37.

61. Butrinto, 497; cf. above, Ch. I, n. 53.

62. Butrinto, 498.

63. *MGH*, Nos. 488, 1277, pp. 444ff., 1411ff. These documents contain both a record of the proceedings of 15 Dec. 1310, and the peace arbitrations of the 16th.

64. Two days after the promulgation of the pact Henry officially cancelled

all existing fines and banishments against the former exiles. A month later he made a similar provision for the dominant Guelf Avvocati. *MGH*, Nos. 498, 1278, pp. 447, 1413f.

65. *MGH*, No. 489 (16 Dec. 1310), pp. 446f. While Henry was in Vercelli he also received homage from ten nobles, among them two of the Marquises of Malaspina, from the Lungiana, a family that later supplied the monarch with many vicars for Lombardy—although not always with the best results; *MGH*, Nos. 491-497 (15-17 Dec. 1310), pp. 448ff. Dino Compagni describes the Malaspina simply as "i falsi fideli" (Bk. III, Ch. 24, p. 253). One Malaspina invested in Vercelli, Moroello, had earlier given Dante refuge and hospitality.

66. *MGH*, p. 447 line 32; No. 1009, par. 7, p. 1054. Berlion de Rivoire was chosen vicar of Vercelli. The next vicar to be appointed (for Novara) was also a Savoyard candidate, Albert de Maloselli, Genoese Guelf relative of Amadeus V; *MGH*, p. 535; cf. Butrinto, 498, and A. de Gerbaix de Sonnaz, *Amè V de Savoie* (cited above, Ch. I, n. 35), 87f.

67. C. Eubel, ed., *Hierarchia catholica medii aevii*, I[2] (Regensberg, 1913), 521; G. Bascape, "I conti palatini del regno italico" (cited above, Ch. I, n. 46), 354, n. 5; Butrinto, 498f.

68. See, e.g., Bonaini, *Acta*, II, No. 16 (Jan. 1311), p. 14, below, Ch. II, n. 94.

69. *MGH*, Nos. 498-499, pp. 451ff.

70. *MGH*, No. 500, pp. 453f.

71. *MGH*, No. 501, pp. 455f. While in Novara, Henry received the homage of the Bishop of Lodi, Egidio dall' Aqua, *MGH*, Nos. 502-505, pp. 456ff.

72. For the claims of Monza, and the investigations, see above, Ch. I, n. 54, Ch. II, n. 53; *MGH*, No. 485 (25 Dec. 1310), p. 440; Butrinto, 501f. Cf. *MGH*, No. 486 (4 Jan. 1311), p. 440f., for Monza's continued claims to be the rightful coronation site and (p. 441 lines 48f): "sedem et coronam regni Ytalie et caput Lombardie." For descriptions of the crown made for Henry, see Villani, IX, Rub. 9; Dino Compagni, Bk. III, Ch. 26, p. 227; *Gesta Trevirorum Integra*, ed. Wyttenbach and Müller (cited above, Ch. II, n. 8), II, 213f.

73. The copy of this invitation sent to Ghiberto da Correggio is extant, and published in *Chron. Parmense*, 118f. It should be noted that Henry addressed this *signore* of Parma only as "Nobili viro Giberto de Coregio fideli suo dilecto." This salutation is conspicuously void of any official designation or recognition of Ghiberto's actual political position as *de facto* ruler of Parma.

74. Butrinto, 499.

75. *MGH*, No. 507, pp. 460f.

76. For the weather conditions see Cermenate, Ch. XVI, p. 38; *Chron. Modoet.*, col. 1097. For a detailed account of the rumored opposition to Henry, see Butrinto, 500f. It is likely that if there had been any truth to the story that Milan teemed with armed Torriani who were prepared to fight the Emperor-elect, the very anti-Torriani chronicler Cermenate would have reported it.

77. Cermenate, Ch. XVI, p. 38.

78. For Henry's stay in Milan (23 Dec. 1310-11 April 1311), see Cognasso, in *Storia di Milano*, ed. G. Treccani degli Alfieri, V, 33-60.

79. *MGH*, No. 508 (24 Dec. 1310), p. 461.

80. *MGH*, No. 509 (27 Dec. 1310), pp. 461f. For the purposes of the

peace pact the dispute between Guido and the Archbishop was ignored, and the Torriani were treated as one single faction, the Visconti as the other.

81. *MGH*, No. 510 (28 Dec. 1310), pp. 463ff.

82. Niccolo de' Buonsignori was already in office as vicar of Milan and its district by 20 Jan. 1311. Bonaini, *Acta*, I, Nos. 91, 92, pp. 133ff., 136f.

83. See above, Ch. I, n. 101.

84. Some of the Cremonese Ghibelline Redenascho family, exiled for over 40 years, had never been in Cremona. For the presence of the above-mentioned persons in Milan at this time, Ferreto, I, 291-295; Bonifazio da Morano, *Chron. Mutinense*, col. 97 (F. della Mirandola). See also docs. of fealty from Cremonese proctors (4 Jan., *MGH*, No. 532, pp. 489f.), of appointment for proctors of Cremonese exiles (8 Jan., Dönniges, *Acta*, II, No. 10, p. 128), of appointment for Modenese exiles' proctor (30 Dec.) and his act of fealty (7 Jan.): Bonaini, *Acta*, I, No. 133, pp. 211ff.; Dönniges, *Acta*, I, No. 36, p. 27. During the days before the Milanese coronation, proctors for the following five cities and one group of exiles pledged fealty to Henry and granted him the power to arbitrate their disputes: 24 Dec.: Como (Dönniges, *Acta*, No. 19, p. 20); 26 Dec.: Crema, Bergamo (*ibid.*, No. 22, p. 21; *MGH*, No. 576, pp. 476f.); 28 Dec.: Piacenza (Bonaini, *Acta*, I, No. 78, pp. 109ff.); 4 Jan.: Pavia, exiles from Como (*MGH*, No. 527, pp. 486f.; Dönniges, *Acta*, I, No. 32, p. 26). During the same period more than ten nobles swore fealty or were invested, most notable among them being Guillelmus de Pusterla (son-in-law of Matteo Visconti), who received an imperial fief of 125 silver marks to be paid him annually in Asti (*MGH*, Nos. 522-524, 31 Dec.-2 Jan., pp. 481ff. G. de Pusterla: No. 522, pp. 581f.).

85. For the Florentine conditions of 10 Nov. 1310, see above, Ch. I, n. 81; for the November discussions, above, Ch. II, n. 5.

86. See Bonaini, *Acta*, II, No. 9 (2 Dec. 1310), pp. 6f. Cf. above, Ch. II, n. 52, for Bolognese spies sent to Henry's court. Even before the King's arrival in Lombardy the Florentine Priory had placed a spy in Asti (see above, Ch. I, n. 36).

87. See B. Barbadoro, ed., *Consigli della Repubblica Fiorentina* (Bologna, 1930) I, Pt. 2, pp. 505, 506 (5, 7 Sept. 1310), proposition 3; pp. 511, 512 (21, 22 Oct. 1310), proposition 2; also p. 509 n.a.

88. See, e.g., Bonaini, *Acta*, II, No. 4 (10 Nov. 1310), p. 4; No. 16 (post 6 Jan. 1311), pp. 13ff.; No. 17 (3 Feb. 1311), pp. 15ff.; Mommsen, *Ital. Analekten*, No. 14 (30 Nov. 1310), p. 26; No. 17 (28 Dec. 1310), p. 27; cf. Caggese, *Roberto*, I, 126f.

89. Bonaini, *Acta*, II, No. 17 (3 Feb. 1311), p. 16; cf. Caggese, *Roberto*, I, 127.

90. See, e.g., Bonaini, *Acta*, II, No. 3 (3 Nov. 1310), p. 3; No. 10 (26 Dec. 1310), pp. 7ff.; No. 12 (4 Jan. 1311), pp. 9f.; No. 19 (4 Feb. 1311), pp. 16ff.; *MGH*, No. 595 (30 March 1311), pp. 554f.; Mommsen, *Ital. Analekten*, No. 13 (20 Nov. 1310), p. 26.

91. Bonaini, *Acta*, II, No. 12 (4 Jan. 1311), pp. 9f.

92. *Ibid.*, II, No. 6 (18 Nov. 1310), p. 5; No. 12 (4 Jan. 1311), p. 10; No. 13 (5 Jan. 1311), pp. 10ff.; No. 14 (8 Jan. 1311), p. 12; No. 16 (Jan. 1311), p. 14; No. 18 (4 Feb. 1311), p. 16.

93. See, e.g., *ibid.*, II, No. 11 (3 Jan. 1311), p. 8; No. 12 (4 Jan. 1311),

pp. 9, 10; No. 13 (5 Jan. 1311), pp. 10ff.; No. 15 (8 Jan. 1311), p. 13; No. 16 (Jan. 1311), pp. 13ff.

94. *Ibid.*, II, No. 16 (Jan. 1311), p. 14.
95. *Ibid.*, II, No. 12 (4 Jan. 1311), p. 9.
96. *Ibid.*, II, No. 14 (8 Jan. 1311), p. 12.
97. *Ibid.*, II, No. 16 (Jan. 1311), p. 14.
98. *Ibid.*, II, No. 13 (5 Jan. 1311), pp. 10f.
99. The humanist Benzo of Alessandria notes that a bas-relief popularly thought to represent Hercules holding a club and traditionally kept in front of the choir in St. Ambrose was removed at Henry's orders and placed in a supine position to form the base for the statues of the King and Queen. This caused much grumbling among the populace, to whom that piece of marble was almost something sacred. It was murmured that until the bas-relief was replaced before the choir there was no hope for the imperial cause. L. A. Ferrai, ed., "Bentii Alexandrini de mediolano civitate opusculum," *Bullettino dell'Istituto Storico Italiano*, No. 9 (1890), p. 33.
100. See Figure 6 entitled "H[enricus] coronat[ur] corone f[er] rea in S[an]cto Ambrosio die Reg[um]." For the *Ordo* of this coronation, *MGH, Leges*, ed. G. H. Pertz, II (Hannover, 1837), 503ff., and F. Ughelli, *Italia Sacra*, IV (Venice, 1729), cols. 801f. See also Henry's letter to the Bishop of Strassburg, *MGH*, No. 518 (7 Jan. 1311), pp. 479f. Henry consigned the crown used for his Milanese coronation to the Church of St. Ambrose 19 April 1311. One of its two bearers was the doctor Bartolomeo da Varignana, White Guelf exile condemned to death by Bologna in 1306. Among the witnesses at the presentation of the crown were Lando of Siena, its creator, and the Florentine exiles, Gherardino Cepperelli de' Malespini and Falcuccio Tebalducci. *MGH*, No. 609, p. 572; cf. G. Fasoli, "Bologna e la Romagna" (cited above Ch. I, n. 74), 29 n. 5; Davidsohn, *Geschichte*, III, 416. See also B. H. Sumner, "Dante and the *regnum italicum*," *Medium Aevum*, I (1932), 2ff., and above, Ch. II, n. 74.
101. *Statuta Civitatis Regii 1311* (in Archivio di Stato of Reggio Emilia), Bk. XIII f. 106r begins "Incipit statuta nova facta et compillata per sapientes electos per consilium generale. Regnante d. [domino] h. [Henrico] Romanorum Rege. sui regni anno primo." It is perhaps possible that for the Reggians "anno primo" began when Henry first appeared in Lombardy in the fall of 1310.
102. The number of knights created by Henry after his coronation in Milan cannot be determined with certainty. Butrinto, 503, says 160; *Chron. Parmense*, 119, says 199; *Chron. Parvum Ripaltae*, 22, says 150; *Cronaca Senese . . . di autore anonimo della metà del secolo XIV*, in *Cronache senesi*, ed. A. Lisini and F. Iacometti, *RR.II.SS.*, n.s., XV, Pt. 6 (Bologna, 1931-1937), 90, says 60. This last source also indicates that Henry knighted a member of each of the Sienese houses of Tolomei, Malavolti, Piccolomini, and Forteguerra.
103. Dino Compagni, Bk. III, Ch. 26, p. 228.
104. For some of Henry's expenses and income during this period, see the tables submitted by the acting treasurer, Simon Philip of Pistoia, *MGH*, No. 1149, pp. 1145f. The income reported dates from 23 Feb. 1311ff., while the expenses date from 10 Dec. 1311—but we cannot state definitely that this indicates the true balance or that Italian income

started so much later than expenses. We must be particularly careful in drawing perhaps unwarranted conclusions, since these figures do not include all the amounts received or spent; cf. the 4,000 florins paid to Philip of Savoy while Henry was in Novara (*MGH*, No. 462, p. 407).

105. On the Milanese gift, see, e.g., Cermenate, Ch. XXI, pp. 44f., and esp. 45, n. 1 (Ferrai's comment and explanation, with references to and quotations from other sources).

106. For the Genoese fealty: *MGH*, No. 567 (28 Jan. 1311), pp. 525f. For the appointment of a proctor by Arezzo: *MGH*, No. 566, pp. 524f. For the Pisan gift: *MGH*, No. 1149, p. 1145—on 23 Feb. 1311, Simon Philip of Pistoia received for Henry "a Banduccio Boncontis dante pro comuni Pisano pro residuo pagamenti LXM flor. aur., quos debebant dicto domino imperatori XXIIIIM IIIIC flor. aur." Homage of the bishops of Como, Aqui, Brescia: *MGH*, No. 535 (8 Jan. 1311), p. 493. For the investiture of Cassone della Torre: *MGH*, No. 538 (21 Jan. 1311), p. 494. The following is a calendar of 15 documents of fealty existing for this period. (The documents for the Veronese exiles and for Albenga are documents appointing proctors only. Unless otherwise indicated, the document was done by the group presently in power in the named cities.) (1) 7 Jan.: Parma, Dönniges, *Acta*, I, No. 34, pp. 26f. (2) 7 Jan.: Modena, exiles, Dönniges, I, No. 36, p. 27. (3) 7 Jan.: Brescia, Dönniges, I, No. 35, p. 27. (4) 8 Jan.: Brescia, exiles, Dönniges, I, No. 38, p. 28. (5) 9 Jan.: Pavia, exiles, Dönniges, I, No. 42, p. 39. (6) 9 Jan.: Piacenza, exiles, Dönniges, I, No. 40, p. 28. (7) 9 Jan.: Parma, exiles, Dönniges, I, No. 39, p. 28. (8) 12 Jan.: Canobbio, Dönniges, I, No. 47, p. 31. (9) 13 Jan.: Mantua, exiles, Dönniges, I, No. 53, p. 32. (10) & (11) 14 Jan.: Reggio, both parties, *MGH*, No. 544, p. 499. (12) 15 Jan.: Lodi, *MGH*, No. 554, p. 511. (13) 15 Jan.: Lodi, exiles, *MGH*, No. 555, pp. 511f. (14) 19 Jan.: Verona, exiles (appointment), Bonaini, *Acta*, I, No. 90, pp. 131ff. (15) 2 Feb.: Albenga—appoints proctors to do fealty, receive confirmation of former privileges, accept new privileges, and request that the rights of the commune now held by others be restored. This last clause refers to an attempt to shake off Genoese control. *MGH*, No. 1279, pp. 1414f.

107. *MGH*, No. 512, pp. 466f.

108. The arbitrations for Como, Parma, Brescia, Piacenza, and Pavia were pronounced respectively on 5, 10, 10, 11, and 12 Jan. 1311. See Dönniges, *Acta*, I, No. 33, p. 26 (Como); *ibid.*, No. 43a, p. 29 (Parma); *ibid.*, No. 44, p. 30 (Brescia); *MGH*, No. 546, p. 502 (Piacenza); *MGH*, No. 530, pp. 488f. (Pavia). All these pacts are extant only in imbreviatures, and it is possible that they differed slightly from the pact for Milan. It would not be surprising, for example, if the fines for each breach of the peace were less for these cities than for Milan—and were more like those declared for Vercelli and Novara (£100 gold) or those later pronounced for Cremona, Reggio *et al.* (£300 gold).

109. *MGH*, No. 533 (14 Jan. 1311), p. 491.

110. *MGH*, No. 534 (14 Jan. 1311), pp. 491ff.

111. *MGH*, No. 545 (14 Jan. 1311), pp. 500ff.

112. The pact issued for Modena on 14 Jan. 1311 was the same as that given Reggio. Dönniges, *Acta*, I, No. 56, p. 33.

113. *MGH*, No. 556 (15 Jan. 1311), pp. 512ff.

114. *MGH*, No. 558 (17 Jan. 1311), pp. 515ff.

115. Cermenate, Ch. XVII, p. 39.
116. *Ibid., loc. cit.;* Mussato, Bk. I, Rub. 12. Matteo Visconti did not remain the only prominent exile to offer the Emperor-elect a gift on the eve of readmission to his native city. On 11 Jan. 1311 Walter de Curte and Manfred Beccaria, Ghibelline rival of Count Philippone Langusco, promised to pay 1,500 florins to Henry and 500 to the Queen within six weeks after they and their followers returned to Pavia. *MGH*, No. 529, p. 488.
117. See G. Sandri, "Il vicariato imperiale e gli inizi della signoria Scaligera in Vicenza," *Archivio Veneto*, ser. 5, XII (1932), 78f.; Mussato, Bk. II, Rub. 7.
118. On 4 Feb. 1311 the Scaligers promised to give Henry all Veronese income pertaining to the Empire. They pledged that no tax would be laid upon Verona without Henry's consent, and that Verona would serve him annually according to the ability of the city and its district (*MGH*, No. 572, pp. 529f.). See also Butrinto, 503f.
119. *MGH*, No. 563, pp. 521ff.
120. *MGH*, No. 564, pp. 523f.
121. *Chron. Parmense*, 119 (for Parma); Bonifazio da Morano, *Chron. Mutinense*, cols. 97f.
122. *MGH*, No. 517, p. 479. Schwalm dates this letter to the Bishop of Strassburg as 1310 Dec. ex. Since it mentions that the coronation has not yet taken place and that Henry has entered Milan, it must have been written ex 23 Dec.—in 6 Jan., and a reference to the fealty of the proctors of Como would place it ex 24 Dec. 1310 (cf. Dönniges, *Acta*, No. 19, p. 20).
123. Gazata, Sagacius, and Petrus, *Chronicon Regiense*, ed. L. A. Muratori, *RR.II.SS.*, XVIII (Milan, 1731), col. 21; cf. Mussato, Bk. I, Rub. 11.
124. See the official list of vicars, *MGH*, No. 579 (mid-Feb. 1311), pp. 534f. The only obvious omissions were Padua and its subject Vicenza, Alba, Alessandria, and Treviso. The absence of vicars for the first two is explained by Henry's negotiations with Padua; for the second two, by their homage to Robert of Anjou. Treviso soon received Pietro di Gaido as its vicar; G. B. Picotti, *I caminesi* (cited above, Ch. I, n. 49), 198, n. 2, 340.
125. Individual vicars were assigned to Monza (previously controlled by Milan), to Val Camonica (subject to Brescia), and to Castrum Razoli (in the Reggian *contado*). *MGH*, No. 579, p. 535. For the importance to Reggio of Castrum Razoli (taken by the Mantuans a few months earlier), see *Statuta Civitatis Regii, 1311*, Bk. XIII, Rub. 24, f. 109ʳ: "Castrum Razoli est alter oculus Communis et Civitatis Regii, quo sublato oculo previo Commune Regii ambulat sicut cecus." On 10 Jan. 1311 Reggio petitioned Henry for the return of Castrum Razoli and of Castrum Novi (captured by the Scaligers, Bonacolsi and Reggian exiles, and consigned to the Di Sesso, leading Reggian Ghibelline exiles). On 12 Jan. 1311 Henry ordered that Castrum Novi be returned to its rightful lord, the Bishop of Reggio (*MGH*, No. 543, p. 499), but he retained Castrum Razoli as a direct holding of the Empire.
126. The Sienese Ghibelline Niccolo de' Buonsignori was vicar in Milan; the White Guelf Guidaloste dei Vergiolesi of Pistoia in Modena (controlled by the Ghibelline Francesco della Mirandola); the Florentine Ghibelline Lamberto Cipriani and Lapo, son of Farinata degli Uberti, re-

spectively in Piacenza and Mantua (controlled by the Ghibelline Bonacolsi). The Florentine Ghibelline papal knight and former imperial legate Ugolino da Vico was still in Chieri. Vanni Zeno of Pisa was made vicar of Verona. Before Zeno's arrival the Scaliger *signori* secretly resigned their positions as captains of Verona. See Sandri, "Il vicariato imperiale" (cited above, Ch. II, n. 117), 78, n. 2, and F. Güterbock, "Veroneser Annalen nach einer Handschrift aus dem Nachlass Sigonio's," *Neues Archiv*, XXV (1900), 69.

127. Guido Cocconato, Count of Radicate, sent to Parma, Francesco Marquis of Cravesana (to Cremona), and the Guelf Albert de Maloselli of Genoa (relative of Amadeus) in Novara were probably candidates of Amadeus and Philip of Savoy and the Marquis of Monferrat. Cocconato was from Monferrat, while Francesco of Cravesana was a personal friend of Philip's (cf. Ventura, cols. 786, 787). On Thomas (or Tolomeo?) Pellicioni, sent to Borgo S. Donnino, see *Chron. Parmense*, 119 lines 33f. Two vicars were chosen from the opportunist Marquises of Malaspina in the Lunigiana (Spineta to Reggio; Marchixetum to Tortona—which city generally opposed the Malaspina. In 1313 Tortona was to complain bitterly against another Malaspina vicar, Azzo; Dönniges, *Acta*, I, Nos. 45a-c, pp. 65f.).

128. On 2 May 1313 Henry's council ordered that the vicar's salary be limited to those of the former podesta and captain combined (*MGH*, No. 963, p. 1005). For Chieri, see above, Ch. II, n. 22. The Reggian statutes specifically designated as compiled under Henry VII (*Statuta Civitatis Regii, 1311*, Bk. XIII) do not treat the vicar's stipend, powers, or limitations; but they do refer to him as "podesta or vicar," e.g., Rub. 71, f. 117v; Rub. 73, f. 118r. The statutes of Vicenza (1311) provided for the vicar's (rector's) salary, to be paid by the commune, and for his family. He was to remain in office six months. See V. Bortolaso, "Vicenza dalla morte di Ezzelino alla signoria scaligera (1259-1311)," *Nuovo Archivio Veneto*, n.s., anno 12, pt. 2, vol. XXIV (1912), 389.

129. See, e.g., *MGH*, No. 987, par. 2, p. 1026; No. 936, par. 5, p. 972; Dönniges, *Acta*, I, No. 33, p. 59; No. 59, p. 68; No. 62, p. 69; No. 95, p. 78. Cf. *Statuti civili . . . di Chieri*, ed. F. Cognasso, Rubrics 3, 19, 35f., 51, 53, 119f., 61f., 122f., 230, 232, 301, 314, also 340, 342 (added in the fall of 1311) for provisions dealing with the vicar's rights and limitations. The detailed discussion of vicarships and general vicarships in O. Felsberg, *Beiträge zur Geschichte des Römerzuges Heinrichs VII. I. Teil: Innere und Finanzpolitik Heinrichs VII. in Italien* (Leipzig, 1886), 16ff., is highly arbitrary and schematized, almost all its proofs are from 1313, and it frequently reads more into source wording than is warranted.

130. Our only notice of a vicar-general for this period is that in Dönniges, *Acta*, I, No. 17 (30 Jan. 1311), p. 137—"Francesco, Count [*sic*] of Cravesana, vicar-general in the city of Cremona and its district."

131. See the discussion in P. Brezzi, "Le relazioni tra i Comuni italiani e l'Impero," *Questioni di storia medioevale*, ed. E. Rota (Como-Milan, 1946), 400ff.

132. Possibly the Mantuan statutes were revised during this period. See C. D'Arco, *Storia di Mantova*, II (Mantua, 1871), containing Books I-III of the *Codice Bonacolsiano*, statutes compiled 1303ff., and III

(Mantua, 1872), containing Bks. IV-X. For the Reggian statutes of 1311, see the beginning of Bk. XIII (above, Ch. II, n. 101). The last rubric, 73, f. 118r, is followed by these lines (cancelled out): "Insuper dominus Guido de Viano vicarius in civitate Regii Serenissimi domino henrici Romanorum Regis ex vigore et baylia sibi concessa et comissa per dictum dominum Regem et omnimodo iure quibus melius potuit, audita provisione suprascripta eam approbavit ratifficavit et confirmavit et fieri et mandari executioni precipit." Guido de Viano only became vicar after the collapse of the rebellion of 25 Feb. 1311, and the city's return to imperial obedience (cf. *MGH*, No. 579, p. 534). At the end of June 1311 he was no longer in office (*Chron. Parmense*, 120; M. Melchiorri, "Vicende della signoria di Ghiberto da Correggio in Parma," 83). On 22 Nov. 1311 the "Wise Men" of Reggio asked the vicar to appoint men "vedere et examinare statuta quae de novo exemplata sunt per Gerundinum de Gerundis et secundum quod providerit quod dictus Gerundinus habeat pro suo labore" (Reggio Emilia, Archivio di Stato, *Provvigioni dei venti Saggi deputati ai negozi del comune*, f. 14r). For Gerundinus as the notary who drew up the statutes in question, see *Statuta Civ. Regii, 1311*, Bk. XIII, Rub. 65, f. 116r-v, Bk. XIV, Rub. 15, f. 125v.

133. *Chron. Parmense*, 119.
134. Gazata, *Chronicon Regiense*, *RR.II.SS.*, XVIII, col. 21.
135. *Loc. cit.*; also E. E. Stengel, ed., *Nova Alamanniae*, I, Pt. 1, No. 81 (s.d.), pp. 38f.; *MGH*, Nos. 550-553. pp. 504-511.
136. *MGH*, No. 641 (post 17 June 1311), p. 604 lines 18f.
137. *MGH*, No. 553 (8 Feb. 1311), pp. 507ff., lists various cities and nobles and their assessments. Venice was assessed third highest, at 28,800 florins a year, Padua fourth, at 20,000. Verona was assigned 13,740, Mantua and Treviso 10,000 each.
138. *MGH*, No. 573 (9 Feb. 1311), p. 530; Butrinto, 504.

NOTES: CHAPTER III. THE FIRST TROUBLES:
FROM MILAN TO GENOA (FEBRUARY—OCTOBER 1311)

1. Butrinto, 502. For further documentation of the following material concerning Milan, including the uprising of 12 Feb. 1311, see F. Cognasso in *Storia di Milano*, ed. G. Treccani degli Alfieri, V, 34ff.
2. *MGH*, p. 1146 lines 19f.
3. Cermenate, Ch. XX, p. 44. See Villani, Bk. IX, Ch. 7, "[Arrigo] che da se non era ricco signore di moneta." Cf. above, Ch. II, n. 8.
4. Cermenate, Ch. XIX, pp. 41ff.
5. *MGH*, No. 565, p. 524.
6. The proctor of Canobbio did fealty on 12 Jan. 1311 (Dönniges, *Acta*, I, No. 47, p. 31). On 20 Jan. Trezzo and Concorezzo separately named proctors to appear before the vicar of Milan and its *contado* (Bonaini, *Acta*, Nos. 91, 92, pp. 133ff., 136f.)
7. 29 Jan. 1311; document published by G. Barelli, "Documenti dell' archivio comunale di Treviglio," *ASI*, ser. 5, XXX (1902), 50f.
8. 9 Feb. 1311, *MGH*, No. 574, pp. 530f., and for the parts there omitted see the inferior ed. by G. Barelli, "Documenti . . . di Treviglio," 52f.
9. Cermenate, Ch. XV, p. 26.

10. Cermenate (Ch. XXIII, p. 50) claims that Henry was warned by the vicar of Milan.
11. Butrinto, 506.
12. *MGH*, No. 580 (20 Feb. 1311), pp. 535ff.
13. 20 March 1311; published by G. Barelli, *ASI*, ser. 5, XXX (1902), 54f., and by J. C. Luenig, ed., *Codex Italiae Diplomaticus*, III (Frankfurt, 1732), col. 207.
14. See, e.g., *Chron. Parmense*, 119f.; Butrinto, 506f.; Cermenate, Ch. XXIX, pp. 65ff.; Mussato, Bk. II, Rub. 1-4; Villani, Bk. IX, Ch. 11. For Asti see Bonaini, *Acta*, I, Nos. 101, 102 (18, 20 Feb. 1311), pp. 147-156, 156-167; also G. Sommerfeldt, "König Heinrich VII. und die lombardischen Städte in den Jahren 1310-1312," *Deutsche Zeitschrift für Geschichtswissenschaft*, II (1889), 113f. In Brescia the nominally Ghibelline Maggi had been in power before Henry's arrival. Events in Brescia are confused and it is impossible to determine which faction began the fighting in February 1311 (Sommerfeldt, pp. 113f.).
15. See, e.g., Butrinto, 506f.; Cermenate, Ch. XXIX, 65ff.; G. Sommerfeldt, "König Heinrich VII. und die lombard. Städte," 114.
16. *MGH*, No. 582 (1311 ante 27 Feb.), pp. 538f.; No. 583 (27 Feb. 1311), pp. 539f.
17. *MGH*, No. 585 (31 March 1311), p. 541.
18. See Bonaini, *Acta*, II, No. 20 (1 April 1311), p. 18.
19. A first installment of over 2,000 florins was in the hands of the royal treasurer before mid-May 1311. The judge appointed for this important task was Cione delle Bellaste of Pistoia, and the well-known humanist Benzo of Alessandria was his notary and assistant. See *MGH*, No. 1149, p. 1145 lines 28f.; No. 989, par. 14, p. 980; No. 1285, pp. 1419ff.; and G. Biscaro, "Benzo da Alessandria" (cited above, Ch. I, n. 110), 287ff.
20. In addition to the chronicle accounts in Butrinto, 508f., Cermenate, Ch. XXIX, pp. 70f., etc., see *MGH*, No. 611 (22 April 1311), pp. 573f., an oath of fealty sworn to the King of the Romans in Lodi by a proctor of that commune.
21. Cf. Jacobus Malvezzi, *Chronicon Brixianum*, ed. L. A. Muratori, *RR.II.SS.*, XIV (Milan, 1729) cols. 966f., for the vicar of Brescia; *Chron. Parmense*, 119f., for the vicar of Parma.
22. See the documents published by F. Güterbock, "Veroneser Annalen" (cited above, Ch. II, n. 126), 70. Cf. H. Spangenberg, *Can Grande I von Scala* (two vols. in one; Berlin 1892-1895), I, 24. For the payment by the Scaligers, see Cortusiis, *RR.II.SS.*, n.s., XII, Pt. 5, Ch. 14, p. 14; cf. the hostile testimony of Ferreto, I, 310; and note *MGH*, p. 1145 line 35, indicating a payment of 17,300 florins to the royal treasurer, "a vicariis de Verona pro seconda solutione." This could not have been the city's contribution to the salary of the Vicar-General in Lombardy, as that was 3,435 florins every three months. We do not know the amount of imperial income due from Verona, and therefore cannot be certain as to the nature of this payment of 17,300 florins.
23. *MGH*, No. 629, pp. 589f. See also *MGH*, No. 630 (10 May 1311), p. 590, and Cortusiis, *RR.II.SS.*, n.s., XII, Pt. 5, Ch. 14, p. 14.
24. Cf. Cognasso, in *Storia di Milano*, ed. G. Treccani degli Alfieri, V, 66ff.
25. Cf. L. Simeoni, *Le Signorie*, I, 54; G. Biscaro, "Benzo da Alessandria" (cited above, Ch. I, n. 110), 307; Cognasso, in *Storia di Milano*, V. 91.)

26. The so-called "Privilege of Liberty" granted Padua the right to select four citizens loyal to the Empire every six months. The monarch was to appoint one of these as vicar of Padua. The vicar was bound by oath to respect the rights, laws, and customs of Padua and its subject, Vicenza (whose custody would now be legalized by perpetual investiture). In return Padua was to pay the imperial treasury 15,000 florins annually, and 60,000 extra when an emperor descended into Italy or was crowned. Vicenza was liberated on 15 April by imperial troops captained by the Bishop of Geneva and Padua's archenemy, the imperial vicar-general of Verona, Can Grande della Scala. The best account of the above events is in Sandri, "Il vicariato imperiale" (cited above, Ch. II, n. 117), 79-95. See also Mussato, Bk. II, Rub. 7, III, 1 (loss of Vicenza), III, 6 (Paduan submission to Henry); Ferreto, I, 311ff. (dealings with Henry; loss of Vicenza), 331ff. (Paduan submission).

27. The privilege of 9 June 1311 did not include the investiture of Vicenza, was valid only six years, and provided that Padua pay the imperial treasury not 15,000 but 20,000 florins annually (*MGH*, No. 626, pp. 587f.). On 10 June the Paduan proctor promised that the treasury would receive an additional 100,000 florins within less than ten weeks, and this did not excuse the city's payment of its share of the Vicar-General's stipend by the following Christmas (*MGH*, No. 628, p. 589).

28. See the chronicle of Pietro da Villola in *Corpus Chronicorum Bononiensium*, ed. A. Sorbelli, *RR.II.SS.*, n.s., XVIII, Pt. 1, vol. II (Bologna, 1938), 318; *MGH*, No. 1045, par. 89, p. 1083.

29. *MGH*, No. 586, pp. 541ff., esp. 543 lines 28f.

30. *MGH*, No. 515, pp. 475f. For a clear statement of Philip's desire that the imperial coronation be delayed, see Clement's letter to Philip, 9 Dec. 1310, *MGH*, No. 467, par. 4, p. 414.

31. See *MGH*, Nos. 604-608 (11–post-19 April 1311), pp. 567ff.

32. *MGH*, No. 594 (1311 ante 30 March), *passim*, esp. par. 2, p. 552, par. 3, p. 553 lines 1f.; *MGH*, No. 596 (5 April 1311), esp. par. 1, p. 556f.

33. See the two sets of instructions for the Florentine ambassadors destined for the papal court, Bonaini, *Acta*, II, No. 12 (4 Jan. 1311), p. 9; No. 20 (1 April 1311), p. 18. Cf. F. Kern, *Die Anfänge der französischen Ausdehnungspolitik*, 311f.

34. *MGH*, No. 514, par. 17, pp. 473f.

35. See Bonaini, *Acta*, II, No. 12 (4 Jan. 1311), p. 10. For Pellagru, cf. above, Ch. II, n. 52.

36. Cf. *MGH*, No. 594 (1311 ante 30 March), par. 2, p. 552; No. 596 (5 April 1311), par. 1, pp. 556f.

37. See *MGH*, No. 595, pp. 554ff. For the Tuscan Guelf conditions, see above, Ch. I, n. 79, Ch. II, nn. 85ff.

38. Clement had never intended to leave even the rights of the Church *within* imperial Italy to the mercies of the outspokenly pacific Henry of Luxemburg. Less than a week before the imperial expedition began its Alpine crossing the Pope appointed a special legate of his own volition and not at the King's behest. His mission was "to augment and maintain ecclesiastical liberty, and spread wide the seeds of tranquility," a precautionary measure for the protection of the rights of the Church in the lands to be visited by the Emperor-elect. *MGH*, No. 440 (8 Oct. 1310), pp. 384ff.; lines quoted are on p. 385 lines 2f.

39. See *MGH*, Nos. 588-592 (4 March 1311), pp. 544ff., all bearing upon the negotiations for French-imperial treaties; *MGH*, No. 596 (5 April 1311), par. 3, pp. 557f.

40. Cf. above, Ch. III, n. 30. The necessity for considering Henry's expedition in its entirety has led this author to modify his earlier opinion that "Pope Clement V found himself *forced* by a concatenation of *circumstances beyond his control* to act in a manner completely contrary to his expressed desires" (see W. Bowsky, "Clement V and the Emperor-elect," *Medievalia et Humanistica*, XII [1958], 69 and 52ff. *passim*).

41. See Bonaini, *Acta*, II, Nos. 16, 17, 22, 23 (Jan. 1311, 3 Feb., 1 April, 1 April 1311), pp. 13ff., 15f., 19f., 20 f. For Robert's attitudes and moves during the winter and spring of 1310-1311, see Caggese, *Roberto*, I, 129ff.

42. Bonaini, *Acta*, II, No. 38 (26 April 1311), pp. 31f.

43. On 2 Dec. 1310, Robert borrowed 24,400 oz. of gold from the Bardi and Peruzzi, of which 284 were to pay for the maintenance of slightly over 150 soldiers in Piedmont for that month (G. M. Monti, *La dominazione angoina*, Doc. XIX, pp. 369f., and p. 127 of the text). In mid-January 1311 he recalled to the Regno all vassals who were abroad or in other parts of Italy (Caggese, *Roberto*, I, 127). In Feb. 1311 Robert ordered his vicar in the Romagna and other royal functionaries to observe scrupulously the statutes and ancient customary rights of Faenza and Forli. Two weeks later he commanded that no novel measures be taken in the Romagnol castles held of Bologna, and granted that city the right to take provisions from the Romagna (Caggese, *Roberto*, I, 129; G. Fasoli, "Bologna e la Romagna" [cited above, Ch. I, n. 74], 29, n. 4).

44. See the references to the Florentine negotiations with Ghiberto da Correggio in a letter from Florence to Siena of 16 April 1311, partially printed in Mommsen, *Ital. Analekten*, No. 27, pp. 30f. For further dealings between Florence and Ghiberto and their outcome, see below Ch. IV.

45. Bonaini, *Acta*, II, No. 20, p. 17.

46. *Corpus Chronicorum Bononiensium*, RR.II.SS., XVIII, Pt. 1, vol. II, 319.

47. Mommsen, *Ital. Analekten*, No. 24, pp. 29f.; Caggese, *Roberto*, I, 130, n. 2.

48. During April 1311 many Bolognese of imperial or Ghibelline sympathies who opposed the Bolognese—Tuscan Guelf alliance left Bologna for Verona, Mantua, and Modena, and there urged the immediate destruction of their native city. See Caggese, *Roberto*, I, 137, n. 1 (doc. of 15 April 1311), and V. Vitale, *Il dominio della parte guelfa* (cited above, Ch. I, n. 74), Doc. XXI.

49. See Bonaini, *Acta*, II, No. 20, pp. 17ff. ("imperatoris Teutonici," p. 18); No. 22, p. 20; No. 23, p. 21; No. 24, p. 22.

50. The implications of this act were not lost upon the Emperor-elect. One of the charges in his first citation of Florence for disobedience was to be that it refused to call him King of the Romans, "suppressing the dignity of his name in opprobrium and disrespect to him." *MGH*, No. 715 (20 Nov. 1311), p. 699.

51. Cf. above, Ch. III, n. 49, see also Bonaini, *Acta*, II, No. 26 (14 April 1311), p. 24.
52. Bonaini, *Acta*, II, No. 20 (1 April 1311), p. 18.
53. For the Cremonese rebellion and the occupation and punishment of the city by Henry of Luxemburg, see A. Cavalcabò, *Le ultime lotte* (cited above, Ch. I, n. 65), 31-39, 41-55; Schneider, *H.VII*, 116ff.; Cognasso in *Storia di Milano,* ed. G. Treccani degli Alfieri, V, 62f.; G. Sommerfeldt, "König Heinrich VII. und die lombardischen Städte," (cited above, Ch. III, n. 14), 119f. The sentence pronounced 10 May 1311 against the Torriani and 71 listed Cremonese rebels is in *MGH,* No. 631, pp. 591ff. The renewed Cremonese oath of fealty to the King of the Romans (10 May) is in *MGH,* No. 632, p. 594. We must rely upon chronicle accounts for the sentence of 29 April 1311.
54. On 3 May 1311 Henry accepted fealty from Soncino in the Cremonese *contado* (north of the city on the west bank of the Oglio River), where he was recognized as immediate lord having all jurisdiction (*MGH,* Nos. 619, 620, pp. 582, 582f.). On 3 Oct. 1311 Henry further guaranteed the independence of Soncino by incorporating it, and the parish of Calcione, into the *camera regis* and specifically stating that they were to be free of all persons or cities (*MGH,* No. 694, pp. 667f.). In late April 1311 Ghiberto da Correggio took advantage of Cremona's weakness and occupied Guastalla (east of the city on the southern bank of the Po) (*Chron. Parmense*, 120). Guastalla had been in Cremonese hands since the twelfth century, and was a key point in Cremona's defense system, as the opposite bank of the Po was controlled by the Cavalcabò fief of Viadana. (Cf. P. Darmstädter, *Das Reichsgut in der Lombardei,* 346, 354; A. Cavalcabò, *Le ultime lotte,* 17ff.) (After Cremona's unsuccessful military alliance with Marquis Azzo VIII of Este, in 1307 Guastalla had fallen to Ghiberto da Correggio. The Cremonese, led by Wm. Cavalcabò, had retaken it peacefully in October 1310.)
55. R. Davidsohn, *Forschungen,* IV, 541.
56. Butrinto, 516. For Giovanni da Castiglione see also Ferreto, I, 294, and *MGH,* p. 1486, col. 3 (index).
57. Richard Tizzone is last mentioned as vicar of Cremona on 5 Aug. 1311. His successor, Geoffrey dei Vergiolesi of Pistoia, first appears on 16 Sept. 1311 (L. Astegiano, ed., *Codex diplomaticus Cremonae* [*Monumenta Historiae Patriae,* ser. 2, XXII; Turin, 1898], II, Nos. 142-144, p. 21). For Da Castiglione's presence in Cremona 16 Nov. 1311, see *MGH,* No. 1221, p. 1274.
58. For the presence of a Cremonese legation in Lodi during that city's insurrection, see Cermenate, Ch. XXX, pp. 71f.
59. Cermenate, Ch. XXXV, p. 79; cf. Butrinto, 515f.
60. For the Brescian rebellion and the events concerning it recounted below see, e.g., Davidsohn, *Geschichte,* III, 435ff.; G. Sommerfeldt, "König Heinrich VII. und die lombardischen Städte" (cited above, Ch. III, n. 14), pp. 110f.; Schneider, *H.VII,* 118ff.; and Cermenate, Chs. XXXV-XLII, pp. 79ff.; Butrinto, 510ff.; Ferreto, I, 328f., 336-465; Mussato, Bk. II, Rub. 9, III, 5, 7, IV, 1-3, 5-6; J. Malvezzi, *Chron. Brixianum, RR.II.SS.,* XIV, cols. 967-976; *MGH,* Nos. 622, 623, 648, 653, 688-691.
61. See, e.g., Villani, Bk. IX, Ch. 10.

62. Dante, Letter VII.
63. The Emperor-elect recalled Matteo and Galeazzo Visconti in mid-April 1311 and permitted them to return to Milan, after less than two months of exile in Asti and Treviso. See Cermenate, Ch. XXIX, pp. 64f.; Ferreto, I, 309. Despite the dubious comportment of the Visconti with respect to the Milanese tumults, the Torriani bore arms against imperial troops, while the Visconti did not. The two rival factions did not share equal guilt.
64. Henry's decision to besiege Brescia may have been reinforced when his brother Walram advised him that he had it upon good authority that the city would fall within a fortnight. Interestingly, that authority was a group of Brescian Ghibelline exiles, desperate at the thought of losing this opportunity of re-entering their native city. Perhaps Walram neglected to add that among the exiles' persuasive arguments was the promise of 20,000 florins if he succeeded in convincing his brother to undertake the siege. Butrinto, 510.
65. For the German troops see John of Victring (cited above, Ch. I, n. 12), II, 21 (Lib. IV, Rec. A, Ch. 9).
66. *MGH*, No. 653, pp. 622f. See also Mussato, Bk. III, Rub. 7; Cermenate, Ch. XXXVII, p. 82; Dino Compagni, Bk. III, Ch. 29, p. 237. See the illustration of Brusati's execution in Figure 12.
67. Cf. the letters sent from Florence to Brescia in Sept. 1311, filled with encouragement and promises of money and troops. Bonaini, *Acta*, II, Nos. 48, 52, 54, 55 (9, 13 & 16, 16, 17 Sept. 1311), pp. 38f., 41f., 42f., 43f. See also Ferreto, I, 329; Dino Compagni, Bk. III, Ch. 30, p. 238; cf. Butrinto, 511.
68. Cermenate, Ch. XXXVII, p. 82.
69. Cf. Mussato, Bk. III, Rub. 7.
70. Dönniges, *Acta*, II, No. 12, pp. 14ff. Among the suspects were Simone degli Avvocati of Vercelli, Count Philippone Langusco's son and heir, and even Richard Tizzone of Vercelli—perhaps still vicar of Cremona.
71. Mommsen, *Ital. Analekten*, No. 33 (14 June 1311), p. 33. For a more fortunate Bolognese spy in the imperial camp during the final month and a half of the siege, see Mommsen, *op. cit.*, No. 42 (10 Nov. 1311), p. 35. Cf. Butrinto, 512f.
72. Butrinto, 508f.
73. Petrus Azarius, *Liber gestorum in Lombardia*, ed. F. Cognasso, *RR.II.SS.*, n.s., XVI, Pt. 4 (Bologna, 1926-1929), 15; Mussato, Bk. XII, Rub. 4.
74. The Dominican Isnard Tacconi, Archbishop of Thebes, had been appointed papal vicar *in spiritualibus* in Rome, and on 13 Aug. 1311 was transferred to the Patriarchate of Antioch (C. Eubel, *Hierarchia catholica*, I², pp. 93, 482). In his reform of Pavia he ordered the Ghibelline Beccaria and De Curte factions to remain outside of the city and its suburbs (*MGH*, No. 656, pp. 625f.). See also G. Sommerfeldt, "König Heinrich VII. und die lombardischen Städte" (cited above, Ch. III, n. 14), 132. Henry of Luxemburg does not appear to have made sufficient use of Isnard Tacconi's statesmanship and talents, and only appointed him as a member of an embassy sent to central and western Lombardy in April 1313 (cf. *MGH*, No. 939, p. 976).
75. The rival Tizzoni and Avvocati of Vercelli called in Philip of Savoy to arbitrate a settlement of their differences. In September 1311 he promulgated a pact ordering that in the future all enmities be

forgotten, and decreeing a fine of 1,000 silver marks for breaches of the peace. The pact specifically ordered that one half of such a fine was to go to the party that had maintained the peace, the other 500 marks to be paid to the Emperor or to Philip in the Emperor's name. For the text of this pact arbitrated 18-30 Sept. 1311, see G. Sommerfeldt, "König Heinrich VII. und die lombardischen Städte," 148-155; cf. G. Ventura, col. 780.

76. *MGH*, No. 660a (15 July 1311), pp. 629ff. For pacts concluded between Matteo Visconti and the Archbishop of Milan in Asti on 4 Dec. 1310, see above, Ch. II, n. 51.

77. For the monetary decree of 10 Aug. 1311 (elaborated and ordered executed in Sept. and Oct.), see *MGH*, No. 669, pp. 638ff. Henry's mintmasters were Florentines—Richard Uguetti and Abizzo di Tano Uguetti. For the Luxemburger's monetary policy, esp. summer 1311—Jan. 1312, see C. Violante, "Per la storia economica e sociale di Pisa nel Trecento. La riforma della zecca del 1318," *Bullettino del Istituto Storico Italiano*, No. 66 (Rome, 1954), 142ff.

78. For this development, and the material in the following paragraphs, see esp. C. Wenck, *Clemens V.*, Ch. IV, Pt. 3, "Die Aussöhnung Philipps des Schönen mit der Curie," 157-163.

79. Cf. *MGH*, No. 514 (24 Dec. 1310), pp. 468ff.

80. *MGH*, No. 612 (1 May 1311), par. 2, pp. 575f.

81. *MGH*, No. 514, p. 473 lines 35ff. Cf. above, Ch. I, nn. 26ff.

82. *MGH*, No. 648, pp. 617f.

83. *Ibid.*, p. 618 lines 9f.: "decet regie benignitatis clementiam, ut cum subditis tuis, quos erroris cecitas a fidelitate regia deducit in devium, misericordie exerceas ubertatem."

84. *Ibid.*, p. 618 lines 16f.: "celsitudinem regiam paterno rogamus affectu et hortamur . . . quod . . . agas misericorditer cum eisdem, et sic erga eos affluentiam tue pietatis exerceas, quod singuli de comunitate predicta tue clementie cognita veritate de tribulationum profundo se liberatos fore letentur. . . ."

85. See, e.g., G. Fasoli, "Bologna e la Romagna," (cited above, Ch. I, n. 74), 34f.

86. *MGH*, No. 650, pp. 619f.

87. *Ibid.*, p. 620 lines 9f.: "Plures . . . duces proditionis capti, fuerunt Dei iusto iudicio et demum ultimo supplicio traditi pro demeritis eorundem."

88. *Ibid.*, p. 620 lines 22f.: "magnificentiam tuam paterno rogamus et hortamur affectu, quatinus proditores predictos . . . tanquam nostros et prefate sedis hostes manifestos et publicos de dicta provincia Lombardie et aliis terris tue dictioni subiectis pro nostra et dicte sedis reverentia facias forbanniri."

89. *MGH*, No. 641 (post 17 June 1311), par. 11, p. 603: "Item petatur a papa, quod scribat terris et civitatibus ecclesie Romane, quod inimicis et rebellibus domino regi [Henrico] non dent auxilium vel favorem nec impediant transeuntes ad dominum nec prohibeant victualia afferri domino et exercitu[i] suo, nec recipiant bannitos a domino rege. . . ."

90. Cf. above, Ch. I, nn. 104f.

91. Two other cardinals appeared before Brescia: Leonardo Patrasso da Guercino, Cardinal Bishop of Albano, and the papal legate Arnald de Faugères (or Frangeriis), Cardinal Bishop of Sabina. A fifth cardinal

went directly to Rome to prepare for the coronation. Cardinal Faugères, raised to the cardinalate by Clement V in Dec. 1310, proved too disinterested in the welfare of Henry VII, who requested his recall and substitution in July 1313 (*MGH*, No. 1006, par. 7, pt. 1, p. 1051). The other four cardinals had been created by Boniface VIII. For the cardinals arrival before Brescia, see, e.g., Cermenate, Ch. XLII, pp. 88f.; J. Malvezzi, *Chron. Brixianum, RR.II.SS.*, XIV, col. 972; Mussato, Bk. IV, Rub. 1; Dino Compagni, Bk. III, Ch. 29, p. 239; and G. Sommerfeldt, "König Heinrich VII. und die lombardischen Städte" (cited above, Ch. III, n. 14), 127.

92. See *MGH*, No. 688 (21 Sept. 1311), pp. 654f. For the conditions expected by Brescia, cf. Mussato, Bk. IV, Rub. 6.

93. For the sentence of 1 Oct. 1311 see *MGH*, No. 689, pp. 655ff. This sentence had at first been drawn up in another form, which differed from the promulgated version only in its much longer and more bitter preamble (*MGH*, No. 691, pp. 660ff.). *MGH*, No. 690, p. 660, contains the Brescian proctor's ratification and acceptance of Henry's sentence against the city.

94. J. Malvezzi, *Chron. Brixianum, RR.II.SS.*, XIV, col. 976.

95. Villani (Bk. IX, Ch. 20) estimates Henry's losses at over three quarters. Cf. Mussato, Bk. IV, Rub. 5; Cermenate, Ch. XLII, p. 89.

96. Bonifazio da Morano, *Chron. Mutinense, RR.II.SS.*, XI, col. 99. F. della Mirandola replaced the Pistoian exile Guidaloste dei Vergiolesi as vicar of Modena. Already on 25 July 1311 Mirandola and two of his relatives had received confirmation of several imperial fiefs (Mommsen, *Ital. Analekten*, No. 34, p. 33).

97. See *MGH*, p. 890 lines 33ff., p. 893 lines 28ff. W. de Curte had long curried royal favor. In January 1311 he had joined with Manfred Beccaria in promising the King of the Romans a handsome gift after his readmission to Pavia (*MGH*, No. 529, p. 488; see above, Ch. II, n. 116). In April he gave Baldwin of Trier a personal cash gift (*MGH*, No. 1150, p. 1149 line 7).

98. See P. Torelli, "Il capitanato del popolo," (cited above, Ch. II, n. 44), 137ff. Possibly P. Bonacolsi received the vicarship for his lifetime.

99. *MGH*, No. 660. pp. 628f.

100. See Gazata, *Chron. Regiense, RR.II.SS.*, XVIII, col. 22; *Chron. Parmense*, 120; Cortusiis, *Chron. de Novitatibus Padue et Lombardie, RR.II.SS.*, n.s., XII, Pt. 5, 14; *MGH*, No. 768, p. 758 lines 41ff. Before the Brescian siege was two months old G. da Correggio had been enfeoffed with Guastalla, which he had seized from Cremona a month earlier (above, Ch. III, n. 54).

101. Mussato, Bk. VII, Rub. 1. Cf. Butrinto, 517f.; *MGH*, No. 1220 (7 Nov. 1311), p. 1271 lines 3ff. See also G. Sommerfeldt, "König Heinrich VII. und die lombardischen Städte" (cited above, Ch. III, n. 14), 135ff.

102. Disappointed too was the nominally Guelf Alberto Scotto, when that aspiring *signore* of Piacenza saw the Veronese Pietro del Mesa appointed vicar of that city in early October 1311 (Ferreto, I, 358; Mussato, Bk. IX, Rub. 9).

103. Villani, Bk. IX, Ch. 20; Ferreto, I, 310f.; Butrinto, 517f.; Mussato, Bk. VII, Rubs. 1, 8; Cortusiis, *Chron. de Novitatibus, RR.II.SS.*, n.s., XII, Pt. 5, 14.

104. *MGH*, No. 695, pp. 668f.

105. Butrinto, 518f.
106. *Chron. Parmense*, 121; Ferreto, II, 6f.
107. Our principal source for the assembly and proceedings at Pavia is Mussato, Bk. IV, Rub. 10. See also Ferreto, II, 3ff. Among the disappointed exiles were the Guelfs Vinciguerra, Count of Sambonifacio of Verona, and William Rossi of Parma, and the Ghibelline Manfred Beccaria of Pavia.
108. Villani, Bk. IX, Ch. 25.
109. See *MGH*, No. 778, p. 771 lines 9ff.
110. Bonaini, *Acta*, II, No. 29 (20 April 1311), p. 26; cf. Nos. 30-43 (20-30 April), esp. Nos. 30, 37, 38.
111. *Cronaca senese attribuita ad Agnolo di Tura del Grasso*, in *Cronache senesi*, ed. A. Lisini and F. Iacometti, *RR.II.SS.*, n.s., XV, Pt. 6 (Bologna, 1931-1937), 313.
112. *Loc. cit.;* Villani, Bk. IX, Ch. 16; Bonaini, *Acta*, II, No. 51 (12 Sept. 1311), pp. 40f.; Davidsohn, *Geschichte*, III, 451f. Among the few Guelfs specifically excluded from the amnesty were Giano della Bella, author of the Ordinances of Justice, and Dante Alighieri.
113. Bologna considered it opportune to grant an annual gift of 200 florins to the Pope's nephew, Cardinal Arnold Pellagru, designated as "the perpetual defender and protector of the commune and people of Bologna." Mommsen, *Ital. Analekten*, No. 31 (10 May 1311), pp. 32f. For dealings of the Tuscan League with Robert of Anjou and his vicars, cf. *ibid.*, No. 30 (27 April 1311), pp. 31f.; No. 38 (13 Oct. 1311), p. 34; also see Caggese, *Roberto*, I, 131ff.
114. Villani. Bk. IX, Ch. 21; Mommsen, *Ital. Analekten*, No. 39 (22 Oct. 1311), p. 34.
115. Villani, Bk. IX, Ch. 21.
116. Mommsen, *Ital. Analekten*, No. 39 (22 Oct. 1311), pp. 34f.
117. Bonaini, *Acta*, II, No. 55 (17 Sept. 1311), pp. 43ff.
118. *Ibid.*, II, No. 48 (9 Sept. 1311), p. 39: "in vestram et nostram et totius Partis, totius Ytalie, necem et periculum retorqueri."

NOTES: CHAPTER IV. WINTER STORMS:
THE EMPEROR-ELECT IN GENOA AND PISA

1. The presentation of the keys is illustrated in G. Irmer, *Die Romfahrt Kaiser Heinrich's VII.*, Pl. 16A. For Henry of Luxemburg in Genoa, see G. Caro, *Genua und die Mächte am Mittelmeer, 1257-1311*, II (Halle, 1899), 400-407; V. Samenek, "Die verfassungsrechtliche Stellung Genuas, 1311-1313," *MIÖG*, XXVII (1906) (cited above, Ch. II, n. 24), 262f., 562f.; Schneider, *H.VII*, 129-137.
2. Cf. Henry's actions in Pavia, and the call of communal representatives to Genoa (above, Ch. III, nn. 104ff.); and Mussato, Bk. V, Rub. 1; Bonaini, *Acta*, II, No. 44 (25 Oct. 1311), p. 52.
3. Ferreto, II, 12; Caro, *Genua*, II, 402.
4. *MGH*, No. 706 (21 Nov. 1311), p. 682 lines 35ff.; cf. Caro, *Genua*, II, 402.
5. *MGH*, No. 703 (13 Nov. 1311), p. 679 lines 5f.; No. 707 (22 Nov. 1311), p. 684 lines 24f.
6. For the act of 14 Nov. 1311, *MGH*, No. 704, 679ff.; for the act at

Milan, 28 Jan. 1311, *MGH*, No. 567, pp. 525f., and above, Ch. II, n. 106.

7. *MGH*, No. 705 (14 Nov. 1311), pp. 681f. For aid given Henry in Genoa on this and other occasions Opizzino Spinola received several grants on 6 Feb. 1312, ten days before the imperial expedition left the city. *MGH*, Nos. 738-739, pp. 728f.

8. See above, Ch. II, n. 32.

9. *MGH*, No. 706 (21 Nov. 1311), pp. 682f. Cf. Samanek, "Die verfassungsrechtliche Stellung Genuas," 265ff.

10. The second reception of authority, *MGH*, No. 708 (22 Nov. 1311), pp. 685ff.; the phrase quoted is on p. 686 lines 36f. For the appointment of a Genoese proctor to ratify the reception, see *MGH*, No. 707 (22 Nov. 1311), pp. 684f.

11. For the institution of the Ancients and the election of the abbot, see *MGH*, No. 710 (s.d.), pp. 691ff. By 24 Dec. 1311 the abbot of the people at the time of Henry's entry, Giovanni di Monticello, had already been replaced by Nicolas di Sauro (*MGH*, No. 716 lines 6f.).

12. The vicarship of Genoa was entrusted to Gobert of Aspromonte, who proved to be a good choice and remained in office a full year. Ferreto, II, 12, calls Gobert an "agnatio" of Henry. For the vicar's installation (between 31 Jan. and 16 Feb. 1312) see Samanek, "Die verfassungsrechtliche Stellung Genuas," 276; also Mussato, Bk. V, Rub. 1.

13. *MGH*, No. 709, pp. 688-691.

14. The phrase quoted is on *MGH*, p. 689 lines 21f. The section specifically referring to the promise of naval service is on p. 698 line 33.

15. *MGH*, p. 688 line 29—p. 689 line 7.

16. Mussato, Bk. V, Rub. 1; Ferreto, II, 12. Cf. Samanek, "Die verfassungsrechtliche Stellung Genuas," 566ff., who points out that although Genoese indebtedness increased markedly under the rule of Henry VII, the administration of the debt neither worsened nor improved.

17. Butrinto, 519f., argues that Henry respected this privilege and accepted "dominium simpliciter ad viginti annos" (519), because "visum fuit regi pro meliori quod ad presens sic dominium reciperet, sperans quod infra viginti annos totum posset recuperare" (520).

18. *MGH*, No. 924, pp. 956ff. On these petitions see Samanek, "Die verfassungsrechtliche Stellung Genuas," 585ff.

19. Henry addressed this letter: "Dilectis nobis vicario nostro, Gubernatoribus, Consilio, populo et Comuni Civitatis Aretii, Gratiam suam et omne bonum." The charge was "quod per Comune Aretii et offitiales ipsius eis [the *contado* nobles] contra antiquam immunitatem eorum de jure et consuetudine observatam datia factiones et alie molestie realiter et personaliter imponuntur." Florence, Archivio di Stato, a badly damaged notarial instrument (parchment), filed under *Atti pubblici*, 22 Jan. 1312. Cf. Mommsen, *Ital. Analekten*, No. 51, pp. 38f.

20. *MGH*, No. 737 (4 Feb. 1312), pp. 727f. While there exists a little evidence concerning Henry's policies towards *contado* towns and nobles, there is far less evidence concerning the relations between the various strata of *contado* society and the communes controlling them, and the way in which those relations affected *contado* dwellers' reactions to Henry.

21. Mussato, Bk. V, Rub. 9.

22. Villani, Bk. IX, Ch. 28; Mussato, Bk. I, Rub. 13, V. 4.

23. Cermenate, Ch. XLII, pp. 91f. Cf. the Queen's intercession for Cremona in April 1311, and for Theobald Brusati during the siege of Brescia (above, Ch. III, nn. 54, 66). Margaret had also interceded for Antonio Fissiraga of Lodi after he joined the rebels in his native city in February 1311 (Cermenate, Ch. XXIX, p. 66; cf. above, Ch. III, p. 100).

24. *MGH*, No. 1287 (Dec. 1311), p. 1423.

25. Mussato, Bk. V, Rub. 8; Ferreto, II, 19f. Caggese, *Roberto*, I, 143, dates this embassy as probably in November 1311.

26. For these Angevin embassies and for Robert's policy during this period, see Caggese, *Roberto*, I, 142ff. During the siege of Brescia two of Robert's envoys had talked inconclusively with Henry's representatives, the Bishops of Liège and Basel. Butrinto, 511.

27. Cermenate, Ch. XLII, p. 92.

28. *MGH*, No. 726, pp. 715-716.

29. Butrinto, 520.

30. Bonaini, *Acta*, II, No. 97 (21 Dec. 1311), pp. 78f. For the activities of John of Gravina in Rome. and for the accounts borne to Henry and the missions he sent to Rome, see *MGH*, No. 1388 (31 March 1312), pp. 1423f. (from H. Finke, ed., *Acta Aragonensia*, I, No. 201, pp. 286ff.); Mussato, Bk. V, Rub. 6, 7; Ferreto, II, 18ff.; Cermenate, Ch. XLII, pp. 92ff.; E. Duprè Theseider, *Roma dal comune di popolo*, 402.

31. E. Duprè Theseider, *Roma dal comune di popolo*, 402, and W. Israel, *König Robert von Neapel und Kaiser Heinrich VII.* (diss.; Hersfeld, 1903), 25, assume that Henry was already aware of Angevin deception and hostility.

32. Caggese, *Roberto*, I, 142-149, argues that Robert was not definitely committed to hostility to Henry; nor was he playing a machiavellian game. He was caught between two attachments: that to Henry, and that to Florence and its allies. He had much to gain and to fear from both, and wished to avoid committing himself at all costs. He also worried that Frederick of Trinacria would attack the Regno if he opposed the King of the Romans. Henry's ambiguity in turn confused and disoriented Robert. The Angevin continued his original tactics of stalling and attempting to escape the necessity for any military engagements. Unfortunately much of Caggese's research cannot be checked, as it is based upon Angevin archival material destroyed during the Second World War.

33. See Davidsohn, *Geschichte*, III, 463ff.; Bonaini, *Acta*, II, No. 69 (5 Nov. 1311), pp. 55f.; Mommsen, *Ital. Analekten*, No. 39 (22 Oct. 1311), p. 34; Villani, Bk. IX, Ch. 27. Cf. above, Ch. III, n. 114.

34. Butrinto, 519, 522ff.; cf. Davidsohn, *Geschichte*, III, 440ff.

35. Cf. Bonaini, *Acta*, II, No. 51 (12 Sept. 1311), p. 40, in which the Priory speaks of "regis Alamanie . . . tirannitatis operibus."

36. Butrinto, 523; *MGH*, No. 715 (20 Nov. 1311), par. 4, p. 699.

37. This conspiracy is poorly related in the chronicles; cf. *Chron. Parmense*, 121; Mussato. Bk. V, Rub. 2; Villani, Bk. IX, Ch. 32; Ferreto, II, 22. For the secret negotiations that Florence was carrying on with G. da Correggio as early as April 1311, see Mommsen, *Ital. Analekten*, No. 27 (16 April 1311), pp. 30f. (and above, Ch. III, n. 44); for rumors of Ghiberto's infidelity, and his suspicious actions in October 1311, see above, Ch. III, n. 106. For the principal documentary sources concern-

ing the conspiracy, see A. Cavalcabò, *Le ultime lotte del comune di Cremona per l'autonomia*, Documents XII-XVI (1 Nov.-6 Dec. 1311), pp. 195-205; L. A. Muratori, *Antiquitates Italicae medii aevii*, IV (Milan, 1741), cols. 615Aff.; M. Melchiorri, "Vicende della signoria di Ghiberto da Correggio in Parma" (cited above, Ch. I, n. 48), Doc. 15 (2 Jan. 1312), pp. 174ff.; Bonaini, *Acta*, II, Nos. 85, 87, 91 (27, 28 Nov., 8 Dec. 1311), pp. 68f., 70f., 73f.; Mommsen, *Ital. Analekten*, No. 44 (24 Nov. 1311), par. 3, p. 36; *ibid.*, No. 46 (23 Dec. 1311), par. 1, p. 37. The most complete modern secondary account of the conspiracy is in A. Cavalcabò, *Le ultime lotte*, pp. 57-71. (P. 58, n. 2, should read 18 Aug. 1312, not 1311. The document C. refers to is in Florence, Archivio di Stato, *Missive*, II, f.35v, and is published in Bonaini, *Acta*, II, No. 191, pp. 155ff. C. was probably misled by a nineteenth-century inventory in the same archive [Luigi Bolgi, *Spogli dei Capitoli, Registri 1-68*].)

38. L. A. Muratori, *Antiquitates Italicae medii aevii*, IV, col. 619D (19 Nov. 1311), "Ghibertus de Corrigia, Potestas Merchadantie Civitatis Parme."

39. See Muratori, *Antiquitates*, IV, cols. 621Bff. (21 Nov. 1311), and the names of the councillors in Reggio Emilia, Archivio di Stato, *Provvigioni dei Venti Saggi*, f. 2r (1 Nov. 1311). The men in question were Ugolinus de Folianus, Bastardus de Canossa, Brancha de Manfredis, and Albertus de Luvixinis.

40. A. Cavalcabò, *Le ultime lotte*, Doc. XII, p. 195.

41. *Ibid.*, Doc. XIII, pp. 196-199. The portion quoted is on p. 197.

42. *Ibid.*, *loc. cit.*

43. *Ibid.*, Doc. XVII, pp. 205-210.

44. *Ibid.*, p. 209 lines 30ff.

45. *Ibid.*, Doc. XIII, p. 196.

46. Chronicle accounts of this second Brescian rebellion are meagre and unsatisfactory: J. Malvezzi, *Chron. Brixianum*, *RR.II.SS.*, XIV, cols. 976-977; Ferreto, II, 29; Villani, Bk. IX, Ch. 32; Mussato, Bk. V, Rub. 2. Most useful is a document published in Dönniges, *Acta*, II, No. 15 (24 Dec. 1311), pp. 24-29: "Processus contra Vicarium Brixiae . . . ," the transcript of an investigation conducted in Brescia after the suppression of the December rebellion. The best secondary account remains G. Sommerfeldt, "König Heinrich VII. und die lombardischen Städte" (cited above, Ch. III, n. 14), 144f., although S. exaggerated greatly in stating that the ringleaders were caught and executed. (For the terms imposed upon Brescia after its capitulation in September 1311, see above, Ch. III, nn. 92f.)

47. *MGH*, No. 1221 (16 Nov. 1311), p. 1274. This request was sent to Brescia by the fierce Luccan exile Giovanni da Castiglione, now designated as "iudex serenissimi principis domini H[enrici] Dei gratia Romanorum regis semper agusti [sic], comes palatii et procurator fisci in Lombardia et Marchia generalis." (For Da Castiglione, see above, Ch. III, n. 56.)

48. *MGH*, No. 1222 (18 Nov. 1311), pp. 1274f., esp. 1274 lines 28ff.

49. Cf. *MGH*, No. 741 (13 Feb. 1312), p. 731 lines 2, 4, 5, and below, Ch. IV, n. 76.

50. On Moroello Malaspina, see above, Ch. II, n. 65. He had served in the imperial army during the siege of Brescia (e.g., *MGH*, No. 625, 6 June 1311, p. 587 line 24). Cf. also citations in *MGH*, p. 1495, col. 3

(index). He appears as Brescian vicar at the time of the December revolt in Dönniges, *Acta*, II, No. 15, pp. 24ff. See also below, Ch. IV, n. 52.

51. For the rectorship of Pietro della Porta, see Dönniges, *Acta*, II, p. 24. For the condition of Brescia during the spring of 1313, see esp. the information collected by two imperial ambassadors in the "Inquisitiones de comite Guernerio et Iohanne de Castilione et de statu civitatis Brixiae," Dönniges, *Acta*, I (29 April-27 May 1313), pp. 165-178. The two ambassadors received from the then vicar of Brescia the names of rebels of the commune who were still fighting against it. These included over 50 small communes, and three lists containing more than 300 individual names (*ibid.*, pp. 130-136). Among the latter we find six of the ten men who along with the vicar Moroello Malaspina were listed as ringleaders of the December 1311 rebellion. These are: Iohaninus condam dni. buetii de Lavellolungo (p. 130); dns. Abbas monasterii sancte Eufemie (p. 130); dns. Aymericus de Salis (p. 131); dns. Iostachinus de Griffis (p. 131, list 2); dns. Brixianus de Lavellolungo (p. 133, list 2); dns. Abbas monasterii Sancti Gervasii (p. 134, list 2). All these men were accused in the inquest of 23 Dec. 1311 (five being named in Dönniges, *Acta*, II, p. 24, and the Abbot of S. Euphemia on p. 26 in the testimony of the first witness, Dns. Albertus de Tangetinis). None of the witnesses at the 23 December investigation, or the men listed as having been imprisoned by M. Malaspina, or of having favored the imperial cause at the time of the December rebellion, are listed among the rebels of 1313. For the rebels who fled Brescia after the collapse of the December revolt see also J. Malvezzi, *Chron. Brixianum*, *RR.II.SS.*, XIV, col. 977 (Dist. 9, Ch. 23).

52. See, e.g., *MGH*, No. 891 (16 Dec. 1312), pp. 904f.; No. 1310 (16-20 Dec. 1312), pp. 1449f.; No. 892 (19 March 1313), pp. 905f. During the spring of 1313, in fact, personal interests worked to place Moroello Malaspina on the side of the Ghibelline faction of Pontremoli in the fighting that raged around that "key and gate for coming from Lombardy into Tuscany." *MGH*, Nos. 961, 962 (ex April-in June 1313), pp. 1002f., 1003f., esp. pp. 1002 lines 34f., 1003 line 25. The passage quoted is on p. 1004 lines 1f.

53. Mussato, Bk. V, Rub. 2.

54. See G. Sandri, "Il vicariato imperiale" (cited above, Ch. I, n. 120), p. 98.

55. For the rebellion of Pavia and Count Philippone Langusco see G. Sommerfeldt, "König Heinrich VII. und die lombardischen Städte" (cited above, Ch. III, n. 14), pp. 142, 146; Mussato, Bk. V, Rub. 2. For the date 19 Jan. 1312 and the marriage of Ghiberto da Correggio with the daughter of Count Philippone on that day, *Chron. Parmense*, 122.

56. Antonio Fissiraga was captured in late October 1311, turned over to the Pavian Ghibelline Manfred Beccaria, and handed on to Matteo Visconti, imperial vicar of Milan, who imprisoned him. Fissiraga died on 20 Nov. 1327 in a Visconti prison. See Butrinto, 521; Ferreto, II, 7f.

57. For a brief treatment of the Guelf seizure of Cremona, see A. Cavalcabò, *Le ultime lotte del comune di Cremona per l'autonomia*, 74ff.

58. Cermenate, Ch. XLIII, p. 99.

59. See, e.g., Butrinto, 516.

60. See above, Ch. III, n. 54.

61. *MGH*, No. 1223, p. 1275. Luzzara lay on the southern bank of the Po, east of Guastalla.

62. A statement of G. da Castiglione, *MGH*, No. 1221 (16 Nov. 1311), p. 1274 line 16.

63. *MGH*, No. 715, pp. 697-701. The principal accusations against Florence were: (1) refusal to quit the siege of Arezzo upon order of the imperial legates during the summer of 1310; (2) receiving and aiding the rebel Guido della Torre; (3) granting a podesta to rebel Cremona; (4) offending imperial messengers in the fall of 1311; (5) aiding rebel Brescia; (6) stating that Henry's followers could be attacked with impunity; (7) denying Henry his rightful title "King of the Romans," and opprobriously designating him "King of Germany"; (8) refusing passage through Florentine territory to Louis of Savoy, appointed Senator of Rome by the Pope; (9) entering into a conspiracy of various cities against the King of the Romans.

64. *MGH*, p. 699, lines 5f. On this phraseology, cf. E. H. Kantorowicz, in *Speculum*, XXXIV (1959), 107, n. 2 (a review of C. T. Davis, *Dante and the Idea of Rome*).

65. *MGH*, p. 698 line 10.

66. *MGH*, No. 716 (24 Dec. 1311), pp. 701-705, the sentence pronounced against Florence. The phrase quoted is on p. 701 lines 39f.

67. *MGH*, No. 721 (29 Dec. 1311), pp. 710f. Henry had already shown a propensity for ordering his vicars to act "sine strepitu et figura iudicii." (Cf. above, pp. 66, 84, 87; also pp. 181, 182.) Cited with G. da Correggio were Giovanni Quilico (or Quirico) de San Vitale of Parma and Opizino da Enzola of Parma. The former was Ghiberto's son-in-law, and appears among the Parmesans who on 19 Nov. 1311 appointed a proctor to enter them into the Guelf League (Muratori, *Antiquitates*, IV, cols. 619Dff.). He was elected podesta of Cremona 3 Feb. 1312 (*Chron. Parmense*, 123). Ghiberto named Opizino da Enzola as his vicar of Borgo S. Donnino early in December 1311, when he procured the rebellion of that town from the Empire (*Chron. Parmense*, 121).

68. *MGH*, No. 768, pp. 757-763.

69. Lucca and Siena were fined 3,000 pounds of gold each, Parma 2,000 and Reggio 1,000. The first two cities could return to grace within 15 days, the last two within 20, after the publication of this sentence of 11 April 1312.

70. Cf. *MGH*, No. 769, p. 763.

71. *MGH*, No. 768, p. 758 line 38.

72. For the granting of the vicarship of Vicenza to Can Grande della Scala, his assumption of authority, and his first acts in office, see G. Sandri, "Il vicariato imperiale" (cited above, Ch. II, n. 117), 99-102.

73. Frederick della Scala was not long his cousin's podesta in Vicenza. Galasinus da Cornano held that office May 1312—27 Jan. 1313 (Ferreto, II, 133, n. 2).

74. G. Sandri, "Il vicariato imperiale," 101.

75. As Count Werner's task was almost entirely military, it was perhaps of relatively small import that he did not understand "Italian" and had to be accompanied by an interpreter (Cermenate, Ch. XLVIII, p. 104).

76. See *MGH*, No. 741 (13 Feb. 1312), pp. 730f., the Captain General's

document of appointment. Cf. O. Felsberg, *Beiträge zur Geschichte des Römerzuges Heinrichs VII.*, 13ff., for the abolition of the office of Vicar-General and the powers and functions of the Captain General.

77. Cermenate, Ch. XLV, p. 101, XLVI, p. 102. According to Cermenate another Milanese representative was Francesco da Garbagnate, the ex-professor who had helped to assure the Luxemburger's acceptance of the exiled Matteo Visconti in 1310.

78. The general assembly at Lodi was followed by a private conference between the Captain General and Matteo Visconti in a monastery near Milan. Count Werner called for a second general meeting at Brescia on 8 March 1312; but unfortunately we are not informed as to the agenda or actions taken at those meetings. (Cf. *MGH*, No. 742, p. 731.)

79. Count Werner restored order in Lodi and imprisoned the erring vicar, Fanus de Drisimo. Mussato, Bk. VII, Rub. 3.

80. The would-be *signore* Alberto Scotto led the imperial recapture of Piacenza. *Chron. Parmense*, 123.

81. Mommsen, *Ital. Analekten*, No. 55 (18 Feb. 1312), p. 40. For the Paduan revolt see Mussato, Bk. V, Rub. 10, VI, 1-2; Cortusiis, *RR.II.SS.*, n.s., XII, Pt. 5, Ch. 14, p. 14; Ferreto, II, 114ff. Even the fact that Paduan representatives (including Mussato) returned from Genoa in these very days with an imperial document assisting the commune in its relations with its former subject Vicenza, could not prevent the declaration of war. The imperial document (*MGH*, No. 735, pp. 725ff., 27 Jan. 1312) announced *inter alia* that Bassiano de' Guaschi (imperial legate to Tuscany in 1310) and Giovanni da Castiglione (Proctor of the Fisc) were being sent to investigate Paduan-Vicentine differences.

82. Mommsen, *Ital. Analekten*, No. 56 (21 Feb. 1312), par. 3, pp. 40f.

83. Ferreto, II, 116; cf. Mussato, Bk. VI, Rub. 1.

84. Ferreto, II, 30 (G. della Torre); Cavalcabò, *Le ultime lotte del comune di Cremona per l'autonomia*, 82, 84f. (W. Cavalcabò).

85. Concerning preparations for the journey from Genoa to Pisa, 16 Feb.-6 March 1312, see Schneider, *H.VII*, 137ff.

86. For Henry's stay and activities in Pisa (6 March-23 April 1312), see, e.g., Schneider, *H.VII*, 139ff.; Ferreto, II, 33-41, with Cipolla's notes.

87. *MGH*, No. 1152, p. 1153 lines 17f., 19ff., indicate two Pisan payments to Henry (between 15 Feb. and 4 May 1312) of 60,000 and 36,800 florins. Davidsohn (*Geschichte*, III, 467) estimates that this first half of the imperial expedition alone cost Pisa at least 180,000 florins.

88. For Pisa's act of fealty of 17 March 1312, see *MGH*, No. 754, pp. 744f.

89. See *MGH*, No. 753 (17 March 1312), pp. 743f. For the list of Ancients previously chosen by the commune, see F. Bonaini, ed., *Breve Vetus seu Chronica Antianorum Civitatis Pisanae*, *ASI*, ser. 1, vol. VI, pt. 2 (1845), 647-792, p. 670.

90. Ferreto, II, 34f.; Butrinto, 529. The Emperor-elect seems to have secured his hold upon Pisa during his month-and-a-half stay in the city. Just prior to leaving it he appointed the exiled Florentine Ghibelline Francesco Tani degli Ubaldini vicar of Pisa. See Ferreto, II, 39f.; cf. *MGH*, No. 881 (7 Nov. 1312), p. 897; Villani, Bk. IX, Ch. 37; Davidsohn, *Geschichte*, III, 467f.

91. Ferreto, II, 37f., lists the above-named men as being present in Pisa. Cf. Villani, Bk. IX, Ch. 37. For Uguccione see P. Vigo, *Uguccione della Faggiuola* (Livorno, 1879); for Castruccio see T. E. Mommsen, "Castruccio e l'impero," in *Castruccio Castracani degli Antelminelli, Miscellanea di studi storici e letterari,* ed. R. Accademia Lucchese (Florence, 1934), 33-45 (trans. in his *Medieval and Renaissance Studies* [Ithaca, N. Y., 1959]), and F. Winkler, *Castruccio Castracani, Herzog von Lucca* (Berlin, 1897).
92. Schneider, *H.VII,* 137.
93. Villani, Bk. IX, Ch. 37.
94. G. Sandri, "Il vicariato imperiale" (cited above, Ch. II, n. 117), 102-108,
95. See G. B. Picotti, *I caminesi e la loro signoria in Treviso dal 1283 a 1312,* 21ff.; H. Spangenberg, *Can Grande I von Scala,* I, 4ff.; Mussato, Bk. VI, Rub. 10; Cortusiis, *RR.II.SS.,* n.s., XII, Pt. 5, Ch. 17, p. 16; Ferreto, II, 127f. Richard da Camino died of his wounds on 12 April 1312.
96. For the insurrection of Asti, and its pacts with Robert of Anjou, see F. Gabotto, *Storia del Piemonte nella prima metà del secolo XIV (1292-1349)* (Turin, 1894), 67ff.; also G. M. Monti, *La dominazione angoina in Piemonte,* 130f. To secure their position, members of the Solari house entered into private agreements with Robert.
97. See *MGH,* No. 751 (10 March 1312), pp. 737ff., the document appointing Henry's proctors to Naples. Cf. Butrinto, 530. For Robert's negotiations with the King of the Romans during this period, see Caggese, *Roberto,* I, 150ff.
98. *MGH,* No. 752 (1 April 1312), pp. 739ff.
99. The principal source for this is a report to James II of Aragon from two of his agents at Vienne, the scene of a Church Council. See H. Finke, ed., *Acta Aragonensia,* I, No. 201, pp. 285-292, reprinted in *MGH,* No. 1288, pp. 1423ff. This Aragonese story finds confirmation in Tolomeo da Lucca, *Historia Ecclesiastica,* excerpt, ed. G. Mollat, in S. Baluzius, *Vitae Paparum Avenionensium,* I (Paris, 1914), 44. See Davidsohn, *Geschichte,* III, 469f., for an exposition of the opinion that this affair was the famous betrayal of Henry referred to by Dante in *The Divine Comedy (Paradise,* XVII, 82), "ma pria che 'l Guasco l'alto Arrigo inganni." Cf. W. Bowsky, "Clement V and The Emperor-elect" (cited above, Ch. III, n. 40), 52.
100. It is possible that on one occasion at least Clement V requested the Tuscan Guelf cities to obey Henry VII. Unfortunately the evidence for this consists of a fragmentary undated document, published by F. Kern, ed., *Acta Imperii Angliae et Franciae,* No. 224, p. 148.
101. See above, Ch. IV, n. 28.
102. It is impossible to be more precise as to Henry's motives for sending proctors to Frederick of Trinacria. The evidence is circumstantial and inconclusive. Cf. Mussato, Bk. V, Rub. 6, 7; Ferreto, II, 18ff.; Cermenate, Ch. XLII, pp. 92ff.; Butrinto, 530. For earlier diplomatic contacts between the two rulers, see above, Ch. IV, nn. 24f.
103. Butrinto, 530; *MGH,* Nos. 765, 766 (s.d.), pp. 754ff. Henry's two envoys were the exiled Florentine Ghibelline nobles, Ubaldini degli Ubaldini (brother of the first vicar Henry appointed for Pisa), and Lamberto Cipriani, Henry's first vicar in Piacenza. The Emperor-elect

wished Frederick of Trinacria to serve him "against all" for one year in person, with 30 galleys and at least 500 mounted knights. Henry in return would aid Frederick against all except the Pope, Church, and "the King of France." No mention is made in the extant official documents of a marriage alliance.

104. *Regestum Clementis Papae V*, vol. IV (Rome, 1886), No. 4782, p. 318 cols. 1f. (See above, Prol., n. 2).

NOTES: CHAPTER V. THE CORONATION—AND AFTER

1. For the material dealt with in this chapter, see esp. the secondary accounts in Schneider, *H.VII*, Ch. V, "Der Kampf um Rom und der Kaiserkronung," 145-164, Ch. VI, "Der Kampf mit Florenz," 165-186; for the events in Rome (without scholarly apparatus), see E. Duprè Theseider, *Roma dal comune di popolo alla signoria pontificia*, 405-422; for the fighting and negotiations with Florence from late August through the winter of 1312-1313, see Davidsohn, *Geschichte*, III, 480-520; for Robert of Anjou, see Caggese, *Roberto*, I, 159-176.

2. The Emperor-elect's two messengers were Bishop Nicolas of Butrinto and the papal notary Pandolfo Savelli. For this mission see Butrinto, 530-534.

3. Butrinto, 534. Duprè Theseider suggests that Butrinto meant only to indicate that the imperial forces were not drawn up in battle order (*Roma dal comune di popolo*, 407).

4. Cardinal Luca Fieschi hastened to Naples to persuade Robert of Anjou to conclude the long-discussed marriage alliance and to serve Henry of Luxemburg honorably. Bonaini, *Acta*, II, No. 136 (20 June 1312), p. 109; No. 137 (20 June 1312), p. 111; No. 138 (20 June 1312), p. 113.

5. See *MGH*, Nos. 781-783, p. 778-781. No. 782, pp. 779ff. contains the Angevin's proposals. Robert's more important conditions are: (1) Henry was to appoint his new son-in-law, Charles of Calabria, Vicar of Tuscany for life. (2) Henry was to receive annually 30,000 florins from Florence, 20,000 from Lucca and 18,000 from Siena, and three months' annual military service in and near Tuscany from 200 knights and 2,000 infantry from Florence, 100 and 1,000 from Lucca, 80 and 900 from Siena, and less in proportion to their ability from the smaller communes. (3) Henry could not interfere in the governments of all these communes as Robert stipulated "quod . . . eligant officiales modo consueto et vicarius [Charles of Calabria] confirmabit." (4) Henry and Robert were to have a common admiral. (5) Robert was to share in choosing the vicars of Lombardy for ten years. (6) The Colonna could not come to the Basilica of St. Peter for the imperial coronation without the permission of the Orsini.

6. See W. Israel, *König Robert von Neapel und Kaiser Heinrich VII.*, 32ff. and Schneider, *H.VII*, 266ff., who argue that Robert made his proposals in order that they might be rejected, since he did not wish to appear the open aggressor against an Emperor-elect who had come to Italy with the approval of his own liege lord, Pope Clement V.

7. Caggese, *Roberto*, I, 155ff.

8. See Caggese, *Roberto*, I, 149-154.

9. See below, Ch. V, nn. 14f.

10. See G. Fasoli, "Bologna e la Romagna," (cited above, Ch. I, n. 74), 40f.
11. See, e.g., Mommsen, *Ital. Analekten,* No. 69 (21 May 1312), par. 2, p. 45; Bonaini, *Acta,* II, Nos. 115, 118, 127, 129 (19 April, 8 May, 7, 11 June 1312).
12. The order to send a scout from Florence is mentioned in Bonaini, *Acta,* II, No. 131 (17 June 1312), p. 105; see also Caggese, *Roberto,* I, 164.
13. *MFH,* No. 1292 (27 June 1312), p. 1431 lines 35f. (from H. Finke, ed., *Acta Aragonensia,* I, No. 210), a report of Christian Spinola in Genoa to James II of Aragon: "Illi de Regno et specialiter gens minuta generaliter dominum imperatorem desiderant et afectant." Even in Sept. 1312, when relations between Henry and Robert were worse, there was still pro-imperial sentiment in the Regno. Cf. Mommsen, *Ital. Analekten,* No. 80 (1 Sept. 1312), p. 48—recording a duel in the northern part of the Regno that was occasioned by the differences between the two monarchs.
14. *MGH,* No. 1291 (4 June 1312), p. 1430 lines 31ff. (from H. Finke, ed., *Acta Aragonensia,* I, No. 208), a report from Christian Spinola.
15. Bonaini, *Acta,* II, Nos. 130, 132, 133 (all 17 June 1312), 134 and 135 (18 June), 136 and 137 (20 June), pp. 104, 105ff.; see Caggese, *Roberto,* I, 164f. It may be no coincidence that it was on 17 June (after the discovery of Robert's treachery) that the Priory sent a scout to seek out the Angevin's troops destined for Rome. See above, Ch. V, n. 12.
16. Bonaini, *Acta,* II, No. 132, p. 106. Cf. above, Ch. II, nn. 34f. (when the King of the Romans similarly excused Robert for his secret dealings with Asti).
17. Bonaini, *Acta,* II, No. 134, p. 107.
18. *Ibid.,* II, No. 137, pp. 110ff.
19. This Florentine accusation may refer to Robert's stay in Florence during the fall of 1310 (above, Ch. I, n. 116), *after* the formation of the Florentine-Bolognese league. Although there is no evidence that Robert directly denied this accusation, his past tactics and those of Florence, and his later reaction to imperial charges (below, Ch. VI) greatly vitiate the strength of the Florentine claim.
20. Bonaini, *Acta,* II, No. 167 (10 Aug. 1312), pp. 137f.
21. *Ibid.,* II, No. 137 (20 June 1312), p. 111.
22. Mommsen, *Ital. Analekten,* No. 76 (3 July 1312), p. 76. This notice is contained in a message sent by Robert to Bologna, requesting that city to send troops to aid him in Rome.
23. See Bonaini, *Acta,* II, Nos. 117 (4 May), 118 (8 May), 122 (19 May), 127 (7 June), 142 (22 June). No. 122, p. 99, urges Perugia to send help to Duke John in Rome, "in defensionem et succursum partis Guelfe totius Italie." Perugia sent 150 cavalry (A. Eitel, *Der Kirchenstaat unter Klemens V.* [Berlin-Leipzig, 1907], 136). See Bonaini, *Acta,* II, Nos. 124 (3 June), 126 (4 June), requesting that Lucca not carry out planned military operations in the Lunigiana or Garfagnana (areas near home), but send all aid possible to Rome.
24. G. Fasoli, "Bologna e la Romagna," (cited above, Ch. I, n. 74), 41, n. 7; Mommsen, *Ital. Analekten,* No. 71 (5-19 June 1312), p. 45.
25. Bonaini, *Acta,* II, No. 126 (4 June 1312), p. 101.
26. Matthew 26:31.

27. Butrinto, 537f.
28. Perhaps, as Caggese asserted (*Roberto*, I, 161), Henry of Luxemburg now actually promised to conclude the marriage alliance with Robert at once (*nunc perficiendi*); but Caggese did not add that this reading is found only in a later addition made to a copy of Henry's petitions to the cardinals in Rome that was sent to Paris in order to inform Philip the Fair of the progress of events (*MGH*, No. 779, p. 775 lines 31ff.). According to Butrinto (537) the French monarch at this time sent letters requesting Roman nobles not to bear arms against Robert. It is possible, however, that these letters were sent later, after Clement V had officially ordered a truce between the Emperor and Robert of Anjou. Cf. below, Ch. V, n. 44.
29. See e.g., Bonaini, *Acta*, II, No. 142 (22 June 1312), p. 116; Mussato, Bk. VIII, Rub. 6.
30. E.g., Mussato, Bk. VIII, Rub. 6; Bonaini, *Acta*, II, No. 144 (26 June 1312), p. 118.
31. *MGH*, No. 1292 (27 June 1312), p. 1431 (from H. Finke, ed., *Acta Aragonensia*, I, No. 210).
32. Mussato, Bk. VIII, Rub. 6.
33. Cf. *MGH*, No. 644 (19 June 1311), pp. 609ff., the *Ordo* that Pope Clement V decreed for the imperial coronation of Henry of Luxemburg. See the discussion in E. Duprè Theseider, *Roma dal comune di popolo*, 414f.
34. Butrinto's statement (539) that Henry VII afterwards swore that he had known nothing of Buonsignori's plans does not completely eliminate the possibility that the Emperor-elect himself instigated the incitement of the Roman mob in order to force the cardinals to crown him in St. John's.
35. For the intrusion during the coronation banquet, see Mussato, Bk. VIII, Rub. 7. See the illustration of the (peaceful) banquet in Figure 19.
36. *MGH*, Nos. 799-800, pp. 799-801: *Constitutio contra haereticos*, etc.; Nos. 801-803, pp. 801-806; Encyclicals. On these documents see M. Maccarrone, "Il terzo Libro della '*Monarchia*'," *Studi Danteschi*, XXXIII (1955), 24, 99, 139.
37. *MGH*, No. 799, p. 800 lines 3ff.
38. *MGH*, No. 801, p. 802 lines 16ff.
39. *MGH*, No. 801, p. 802 lines 27f. On the obvious and time-worn nature of this thesis, cf. E. H. Kantorowicz, in *Speculum*, XXXIV (1959), 107. It is interesting to note, however, that on 13 June 1312 the Senator of Rome granted Henry, "Romanorum rex semper augustus," and his officials permission to exercise civil and criminal jurisdiction in Rome during his stay—but not to the prejudice of papal rights over Rome (*MGH*, No. 789, pp. 787f.). But how this grant affected Henry as *emperor* is debatable. (Cf. the discussion in Ch. VI, below, on "Legality and Polemic.")
40. *MGH*, No. 799, p. 800 lines 21ff.
41. Responses are published in *MGH*, No. 810 (s.d.), pp. 811f., from Clement V; No. 811 (s.d.), pp. 812ff., from Philip the Fair; No. 812 (30 April 1313), p. 814, from Edward II of England.
42. *MGH*, No. 811, p. 813 lines 22ff.
43. Finke, ed., *Acta Aragonensia*, I, No. 219, p. 327 (reprinted in *MGH*,

p. 1432, n. 1), a report of 8 Feb. 1313 to the King of Aragon, stating that in a consistory on 26 Jan. 1313 Clement V recognized Henry as Roman Emperor for the first time. A Florentine letter of 20 July 1312 contains an interesting story—not confirmed elsewhere—to the effect that on 2 July the Pope dispatched letters permitting the cardinals in Rome to crown Henry wherever they desired, and commanding Duke John of Gravina to leave the city within three days of receiving the orders. But anti-imperial nobles and prelates convinced the Pope that he was in error, and would greatly jeopardize Robert and his allies. The Pontiff rescinded the earlier orders and commanded that Robert be told to act as he saw fit. Bonaini, *Acta*, II, No. 156, p. 127.

44. See F. Kern, *Acta Imperii, Angliae et Franciae*, No. 227 (19 June 1312), pp. 150f.; the papal lament over the present fighting between "the Kings Henry of the Romans and Robert of Sicily," with the complaint it could hinder the launching of a crusade to the Holy Land, and compassion for horrors suffered by Rome, whose citizens are "special sons of the Roman Church [peculiares Romane ecclesie filii]." In this document Clement commands the one year truce between Henry and Robert by reason of his "Apostolic authority" and the papal *plenitudo potestatis*. The person who infringes upon this truce is threatened with personal excommunication and an interdict upon his lands. See *MGH*, No. 1045 (July 1313), nos. 3-7, p. 1079, for a listing of five official documents (no longer extant) dealing with the papal truce, the orders to leave Rome and not to invade the Regno, and not to return to Church lands. Cf. also *MGH*, No. 841 (6 Aug. 1312), pp. 844ff., Henry VII's responses to the cardinals concerning the various papal demands. For Clement's fear that Henry might linger in Rome and act as sovereign there, see M. Maccarrone, "Il terzo Libro della 'Monarchia,'" *Studi Danteschi*, XXXIII (1955), 94f.; cf. C. T. Davis, *Dante and the Idea of Rome*, 159ff.

45. See *MGH*, Nos. 839-842, pp. 841-848; cf. Butrinto, 541f., and below, Ch. VI.

46. This last was certainly true. We have already noted that the Angevin accepted the signory of Asti in April 1312 (above, Ch. IV, n. 96). During that same spring and summer his seneschal received the castles of Casale and Valenza (*MGH*, No. 848, p. 856 lines 15ff.; cf. F. Cognasso in *Storia di Milano*, ed. G. Treccani degli Alfieri, V, 83). Unlike the Emperor, Robert was pleased by the papal truce, as it allowed him to avoid temporarily a serious conflict with Henry VII and at the same time to save face with his Tuscan allies. In fact, Robert immediately began to request that these allies be included in the truce. Cf. *MGH*, Nos. 843, 844 (14 Aug. 1312), pp. 849, 849f. (No. 844 is a letter seeking aid from Philip the Fair.) Robert sought the inclusion of the Guelfs even though Florence had written him arguing that the truce would only aid the Ghibellines and give Henry time to procure reinforcements from north of the Alps. Bonaini, *Acta*, II, No. 167 (10 Aug. 1312), pp. 136ff.

47. *MGH*, No. 840 (6 Aug. 1312), p. 843. On the nature of Henry's oath see also below, Ch. VI; cf. Schneider, *H.VII*, 307, n. 34 and the literature there cited.

48. *MGH*, Nos. 815-823 (4 July 1312), pp. 816-826; see also Butrinto, 539f.

49. While Henry remained loyal to his treaties and excepted Philip IV and his successors, Frederick excepted his elder brother, the King of Aragon, and his successors.

50. See *MGH*, No. 820 (4 July 1312), p. 823. Frederick's seneschal and proctor during these negotiations, Manfred of Claramonte, Count of Mohacs, received an annual fief of 200 silver marks from the Emperor. Manfred's oath of fealty to Henry contained the promise to serve "contra omnem hominem" except Frederick (*MGH*, No. 825, 5 July 1312, pp. 827f.). See *MGH*, No. 826 (5 July), pp. 828f., for the grant of 200 marks.

51. *MGH*, No. 822 (4 July 1312), p. 824 line 37.

52. Although Henry VII insisted on keeping the captured Tuscan Count of Bisenzio, the prisoner soon eluded his captors. See Ferreto, II, 72.

53. Having nothing else to do in Rome, Duke John of Gravina left the city at the end of August (Caggese, *Roberto*, I, 176). Almost immediately upon Henry VII's withdrawal all traces of his power in Rome began to disappear. During the second week of September the imperial garrison in the city was withdrawn. The Guelf Orsini expelled John of Savigny, the Burgundian noble in Henry's following who had been elected captain of the people. But wearied and disgusted by Robert's failure to arrive, the Orsini could not see the sense of further hostilities. A general pacification became the order of the day, Orsini and Colonna exchanging the kiss of peace and contracting marriages. In place of the ousted captain of the people, two nobles (an Orsini and a Colonna) were elected Senators of Rome. Why should men continue fratricidal slaughter in the name of an emperor who left the city and of an Angevin king who never arrived? Rome returned to the role of a relatively unimportant city in the Papal States. See E. Duprè Theseider, *Roma dal comune di popolo alla signoria pontificia*, 421ff.

54. Cf. *MGH*, No. 1154, pp. 1184-1190, and No. 1155, esp. p. 1190 lines 13ff.

55. *MGH*, No. 831 (8 July 1312), pp. 832f.; the phrase quoted is on p. 833 lines 7f. The substitution of toll rights, etc., for a cash remuneration may have proven unpopular, as it was not always easy to make the designated northern castle or town effect the ordered payment. In December 1312 Baldwin of Luxemburg, Archbishop of Trier, asked his brother the Emperor to order two castles to pay him money that he had been promised five months earlier. See *MGH*, No. 889 (8 Dec. 1312), pp. 902f.; the grant was made 18 July 1312 (*MGH*, No. 833, pp. 834f.).

56. *MGH*, No. 845 (15 Aug. 1312), p. 850. For other grants of July-Aug. 1312, cf. above, Ch. V, n. 50 (to Manfred of Claramonte), and *MGH*, No. 834 (18 July 1312), p. 836 (to Count Dietrich of Katzenellenbogen for services he had done and was doing in Italy).

57. For the above paragraph, see Ferreto, II, 66, n. 2, 69; Butrinto, 542 (offer to the Colonna); Bonaini, *Acta*, II, No. 150, pp. 122f. (noting that the Angevin forces in Rome granted a safe-conduct pass to Rudolf of Bavaria); Davidsohn, *Geschichte*, III, 480.

58. Mommsen, *Ital. Analekten*, No. 84 (6 Sept. 1312), p. 49; see *ibid.*, No. 90 (17 Sept. 1312), p. 50. Even Reggio, hard pressed by imperial attacks, sent 20 knights to Tuscany in response to a Florentine request (*ibid.*,

No. 92, 22 Sept. 1312, p. 51). For the large contingents of allied troops in Florence at the beginning of its battle with the Emperor, cf. Villani, Bk. IX, Ch. 47, who lists, among others, 600 cavalry and 3,000 infantry from Lucca, 600 and 2,000 from Siena, 400 and 1,000 from Bologna, 300 and 1,500 from the Romagna. See also Ferreto, II, 82, n. 1, and the sources there cited and partially quoted.

59. See G. Fasoli, "Bologna e la Romagna" (cited above, Ch. I, n. 74), 43, and three letters published by Fedor Schneider in "Untersuchungen zur italienischen Verfassungsgeschichte, II. Staufisches aus der Formelsammlung des Petrus de Boateriis—Anhang II, Analekten zur Römerzug Heinrichs VII.," *Quellen und Forschungen aus italienischen Archiven und Bibliotheken*, XVIII (1926), 255-266. Letter II (pp. 262f.), from G., son of Francesco della Mirandola, to Can Grande della Scala "Captain General of the city of Verona," tells of the defeat of Baggiovara and requests aid. Letter III (p. 263), is Can Grande's response, that he is at present occupied with fighting in the Vicentine district, but will soon aid Modena. Letter IV (p. 264), Count Duffus de Panico, a Bolognese exile captured by the Bolognese at Baggiovara, requests Ghiberto da Correggio to intercede for him with his captors. (All three letters are s.d.)

60. See Bonifazio da Morano, *Chron. Mutinense, RR.II.SS.*, XII, cols. 99f., who dates the Bonacolsi assumption of power in Modena as Thursday, 4 Oct. 1312. But Thursday was 5 October, and this is the date given for the same event in the briefer version of the *Annales veteres mutinensium*, ed. L. A. Muratori, *RR.II.SS.*, XI, col. 78. See also Ferreto, II, 110. For the truce with Reggio, see Mommsen, *Ital. Analekten*, No. 101 (4 Dec. 1312), p. 53, and below, Ch. VI, nn. 106ff. The Modenese request that the Bonacolsi, and none other, be made their vicar was probably presented to Henry VII in mid-May 1313. Dönniges, *Acta*, I, No. 82, p. 75.

61. For the following events in Vercelli, see F. Gabotto, *Storia del Piemonte nella prima metà del secolo XIV*, pp. 70, 243f. Mussato, Bk. VII, Rub. 8-9 is a useful chronicle source.

62. F. Gabotto, *Storia del Piemonte*, 71.

63. On Philip of Savoy's possible guilt, and his dynastic interests, cf. G. Sommerfeldt, "König Heinrich VII. und die lombardischen Städte" (cited above, Ch. III n. 14), 142ff.

64. Butrinto, 544f. For Henry VII's itinerary, see F. Ludwig, *Untersuchungen über Reise- und Marschgeschwindigkeit*, 78f.

65. *MGH*, No. 848, pp. 854ff. (the citation of 12 September). Robert did not appear before the Emperor by 21 Jan. 1313, the day the citation was removed from the Arezzo cathedral (*MGH*, No. 849, pp. 856f.). It was probably during this period (the early fall of 1312) that Henry VII initiated a new legal action against the commune of Florence and a number of specifically cited Florentines. The citation enumerated the crimes committed against the Emperor during the past spring and summer, particularly in Rome. The citation, unfortunately lost, is mentioned in a condemnation of Florence and certain of its citizens, promulgated 12 Dec. 1312 because the accused had not appeared to answer the charges (*MGH*, No. 890, pp. 903f.). Cf. Butrinto, 546, "Utrum in civitate Tiburtina, vel in Cortona, vel in Aretio in-

ceperint citationes regis Roberti et multarum personarum et civitatum rebellium non recordor." On these citations and ensuing legal proceedings and polemic, see below, Ch. VI.

66. Schneider, *H.VII*, 175, n. 33; cf. above, Ch. V, n. 58.

67. The Italian captains were Uguccione della Faggiuola and Frederick of Montefeltro. *Anonymi Itali Historia*, ed. L. A. Muratori, *RR.II.SS.*, XVI (Milan, 1730), col. 278; cf. Ferreto, II, 78.

68. Butrinto, 544f.

69. See Butrinto, 549f.; cf. Cermenate, Ch. LII, p. 110; Villani, Bk. IX, Ch. 47.

70. Butrinto, 551.

71. Butrinto, 547f.

72. Butrinto, 551f.; Davidsohn, *Geschichte*, III, 511.

73. Butrinto, 555. Dino Compagni, Bk. III, Ch. 34, pp. 252f.: "Siena puttaneggiava: che in tutta questa guerra non tenne il passo a' nemici, ne dalla volontà de' Fiorentini in tutto si partì." The podesta of Pistoia came to the imperial camp and frankly stated that "even if the other cities did not want [to conclude] convenient pacts, he still wished them for his own." Henry VII found his propositions unsatisfactory (Butrinto, 554). While the Emperor was still in Tivoli, several prominent Florentine private citizens (one was Pino della Tosa, podesta in Brescia during the siege of 1311) tried to negotiate a peace for their city through the offices of Richard Uguetti, a Florentine exile and master of the imperial mints in Italy. But they did not appear for a planned second meeting, probably realizing that the terms they proposed would be unacceptable to the Priory (Butrinto, 543f.; Davidsohn, *Geschichte*, III, 480f.).

74. See 14 documents appointing proctors to swear fealty to Henry VII, and actual oaths of fealty, publ. in *MGH*, Nos. 851-865, pp. 858-871, and 16 others cited, *ibid.*, p. 858, n. 2. Cf. Butrinto, 549f.

75. The only significant exception was Poggibonsi, which Henry made his temporary headquarters and rechristened with the defiant name "Mount Imperial."

76. *MGH*, No. 853, p. 861 lines 27ff.

77. *MGH*, No. 860, p. 867 lines 27ff.

78. *MGH*, No. 863, p. 869 lines 25ff.

79. *MGH*, No. 865, p. 870 lines 41ff.

80. That Henry had little faith in the promises of his newly acquired Tuscan subjects may be seen, for example, from the safe-treatment and safe-conduct passes issued them. They were not to be molested "so long as they remain in obedience to the said lord our Emperor" (*MGH*, No. 866, 6 Dec. 1312, p. 871; see also *MGH*, No. 867, 4 Jan. 1313, p. 872).

81. Cortona declined to declare itself openly for the Emperor-elect and to do him fealty publicly when his messengers, Nicolas of Butrinto and Pandolfo Savelli, visited it in the fall of 1311. The commune explained that it feared attacks from neighboring anti-imperial Perugia, Città di Castello and Gubbio (Butrinto, 527). But as the commune then promised, it appointed a proctor to do fealty to Henry when he was in Pisa (*MGH*, No. 757, 17 March 1312, pp. 747f.). Perhaps because of claims made upon it by the Bishop of Arezzo, Cortona asked to be taken into the Emperor's protection as part of the *camera regis* when he

stopped there in September 1312. This Henry VII did on 6 Sept., wishing, as he explained, that the commune enjoy its imperial liberty "as best it can"! (*MGH*, No. 846, pp. 850ff.; the phrase quoted is on p. 852 line 33. See also Butrinto, 545.) Yet Cortona rapidly lost interest in the imperial cause. By April 1313 the imperial council received a report from Frederick of Montefeltro, vicar of Arezzo, stating that Cortona was disobedient and that "nus de celes parties [in Cortona] nest feables au segnour [Henry VII] par amour for que soulement par temour" (Dönniges, *Acta*, I, No. 20, p. 56).

82. Cermenate, Ch. LIII, p. 113.
83. Borgo S. Donnino fell to the pro-imperial forces on 13 Jan. 1313; M. Melchiorri, "Vicende della signoria di Ghiberto da Correggio in Parma" (cited above, Ch. I, n. 48), 125, 126f.; cf. Mussato, Bk. XII, Rub. 5.
84. On the Lozzo conspiracy see Mussato, Bk. X, Rub. 2-3, XII, 3; Cortusiis, *RR.II.SS.*, n.s., XII, Pt. 5, Ch. 19, p. 18; Ferreto, II, 138ff.; H. Spangenberg, *Can Grande I von Scala*, I, 60f.
85. The Trevisan Guelf nobles expelled Guecello da Camino from their city because he was dealing with the Emperor and appeared to be planning to change sides in the Italian war. This ended 29 years of Da Camino rule in Treviso. See Mussato, Bk. X, Rub. 1; H. Spangenberg, *Can Grande*, I, 62.
86. On 5 Nov. 1312 in Pavia the Torriani signed a pact promising Robert of Anjou the signory of Milan once it was captured. See F. Cognasso, in *Storia di Milano*, ed. G. Treccani degli Alfieri, V, 82, 83f., and *MGH*, No. 1008, p. 1053 par. 6.
87. Caggese, *Roberto*, I, 183ff.
88. H. Finke, ed., *Acta Aragonensia*, I, No. 219 (8 Feb. 1313), p. 327 (reprinted in *MGH*, p. 1432, n. 1), a report to James II of Aragon that on 26 Jan. 1313 the Pope had added Ferrara to Robert's rectorship. See also Bonaini, *Acta*, II, No. 304 (13 March 1313), p. 236f.
89. See Davidsohn, *Geschichte*, III, 509f. Butrinto (554), an eyewitness, states that Henry VII was wrong to refuse Robert and the Count of Blankenheim permission to leave. Cermenate, Ch. LIV, p. 114, claims that Robert received permission. Villani, Bk. IX, Ch. 48, is silent on this point. See also Schneider, *H.VII*, 180.

NOTES: CHAPTER VI. THE FINAL CRISIS

1. See above, Ch. V, nn. 44f.; cf. *MGH*, No. 1003 (12 June 1313), pp. 1044ff. and Schneider, *H.VII*, 185, 187, 188, 190. For Henry's continued determination to invade the Regno, cf. *MGH*, No. 1296 (30 April 1313), p. 1437, and Nos. 979, 980 (7 May 1313), pp. 1012f., 1013f., directed to Frederick of Trinacria.
2. For this embassy see esp. *MGH*, Nos. 1004-1008, pp. 1046-1053; No. 1037, p. 1075 lines 11ff.; Mussato, Bk. XVI, Rub. 4; Butrinto, 559 (esp. n. 4); Cermenate, Ch. LXII, p. 125. See Henry's protest of 4 July 1313, *MGH*, No. 1004, pp. 1046f. The embassy included Count Amadeus of Savoy, Henry of Trent (acting imperial chancellor), and Nicolas of Butrinto.
3. Butrinto, 560.
4. Bonaini, *Acta*, II, No. 288 (19 Feb. 1313), pp. 220f.

5. *Ibid.*, II, No. 355, pp. 271f.
6. *Chron. Parmense*, 127; Mussato, Bk. XII, Rub. 5; Bonaini, *Acta*, II, No. 314 (31 March 1313), p. 243.
7. Bonaini, *Acta*, II, No. 315 (31 March 1313), p. 244; Dönniges, *Acta*, I, No. 39 (ex mid-April—in 6 May 1313), p. 61.
8. Angevin soldiery scored impressive victories over imperial forces in northwestern Italy. See, e.g., Mussato, Bk. XII, Rub. 7; F. Gabotto, *Storia del Piemonte nella prima metà del sec. XIV*, 72.
9. *Chron. Parmense*, 127 (mid-May 1313).
10. See Caggese, *Roberto*, I, 88ff.; cf. B. Barbadoro, ed., *Consigli* (cited above, Ch. II, n. 87), I, vol. 2, p. 619 (1 May 1313), pp. 621f. (14, 20 May).
11. *MGH*, No. 915 (23 Feb. 1313), pp. 929-933.
12. *MGH*, No. 916 (23 Feb. 1313), pp. 933-951.
13. Villani, Bk. IX, Ch. 49. The Florentine chronicler adds that Henry VII gave Opizzino Spinola of Genoa and the Marquis of Monferrat the right to coin imitation florins. For Henry's attempt to establish an imperial coinage in Italy, see above, Ch. III, n. 77.
14. *MGH*, Nos. 929-930 (2 April 1313), pp. 965f. (*Edictum de crimine laesae maiestatis*); Nos. 931-932 (2 April 1313), pp. 966ff. (*Declaratio quis sit rebellis*).
15. *MGH*, No. 929, p. 965 lines 26f. For this imperial assumption of traditional anti-hierocratic arguments, see esp. M. Maccarrone, "Il terzo Libro della '*Monarchia*,'" *Studi Danteschi*, XXXIII (1955), 79, n. 1.
16. F. Gabotto, *Storia del Piemonte nella prima metà del sec. XIV*, 73, dates these bans and fines as 14 July 1313, but see the comment of L. A. Ferrai, in Cermenate, p. 121, n. 1 (there read 1313 for 1318). Cermenate, Ch. LIX, pp. 120f., describes at length (but supplies no date) an imperial condemnation of Pavia and of more than 50 listed Pavians, including Count Philippone. See also Butrinto, 558f.
17. *MGH*, No. 982, pp. 1017-1023. This sentence lists over 100 Paduans, among them the historian and poet Albertino Mussato. Those owing services to any of the condemned could be acquitted of half if they assigned the other half to the imperial fisc. See also *MGH*, No. 783 (25 May 1313), pp. 1023f., the order for the publication and execution of the sentence against Padua.
18. See Mommsen, *Ital. Analekten*, No. 209 (21 Oct. 1331), p. 92: Florence expresses the desire to have Henry VII's sentences cancelled. *Ibid.*, No. 445 (10 April 1355), p. 183: an expression of the same desire, to be communicated to Charles IV. *Ibid.*, No. 142 (26 Nov. 1320), p. 68: a professor of civil and canon law, requested to give an opinion as to the validity of Henry VII's sentence depriving the Bishop of Volterra of his imperial lands and privileges, judges that the sentence is still in effect. *Ibid.*, No. 143 (16 Dec. 1320), pp. 68f., Volterra is troubled by and investigates Henry VII's sentence depriving the Bishop of Volterra of his imperial lands and privileges. *Ibid.*, No. 286 (19 Feb. 1355), p. 119, and No. 289 (18 May 1355), pp. 120f.: Charles IV cancels his grandfather's sentence against the Bishop of Volterra, and restores the latter's confiscated lands and rights. See also F. Ercole, *Dal comune al principato*, 160-163, esp. the documentation in 160, n. 1. Cf. P. Brezzi, "Le relazioni tra i comuni italiani e l'impero," in E. Rota, ed., *Questioni di storia medioevale*, 403f.

19. Milanzo's opinion is publ. in *MGH*, No. 981 (s.d.), pp. 1015ff. For Henry's citation of Bologna, see esp. Mommsen, *Ital. Analekten*, No. 118 (8 May 1313), pp. 58f., and G. Fasoli, "Bologna e la Romagna" (cited above, Ch. I, n. 74), 48ff.
20. *MGH*, No. 946 (2 April 1313), pp. 985-990.
21. Butrinto, 561.
22. *MGH*, No. 948 (12 May 1313), p. 993.
23. *MGH*, No. 947 (s.d.), pp. 991-993.
24. See above, Ch. V, nn. 45ff.
25. E. E. Stengel, ed., *Nova Alamanniae*, I, Pt. 1, No. 90, pp. 44-52.
26. *Ibid.*, par. 6, p. 50.
27. *Ibid.*, par. 4, p. 50.
28. *MGH*, No. 1248 (ex Aug. 1312-in 26 April 1313), pp. 1308-1317, perhaps written by the Sicilian jurist Giovanni di Calvaruso. Cf. M. Thilo, *Das Recht der Entscheidung über Krieg und Frieden im Streite Kaiser Heinrichs VII. mit der römischen Kurie* (Berlin, 1938), 8ff. (and the review in *Deutsches Archiv*, IV [1941], 329f.); Schneider, *H.VII*, 339f.; F. Bock, *Reichsidee und Nationalstaaten* (Munich, 1943), 135f.
29. *MGH*, pp. 1312f.
30. *MGH*, p. 1312 lines 11f. This use of the commonplace concept of Christian reverence to explain the Emperor's relation to the Pope will of course recall to the reader the last line of Dante's *Monarchia* (III, 16), and his discussion of "reverentia" in the *Convivio*, IV, viii, 11-16.
31. *MGH*, pp. 1314f.
32. *MGH*, p. 1315 lines 18ff.; cf. c. 22, *D.LXIII*.
33. Dante, *Monarchia*, ed. G. Vinay (Florence, 1950), I, 2. For a resumé of recent scholarship on dating *M.*, see C. T. Davis, *Dante and the Idea of Rome*, 263ff. On *M.* as political philosophy, see A. P. D'Entrèves, *Dante as a Political Thinker*, 41ff.; G. Vinay, *ed. cit.*, pp. vf. For the relation between *M.* and contemporary polemic, see esp. M. Maccarrone, "Il terzo Libro della '*Monarchia*,'" *Studi Danteschi*, XXXIII (1955), *passim*; cf. C. T. Davis, *op. cit.*, 178-187 for *M.* and five pieces of contemporary polemic.
34. See Dante, *Monarchia*, III, xvi, 11f. and *MGH*, No. 801, p. 802 lines 11ff. Cf. Maccarrone, *op. cit.*, 119f. (and above, Ch. V, n. 38).
35. See, e.g., Maccarrone, *op. cit.*, 62ff.
36. *Ibid.*, 137.
37. See E. H. Kantorowicz, *The King's Two Bodies*, Ch. VIII, "Man-Centered Kingship: Dante," pp. 451-495. The passages quoted are on pp. 457, 463, 465.
38. *MGH*, No. 1251 (ex 29 June 1312), pp. 1342-1362, esp. pp. 1345 par. 7, 1348 par. 8. Cf. Davis, *Dante*, 180f.
39. *MGH*, pp. 1353f.
40. *MGH*, p. 1346 lines 41ff.
41. The legal treatise is publ. in *MGH*, No. 1250 (post 26 April 1313), pp. 1320-1341, and is an elaboration of the questions set out in *MGH*, No. 1249, pp. 1317-1320. The argument of "foreign provinces" is treated in *MGH*, No. 1250, pp. 1333f.; that attacking the universality of the Empire, on pp. 1338f. Davis, *Dante*, 180, has noted the treatment of "*Romanum imperium habet fines*" (*D*. 50, 1, 33), the arguments centering on the Empire's violent origins (*MGH*, p. 1339), and those

attacking *"Roma communis est patria" (MGH,* p. 1330). For the complexity and unwieldiness of the problem of the Empire's universality,
see the remarks of E. H. Kantorowicz in *Speculum,* XXXIV (1959), 107,
esp. n. 5.

42. *MGH,* pp. 1331f.
43. F. Kern, ed., *Acta Imperii, Angliae et Franciae,* No. 295 (post 26 April
    1313), pp. 244-247. (Cf. Davis, *Dante,* 184f.). In addition to Kern, No.
    295, the following tractates were written to deny the validity of
    Henry's sentence against Robert: *MGH,* Nos. 1254, 1255 (post 24 Aug.
    1313), pp. 1373-1378, 1378-1398; and [Tolomeo da Lucca] *Tractatus de
    Jurisdictione Ecclesie super Regnum Sicilie et Apulie in quo ostenditur
    quadrupliciter ad ipsam solam Ecclesiam pertinere,* in S. Baluzius and
    J. D. Mansi, *Miscellanea,* I (Lucca, 1761), cols. 468-473. This last tract
    is particularly interesting as its main argument is based primarily upon
    a historical analysis of the actual rule of southern Italy, treated in
    detail from the Norman conquest of the eleventh century.
44. *MGH,* No. 1252 (post 6 Aug. 1312—in 24 Aug. 1313), pp. 1362-1369.
45. *MGH,* No. 1253 (post 24 Aug. 1313), pp. 1369-1373.
46. The argumentation in *MGH,* No. 1253, par. 2, pp. 1369f. (that the
    Empire originated in violence, and hence its consequent disruption is
    only a return to an ancient, natural condition) is perhaps derived from
    F. Kern, ed., *Acta Imperii, Angliae et Franciae,* No. 295, par. 8, pp. 246f.
47. *MGH,* pp. 1371ff.
48. *MGH,* p. 1372, par. 10. Even Giovanni da Cermenate, a partisan of
    Henry VII and a Ghibelline follower of Matteo Visconti, could write:
    "Theutonicus furor effraenis factus exultat nimis, et licentius in quosli-
    bet cives saevire coepit," and "ridet Theutonus et omnis barbarus, qua
    utitur, amentia vestra [Mediolani civium] gaudens" (Ch. XXIX, p.
    62 lines 144f., 158f.). Henry VII's expedition helped, perhaps, to de-
    velop a strong distaste among many Italians (both Guelf and Ghibel-
    line) for northerners in general and Germans in particular. The entire
    question of Italian attitudes towards non-Italians during the late middle
    ages and early Renaissance merits a serious independent study, as free
    as possible of nationalistic preconceptions and prejudices.
49. Cf. Bonaini, *Acta,* II, No. 137 (20 June 1312), p. 111, and above, Ch.
    V, n. 20. The Angevins themselves abandoned this drastic remedy after
    a few years, when changes in the international scene dictated other
    policies. See G. Tobacco, "Un presunto disegno domenicano-angoino
    per l'unificazione d'Italia," *Rivista Storica Italiana,* LXI (1949), 492ff.
50. *Pastoralis cura* and *Romani principes* are printed in E. Friedberg, ed.,
    Corpus Iuris Canonici, II (Leipzig, 1881), c. un *Clem.* II, 9 and c. 2
    Clem. II, cols. 1147-1150, 1151-1154, and in *MGH,* Nos. 1165, 1166,
    pp. 1207-1211, 1211-1213. Still valuable is G. Lizerand, "Les constitu-
    tions 'Romani principes' et 'Pastoralis cura' et leurs sources," *Nouvelle
    revue historique du droit français et étranger,* XXXI (1913), pp. 725-
    757. On *Pastoralis cura* see also G. M. Monti, *Cino da Pistoia giurista*
    (Città di Castello, 1924); *id., Cino da Pistoia. Le quaestiones e i con-
    silia* (Milan, 1942); P. S. Leicht, "Cino da Pistoia e la citazione di Re
    Roberto da parte d'Arrigo VII," *ASI,* CXII (1954), 313-320; E. Will,
    *Die Gutachten des Oldradus de Ponte zum Prozess Heinrichs VII. gegen
    Robert von Neapel* (Abhandlungen zur mittleren und neueren Ge-
    schichte, LXV; Berlin-Leipzig, 1917).

51. Henry VII arrived in Pisa 10 March 1313 and left 8 August. F. Ludwig, *Untersuchungen über Reise- und Marschgeschwindigkeit im XII. und XIII. Jahrhundert*, 80.
52. Mussato, Bk. VIII, Rub. 6; R. Sardo, *Cronaca Pisana* (ed. cited above, Ch. I, n. 70), Ch. 52, p. 94.
53. Cf. G. Volpe, "Pisa, Firenze e Impero," *Studi Storici*, XI (1902), 312; *MGH*, p. 1153 lines 19ff., p. 1184 lines 5f., p. 1191 line 40–p. 1192 line 2.
54. *MGH*, No. 900 (26 Dec. 1312), pp. 913ff.
55. Dönniges, *Acta*, II, No. 2, pp. 95f. For a discussion of this document on Pisan income dictated by Vanni Zeno dei Lanfranchi, see G. Volpe, "Pisa, Firenze e Impero," 310. For Vanni Zeno, cf. above, Ch. II, nn. 3, 126.
56. *MGH*, No. 1292 (27 June 1312), p. 1431 lines 39f.; a report of Christian Spinola (from H. Finke, ed., *Acta Aragonensia*, I, No. 210).
57. *MGH*, No. 1294 (1 March 1313), p. 1433 (from H. Finke, ed., *Acta Aragonensia*, I, No. 220).
58. Dönniges, *Acta*, I, No. 5 (6 or 7 April 1313), pp. 51f. See also a series of ordinances regulating the sale of food and drink in Pisa, *ibid.*, I, No. 73, pp. 71f.
59. Dönniges, *Acta*, I, No. 104 (11 June 1313), p. 80; cf. *MGH*, No. 1294 (1 March 1313), p. 1433 (from H. Finke, ed., *Acta Aragonensia*, I, No. 220).
60. See *MGH*, No. 987 (22 May 1313), par. 12, p. 1028. With mainly Pisan troops the imperial Marshal, Henry of Flanders, captured Pietrasanta during the first week of June 1313. See Mussato, Bk. XIII, Rub. 8; Cermenate, Ch. LXII, pp. 125f.; *Diario di Ser Giovanni di Lemmo da Comugnori*, p. 184, ed. L. Passerini, in *Documenti di storia italiana*. VI: *Cronache dei secoli XIII e XIV* (R. Deputazione toscana di storia patria; Florence, 1876).
61. See *MGH*, Nos. 979, 980 (7 May 1313), pp. 1012f., 1013f.
62. *MGH*, No. 934, pp. 969f.
63. Dönniges, *Acta*, I, No. 2, pp. 100-103 (p. 103 [14 May] Uguccione is called "vicar-general."). This embassy also granted individual Genoese permission to sail ships against the rebels, provided that they gave security to attack only rebels (*MGH*, No. 934, p. 970). (For such a request by a Genoese, and the reply of Henry's council, see *MGH*, No. 935 [7 April 1313], p. 971. In this case, the council ordered the vicar of Genoa to grant such permission if he had no just cause for objection, and if he had objections to communicate them to the Emperor.) Christian Spinola in Genoa reported the imperial request for 25 galleys to King James II of Aragon, with the comment that it would be approved despite a division of opinion in the city. *MGH*, No. 1295 (22 April 1313), p. 1434 (from H. Finke, ed., *Acta Aragonensia*, I, No. 221). For the privileges of 27 March 1313 see *MGH*, No. 927, pp. 962ff., and below, Ch. VI, nn. 94f.
64. *MGH*, No. 981, p. 1016 line 11.
65. *MGH*, No. 937 (6 April 1313), pp. 973f.
66. *MGH*, No. 981, pp. 1015f., contains Milanzo's suggestions. For the embassy to Venice (27 May 1313), see *MGH*, No. 989, pp. 1033f. It was first to visit Mantua, Verona, and Treviso. The envoys were Domenicus Dugneyo, Geoffrey dei Vergiolesi of Pistoia (last imperial vicar

of Cremona before its capture by the Guelfs in Jan. 1312), Giovanni da Castiglione of Lucca (Proctor of the Fisc in Lombardy), and Milanzo of Bologna. See also *MGH*, No. 963 (2 May 1313), par. 3, p. 1005.

67. See *MGH*, Nos. 893-899 (18 Dec. 1312—5 May 1313), pp. 906-913. These include the calls for troops, the document of appointment of the imperial messengers, the postponement of the date of assembly, and the response of Besançon to the Emperor's request. For the diet at Nuremberg (Jan. 1313), and the failure of many troops to leave for Italy before mid-August, see *Cron. Aulae Regiae* (cited above Ch. I, n. 12), I, Ch. 110, pp. 323f. Henry VII appears to have sought more than troops from the north. Chronicle accounts and a report of Christian Spinola indicate that he sent his brother, Baldwin of Trier, to Germany in mid-March 1313 to arrange, among other things, for a Habsburg marriage alliance—a union between Henry himself and Catherine, daughter of the late Emperor-elect Albert. But while the Emperor's mother, and his daughter (the destined daughter-in-law of Frederick of Trinacria) began the trip to Italy in the company of Duke Leopold of Austria, we find no further mention of Catherine and may presume that the Luxemburg diplomacy had failed. See J. H. Wyttenbach and M. F. J. Müller, eds., *Gesta Trevirorum Integra*, II, p. 229 (noting that Baldwin left Pisa 19 March and entered Trier 15 May 1313); Mussato, Bk. XII, Rub. 6; *MGH*, No. 1295 (22 April 1313), pp. 1433f. (from H. Finke, ed., *Acta Aragonensia*, I, No. 221) (Christian Spinola's report); *Cron. Aulae Regiae*, I, Ch. 110, p. 334; John of Victring (cited above, Ch. I, n. 12), II, p. 26 (Lib. IV, Rec. A, Ch. 11).

68. The Ghibelline chief and imperial vicar of Milan, Matteo Visconti, for example, had not paid one gold piece for more than a year and a half, and owed the treasury 37,500 florins. For this debt, see above, Ch. III, n. 99, and below, Ch. VI, n. 72.

69. E.g., Galeazzo, oldest son and heir of Matteo Visconti, Frederick della Scala, cousin of Can Grande, Bonaventura (called Butirone), younger brother of Passerino Bonacolsi of Mantua, and Philip of Savoy.

70. For the above two paragraphs, see *MGH*, No. 923, pp. 954f., and esp. *MGH*, Nos. 937, 939-940, pp. 973f., 976-983, the instructions for three separate embassies dispatched on 6 April 1313 to Venice and the Veneto, central and western Lombardy, and the Trevisan March. For credentials and letters of safe conduct for the two men sent to the March, see *MGH*, Nos. 921-922, pp. 953f., 954. Of the eleven legates sent out on 6 April (including three to Genoa, *MGH*, No. 934, p. 969), at least five were well-known Ghibellines or White Guelfs: the Florentine banker Vermiglio degli Alfani (above, Ch. I, n. 37), Geoffrey dei Vergiolesi of Pistoia, and three Pisans—Jacob Fasoli, Lelmo Boglio dei Galandi, and Giovanni Rossi dei Galandi. Among the remaining six legates were Isnard Tacconi, Archbishop of Antioch (above, Ch. III, n. 74), and Antonio Surdi of Piacenza, "iudex aulae regiae" (see *MGH*, No. 751, p. 738). Note too that three of the four legates sent to Mantua, Verona, Treviso, and Venice 27 May 1313 were Ghibelline or White Guelf exiles. See above, Ch. VI, n. 66.

71. See the day-by-day account of their travels and experiences given Henry by Giovanni Rossi dei Galandi of Pisa and Vermiglio degli Alfani of Florence, sent on 6 April 1313 to Verona, Vicenza, Mantua, Modena, and Brescia, in Dönniges, *Acta*, I, pp. 123-165. This includes lists of

rebels of the various communes, names of Tuscans in Lombardy, and summaries of the legates' dealings with communal vicars, podestas and councils, and with individual lay lords and prelates. It is interesting to note that the legates were forced to pay tolls even by the Ghibelline, pro-imperial Marquises of Malaspina and at a bridge possessed by Milan (Dönniges, I, 123f.).

72. See *MGH*, No. 950 (5 May 1313), pp. 994f. (Brescia); No. 955 (28 May 1313), pp. 997f. (Modena); cf. No. 956 (30 May 1313), p. 998. For Matteo Visconti see *MGH*, No. 960, par. 15, pt. II, p. 1001; No. 1020, par. 4, p. 1063; cf. above, Ch. VI, n. 68; Ch. III, n. 99.

73. Mussato, Bk. XIII, Rub. 6.

74. Butrinto, 554f. See, e.g., *MGH*, Nos. 971, 984, 985, 1027-1029.

75. Butrinto, 553. See, e.g., *MGH*, Nos. 964, 1026, 1035, 1300.

76. Butrinto, 555. See, e.g., *MGH*, Nos. 971 (par. 1), 975, 976.

77. *MGH*, No. 919, pp. 952f. For the grant of 15 Aug. 1312, *MGH*, No. 845, p. 850.

78. *MGH*, No. 908, pp. 921f., for the grant of 21 Jan. 1313; No. 971, p. 1007, for that of 16 May. The Count of Buchek (commander of the imperial forces left behind in Rome after the Emperor's withdrawal) received 100 silver marks in the form of an office in Germany because "at present we cannot pay" (*MGH*, No. 976, 20 May 1313, pp. 1010f.). On 16 July 1313 Thomas of Siebenborn received the hereditary noble fief of 2,000 small gold florins a year. Thomas, "camerarius noster," was to serve with 20 armed knights three months a year, and to do other services named "in registro camere nostro" (E. E. Stengel, ed., *Nova Alamanniae*, I, Pt. 1, No. 95, pp. 55f.).

79. On 16 April 1313 Henry VII recognized a debt of 8,000 florins to his brother-in-law, Amadeus of Savoy, for services done in Italy to 1 Jan. 1313 (*MGH*, No. 944, p. 985). By mid-July he owed his treasurer, Egidius of Liège, 2,472 florins (*MGH*, No. 1036, 13 July 1313, p. 1074). Cf. *MGH*, No. 888 (4 Dec. 1312), p. 902, the recognition of a debt of 1,440 florins and four tourneois to Henry of Rapoltstein, for service to 1 Nov. 1312.

80. (1) On 3 Oct. 1311 Henry of Luxemburg had assumed Soncino (in the Cremonese *contado*) into the *camera imperii*, *MGH*, No. 694, pp. 667f. (see above, Ch. III, n. 54). On 13 March 1313 he gave it in hereditary fief to Count John of Forest. If it yielded less than 4,000 florins a year he was to collect the difference from the treasury, if more, to render the difference to the treasury. In return he was to serve Henry in Italy for three months a year with 40 knights (*MGH*, Nos. 985, 1312, pp. 1024f., 1451f.; Butrinto, 554). At some unknown later date this castle was granted to the Marshal, Henry of Flanders, who resigned it 20 May 1313 (*MGH*, No. 984, p. 1024). (2) On 14 July 1313 Pontremoli, at the northern end of the Magra Valley, part of the *camera regis*, was given in hereditary fief to the Counts of Lavagna (*MGH*, No. 1035, p. 1073). An important member of this family, Cardinal Luca Fieschi, had greatly aided Henry since his arrival in Italy in Aug. 1311. (3) On 22 May 1313 part of the *contado* of Como was granted in fief to Eugene, "advocato de Ametzia," whom Werner of Homburg had informed the Emperor would come to Italy on 2 Feb. 1314 to serve for a year with 40 soldiers (*MGH*, Nos. 977, 978, pp. 1011, 1011f.). (4) According to a somewhat unreliable chronicle, Simon Philip of Pistoia,

who had assisted Henry since the summer of 1310, received Crema in fief (G. Flamma, *Manipulus Florum*, *RR.II.SS.*, XI, Milan, 1727, col. 722).

81. On 6 Feb. 1312 Opizzino Spinola of Genoa received the vicarship of Sarzana and was ordered to seize it from the rebels (*MGH*, No. 739, p. 729).

82. *MGH*, No. 914 (22 Feb. 1313), pp. 927ff.; Butrinto, 553. Count Amadeus was forbidden to remove the imperial bans against the city, and all *regalia* and services due the Empire from Asti and its *contado* were reserved to Henry VII and his successors. On 3 June 1313 Henry commanded Philip of Savoy to surrender to his uncle a group of forts he held in the Asti *contado*, but by 15 July Philip had shown no sign of obeying and was sent another imperial directive. See *MGH*, Nos. 990-994 (3 June-15 July 1313), pp. 1034ff. On the differences between Philip and Amadeus of Savoy, cf., below, Ch. VI, nn. 103, 129.

83. *MGH*, No. 1300 (8 May 1313), p. 1440 (act of donation); No. 964 (6 May 1313), p. 1005 (notarial note). At this time Henry invested Manfred IV with the Marquisate of Saluzzo, an action he had refused to perform in 1310 because the marquis had done homage to Robert of Anjou (*MGH*, Nos. 1297-1299, 6-8 May 1313, pp. 1438f.; No. 964, par. 2, p. 1005. On the events of 1310 see above, Ch. II, p. 58). Two months after he received Alba from Henry VII, Manfred of Saluzzo resigned it along with several neighboring communes, while he was hard-pressed in battle. See *MGH*, No. 1314 (14 July 1313), p. 1453, and F. Gabotto, *Storia del Piemonte nella prima metà del sec. XIV*, 74, and *id.*, *Asti e la politica sabauda al tempo di Guglielmo Ventura* (Biblioteca della Società Storica Subalpina, XVIII; Pinerolo, 1903), 354.

84. *MGH*, No. 984 (20 May 1313), p. 1024; Butrinto, 554.

85. *MGH*, No. 988 (22 May 1313), par. 4, 5, p. 1030; cf. Dönniges, *Acta*, I, No. 77, p. 73.

86. *MGH*, No. 939 (6 April 1313), par. 8, VI, p. 978, par. 11, pp. 979f.; Dönniges, *Acta*, I, No. 60, p. 68; No. 39, pp. 61f.; No. 78, pp. 73f. The marquis did not receive the vicarships of Ivrea and Canavese.

87. *MGH*, No. 1009 (25 June 1313), pp. 1053f. This includes (par. 6, 7, p. 1054) the requests Philip made on behalf of his cousin, Louis of Savoy, including one for 20,000 florins for services rendered in Rome.

88. *MGH*, No. 939 (6 April 1313), par. 8, sect. 5, p. 978, par. 9, pp. 978f., par. 10, esp. sect. 3, p. 979. Matteo reported that only the untiring efforts of Milan and its vicar held the enemy at bay and retained loyal communes. While this was true, for example, in the case of Brescia, the Visconti purposely underestimated the importance of the presence and activities of the Captain General in Lombardy in order to exaggerate his own value.

89. Cf. F. Cognasso, in *Storia di Milano*, ed. G. Treccani degli Alfieri, V, 91. G. Biscaro, "Benzo da Alessandria" (cited above, Ch. I, n. 110), 307, 308ff., has pointed out how Matteo probably created embarrassments and difficulties for Cione delle Bellaste of Pistoia, the judge appointed to study the condition of rebel goods and properties after the tumults of Feb. 1311. Matteo may even have imprisoned him to prevent the discovery of his own complicity in the rebellion and his

seizure of Torriani holdings, and because Matteo did not wish to see the confiscated rebel money leave Milan. See also *MGH*, No. 939 (6 April 1313), par. 14, p. 980. For Cione's appointment and activities, see above, Ch. III, n. 19.

90. *MGH*, No. 1021, pp. 1063f. This petition contains requests by Galeazzo Visconti, by Manfred Beccaria of Pavia (now allied with the Visconti), and by a castellan in the Milanese *contado*.

91. In March 1313 Simon Crivelli succeeded a Malaspina as vicar of Novara. Luchino Visconti replaced Simon in July. See P. Azarius, *Liber gestorum in Lombardia*, ed. F. Cognasso, *RR.II.SS.*, n.s., XVI, Pt. 4 (Bologna, 1926-1929), 19, n. 4.

92. Technically Piacenza was held by imperial forces battling Guelf exiles. Actually two parties contested it, both claiming to represent the Empire and having an imperial vicar. Outside the walls was the faction of Ubertino Lando, *locum tenens* of a "vicar of the imperial party of Piacentine exiles." Within the city, by the side of Muzio of Modena, "imperial vicar," was Alberto Scotto—once more on the side of the Empire after having turned against it only three months earlier. This complicated tangle only becomes clearer if we forget both the terms "Guelf" and "Ghibelline," and the Emperor's presence in Italy, and recall that for many years before Henry's arrival and the revival of those partisan terms, Alberto Scotto and Ubertino Lando had led the two opposing factions that continually battled for domination of Piacenza. See *MGH*, No. 1225 (21 April 1313), pp. 1280-1286, the peace arbitration made for Piacenza by Baldwin of Trier.

93. See *MGH*, No. 1226 (21 April 1313), pp. 1287f. (Bobbio); No. 1227 (21 April 1313), pp. 1288ff. (Lodi).

94. Butrinto, 558. For the privilege of 27 March 1313, see *MGH*, No. 927, pp. 962ff.

95. *MGH*, No. 925, pp. 958-961. See also No. 926, pt. II, p. 962, a notary's outline of the imperial council's recommendations concerning each of the 16 sections of the petition. Almost all were rejected outright or accepted in a form that destroyed their scope. Henry also had to fence with a mass of petitions from the men upon whom he relied most heavily for support in Genoa, the Ghibelline Spinola and Doria. See *MGH*, Nos. 1014-1016 (June ex-July in, 1313), pp. 1056ff.; Dönniges, *Acta*, I, No. 78, pp. 73f., No. 97, p. 79 (petitions from Opizzino Spinola); No. 71, p. 71, No. 77, p. 73 (from Bernabo Doria).

96. See also *MGH*, No. 965 (2-6 May, 1313), pp. 1005f. (Arezzo); No. 1018, pp. 1060f. (Savona; incl. a plea for liberation from Genoese rule). Cf. the difficulties created for the imperial administration by Bergamo and its vicar, Tancred dei Vergiolesi of Pistoia; *MGH*, No. 939 (6 April 1313), par. 8, sect. 5, p. 978, par. 9, pp. 978f., par. 10, esp. sect. III, p. 979.

97. Cf. the struggle of Savona (in the western Riviera) against the Doria, Spinola, and its own bishop, who styled himself "the servant of the servants of his imperial majesty." (See *MGH*, Nos. 1017-1019, pp. 1060-1063; quoted phrase is on p. 1062 line 5). In the eastern Riviera the Counts of Lavagna (incl. Cardinal Luca Fieschi) tried to escape the many restrictions Genoa had imposed upon them. During the summer of 1313 they gained important imperial concessions, including the grant

of Pontremoli in fief (See *MGH*, Nos. 1032-1035, pp. 1070-1073). But Henry VII did not concede the counts' most sweeping demands, as it would have too greatly weakened Genoese supervision of the Riviera, and because the Emperor benefitted from the unity of rule obtained by administering the entire Riviera through a central direction at Genoa (cf. V. Samanek, "Die verfassungsrechtliche Stellung Genuas" [cited above, Ch. II, n. 24], 576).

98. See *MGH*, No. 987 (22 May 1313), pp. 1026ff.; No. 988 (22 May 1313), pp. 1029ff.; Dönniges, *Acta*, I, No. 90, pp. 77f.; No. 91, p. 78; No. 98, p. 78.

99. See *MGH*, Nos. 1032-1035, pp. 1070ff. Some Malaspina fought pitched battles against the Ghibellines of Pontremoli, while that city itself was rent with discord. *MGH*, Nos. 961-962, pp. 1002ff., esp. 1002, par. 1, 3.

100. See *MGH*, No. 891 (16 Dec. 1312), pp. 904f.; No. 1310 (16-20 Dec. 1312), pp. 1149f.; No. 892 (19 March 1313), pp. 905f.

101. See Dönniges, *Acta*, I, Nos. 45a-c, pp. 65f.; No. 48, pp. 66f.; No. 77, par. 1, p. 73; No. 78, par. 4, p. 73.

102. See *MGH*, No. 997, pp. 1040f. Hostilities had broken out between John of Vienne and the Count of Savoy during the first siege of Brescia, causing Henry of Luxemburg to order a truce between them 17 July 1311 (*MGH*, No. 662, pp. 632ff.). Exactly two years later the Emperor attempted to win John's support by releasing him from his fealty to Robert of Anjou and making him an immediate vassal of the Empire (*MGH*, No. 1038, 17 July 1313, pp. 1074f.).

103. See above, Ch. VI, nn. 69, 82, Dönniges, *Acta*, I, No. 70, p. 70; F. Gabotto, *Storia del Piemonte nella prima metà del sec. XIV*, 71.

104. Above, Ch. VI, n. 85.

105. For the legates' order to undertake the investigation, see *MGH*, No. 939 (6 April 1313), par. 13, p. 987. See the detailed account of the inquest, covering the period 29 April-27 May 1313, with summaries of the testimony of 27 witnesses, in Dönniges, *Acta*, I, 165-178.

106. *MGH*, No. 939, p. 1032 lines 16ff.

107. For the above two paragraphs, see *MGH*, No. 939, par. 1, pp. 1032f. Francesco della Mirandola must have been ransomed or received from the Bolognese in a prisoner exchange. See above, Ch. V, nn. 59f.

108. For the evidence against Bonacolsi, see esp. Mommsen, *Ital. Analekten*, No. 101 (4-29 Dec. 1312), p. 53, from the Reggian Defense Council; No. 81 (1 Sept. 1312), p. 48, from the Reggian Council of the Twenty Wise Men; the Guelf chronicler, Alberto de Bezano (cited above, Ch. I, n. 51), 82; Bonifazio da Morano, *Chron. Mutinense*, *RR.II.SS.*, XI, cols. 99f.; and above, Ch. V, n. 60.

109. Imperial forces had already proven their worth in the Lunigiana and Versilia, capturing Sarzana and Pietrasanta. On 9 Aug. 1313 Galeazzo Visconti, vicar of Piacenza, and German troops shattered an attack by Philippone Langusco of Pavia and Ghiberto da Correggio. Count Philippone, wounded and captured, was dispatched to Matteo Visconti's prisons in Milan. See Cermenate, Ch. LXIII-LXV, pp. 126ff.; *Chron. Parmense*, 130; Mussato, Bk. XV, Rub. 7. On 17 July 1313 Galeazzo had sent an "embassy" composed of some leading Piacentine Ghibellines and Guelfs, including Alberto Scotto, to his father in

Milan, in order to assure continued order in Piacenza. Matteo released the Ghibellines but retained Scotto and the other Guelfs. Cf. Mussato, Bk. XV, Rub. 6.

110. See Villani, Bk. IX, Ch. 51. For the period 8-24 Aug. 1313 (to the death of Henry VII), see Davidsohn, *Geschichte*, III, 537-547, and Ferreto, II, 89-98 (esp. Cipolla's notes). For the plan to sail the imperial fleet from Ostia 1 Sept., see Ferreto, II, 89. We do not know why Henry VII left Pisa before his brother Baldwin of Trier arrived with reinforcements that included Duke Leopold of Austria and King John of Bohemia.

111. See Cermenate, Ch. LXIV, p. 133; Mussato, Bk. XVI, Rub. 6; Ferreto, II, 91f. Cf. Bonaini, *Acta*, II, Nos. 330, 331 (12, 18 May 1313), pp. 252f., 253f., Florentine reports that the Sienese and the Luccans had been dealing secretly with Henry VII. See also Davidsohn, *Geschichte*, III, 543.

112. Soon after Henry's death a rumor circulated that his Dominican confessor had poisoned him. This story was not even universally believed at the time, and has been completely discredited by modern scholarship. For the Emperor's final illness and death, see, e.g., Davidsohn, *Geschichte*, III, 544-547; Schneider, *H.VII*, 191ff., Ferreto, II, 93, n. 1. See the illustration of Henry VII's funeral monument in Figure 29, and of the second monument carved by the Sienese Tino di Camaino in 1315, in G. Irmer, *Die Romfahrt Kaiser Heinrich's VII.*, following Pl. 37 or in L. Salvatorelli, *L'Italia comunale*, 770.

113. Sardo, *Cronaca pisana* (cited above, Ch. I, n. 37), Ch. 54, p. 95. For reactions to the Emperor's death among his partisans and enemies, see Davidsohn, *Geschichte*, III, 548ff.

114. Bonaini, *Acta*, II, No. 355, pp. 278f.

115. *Chron. Parmense*, 130.

116. For events in Italy immediately after the death of Henry VII, and for a general discussion of the political and military map that resulted, see, e.g., L. Simeoni, *Le Signorie*, I, 10-25; L. Salvatorelli, *L'Italia comunale*, 775ff.; R. Caggese, *Dal concordato di Worms*, 438ff. For more detailed studies, see, e.g., Caggese, *Roberto*, I, 198ff.; H. Spangenberg, *Can Grande I von Scala*, I, 76ff.; F. Cognasso, in *Storia de Milano*, ed. G. Treccani degli Alfieri, V, 100ff.; E. G. Léonard, *Les angevins de Naples*, 222ff.; G. M. Monti, *La dominazione angoina in Piemonte*, 135ff.; A. Cavalcabò, *Le ultime lotte . . . di Cremona*, 104ff.

117. Henry of Flanders, Marshal of the army, refused the Pisans' offer of the signory of their city. Frederick of Trinacria, who arrived in Pisa shortly after the Emperor's death, also left without accepting the offered signory, as the commune would not agree to cede him Sardinia.

118. Cavalcabò, *Le ultime lotte*, 105f.; Ferreto, II, 111f., esp. 111, n. 3. The pact between the Ghibellines ruling Brescia and the Guelf exiles controlling most of the *contado* is published by F. Odorici, in *Monumenta Historiae Patriae*, XVI, Pt. II (*Leges Municipales*, II, Pt. II) (Turin, 1876), cols. 1835-1873. Among its provisions were the cancellations of all sentences levied against the city by the late Emperor, and the mutual pardon of all war offences by Guelfs and Ghibellines (Art. 16, col. 1843). The commune considered it prudent to establish good relations with its last vicar, Francesco Malaspina, appointed by Henry VII 3 July 1313. He was to be paid as if he had served until 1 Jan.

1314, pardoned any wrongs he may have committed as vicar, and together with his "family" honorably acquitted of his office (Art. 114, cols. 1870f.).

119. Inability to compensate German mercenaries seems to have caused the quarrel between Matteo Visconti and Count Werner of Homburg, which led to Werner's returning home with his soldiers. See *Chron. Modoet.*, *RR.II.SS.*, XII, col. 1109; cf. Cermenate, p. 135, n. 3.

120. In October 1313 soldiers Matteo Visconti sent to join other Ghibellines and Parmesan Guelf exiles in a battle near Borgo S. Donnino bore three separate standards into the fight: those of the Empire, of Milan, and of Matteo Visconti. *Chron. Parmense*, 131.

121. G. De Vergottini, "Vicariato imperiale e signoria," in *Studi di storia e diritto in onore di Arrigo Solmi*, I (Milan, 1941), 43-64, esp. p. 60.

122. 20 Sept. 1313. Published by C. Erdmann, "Vatikanische Analekten zur Geschichte des Ludwigs des Bayern. Anhang A.," *Archivalische Zeitschrift*, ser. 3, vol. VIII (Munich, 1932), 1-47, on p. 43. This action was taken upon the proposal of the podesta, Janatius de Salimbene, and of the Ancients. It is interesting to note that Milan thought that it could legitimately confer the rights of high and low justice.

123. See G. Biscaro, "Benzo da Alessandria" (cited above, Ch. I, n. 110), 307, n. 2, 308, n. 1. Cf. Ferrai, in Cermenate, 136, n. 1, for the consolidation of the Milanese *contado*. The judge appointed to deal with rebel goods was "d. Beccario de Beccaria." The Pavian Ghibelline Beccaria family became a satellite of the Visconti, although it nominally controlled Pavia from 1315 to 1357. The Visconti named Pavian podestas and garrisoned troops in that city. See G. C. Bascapè, "I conti palatini" (cited above, Ch. I, n. 46), 376; also Cognasso, in P. Azarius, *Liber gestorum in Lombardia*, *RR.II.SS.*, n.s., XVI, Pt. 4, p. 16, n. 1.

124. For this expansion of Visconti rule, see, e.g., L. Simeoni, *Le Signorie*, I, 91; Cognasso in P. Azarius, pp. 16, n. 1, 18, n. 7 (Vercelli), 20, n. 1 (Alessandria and Tortona). Some neighboring cities soon passed out of the Visconti orbit.

125. The Scaliger vicarship is carefully guarded in the Veronese statutes of 1329. Cf. L. Simeoni, *Le Signorie*, I, 55f., and the analysis of these unpublished docs. in H. Spangenberg, *Can Grande I von Scala*, II. The Mantuan statutes (compiled 1303-1328) similarly guard the Bonacolsi vicarship of Mantua. See C. D'Arco, *Storia di Mantova*, II (Mantua, 1871), containing Bks. I-III of the statutes, and *id.*, *op. cit.*, III (Mantua, 1872), containing Bks. IV-X. Note esp. Bk. V, Rub. 18 (D'Arco, III, 99); Bk. VI, 42 rubrics (D'Arco, III, 123-155), esp. Rub. 1, "De vicaria dominorum Raynaldi et Botirone fratrum de Bonacolsis." (Raynoldo was the correct name of "Passerino" Bonacolsi.)

126. H. Spangenberg, *Can Grande I von Scala*, I, 78f.

127. See, e.g., E. G. Léonard, *Les angevins de Naples*, 226f.

128. See, e.g., P. Brezzi, in E. Rota, ed., *Questioni di storia medioevale*, 403f.; F. Niccolai, *Città e signori* (Bologna, 1941), 119ff.

129. Count Amadeus and Philip of Savoy settled their principal differences by arbitration in late Oct. 1313. Gabotto, *Storia del Piemonte nella prima metà del sec. XIV*, 175.

130. See the grant of 14 March 1314, in *MGH*, No. 1164, pp. 1205f. Several

modern authors state that Robert received this appointment as a weapon against Matteo Visconti of Milan, most powerful of the Ghibelline *signori* after the demise of Henry VII. Cf. E. G. Léonard, *Les angevins de Naples,* 224; G. M. Monti, *La dominazione angoina in Piemonte,* 138; C. Capasso, "La signoria viscontea e le lotte politico-religiose con il papato nella prima metà del secolo XIV," *Bollettino della Società Pavese di Storia Patria,* VIII (1908), 276.

Select Bibliography

MANUSCRIPT SOURCES

Florence, Archivio di Stato, *Atti Pubblici,* 22 Jan. 1312.

———, ———, *Missive,* II.

Reggio Emilia, Archivio di Stato, *Provvigioni dei venti saggi deputatiai negozi del comune* (Nov. 1311).

———, ———, *Statuta Civitatis Regii, 1311.*

PRINTED SOURCES (EXCEPT CHRONICLES)

Astegiano, L., ed., *Codex diplomaticus Cremonae,* II (*Monumenta Historiae Patriae,* ser. 2, XXII; Turin, 1898).

Baluzius, Stephanus and Mansi, J. D., *Miscellanea,* I (Lucca, 1761).

Barbadoro, B., ed., *Consigli della Repubblica Fiorentina,* in 2 vols. (Bologna, 1930-1931).

Barelli, G., "Documenti dell' archivio comunale di Treviglio," *ASI,* ser. 5, XXX (1902), 1-70.

Böhmer, J. F., ed., *Acta Imperii Selecta* (Innsbruck, 1870).

———, *Regesta imperii, 1246-1313. Die Regesten des Kaiserreiches unter Heinrich Raspe, Wilhelm, Richard, Rudolf, Adolf, Albrecht, und Heinrich VII.* (Stuttgart, 1844-1857).

——— and Redlich, O., eds., *Regesta imperii,* new ed., VI, 1: *Die Regesten des Kaiserreiches unter Rudolf, Adolf, Albrecht I. und Heinrich VII. 1273-1313.* Abt. 1. *Rudolf 1273-1291* (Innsbruck, 1898).

Bonaini, F., ed., *Breve vetus seu chronica vetus antianorum civitatis pisanae ab an. dom. inc. mcclxxxix ad an. mccccix,* in *ASI,* ser. 1, VII, pt. II (1845), 647-792.

———, see Henry VII.

Clement V, *Regestum Clementis Papae V ex Vaticanis archetypis . . . nunc primum editum cura et studio monachorum ordinis Sancti Benedicti,* 8 vols. (Rome, 1884-1892).

Cognasso, F., ed., *Statuti civili del comune di Chieri, 1313* (Biblioteca della Società Storica Subalpina, LXXVI, pt. II; Pinerolo, 1913).

Corpus iuris canonici, ed. E. Friedberg, 2 vols. (Leipzig, 1879-1881).

Corpus iuris civilis (critical ed., Berlin)
  Vol. I. *Institutiones,* ed. P. Krueger (16th ed., 1954).
  ———. *Digesta,* ed. T. E. Mommsen and P. Krueger (16th ed., 1954).
  Vol. II. *Codex Iustinianus,* ed. P. Krueger (11th ed., 1954).
  Vol. III. *Novellae,* ed. R. Schoell and W. Kroll (6th ed., 1954).

Dante Alighieri, *Le opere di Dante, testo critico della Società Dantesca Italiana,* ed. M. Barbi *et al.,* 2 vols. (Florence, 1921).

———, *Monarchia,* ed. G. Vinay (Florence, 1950).

———, *Monarchy and the Three Political Letters,* trans. D. Nicholl and C. Hardie (London, 1954).

D'Arco, C., ed., *Codice Bonacolsiano,* in his *Storia di Mantova,* II, III (Mantua, 1871-1872).

Dönniges, W., see Henry VII.

Erdmann, C., ed., "Vatikanische Analekten zur Geschichte Ludwigs des Bayern. Anhang A.," *Archivalische Zeitschrift,* ser. 3, VIII (1932), 1-47.

Eubel, C., ed., *Hierarchia catholica medii aevii,* I, 2nd ed. (Regensberg, 1913).

Finke, H., ed., *Acta Aragonensia,* 3 vols. (Berlin-Leipzig, 1908-1922).

Graevius, J. G., ed., *Thesaurus antiquitatum et historiarum Italiae,* 9 vols. in 30 (Leyden, 1704-1725); esp. III, Pt. I (1704).

Henry VII, *Acta Henrici VII,* ed. F. Bonaini, 2 vols. (Florence, 1877).

———, *Acta Henrici VII,* ed. W. Dönniges, 2 vols. (Berlin, 1839).

Kern, F., ed., *Acta Imperii, Angliae et Franciae ab anno 1267 ad annum 1313* (Tübingen, 1911).

Luenig, J. C., ed., *Codex Italiae diplomaticus,* 4 vols. (Frankfurt, 1725-1735).

Mommsen, T. E., ed., *Italienische Analekten zur Reichsgeschichte des XIV Jahrhunderts (1310-1378)* (Schriften der Monumenta Germaniae Historica, XI; Stuttgart, 1952).

Muratori, L. A., *Antiquitates italicae medii aevii,* 6 vols. (Milan, 1738-1742), esp. IV (1741).

Odorici, F., ed., *Statuta civitatis Brixiae, 1313,* in *Monumenta Historiae Patriae,* XVII, Pt. 2 (*Leges Municipales,* IV, 2) (Turin, 1876), cols. 1585-1914, and intro., cols. 1584, 275-280.

Pertz, G. H., ed., *Monumenta Germaniae Historica, Leges,* II (Hannover, 1837).

Schneider, Fedor, "Untersuchungen zur italienischen Verfassungsgeschichte. II. Staufisches aus der Formelsammlung des Petrus de Boateriis. Anhang II. Analekten zum Römerzug Heinrichs VII.," *Quellen und Forschungen aus italienischen Archiven und Bibliotheken,* XVIII (1926), 256-266.

Schwalm, J., ed., *Monumenta Germaniae Historica, Const.,* IV, 3 (Hannover-Leipzig, 1904-1906); IV, 4 (Hannover-Leipzig, 1906-1911).

Stengel, E. E., ed., *Nova Alamanniae,* I, Pt. 1 (Berlin, 1921).

Ughelli, F., *Italia sacra,* IV (Venice, 1729).

PRINTED SOURCES: CHRONICLES

Agnolo di Tura del Grasso, *Cronaca senese attribuita ad Agnolo di Tura del Grasso detta la cronaca maggiore,* in *Cronache senesi,* ed. A. Lisini and F. Iacometti, *RR.II.SS.,* n.s., XV, Pt. 6 (Bologna, 1931-1937).

Alberto de Bezano, *Alberti de Bezanis abbatis S. Laurentii Cremonensis cronica pontifica et imperatorum,* ed. O. Holder-Egger (Monumenta Germaniae Historica, SSRG in usum scholarum, LII; Hannover-Leipzig, 1908).

Annales Mediolanenses (1230-1402), ed. L. A. Muratori, *RR.II.SS.,* XVI (Milan, 1730).

Annales veteres mutinensium, ed. L. A. Muratori, *RR.II.SS.,* XI (Milan, 1727).

Anonymi Itali Historia, ed. L. A. Muratori, *RR.II.SS.,* XVI (Milan, 1730).

Azarius, Petrus, *Liber gestorum in Lombardia,* ed. F. Cognasso, *RR.II.SS.,* n.s., XVI, Pt. 4 (Bologna, 1926-1929).

Bazano, Johannes de, *Chronicon Mutinense,* ed. T. Casini, *RR.II.SS.,* n.s., XV, Pt. 4 (Bologna, 1919).

Benzo da Alessandria, "Bentii Alexandrini de mediolano civitate opusculum," ed. L. A. Ferrai, *Bullettino dell' Istituto Storico Italiano,* No. 9 (1890), 15-36.

Bonifazio da Morano, *Chronicon Mutinense, auctore Bonifacio de Morano,* ed. L. A. Muratori, *RR.II.SS.,* XI (Milan, 1727).

Butrinto, Nicolas of, *Nicolai episcopi Botrontinensis Relatio de Itinere Italico Henrici VII Imperatoris ad Clementem V Papam,* in vol. III, Stephanus Baluzius, *Vitae Paparum Avenionensium,* ed. G. Mollat (Paris, 1921), 491-561.

Cermenate, Giovanni da, *Historia Iohannis de Cermenate notarii mediolanensis de situ ambrosiane urbis . . . ab initio at per tempora successive et gestis imp. Henrici VII,* ed. L. A. Ferrai (Fonti per la storia d'Italia, II; Rome, 1889).

Chronicon Brixianum, see Malvezzi, Jacobus.

Chronicon Parmense, ed. G. Bonazzi, *RR.II.SS.,* n.s. IX, Pt. 9 (Città di Castello, 1902).

Chronicon Modoetiense, see Morigia, Bonincontro.

Chronicon Parvum Ripaltae, seu chronica pedemontana minora, ed. F. Gabotto, *RR.II.SS.,* n.s., XVII, Pt. 3 (Città di Castello, 1912).

Chronicon Regiense, see Gazata.

Corpus chronicorum Bononensium, ed. A. Sorbelli, *RR.II.SS.,* n.s., XVIII, Pt. 1, vol. 2 (Bologna, 1938).

Cortusiis, Guillelmus de, *Guillelmi de Cortusiis Chronica de Novitatibus Padue et Lombardie,* ed. B. Pagnin, *RR.II.SS.,* n.s., XII, Pt. 5 (Bologna, s.d. [*c.* 1941]).

Cronaca senese dei fatti riguardanti la città e il suo territorio, di autore anonimo della metà del secolo XIV, in *Cronache senesi,* ed. A. Lisini and F. Iacometti, *RR.II.SS.,* n.s., XV, Pt. 6 (Bologna, 1931-1937).

Cronaca pisana, see Sardo, R.

Cronica Aulae Regiae, ed. J. Loserth, in *Die Königsaaler Geschichtsquellen (Fontes Rerum Austriacarum, Scriptores,* VIII; Vienna, 1875).

Dino Compagni, *La Cronica di Dino Compagni,* ed. I. del Lungo, *RR.II.SS.,* n.s., IX, Pt. 2 (Città di Castello, 1916).

Ferreto de' Ferreti, *Historia rerum in Italia gestarum,* ed. C. Cipolla, 3 vols. (Fonti per la storia d'Italia, XLII-XLIII; Rome, 1908-1920).

Flamma, Galvaneus, *Galvanei Flammae Manipulus Florum sive Historia Mediolanensis* . . . , ed. L. A. Muratori, *RR.II.SS.,* XI (Milan, 1727).

Gazata, Sagacius, and Petrus, *Chronicon Regiense,* ed. L. A. Muratori, *RR.II.SS.,* XVIII (Milan, 1731).

Gesta Balduini Trevirensis, in *Gesta Trevirorum Integra,* II, ed. J. H. Wyttenbach and M. F. J. Müller (Trier, 1838).

Giovanni di Lemmo da Comugnori, *Diario di Ser Giovanni di Lemmo da Comugnori,* ed. L. Passerini, in *Documenti di storia italiana,* VI: *Cronache dei secoli XIII e XIV,* R. Deputazione toscana di storia patria (Florence, 1876).

Guido di Filippo dell' Antella, *Ricordi di cose familiare scritti da varie persone. Ricordi di Guido dell' Antella,* ed. F. Polidori, *ASI,* ser. 1, IV, pt. II (1843), 3-24.

John of Victring, *Johannis abbatis Victoriensis liber certarum historiarum,* ed. Fedor Schneider, 2 vols. (Monumenta Germaniae Historica, SSRG in usum scholarum, LV-LVI; Hannover-Leipzig, 1909-1910).

John of Winterthur, *Die Chronik Johanns von Winterthur,* ed. F. Baethgen and C. Brun (Monumenta Germaniae Historica, SSRG, n.s., III; Berlin, 1924).

Loserth, J., ed., see *Cronica Aulae Regiae.*

Malvezzi, Jacobus, *Chronicon Brixianum,* ed. L. A. Muratori, *RR.II.SS.,* XIV (Milan, 1729).

Mathias of Neuenberg, *Mathiae de Nuwenberg Chronica,* ed. A. Hofmeister, 3 vols. (Monumenta Germaniae Historica, Scriptores, n.s., IV, Pt. 1-3; Berlin, 1924-1937).

Merula, G., *Antiquitatis Vicecomitum libri X,* in J. G. Graevius, ed., *Thesaurus antiquitatum et historiarum Italiae,* III, Pt. I (Leyden, 1704), 9-240.

Morigia, Bonincontro, *Bonincontri Morigiae Chronicon Modoetiense,* ed. L. A. Muratori, *RR.II.SS.,* XII (Milan, 1728) .

Mussato, Albertino, *Albertini Mussati Historia Augusta,* ed. L. A. Muratori, *RR.II.SS.,* X (Milan, 1727).

Sardo, Ranieri, *Cronaca Pisana di Ranieri Sardo dall' anno*

962 sino al 1400, ed. F. Bonaini, *ASI,* ser. 1, VI, pt. II (1845),
281-377.

Tolomeo da Lucca, *Historia ecclesiastica,* excerpt, in vol. I,
Stephanus Baluzius, *Vitae Paparum Avenionensium,* ed. G.
Mollat (Paris, 1916), 24-53.

Ventura, Guilielmus, *Memoriale Guilielmi Venturae civis astensis,* ed. C. Coelestinus, in *Monumenta Historiae Patriae,* V
(Scriptores, III) (Turin, 1848).

Villani, Giovanni, *Cronica di Giovanni Villani a miglior lezione
ridotta,* 4 vols. (Florence [Magheri], 1823-1825).

MODERN WORKS

Bascapè, G. C., "I conti palatini del regno italico e la città di
Pavia dal comune alla signoria," *Archivio Storico Lombardo,*
ser. 7, LXII (1935), 281-377.

Belotti, B., *Storia de Bergamo e dei Bergamaschi,* 3 vols. (Milan,
1940).

Biscaro, G., "Benzo da Alessandria e i giudizi contro i ribelli a
Milano nel 1311," *Archivio Storico Lombardo,* ser. 4, VII, an.
34 (1907), 281-316.

Bock, F., *Reichsidee und Nationalstaaten* (Munich, 1943).

Bortolaso, V., "Vicenza dalla morte di Ezzelino alla signoria
scaligera (1259-1311)," *Nuovo Archivio Veneto,* n.s., an. 12,
pt. 2, vol. XXIV (1912), 5-53, 336-394.

Bowsky, W., "Clement V and the Emperor-elect," *Medievalia
et Humanistica,* XII (1958), 52-69.

———, "Dante's Italy: A Political Dissection," *The Historian,*
XXI (1958), 82-100.

———, "Florence and Henry of Luxemburg, King of the
Romans: The Rebirth of Guelfism," *Speculum,* XXXIII
(1958), 177-203.

Brezzi, P., "Le relazioni tra i comuni italiani e l'impero," in
Questioni di storia medioevale, ed. E. Rota (Milan-Como,
1946), 385-411.

Brosien, H., "Heinrich VII. als Graf von Luxemburg," *Forschungen zur deutschen Geschichte,* XV (1875), 475-511.

Butler, W. F., *The Lombard Communes* (London-New York,
1906).

Caggese, R., *Dal concordato di Worms alla fine della prigionia di Avignone (1122-1377)* (Turin, 1939).

――――, *Roberto d'Angiò e i suoi tempi*, 2 vols. (Florence, 1921-1930).

Capasso, C., "La signoria viscontea e le lotte politico-religiose con il papato nella prima metà del secolo XIV," *Bollettino della Società Pavese di Storia Patria*, VIII (1908).

Caro, G., *Genua und die Mächte am Mittelmeer, 1257-1311*, 2 vols. (Halle, 1895-1899).

Castruccio Castracani degli Antelminelli, Miscellanea di studi storici e letterari, ed. R. Accademia Lucchese (Florence, 1934).

Cavalcabò, A., *Le ultime lotte del comune di Cremona per l'autonomia* (R. Deputazione di Storia Patria per la Lombardia, sezione di Cremona. Biblioteca storica cremonese, I; Cremona, 1937).

Cessi, R., *Storia della Repubblica di Venezia*, 2 vols. (Milan-Messina, 1944-1946).

Cibrario, L., *Delle storie di Chieri libri quattro con documenti*, I, II (Turin, 1827).

Cognasso, F., "L'unificazione di Lombardia sotto Milano," in G. Treccani degli Alfieri, ed., *Storia di Milano*, V (Milan, 1955), 3-564.

Darmstädter, P., *Das Reichsgut in der Lombardei und Piemont (568 bis 1250)* (Strassburg, 1895).

Davidsohn, R., *Forschungen zur Geschichte von Florenz*, 4 vols. (Berlin, 1896-1908).

――――, *Geschichte von Florenz*, 4 vols. (Berlin, 1896-1927).

Davis, C. T., *Dante and the Idea of Rome* (Oxford, 1957).

D'Entrèves, A. P., *Dante as a Political Thinker* (Oxford, 1952).

De Vergottini, G., "Origini e sviluppo storico della comitatinanza," *Studi Senesi*, XLIII (1929), 347-481.

――――, "Vicariato imperiale e signoria," in *Studi di storia e diritto in onore di Arrigo Solmi*, I (Milan, 1941), 43-64.

Dönniges, W., *Geschichte des deutschen Kaisertums im vierzehnten Jahrhundert*, I: *Kritik der Quellen für die Geschichte Heinrichs des VII des Luxemburgers* (Berlin, 1841).

Duprè Theseider, E., *Roma dal comune di popolo alla signoria pontificia (1252-1377)* (Storia di Roma, XI; Bologna, 1952).

Eitel, A., *Der Kirchenstaat unter Klemens V.* (Abhandlungen zur mittleren und neueren Geschichte, I; Berlin-Leipzig, 1907).

Elze, R., "Die 'Eiserne Krone' in Monza," Ch. XIX of P. E. Schramm, *Herrschaftszeichen und Staatssymbolik,* II (Schriften der *MGH, X,* Pt. 2; Stuttgart, 1955), 450-479.

Ercole, F., *Dal comune al principato* (Florence, 1929).

Ermini, G., *Stato e chiesa nella monarchia pontificia dei secoli XIII e XIV* (Bologna, 1932).

Fasoli, G., "Bologna e la Romagna durante la spedizione di Enrico VII," *R. Deputazione di Storia Patria per l'Emilia e la Romagna. Atti e Memorie,* IV (1938-1939), 15-54.

Felsberg, O., *Beiträge zur Geschichte des Römerzuges Heinrichs VII.* I Teil: *Innere und Finanzpolitik Heinrichs VII. in Italien* (diss.; Leipzig, 1886).

Fiumi, E., "Sui rapporti economici tra città e contado nell' età comunale," *ASI,* an. 114 (1956), 18-68.

Fournier, P., *Le royaume d'Arles et de Vienne 1138-1378* (Paris, 1891).

Gabotto, F., *Asti e la politica sabauda in Italia al tempo di Guglielmo Ventura* (Biblioteca della Società Storica Subalpina, XVIII; Pinerolo, 1903).

————, *Storia del Piemonte nella prima metà del secolo XIV, 1292-1349* (Turin, 1894).

Gerbaix de Sonnaz, A. de, *Amé V de Savoie et les Savoyards à l'expedition de l'empereur Henri VII de Luxembourg à Rome (1308-1313)* (Thonon-les-Bains, 1903).

Gualazzini, U., *Il "populus" di Cremona e l'autonomia del comune* (Biblioteca della Rivista di Storia e del Diritto Italiano, XIV; Bologna, 1940).

Güterbock, F., "Die Veroneser Annalen nach einer Handschrift aus dem Nachlass Sigonio's," *Neues Archiv,* XXV (1900), 37-79.

Haase, K., *Die Königskrönungen in Oberitalien und die eiserne Krone* (diss.; Strassburg, 1901).

Heidemann, J., *Peter von Aspelt als Kirchenfürst und Staatsmann* (Berlin, 1875).

Herlihy, D., *Pisa in the Early Renaissance* (New Haven, 1958).

Irmer, G., *Die Romfahrt Kaiser Henrich's VII. im Bildercyclus des Codex Balduini Trevirensis* (Berlin, 1881).

Israel, W., *König Robert von Neapel und Kaiser Heinrich VII. Die Ergebnisse bis zur Krönung in Rom* (Berlin, 1903).

Kampf, H., "Zu einem Imbreviaturenbuch und einem Register Bernards de Mercato," *Mitteilungen des Instituts für öster-*

reichische Geschichtsforschung, Erg. Bd., XIV (1939), 391-409.
Kantorowicz, E. H., *The King's Two Bodies* (Princeton, 1957).
Kern, F., *Die Anfänge der französischen Ausdehnungspolitik* (Tübingen, 1910).
———, "Die Reichsgewalt des deutschen Königs nach dem Interregnum," *Historische Zeitschrift*, CVI (1911), 39-95.
Kretschmayr, H., *Geschichte von Venedig*, 3 vols. (Gotha, 1905-1934).
Leicht, P. S., "Cino da Pistoia e la citazione di Re Roberto da parte d'Arrigo VII," *ASI*, CXII (1954), 313-320.
Léonard, E. G., *Les angevins de Naples* (Paris, 1954).
Lizerand, G., "Les constitutions 'Romani principes' et 'Pastoralis cura' et leurs sources," *Nouvelle revue historique du droit français et étranger*, XXXVII (1913), 725-757.
Ludwig, F., *Untersuchungen über Reise- und Marschgeschwindigkeit im XII. und XIII. Jahrhundert* (Berlin, 1897).
Maccarrone, M., "Il terzo Libro della 'Monarchia'," *Studi Danteschi*, XXXIII (1955), 5-142.
Melchiorri, M., "Vicende della signoria di Ghiberto da Correggio in Parma," *Archivio Storico per le Provincie Parmensi*, n.s., VI (1906) [1907], 1-201.
Mollat, G., *Les papes d'Avignon (1305-1377)*, 9th ed. (Paris, 1949).
Mommsen, T. E., "Castruccio e l'Impero," in *Castruccio Castracani degli Antelminelli, Miscellanea . . .* (Florence, 1934), 33-45 (trans. in his *Medieval and Renaissance Studies* [Ithaca, N. Y., 1959]).
Monti, G. M., *Cino da Pistoia giurista* (Città di Castello, 1924).
———, *Cino da Pistoia, Le quaestiones e i consilia* (Milan, 1942).
———, *La dominazione angoina in Piemonte* (Biblioteca della Società Storica Subalpina, CXVI; Turin, 1930).
Niccolai, F. *Città e signori* (Bologna, 1941).
Ottokar, N., *Il comune di Firenze alla fine del dugento* (Florence, 1926).
Picotti, G. B., *I caminesi e la loro signoria in Treviso dal 1283 a 1312* (Livorno, 1905).
———, "Qualche osservazione sui caratteri delle signorie italiane," *Rivista Storica Italiana*, X (1926), 6-30.
Ranke, L. von, *Weltgeschichte*, IV (Leipzig, 1896).

Runciman, S., *The Sicilian Vespers* (Cambridge, 1958).

Salvatorelli, L., *L'Italia comunale dal secolo XI alla metà del secolo XIV* (Storia d'Italia Illustrata, IV; Milan, 1940).

Salvemini, G., *Magnati e popolani in Firenze dal 1280 al 1295* (Florence, 1899).

Salzer, E., *Ueber die Anfänge der Signorie in Oberitalien* (Berlin, 1900).

Samanek, V., "Der Marschall des Kaisers in nachstaufischen Reichsitalien," *Quellen und Forschungen aus italienischen Archiven und Bibliotheken*, XIV (1911), 38-67.

———, "Die verfassungsrechtliche Stellung Genuas, 1311-1313," *Mitteilungen des Instituts für österreichische Geschichtsforschung*, XXVII (1906), 237-314, 560-628.

Sandri, G., "Il vicariato imperiale e gli inizi della signoria scaligera in Vicenza," *Archivio Veneto*, ser. 5, XII (1932), 73-128.

Schneider, Friedrich, *Kaiser Heinrich VII.* (3 Hefte, continuously paged; Greiz-Leipzig, 1924-1928).

Simeoni, L., *Le signorie, 1313-1559*, 2 vols. (Storia politica d'Italia; Milan, 1950).

———, "Signorie e principati," in *Questioni di storia medioevale*, ed. E. Rota (Milan-Como, 1946), 413-454.

Sommerfeldt, G., *Die Romfahrt Kaiser Heinrichs VII. (1310-1313)*, Teil I (all published) (diss.; Königsberg, 1888).

———, "König Heinrich VII. und die lombardischen Städte in den Jahren 1310-1312," *Deutsche Zeitschrift für Geschichtswissenschaft*, II (1889), 97-155.

Soranzo, G., *La guerra fra Venezia e la S. Sede per Ferrara (1308-9)* (Padua, 1905).

Spangenberg, H., *Can Grande I von Scala*, 2 vols. (Berlin, 1892-1895).

Stengel, E. E., *Avignon und Rhens* (Weimar, 1930).

Sumner, B. H., "Dante and the *regnum italicum*," *Medium Aevum*, I (1932), 1-23.

Thilo, M., *Das Recht der Entscheidung über Krieg und Frieden im Streite Kaiser Heinrichs VII. mit der römischen Kurie* (Berlin, 1928).

Tobacco, G., "Un presunto disegno domenicano-angoino per l'unificazione d'Italia," *Rivista Storica Italiana*, LXI (1949), 489-525.

Torelli, P., "Capitanato del popolo e vicariato imperiale come elementi costitutivi della signoria bonacolsiana," *R. Accademia Virgiliana di Mantova, Atti e Memorie,* n.s., XIV-XVI (1923), 73-221.

Treccani degli Alfieri, G., ed., *Storia di Milano,* V (Milan, 1955).

Ullmann, W., "The Development of the Medieval Idea of Sovereignty," *English Historical Review,* LXIV (1949), 1-35.

Valeri, N. *et al., Storia d'Italia,* I: *Il Medioevo* (Turin, 1959).

Vigo, P., *Uguccione della Faggiuola* (Livorno, 1879).

Villari, P., *I primi due secoli della storia di Firenze* (2nd ed.; Florence, 1905) (*The First Two Centuries of Florentine History,* trans. by L. Villari, from 2nd Italian ed. [London, 1908]).

Violante, C., "Per la storia economica e sociale di Pisa nel Trecento. La riforma della zecca del 1318," *Bullettino dell' Istituto Storico Italiano,* No. 66 (1954), 129-205.

Vitale, V., *Il dominio della parte guelfa in Bologna (1280-1327)* (Bologna, 1901).

Volpe, G., "Pisa, Firenze, Impero al principio del 1300 e gli inizi della signoria civile a Pisa," *Studi Storici,* II (1902), 177-203, 293-337.

Wenck, C. R., *Clemens V. und Heinrich VII.* (Halle, 1882).

Will, E., *Die Gutachten des Oldradus de Ponte zum Prozess Heinrichs VII. gegen Robert von Neapel* (Abhandlungen zur mittleren und neueren Geschichte, LXV; Berlin-Leipzig, 1917).

Winkler, F., *Castruccio Castracani, Herzog von Lucca* (Berlin, 1897).

Index

References to the text refer also to material in the pertinent reference notes, and reference notes are only separately indexed when they contain material differing substantially from that in the text. The index of subjects, while not complete, it is hoped will prove useful. In addition to standard abbreviations (abp. = archbishop, bp. = bishop, ct. = count, k. = king, marq. = marquis), note that Cl.V = Pope Clement V, H. = Henry VII, Robt. = Robert of Anjou. Material pertaining to many Italian cities is also separately indexed under the entries "Oath (s)," "Peace Arbitrations," and "Sentences."